PATTERNS FOR AMERICA

PATTERNS FOR AMERICA

MODERNISM AND THE CONCEPT OF CULTURE

Susan Hegeman

PRINCETON UNIVERSITY PRESS   PRINCETON, NEW JERSEY

Library of Congress Cataloging-in-Publication Data

Hegeman, Susan, 1964–
Patterns for America : modernism and the concept of culture. / Susan Hegeman.
p.   cm.
Includes bibliographical references and index.
ISBN 0-691-00133-2 (cloth : alk. paper). —ISBN 0-691-00134-0 (pbk. : alk. paper)

1. American literature—20th century—History and criticism. 2. Modernism (Literature)—
United States. 3. Literature and anthropology—United States—History—20th century.
4. Culture—Social aspects—United States—History—20th century. 5. National
characteristics, American, in literature. 6. United States—Civilization—20th century.
7. Modernism (Aesthetics)—United States. 8. Arts, Modern—20th century. 9. Arts,
American. I. Title.
PS228.M63H44   1999
810.9′112—dc21   98-37761   CIP

This book has been composed in Times Roman
The paper used in this publication meets the minimum requirements of
ANSI/NISO Z39.48-1992 (R1997) (*Permanence of Paper*)

http://pup.princeton.edu

Printed in the United States of America

10 9 8 7 6 5 4 3 2 1

10 9 8 7 6 5 4 3 2 1

For my grandparents

Contents

Acknowledgments _____

OVER THE COURSE of the eight years spent writing this book, I have been affiliated with four different universities in four different parts of the country. Each place carries with it its own happy memories of intellectual and personal debts incurred.

I begin with a word of thanks to my teachers, Fredric Jameson, Thomas J. Ferraro, Richard G. Fox, and especially Janice Radway and Barbara Herrnstein Smith. I am still occasionally struck, and flattered, and grateful, that they trusted me enough to take on a topic like this for a dissertation, as I am for the support and interest they have shown in it since I left Duke. The greatest compliment I could give any teacher applies to them—that their passions, ideas, and examples continue to engage and inspire me.

I was materially supported in the completion of this project by a Career Development Grant from the University of California at Berkeley and by a summer research grant from the University of Florida. Especially important was my year as the William S. Vaughn Visiting Fellow at the Robert Penn Warren Center for the Humanities at Vanderbilt University, which allowed me the time, space, and ideal collegial environment for finishing this book the way I wanted. Mona Frederick, associate director of that center, cannot be thanked enough for her gifts of hospitality, endless logistical help, and her bountiful supply of wit and wisdom. Sherry Willis provided good company and valued secretarial help. I am also indebted to the participants in the Humanities Center seminar "The Question of Culture." Jay Clayton, Beth Conklin, James Epstein, Yoshikuni Igarashi, Konstantin Kustanovich, Jane Landers, Richard A. Peterson, Karen Shimakawa, and Mark Wollaeger offered stimulating discussions, critical readings of my work, timely professional advice, lots of references and research tips, and good company during my year at Vanderbilt.

There, and elsewhere, numerous colleagues, students, advisors, and friends have left their mark on my thinking, and on this project. These also include Rita Barnard, Mitchell Breitwieser, James Buzard, John Evelev, Vivien Green Fryd, Dorothy Hale, Tace Hedrick, Abdul JanMohamed, Anne Goodwyn Jones, Caren Kaplan, Rebecca Karl, Amitava Kumar, John Leavey, David Leverenz, Molly Mullin, Samuel Otter, Malini Johar Schueller, Susan Schweik, Stephanie Smith, and the participants in my graduate classes, "Theorizing Culture," at Berkeley, and "Reading the Literary Academy," at Florida—especially David Zimmerman, who also provided research help. Mei Lin Chang, at *Common Knowledge*, significantly improved the prose of an earlier version of Chapter 7. My parents, Sally and George Hegeman, provided general counsel, facetious suggestions for book titles, and (wearing their professorial hats) thoughtful answers to my sometimes muddled questions about Darwin, genetic theory, and other matters scientific. At Princeton University Press, Mary Murrell's professionalism and patient good humor calmed me down considerably about the process of publication. I am especially grateful to Robert Seguin, for reading many drafts of my work over the years; to Sheryl Kroen, for keeping me focused on the big picture, in terms of this project and in all other ways, during a difficult transitional year; and to Marc Manganaro, for his ongoing interest in this project, and for his extremely thorough and generous comments on a draft of this book. He and two anonymous readers saved me from numerous infelicities and encouraged me to sharpen my argument in important ways. Finally, and as always, I owe my biggest thanks to Phil Wegner: editor, coach, cook, companion, fellow sufferer, the person who taught me everything I know about utopian desires. What was best about writing this book was writing it with him.

PATTERNS FOR AMERICA

Introduction _____

The Domestication of Culture

THIS IS A BOOK about the idea of culture as it was understood and deployed in early-twentieth-century United States, a moment when, as the anthropologists A. L. Kroeber and Clyde Kluckhohn put it, "the idea of culture, in the technical anthropological sense," had become "one of the key notions of contemporary American thought." Writing from midcentury, they also noted that, used ubiquitously, the term was in danger of losing whatever precision it might have possessed "in the technical sense": "Psychiatrists and psychologists, and, more recently, even some economists and lawyers, have come to tack on the qualifying phrase 'in our culture' to their generalizations, even though one suspects it is often done mechanically in the same way that mediaeval men added a precautionary 'God Willing' to their utterances."[1]

We should recognize the problem. "Culture" is still everywhere—still a "keyword" in our various conversations about ourselves and others, still somehow connected to what we understand to be a usage derived from anthropology, still a confusing tangle of connotations, and still perhaps so overused as to have become the stuff of slightly pious platitude.[2] On the other hand—precisely because of this interesting combination of ambiguity and discursive centrality—"culture" is also a word that has received an enormous quantity of philological and historical attention. Thus, we may be generally certain of a long and complex history of the term, most commonly (and plausibly) beginning with the Romantic nationalism of Johann Gottfried Herder and his contemporaries, or, in the British context, with the history of industrialism and the thought of eighteenth- and nineteenth-century figures such as Edmund Burke, Thomas Carlyle, and Matthew Arnold.[3]

However, I will focus instead on a moment that I see as in effect *necessitating* the broader project of locating the origins and meanings of "culture." For, I would suggest that the very phenomenon that Kroeber and Kluckhohn described, and the context of current debates surrounding "culture" in the United States, is largely the product of a more recent moment, the first half of this century, when the term emerged and was elaborated upon in a diversity of interesting sites: in the social and aesthetic criticism of the modernist little magazines as well as in the work emerging from the newly academicized disciplines of anthropology and sociology.[4] But perhaps most remarkably, what Kroeber and Kluckhohn saw as "culture, in the technical anthropological sense" emerged in this period as an important presence in the wider, *public* discourse.

The new accessibility of, and interest in, the idea of "culture" in this period was noted over a decade ago in a brilliant essay by the historian Warren Susman. In "The Culture of the Thirties," Susman argued, "It is not too extreme to propose that it was during the Thirties that the idea of culture was domesticated, with important consequences. Americans then began thinking in terms of patterns of behavior and belief, values and life-styles, symbols and meanings. It was during this period that we find, for the first time, frequent reference to an 'American Way of Life.' "[5] Alluding to Ralph Waldo Emerson's 1867 prediction of the "gradual domestication of the idea of Culture" in the United States, Susman described its *achievement* in the thirties as being a rather different thing than the national *Bildung* Emerson had imagined.[6] Specifically, he saw this particular version of the concept as enabling a wide spectrum of Americans to do two new things: to understand themselves as participating in a distinctive "American" culture, and to see this culture as a set of patterns, values, and beliefs roughly comparable to those of other cultures. Crucially, this moment of culture's domestication was one of both national self-perception and critical *estrangement*; "culture" may have hit home to many Americans, but it left them thinking about themselves and their allegiances in a newly relational, contextual, and often critical way. It is this particular way of thinking culturally that interests me, in that it suggests the construction of group identities of a decidedly uneasy and reflexive kind.

I will suggest that the vision of "culture" that enabled this estranged perception of collective identity is a complexly modernist one, related to other estrangements of context and perception that so influenced the more experimental artistic movements of the period. I see this popular embrace of a spatial "culture" as answering a particular descriptive need in the modernist moment, when older conceptions of history and temporality had begun to seem, for various reasons, no longer adequate to explaining the specific experiences of alienation and difference Americans felt from others in their communities, their nation, the world. More specifically, "culture" offered an important conceptual framework for articulating the often uneasy and uneven experience of the achievement of modernity. Thus, the period of the thirties is the moment of "culture's" domestication precisely because it is also when the problem of uneven modernity—then being aggressively addressed by the antipoverty and infrastructural development programs of the New Deal—was a topic of such intense social and political concern.

But the period of the thirties is also central to my description of the meanings of "culture" in the United States because it is in this moment that we are best able to see the real complexity of this spatial rearticulation of culture. Though the term suggested the existence of a range of relatively equivalent, historically concurrent sites, it also suggested another spatial arrangement of difference, in the clear articulation of *hierarchies* of taste. In Chapter 5, I will show how both of these axes of cultural difference—one horizontal, one vertical—*converged* in this period, in the concept of the "middlebrow," which was also strongly associated with a specific geographic location: the Midwest.

The "culture" I am interested in describing was, in other words, employed in the service of a complex mix of often overlapping impulses: the desire to locate the "truth" of a particular social reality; the desire to demarcate the good from the bad, the real from the false, insiders from outsiders. It also involved a revision of historical thinking, challenging teleological models of human advancement by suggesting a range of possible sites, possible ways of doing things and being human. These impulses, in turn, were related to the significant social and political challenges of the moment. "Cultural" rhetoric was deployed to talk not only about what it meant to experience a uniquely "American" way of life, but to address such problems as immigration and assimilation; the personal experiences of group belonging and alienation; and questions of what constituted the best, or purest, expressions of a group of people, be they the "folk," the nation, or a region in the nation.

Because I see changes in the usage of "culture" as indicative of something more than a rhetorical phenomenon (and because I don't pretend to have exhaustively surveyed the field of instances of the word "culture" in this period), I will resist here and elsewhere the temptation to belabor specific usages of the term, in favor of addressing what I see as the larger "cultural" logics at work in the period. Nevertheless, there are a number of points of terminological confusion that may be addressed at the outset, the first involving the difficult relationship between "culture" and a related concept, "civilization."

As Lewis Mumford put it in 1926, "civilization and culture . . . are not exclusive terms; for one is never found without at least a vestige of the other."[7] A careful reader of the following pages will find ample evidence to suggest that there was a strong degree of interchangeability between the two words, as many of the writers I cite do seem to use these terms (along with "society," "national genius," and a few others) as near synonyms. Nevertheless, certain distinctions between the connotations of the two words also emerge. Perhaps most trivially, "civilization" implies something a bit more rhetorically grand than "culture," as, for example, when Randolph Bourne hyperbolically states, "The Middle West is the apotheosis of American civilization."[8] For Mumford, the key distinction between "civilization" and "culture" was glossed as the difference between "the material fact and the spiritual form"—a distinction not dissimilar to that made by a number of social scientists of the early twentieth century (though it was also common to see "culture" described as the material, and "civilization" as the spiritual).[9] Perhaps most significant for this study, however, is each term's connotation of a particular relationship of part to whole, and of a particular orientation toward history. Thus, Edward Sapir defines "culture" as "civilization in so far as it embodies the national genius,"[10] showing that "civilization" connotes a general state, while "culture" refers to a particular (here, national) context. Frequently, "civilization" implies a level of human achievement, often in the context of a teleological view of human progress. Thus, to take a well-known example, the nineteenth-century American ethnologist Lewis Henry Morgan charted the "ethnical periods" of human development from stages of "savagery," to "barbarism," to "civilization."[11] "Culture," on the other hand, often implies something both more specific and more universal than "civilization," in that it refers to the distinctive "genius" of a *particular* group of people, and yet also describes a common condition of all people, all of whom have their own form of a "culture." "Culture" and "civilization" thus imply different kinds of relationships between groups of people. Where "civilization" invites comparisons of advancement with the "savage" others, "culture" allows for the possibility of a comparative operation in which one's own group's particular "genius" may be understood in the context of those of other people, irrespective of levels of "advancement." This broad distinction holds not only in the earlier moments of the articulation of the culture concept, when "culture" was occasionally employed to counter teleological accounts of the achievement of "civilization," but in the latter years discussed in this study, those immediately preceding and following World War II, when "civilization" can be said to have made something of a comeback in American discourse, in phrases including "Western civilization" and "American civilization." In this moment of crisis, an imperiled "civilization" apparently connoted a greater sense of urgency than did an imperiled "culture." But in this choice of terminology, what was also being recaptured was something of this earlier teleological connotation of the term, in which America (or the West) was also viewed as having achieved a certain—advanced—stage of development.

It should also be noted that I don't belabor another rhetorical distinction commonly made in discussions of the usage of the word "culture": the one that separates the aesthetic ideal of "high culture" (*Bildung*, "the best that has been thought and said," etc.) from "culture" as a purely descriptive term of social scientific discourse. This is precisely because I regard the "culture" of this period—particularly in its connotations as the "spirit" of a group of people, or the "national genius," or "the American way of life"—as often subsuming *both* of these ideas. In this sense, I see myself as participating in a tradition of thinking about "culture" and its contexts that explicitly challenges the still-common assumption that the gesture of "cultural" description and intercultural comparison is somehow distinct from the one of cultural evaluation and judgments of taste. This presumed separation between these two "cultural" operations is often articulated in terms of a species of unfortunate linguistic accident, in which two separate intellectual trajectories just happened to converge on the same word, "culture." One of these trajectories is seen as having emerged from a relativist, comparativist anthropology; the other, from aesthetics, which is seen as evaluative, discriminating, and therefore *anti*relativist.[12]

As we shall see, this characterization of "culture's" history, and its resulting paradox, can be dismantled in a number of ways. But for the purposes of introduction, it is especially important to point out that the idea of "relativism" upon which this account's contradiction stands, has, like "culture," its own historical baggage in need of unpacking. During the historical moment in which I am interested, anthropologists were not committed in any rigorous way to relativism in its common contemporary sense as an epistemological, antifoundational position. Rather, relativism in this moment often went hand in hand with a foundational belief in scientific rationality and the commonality of humankind, and served, rather, as a largely *ethical* gesture, which refuted the validity of intercultural assessments of human worth.[13] Given this more humanistic understanding of relativism (which I will specify as *moral relativism*), it is possible to imagine how it could have coexisted uncontradictorily with foundational theories of value, including aesthetic value.

Though it is thus clear that the bipartite history of culture (as on the one hand "anthropological" and on the other hand "aesthetic") is inadequate to explain the nuances of cultural discourse, I nevertheless somewhat replicate its structure in my own account—in order to refute it. Central figures in my narrative of "culture" in early-twentieth-century United States may easily be divided into the categories of "anthropological" and "literary" intellectuals. However, I follow Susman's description of the culture of the thirties to specify these groups further. While we may easily recognize in his point, quoted above, the presence of anthropological ideas of "culture," which introduced the language of discrete patterns, symbols, and beliefs, the other relevant influence in his characterization of a fully domesticated culture concept is a *nationalist* one, which introduced the very possibility that the United States possessed a distinctive, valuable "culture" of its own. Thus, in my bipartite structure, I specify a group of intellectuals that was particularly influential in the theorization, promotion, and creation of distinctively American arts traditions within the context of the international movement of aesthetic modernism. This group includes Van Wyck Brooks, Randolph Bourne, Waldo Frank, Paul Rosenfeld, and Constance Rourke among the critics and promoters, and Jean Toomer, Hart Crane, Sherwood Anderson, and Alfred Stieglitz among the artists. I discuss their work in connection, and in comparison, with that of key figures in the early history of American anthropology, particularly Franz Boas and his students Edward Sapir, Alfred Louis Kroeber, Ruth Benedict, and Margaret Mead.

There is a strong institutional tradition that connects these Boasian anthropologists to the creation of a humanist "anthropological" culture concept. Indeed, their emphasis on "culture" as a central concept of the discipline has been seen to distinguish American anthropology from the approaches developed in other countries, where the term has been of less theoretical significance.[14] Similarly, Brooks and his peers have long been recognized as having formed their own tradition, representing a distinctive cultural-nationalist strain in American criticism. However, my narrative will trouble both of these descriptions in a number of respects. Not only will I emphasize the complexly modernist contexts of their projects, but I will show how both Brooks and Boas were important, but ultimately displaced, predecessors of the fully domesticated culture concept.

In my narrative, it will become clear that, while both Brooks and Boas instantiated different strands of the discourse of "culture," its permutations were often altogether different from what they had themselves envisioned. Thus, it is significant that Boas was an uneasy and contradictory supporter of the work of students such as Benedict and Mead, who represent the most important anthropological contributors to the culture concept in its popular form. Similarly, I think it highly unlikely that Brooks saw himself as the spokesman of a genial middlebrow cultural position that he was later taken to be. Thus, I take some pains in this narrative to show how it is that figures like Alfred Kroeber, Edward Sapir, Randolph Bourne, and Waldo Frank were crucial mediators in the elaboration of discourses founded elsewhere, under a diversity of historical and institutional imperatives.

Before addressing what I will insist is these groups' *convergent* project of elaborating on "culture," I should note some significant social and institutional differences between the figures who represent the two strands of my discussion. While the "cultural critics" represented an older model of the relatively autonomous literary intelligentsia, the anthropologists were on the vanguard of the present pattern of intellectual life in the United States in which "traditional intellectuals" depend on the credentialing and financial support of the academy.[15] The academic institutionalization of anthropology, in which one was trained and credentialed as a professional within the academy, was part of a more general trend around the turn of the century which saw the consolidation of a wide variety of new professional statuses and a corresponding emergence of the "professional-managerial" strata of the dramatically expanding middle class.[16] Professionalization had the important benefit of allowing for some upward mobility for those who had access to training and professional certification. This was especially evident in new fields like anthropology and the other emerging social science disciplines, which were far less affected by the social exclusivity which in that period pervaded the humanities. Thus, professional anthropology accommodated scholars from a remarkable diversity of backgrounds who were otherwise not well represented in the academy, including Jews, members of the working class, women, immigrants, and bohemian proponents of diverse radical opinions.

Situated in polyglot New York, Boas's department at Columbia was particularly diverse. Boas and Sapir were both Jewish immigrants from Germany

(Boas as a young man, Sapir as a child), while Kroeber was a second-generation immigrant whose first language, and cultural allegiance, was German.
Among others of Boas's students at Columbia University, Paul Radin was a
Jewish immigrant from Poland, Robert Lowie emigrated as a child from Aus-
tria, and Alexander Goldenweiser was born in Russia. Many, including Sapir,
Lowie, and Alexander Lesser, grew up in the ethnically diverse, working-class
neighborhoods of New York City.[17] Boas was also remarkably open and encouraging of women students. According to Judith Modell, before World War
II (and before the GI Bill, which encouraged the enrollment of veterans) almost
half of Columbia's anthropology PhDs were granted to women. Among Boas's
more pragmatic reasons for supporting women graduate students were that he
felt that their fieldwork uncovered things to which men didn't have access, and
that he perceived women to be less in need of economic support. Indeed, several eminent women anthropologists of this period, including Benedict, Mead,
and Elsie Clews Parsons were from comfortably bourgeois families. However,
it is also true that the presence of these strongly feminist anthropologists was
to a great degree self-perpetuating. In the years around World War I, when (as
we shall see in Chapter 2) Boas was most at odds with the Columbia administration for his public political statements, the wealthy Parsons provided the
funds for Boas and his students to conduct their fieldwork, and paid the salary
of Boas's secretary. This unique financial arrangement further encouraged the
participation of women in the department, for the feminist Parsons—an extremely prominent and controversial writer on the family and sexual morality—was particularly interested in promoting women's careers. Two of the
secretaries whom Boas hired with her support, Esther Schiff Goldfrank and
Ruth Bunzel, were eventually sent into the field, and thence into careers as
anthropologists.[18]

The wider group of "Boasians" was a large and extremely diverse one, since
Boas either directly trained, or strongly influenced, the careers of numerous
anthropologists over a period of more than forty years of graduate instruction.[19]
There are, however, a number of ways in which a specific lineage and group
identity could be created for the Boasians I discuss in these pages: Kroeber,
Sapir, Benedict, Mead, and Boas himself. Most generally, we might follow
Marshall Sahlins's taxonomy to see them as united by a common emphasis on
culture as a system of meaning-making. In this respect, they are united with
more recent figures in the field including Claude Lévi-Strauss and Clifford
Geertz.[20] More specifically, however, their commonality may be found in, first,
their direct participation and intervention in broader cultural debates of their
day, and second, in a specific intellectual trajectory, delineated both by an
increasing interest in the relationship between culture and *mentalité*, and in the
theories and methods of psychology. It is this strain of Boasian thinking about
"culture" that had the greatest impact on the popular imagination.

The other group that emerges in these pages is, by contrast, that of the more fluidly allied one that Waldo Frank called the "culture critics."[21] By this name, he designated the generally left-leaning and bohemian New York writers and editors of such journals as the *New Republic*, the *Masses*, the *Soil*, and the *Seven Arts*, but I will here give special attention to Frank, Randolph Bourne, Van Wyck Brooks, Brooks's protégée Constance Rourke, and several of the artists they championed, including Sherwood Anderson, Hart Crane, and Jean Toomer. Their identity as a group was most coherent from around the First World War until the early thirties and the creation of the cultural organs of the Popular Front. Thereafter, my account of this bohemian literary world becomes somewhat more dispersed. In some respects adopting the "culture critic" mantle, but to new ideological ends, are the younger critics of the *Partisan Review*, including Dwight Macdonald, Lionel Trilling, and Clement Greenberg; their work, and the work of James Agee, an artist they championed, is central to my discussion of the World War II period. I also address at some length two other figures who have only an indirect relationship to the "culture critics": writer Nathanael West and painter Thomas Hart Benton. Both appearing in my discussion of the thirties, these two figures may be thought of as representing a certain antithesis, Benton offering a vehement populist polemic for American regionalism, while West engages in a kind of critical dismantling of *all* the various competing cultural rhetorics of his moment.

These writers and artists can be fairly called "culture critics" in two senses—both in terms of their investments in the arts and letters, and in terms of the larger critiques of American culture in which they engaged. In the earlier parts of the century, Brooks, Bourne, and Frank shared a critique of American life based on what they perceived to be the ugliness and moralism of the world of their Victorian parents. They argued that the Victorian world into which they were born (of which an almost religious worship of "Culture" was a significant feature) inhibited both the creation of a healthy American culture, and the personal fulfillment of the individuals who could comprise that culture.

Though separated by age, political beliefs, and the influence of different formative historical events, members of this larger group (excluding, perhaps, West, who was beholden to the Hollywood studio system) are all exemplars of what Russell Jacoby has called the "public intellectual." Largely based in New York, they made their livings outside the confines of the academy, and worked within and for the relatively narrow audience of the educated urban elite. Though Jacoby hardly mentions Brooks, Bourne, and Frank, they were the mentors of a number of figures whom Jacoby calls the "classical American intellectuals," including Kenneth Burke, Lewis Mumford, and Edmund Wilson.[22] The earlier figures could, in fact, be seen as the models for this nonacademic intellectual niche.

As we shall see, these different contexts were themselves significant in a number of respects for the way they influenced, and in some cases were influenced by, thought on "culture." But my narrative will not support the common one (made by the postwar New York intellectuals and reiterated by Jacoby) of "captured" intellectuals in the university, versus the "free" and autonomous life of the public intellectual. Though a few of the anthropologists I discuss, notably Mead and Benedict, did allow their research agendas to conform to the interests of their government sponsors during World War II and after, I can think of no better example of Jacoby's critical public intellectual than Boas, whose conception of himself as an autonomous, and activist, scholar was in some sense predicated on his position *within* the academy. Boas wielded his authority as a professional—therefore presumably critically detached—intellectual very effectively in his courageous and often public campaigns against scientific attempts to justify racism and against U.S. participation in World War I. It would be churlish indeed to see Boas's public interventions as being in any simple way self-serving. Though Boas's public views arguably enabled the furtherance of both his own prestige and that of anthropology as a discipline, they also caused him a great deal of immediate political and financial grief (he was, for example, harassed by the Columbia University administration for years after making his public antiwar statements). Similarly, though Boas's background as both a Jew and a German immigrant strongly influenced his antiracist and antiwar positions, he encouraged the widest possible application of his ideas in the service of other antidiscriminatory agendas.

It is the very public nature of the discourses of both these groups, anthropologists and culture critics alike, that further supports my emphasis on their shared "cultural" project, the pieces of which included a reconception of the social geography; the place of the individual, and of individual talent, within society; and the relationship of cultural and political centers to their margins. This shared project also had its specific social context, in a bohemian milieu shared by both groups. As residents of New York in the early decades of this century, the anthropologists and literary bohemians freely intermingled in such locations as meetings of Felix Adler's Ethical Culture Society (to which both Boas and Frank had strong connections), or at the literary clubs that dotted Greenwich Village. Robert Lowie, a prominent member of the first generation of Boas's students that also included Sapir and Kroeber, described his experience in one such literary club as follows:

[At the Liberal Club] one met a motley crew of poets, authors, journalists, editors, publishers, reformers, and radicals—some of them members, many of them guests. Dr. Grant introduced Carl [Gustav] Jung on the latter's first American visit, and we heard an enthralling talk on folklore from a psychological point of view. Robert Henri enlightened us about the first American exhibition of modernist painting and sculpture. Edna St. Vincent Millay and Amy Lowell read from their poems. Jacques Loeb expounded the latest advances in physical science. The notorious Frank Harris

thrilled an audience with a two-hour lecture on Shakespeare. In the basement restau-
rant of the Greenwich Village headquarters one might dine at the same table with
Bill Hayward of the Industrial Workers of the World or with Jim Larkin, the Irish
labor leader. Upstairs during the dance craze of the period members even learned the
latest tango steps to the tune of "Maurice Irrésistible."[23]

This rich interchange between uptown and downtown, the anthropological
and the literary, is also personified in the figure of Elsie Clews Parsons, a
founder of the *New Republic*, and a friend to such notable figures as Bourne,
Walter Lippmann and Charlotte Perkins Gilman. Parsons, a leading spokes-
woman for women's suffrage, birth control, and other feminist causes, would
become under Boas's tutelage a prominent anthropologist of the American
Southwest. We may also cite as interesting examples of the fluid exchanges
that occurred in this world Constance Rourke's acknowledgment of her friend
Ruth Benedict's influence on her work, and Edward Sapir's memorial essay
for Bourne after his death in 1918. In fact, despite the eventual dispersal of
many of the Columbia anthropologists to far-flung universities, many remained
steady contributors of essays, opinion pieces, and (in the case of Sapir and
Benedict) poetry to the important magazines for which Brooks and his colleagues also wrote.

I begin my story of these figures and of the domesticated culture concept in
Chapter 2, with a reexamination of the heroic origin story of the anthropological idea of "culture." My account of Boas's legacy stresses that his contribution
to "culture" was a product of both the internal development of anthropology
as a profession and wider developments in the social discourse, especially the
nationalism precipitated by the onset of World War I. I describe his specific
achievement as residing within a critique of progressivist visions of human
difference, which would ultimately result in the new spatial articulation of the
culture concept. However, Boas's largely critical gesture only hesitantly allowed for the attribution of positive content to "culture." I thus turn to the
work of W. E. B. Du Bois, Horace Kallen, and Randolph Bourne to show how,
in the same period, this spatial culture could then be deployed to address the
issue of national and subnational group identity. It was the pressure of finding
a strong ethical position against U.S. involvement in World War I that would
finally encourage Boas also to use "culture" in this way.

A nagging problem presented by these national and subnational constructions of cultural identity was the question of the *individual*'s position within
the cultural context. What was one to make of the person who did not seem to
fit neatly into his or her culture? By addressing the work of Van Wyck Brooks
and Edward Sapir together in Chapter 3, I show how closely this theoretical
question about individual agency in culture was related to the general concern
of the period over personal alienation in the context of an increasingly massified urban world. In trying to grapple with this question, however, both of

these writers were forced to express deep doubts about the very idea of a national culture. Incapable of seeing an alternative to personal alienation, they also began to see "culture" of any form as impossible, since its existence requires the resolution of irresolvable divisions—divisions that were, in turn, also endemic to the characters of individuals. Brooks's famous articulations of these splits, using the terms "Puritan" and "Pioneer," and "highbrow" and "lowbrow," inspired in subsequent writers not only an obsession with the failures of American culture, but new characterological and hierarchical vocabularies for thinking about the American context. Like Boas's deployment of "culture" as a descriptor of social spaces, Brooks and Sapir were also engaged in a revision of historical models into spatial, hierarchical conceptions of cultural difference.

After discussing Edward Sapir's fascinating, but failed, attempt to employ a dialectical structure to resolve this problem of splits and divisions between the individual and culture, I turn, in Chapter 4, to what is in effect an imaginary resolution of this problem, found in the work of anthropologist Ruth Benedict and culture critic Waldo Frank. I read both Frank (in *Our America*) and Benedict (in *Patterns of Culture*) as attempting to get around some of the problems of the limitations of culture that Brooks and Sapir had described, by appropriating their own versions of Brooks's characterological device and placing these characters into actually existing regional locales. For them, "cultures" were understood as a spatial range of possibilities open to the cultural traveler (or armchair anthropologist) disappointed with his or her milieu. In their influential descriptions, a given culture could be conceived that was not only the individual's authentic, unalienated homeland, but a resolution to the problems of fragmentation and unevenness that had made American culture seem like such an impossibility to Brooks and Sapir. This fully spatial "culture," deeply indebted to a modernist fascination with the estranging possibilities of the cultural other, becomes the version of culture that is, following Susman's description, domesticated in the 1930s.

Chapter 5 then addresses the context of this popular usage of culture, to offer some complications to Susman's vision. In this politically charged decade, "culture" indeed became an important term in American social criticism—often in conjunction, not coincidentally, with documentary, a kind of popularized ethnography.[24] And yet, given the explicitly estranging quality of much "cultural" discourse, it also produced a controversial map of differences within the American political landscape. Concern with regional diversity and the development of class-based artistic movements led to a complex competition over the contours of "culture," in which "culture" eventually became associated with a static social fiction known as "Middle America." While those who identified with "Middle America" as a region used this concept as a positive descriptor of "real" America, the construct suggested to many members of the urban cultural elite a stratum of debased, or possibly even dangerous, cultural taste: the "middlebrow," a terminal convergence of both spatial and hierarchical strands of "culture's" modernist genealogy.

In Chapter 6, I address this highly contestatory "cultural" landscape in the period of World War II and shortly thereafter, when, for specific political and social reasons, the critical and estranging implications of the idea of culture are strongly challenged, by both anthropologists and cultural critics alike. Thus, I read James Agee and Walker Evans's *Let Us Now Praise Famous Men*, the notoriously difficult documentary book on Southern tenant farmers, as reflecting an emerging "highbrow" rejection of the middlebrow and populist implications of the documentary form, and, indeed, suggesting a rejection of the project of cultural representation altogether. Meanwhile, among highbrow critics, including Dwight Macdonald, Clement Greenberg, T. S. Eliot, and Ezra Pound, "culture" was also being redeployed—not as the populist term it had occasionally been in the thirties, but against the tastes of the masses. A new vocabulary of degraded taste was beginning to emerge: "masscult," "midcult," "Kulchur," "kitsch." Meanwhile, social-scientific versions of culture, developing in the context of a new academic-government partnership, increasingly tended toward similarly antirelativist visions of culture as, on the one hand connoting the total space of a hegemonic "Western civilization," and on the other, the equally ideological spaces of reified national characters. I argue that, around the onset of World War II, the changing institutional situation of social scientists, combined with the anti-institutional obsessions of some literary intellectuals, finally suggested a division in the culture concept itself. I believe that the historical narrative, which sees a deep division between "anthropological" and "literary" usages of culture, is a product not of the actual histories of these fields, but rather of *this* moment.

Finally, my conclusion addresses some of the consequences of this split in our postmodern context. I take as my texts some members of one of the more curious genres of "cultural" description being circulated today, which offer proposals for getting rid of "culture" as an obsolete, or even meaningless term. I read this gesture as the postmodern legacy of the relationship between modernism and "culture," and suggest that it reveals a larger anxiety about totalizing theory in the postmodern context. I will argue, however, that this very lack of totalizing theory is precisely the site upon which a recuperation of certain features of the modernist discourse of "culture" might be most beneficial.

But to get to that point—and to begin my account of the domestication of culture and its effects—I must first offer an account of how we might think about modernism in relation to culture in the context of pre–World War II United States. This is the topic of the next chapter.

1

Modernism, Anthropology, Culture

THERE ARE A NUMBER of ways that one might delineate a relationship between the concept of culture and the aesthetic and intellectual period we call modernism. Indeed, as it will become clear, I see this connection as multiply inflected. But, for the purposes of beginning, I will start by observing that the rhetoric of "culture" itself conforms neatly to certain modernist ideologies.

Critical accounts of "culture" as a term—of which there are sufficient examples to comprise something like a genre—almost always begin with vexation, and exclamations at the word's ambiguity. For Raymond Williams in *Keywords*, "Culture is one of the two or three most complicated words in the English language." More recently, the prominent anthropologist Eric R. Wolf singled out culture for a discussion of "perilous ideas," while Stephen Greenblatt's entry in *Critical Terms for Literary Study* begins by arguing that the traditional definition of culture by E. B. Tylor "is almost impossibly vague and encompassing, and the few things that seem excluded from it are almost immediately reincorporated in the actual use of the word."[1]

The rhetorical function of this encounter with ambiguity and even "peril" is to bring coherence out of confusion, to show how the terminological anxiety can be banished. To this end, culture's definers often suggest its vexatiousness results from a kind of internal paradox, an uneasy cohabitation of opposed meanings. There are a number of versions of this paradox, the most common being the observation that culture has something to do with both "legitimate," or "high" culture and mass, everyday, or popular phenomena. The salient antithesis is then historicized, and frequently in such a way that one piece of the opposed set of ideas becomes a historical artifact, while the other, newer usage marks a kind of terminological revolution. Thus, Clifford Geertz defined the emergence of contemporary usages of "culture," whose salient feature for him is the emphasis on the particularity of human contexts, as a correction of the Enlightenment conception of the "uniformity" of human experience.[2]

More frequently, however, the culture that is imaginatively swept away is defined as the "Arnoldian" view of culture as the attainment of social and aesthetic perfection. Like its related Victorian models of progress, this culture suggests a strict hierarchy of aesthetic, moral, and political value, which places the beloved objects and practices of the elite (and hence the elites themselves) in a position of superiority. This culture, in other words, is seen as part and parcel of the nineteenth-century legacy of racism, sexism, classism, and vulgar nationalism. Against this culture, we witness the rise of what is often called the "anthropological" definition of the term, which is more synonymous with custom, connoting both the special and the mundane life ways of a given group of people. Rather than emphasizing hierarchy, this culture is comparative and relativist in structure; its function is the dispassionate description of difference, not superiority.

It is this narrative that seems typically modernist to me. Both dispassionately professional *and* comprising an avant-garde, the anthropologists are the heroes of this story, dramatically undoing the legacy of a Victorian predecessor in order to—paraphrasing Ezra Pound's famous slogan—make "culture" new. Like other great modernist thinkers, including Nietzsche, Freud, Heisenberg, and Einstein, the anthropologists are here taken to be paradigm shifters and world expanders, offering us shockingly new ways of understanding the world, and the foils (their descriptions of the culture of the "primitive" other) by which we may encounter, and release ourselves from, the Victorian narrowness and hypocrisy of church, parlor, and school. Given this narrative, it is not a surprise that this new "anthropological" definition of culture is often periodized as arising around the turn of the twentieth century, the moment historically coincident with the beginnings of the great modernist experiments of art and literature.[3] In the United States, it is usually the work of one particular anthropologist, Franz Boas, that is cited in this context. As Carl N. Degler put it, "Boas, almost single-handedly, developed in America the concept of culture, which, like a powerful solvent, would in time expunge race from the literature of social science."[4]

It is probably wise to be suspicious of accounts that rest such changes on the shoulders of one individual, and indeed, much of the next chapter will be devoted to qualifying this mythical-heroic reading of Boas and his specific role in the development of the culture concept. Similarly, we should question this narrative's caricature of the Victorian contribution to the development of the culture concept, which, others have shown, was not only significant but was complexly bound up with the developing field of anthropology.[5] I will show in Chapter 3 how one of the central figures of my narrative, Van Wyck Brooks, is both an important modernist theorizer of "culture," and deeply indebted to the work of that most central of Victorian theorizers of "culture," Matthew Arnold. But even aside from the issues of periodization that immediately emerge when attempting to understand the transition from the Victorian to modernist views of "culture," it may seem perverse for other reasons to draw a connection between the "anthropological" usage of "culture" and the aesthetic modernism of the early twentieth century. Though a number of modernists were fascinated by anthropological researches, they were far less interested in the "cutting edge" work of the likes of Boas than in that of evolutionary comparativists like Sir James G. Frazer and E. B. Tylor, figures against whom Boas positioned much of his work.[6] Indeed, it would be easy to see a plural, relativist, antiracist "anthropological" culture concept as *antithetical* to an aesthetic tradition that has long been associated not only with a mandarin preoccupation with formal play, but with a limited set of works belonging to T. S. Eliot's disembodied "mind of Europe."[7] Rather than suggesting pluralism, the typical heroes of a traditional modernist criticism such as Eliot and Ezra Pound might actually suggest the opposite: elitism, racism, even fascism.

Indeed, Lawrence W. Levine has recently argued that the Boasian cultural revolution may never have happened in the exalted realms of art, where hierarchical views of aesthetic value were fully entrenched. Levine writes:

> In the late nineteenth century, and well into the twentieth, culture became an icon as never before. Even while anthropology was redefining the concept of culture intellectually, aesthetically it proved remarkably impervious to change; it remained a symbol of all that was fine and pure and worthy. Whatever Franz Boas and Ruth Benedict might have meant by culture, and however influential their meaning ultimately was, Charlie Chaplin knew what the *society* meant by Culture.[8]

Levine's work contributes to our picture of another significant "cultural" event associated with modernism: the emergence of what Andreas Huyssen has called the "great divide" between "high" culture, and popular or "low" culture.[9] The elements in this change included the establishment in the latter half of the nineteenth century of museums, symphonies, universities, and other institutions of "legitimate" culture by a burgeoning middle class interested in consolidating its cultural capital—an event paralleled by the emergence of an increasingly massified popular culture in film, radio, advertising, and public entertainments.[10] In Levine's view, cultural distinction replaced other forms of social hierarchy, enabled new strategies of social control, and segregated both publics and cultural forms into categories of distinction: "highbrow," "lowbrow," "middlebrow." Thus, for Levine, high culture's "sacralized" status changed little under the pressure of anthropological developments. He implies that if culture's meaning changed, it changed only among those who already had access to elite forms and tastes.

However, there are a number of ways we might complicate Levine's point about the intractability of this view of culture. Not only was there a great deal of interborrowing between "high" and "low" forms in the modernist moment,[11] but the audiences for these forms were more versatile than Levine grants. In this regard, we might point to the fact that broadcasts of classical music were some of the earliest and most popular programs on commercial radio.[12] These broadcasts, in turn, enabled new mass-cultural uses for classical music such as in Disney's *Fantasia* and in Bugs Bunny cartoon spoofs of Italian operas; both relied on the existence of an audience ready to both appreciate and have fun with "highbrow" music. Indeed, Levine's own example of Charlie Chaplin offers a fascinating example of the complexities of cultural stratification in this period. Chaplin, a self-described "high lowbrow," conjoined British music-hall comedy, Hollywood sentimentality, and pointed social criticism in a mixture that brought him the admiration and acquaintance of such (purely?) "highbrow" intellectuals as Edmund Wilson, Waldo Frank, James Agee, and Sergei Eisenstein. Walter Benjamin wrote approvingly of his work, and Hart Crane's poem "Chaplinesque" was inspired by the actor's performance in *The Kid*. As Frank put it, "The most popular artist of our time was also the deepest."[13]

Similarly, I think Levine is too quick to discount anthropology's impact on popular discourse. After the Second World War, something recognizable as the "anthropological" culture concept had such widespread usage that two of anthropology's more prominent practitioners were led to wonder, "Why has [the concept] rather suddenly become popular in the United States, to the point that such phrases as 'Eskimo culture' appear even in the comic strips?"[14] By the thirties, something like the anthropological version of "culture" was well assimilated into the popular consciousness of many Americans; in Chapter 5, I will address the politics of regionalism as an example of this new familiarity with "culture." But Levine is entirely right to insist on the persistence of hierarchical conceptions of culture long after the emergence of other, more clearly relativist, versions of the term: while Boas may have done much to "expunge" scientific racism from the social sciences, he certainly did not exile the idea of strata of taste and value from public, or even anthropological, discourse. In this sense, I will in fact extend Levine's point to argue not only that a vernacular conception of high culture persisted, but also that in the more elite realms of intellectual discourse, relativist and hierarchical conceptions of the term coexisted and even intermingled.

Given that much of Matthew Arnold's influential description of culture was informed by nineteenth-century ethnological assumptions, or that the system of designating taste strata via the language of "highbrow" and "lowbrow" is itself derived from the pre-anthropological pseudoscience of phrenology, the connection between "anthropological" and "aesthetic" discourse is not difficult to prove.[15] Likewise, we must see the so-called anthropological version of the concept as emerging from a complex tangle of discourses relating to the politics and theory of race, theories of human evolution, debates on nationalism and antinationalism, Enlightenment notions of human equality, Romantic conceptions of organic unity, ideas on public education, views of the public and private good, and, in fact, theories of value and aesthetics. Though the usages of the concept were consolidated under the pressure of specific polemics and disciplinary configurations, I will thus follow Raymond Williams in arguing that the various versions of "culture" have long been intertwined. Rejecting origin stories of the term that suggest otherwise will not only help us see "culture" more vividly but avoid a self-mythologization of modernism as a clean and self-evident break from its past.

Thus I will offer a narrative of "culture" that emphasizes complexity, or at least resists quick distinctions and histories marked by dramatic ruptures. I will, however, retain one feature of the traditional rhetoric of "culture": I too will focus on its apparent containment—or, perhaps better, neutralization—of contradictions. Arnold's culture is once again exemplary here, as a rhetorical attempt to mediate between (indeed, to wish away) the class warfare of English society, via a complex architecture of oppositions: between Hebraism and Hellenism, Barbarians and Philistines, anarchy and authority. However, I am more interested in emulating Raymond Williams's extended engagement with "culture," which takes up Arnold's project in a much more rigorous and troubled attempt to understand the tensions between high culture and daily life, the traditional and the newly created, the individual and the collective, the general construct and the specific instance, theory and practice. Given these complexities, the term often seems less definable than describable—as when Williams offers us "cultural" definition via a bus trip that takes us through the totality of social life as he once experienced it: past a cathedral containing the *mappa mundi* and the cinema showing a "cartoon version of *Gulliver's Travels*," through the city and into the country, past "grey Norman castles" and the "steel rolling-mill."[16]

Of course, the things Williams points out along the way were selected for their value in illustrating through juxtaposition the contradictions he was interested in, and thus he did not offer us, in this foray, anything like an exhaustive "cultural" map of the Welsh borderlands. The same will be true on my bus trip: I will similarly avoid a comprehensive mapping of all the various debates and nuances of the discourse of "culture" in the time and period in which I am interested. However, as a point of method, I do feel that "cultural" specificities need to be addressed as a way of illuminating, and correcting, the cultural generality. Thus, though largely a theoretical treatment of the idea of "culture," this book is very much about a place, a time, and a set of discourses. Put another way, I am interested in the tension residing in the fact that the same historical moment, roughly the first forty years of this century, saw the creation of *both* the anthropological culture concept and an elaboration of such ideas as "mass culture" and "middlebrow culture," not to mention "kitsch," "Kulchur," and "masscult." These different "cultures," residing uneasily together, seem to me to offer a startling key to the intellectual, artistic, and social life of what I will call the "modernist" moment.

The Culture of Modernism

Modernism is for me first and foremost a periodizing concept, characterized by a nexus of related historical, intellectual, technological, and aesthetic developments, rather than by a set of formal traits or styles.[17] Thus, it does not seem impossible to talk about the discipline of anthropology itself as fundamentally modernist in its conception—a point to which I will return at a later place in this chapter. First, however, I will address the question of how we may think about modernism as a specific historical period.

The historical and intellectual keys to modernism are well established, and rehearsed: the horror of the First World War; the development of the scientific concepts of relativity and uncertainty; Freud's theory of the unconscious and infantile sexuality; the development and proliferation of consumer culture; the invention of the camera, the automobile, the street light, steel-frame architecture, sound recording, the moving picture; the consolidation of the globe-spanning European empires and the emergence of the United States as a central economic and military power. To this list we might profitably add what Perry Anderson has called "the imaginative proximity of social revolution," providing the hope and fear of radically disruptive changes to come.[18]

Perhaps just as crucially as any of these elements, modernism was characterized by self-consciousness, especially a distinctive self-awareness of the rapidity of change, and distance from the past. But largely because of this self-consciousness, it is both a historical period, and an ideology, offering us a fully presented story about the meaning of its own historicity.[19] One danger, then, of talking about modernism is of falling into an acceptance of its own reification as the historical fact of the period, its import, its context. This book will thus attempt to walk a fine line between two modernisms, one historical, the other a self-presentation of the historical, produced both by modernists themselves, and those (like the New York intellectuals, discussed in Chapter 6) who have claimed the role of preserving its legacy. I will do this by addressing the period in terms of another seemingly self-contradictory idea: *American modernism*.

Just as I am interested here in both an ideological critique of modernism and a characterization of it, so am I also interested in both interrogating and explicating its American context: my claim is exceptionalist to the extent that I believe that modernism did take on specific forms in the United States between 1900 and 1950, brought about by, among other things, thoroughly ideological views about the existence, and nature, of a uniquely American "culture." This will, no doubt, seem to some a departure from both recent and traditional scholarship on modernism, which has long held that modernism was by definition international, perhaps a product of rootlessness itself, but certainly belonging to the cosmopolitan avant-gardes of a few European capitals.[20] This view—one often produced and promoted by the artists most firmly associated with the period—has thus typically emphasized the significance of Pound and Eliot's London; the Paris of Montparnasse and Shakespeare and Company; Prague; Vienna; Zurich; Berlin; and the newly international context of an émigré-filled World War II–era New York. Needless to say, such a vision severely limits American modernism's participants—to a handful of Parisian exiles, and those who served in the Great War. Or, Midwesterner Sherwood Anderson becomes a modernist (by some closed canonical calculus) only via the influence of Gertrude Stein, who was in turn, of course, influenced by cubism. Needless to say, such a view of modernism, already somewhat impoverished in its explanatory power, also supports an analysis of a relatively closed set of autonomous authors and their works.

Meanwhile, risking the charge of exceptionalism, a number of scholars have addressed the presence of U.S.-based avant-gardes, in Harlem, Chicago, and Greenwich Village. In addressing these indigenous modernisms, a number of writers have revealed the enormous creative diversity of the period: along with cubist painting, jazz is now recognized as a key influence; the supposed opposition between formal experimentation and political activism has been revised and complicated; and the intercultural and interracial quality of aesthetic experimentation—and cultural production generally—is finally revealed and addressed.[21]

But if the idea of modernism—to say nothing of American modernism—is to be critically useful, it must do more than provide us with a canon against which to produce countercanons. Indeed, the idea of modernism will likely remain a quasi-evaluative term unless we turn at some point to questions of historiography, and the question of American modernism will be open to charges of provincialism, unless we can account for it in terms of an international context. What would happen if we understood this wider context in conjunction with Stein's fascination with the fact that her birthplace was Allegheny, Pennsylvania (or is it merely a collection of syllables?), or really came to grips with the paradoxes of Pound's origins in Idaho?[22]

One place to bridge the gap between modernism's internationalism and the American context is with an account of modernism that takes seriously the centrality of the ideology of *Americanism* to modernist theory and practice. For intellectuals from Italy to Russia to Japan, "America" was taken to be synonymous with the massified modernity that presented such an object of combined horror and fascination. This "America" could be called the homeland of modernism insofar as such quintessentially American phenomena as jazz, the skyscraper, Henry Ford's assembly line, and the movies provided inspiration for its characteristic experiments in space, form, imagery, and tempo. For Le Corbusier, to take but one well-known example, modern architecture began with the North American grain elevator.[23] Far from refuting the idea that modernism was an international movement, such a view, rather, pulls the American social context of industrialization and mass culture into the foreground of the international debates about the modernist experiment.

Of course, this association of "America" with modernity itself is also part of modernist mythology. For, if the modernity of the American scene was such a crucial inspirational source of modernism, why did all those American expatriates go to Paris; why would Faulkner write about life in the rural South; or why would Georgia O'Keeffe abandon her fascination with New York skylines to paint in the rural environs of Taos, New Mexico? Why, on the other hand, would Futurist and Constructivist celebrations of the machine emerge in industrially underdeveloped Italy and Russia, while at the same time the far more technologically advanced United States was the home of the reactionary, antitechnological, literary-political movement of the Southern Agrarians?[24]

These questions necessitate that we turn to an issue central to the historicization of modernism: namely, the complex relationship between modernism as a practice and the experience of modernity itself.[25] This experience, rather than reflecting a seamless parade of jazz, cars, and steel, is, rather, marked by a perception of uneven development, and even friction, between those sites of modernization's greatest impact and the places that it touched less completely. Thus, as Fredric Jameson has argued, modernism can be best characterized by "the coexistence of realities from radically different moments of history— handicrafts alongside the great cartels, peasant fields with the Krupp factories or Ford plant in the distance."[26] We may now see that the fascination with America for Gramsci or for the intellectuals of a modernizing Japan was precisely in the way that it *imaginatively* figured for a full modernity imperfectly realized in their own context.

I stress the word *imaginatively* because the reality of the American context was decidedly more complicated than such visions suggest. It is clear that in certain respects the United States of the early twentieth century was more modernized than was Europe, particularly in regard to the development of industry, mass media, and consumer culture. For example, in 1934 over 43 percent of all the radio sets owned worldwide were owned by Americans.[27] However, as Jameson's allusion to the Ford plant suggests, this did not mean that the United States experienced its modernity in a uniquely uniform fashion. Indeed, it could well be that the very things that made the United States more advanced compared to other nations also heightened the experience of difference *among* Americans in different regions, where modernization was differently experienced.

The U.S. pattern of development in the early twentieth century can be characterized by the presence of a highly developed urban and industrial core in the Northeast and upper Midwest, surrounded by an extensive and often still remote rural periphery. In a sense, this periphery extended well beyond the borders of the nation into eastern and southern Europe, which served around the turn of the century as the source of a seemingly limitless supply of immigrant labor. But within the United States itself, the South, the mountain West, and the plains Midwest were also peripheral, serving the industrial core and the centers of capital by supplying not only laborers (especially during the mobilization for World War II), but also agricultural products and other extracted raw materials.[28] Residents of these peripheral parts of the United States not only had comparatively limited access to the consumer goods and mass cultural forms that were transforming the lives of those in the urban core, they also often lacked access to basic modern infrastructure. Indeed, in the respect of infrastructural development, the United States as a whole was rather backward, lagging far behind western Europe and even remote settler colonies such as New Zealand in providing such basic services as electrification to its rural areas. Before the New Deal, fewer than 5 percent of the farms in the South and the Great Plains were on the electrical grid.[29] The absence of this infrastructure meant that only a few farmers in these regions (those who could afford costly home generators) could enjoy such modern amenities as up-to-date farm equipment, safe and reliable lighting, washing machines, and the electrical water pumps that made indoor plumbing a practical possibility.[30] Lack of electrification also more or less precluded the enjoyment of radio and phonograph records, features of the new mass culture that was quickly transforming the tastes, habits, and attitudes of urban Americans. We may now qualify the picture of a homogenous modernity suggested by the fact that Americans as a whole owned 43 percent of the world's radios in 1934, by pointing out that these sets were owned by only 60 percent of American households.[31]

Needless to say, geographic differences in the experience of modernity could only heighten the already existing tensions between regions of the United States. These tensions are part of the context for a number of well-known conflicts of this period, including the battle over the teaching of evolutionary theory in the 1925 Scopes "Monkey" trial in Tennessee and the protracted debate over prohibition, which was widely opposed in the cities but strongly supported outside of the urban centers. In political conflicts such as these, the rural periphery, slowly becoming linked to the urban centers via infrastructural improvements and a nascent mass media, expressed its horror over the social changes brought about by modernization, and doubtless also its resentment over the cultural and political power of the urban centers. This horror is expressed most directly in the Agrarians' manifesto, *I'll Take My Stand*.[32] From the other side of the cultural divide, members of the urban elite such as H. L. Mencken expressed their disdain for the provinces by frothing over the anti-alcohol prejudices of the "booboisie," and calling the South and Midwest the "Sahara of the Bozarts." Meanwhile, Harold Ross created the *New Yorker* magazine, which proudly declared its urban identity with the slogan, "Not for the old lady in Dubuque." Never before (nor since) in the United States were issues of taste and cultural value articulated in such geographic terms.

Given what we may now see as the geographic context of the cultural great divide, we may now turn to the "high" culture of the period, and see how often its interesting producers addressed, in similarly geographical terms, the paradoxes and unevenness of America's progress toward modernization. Willa Cather, W. E. B. Du Bois, William Faulkner, Zora Neale Hurston, William Carlos Williams, and many others may be said to have followed Pound's famous injunction to "make it new" *within* the context of what might be described as the provincial, and the geographically and culturally marginal. By locating their work in rural Nebraska or Mississippi, Eatonville, Florida or

Paterson, New Jersey, in the often painful contact zones between the past and the present, these writers registered the conflicts and paradoxes of America's uneven modernity. Nor were writers alone in this interest in addressing the vernacular and the regional; the same interest may be found in the "prairie school" architecture of Frank Lloyd Wright, and in the settings and ideas in the music of Charles Ives and Aaron Copland. This book addresses the work of several other modernist figures, including Sherwood Anderson, Waldo Frank, Jean Toomer, Hart Crane, Thomas Hart Benton, Nathanael West, and James Agee, whose work was variously situated within, and commented upon, this American—geographical—cultural divide.

By insisting on these provincial and vernacular interests in the context of modernism—so long defined in terms of the experience of historical rupture, rejection of the aesthetics of the past, making things new, and so forth—we may begin to find a way to think about modernism's project in terms that do not excessively privilege the modernists' own self-presentation of their efforts, as enacting radical breaks from history. Instead, what we have is a more historically embedded modernism in which its creators can be seen to have held the relationship between past and present, and center and periphery, in dialectic tension. Neither embracing the past in a decidedly unmodernist nostalgia nor celebrating the massified present—or future—uncritically, these *peripheral* modernists, rather, registered the historical specificity of their moment.

This point might be made more completely by examining the relationship between the modernism I am describing here and what is confusingly called *anti*modernism. This term would seem to refer to a position critical of modernist art or ideas—a position which, as we will see, certainly had its spokesmen, including Thomas Hart Benton, and (more complexly) Van Wyck Brooks. However, I am interested here in the "antimodernist" movement preceding and in some respects anticipating modernism, that—following the lead of socialist William Morris—attempted to address the problem of worker alienation in industrial society through a revitalization of handicraft traditions. Though this antimodernism was explicitly backward-looking in its fascination with preindustrial technology (indeed, the premodern Middle Ages were a favored model), a number of the craftspeople and architects inspired by the antimodernism of Morris and others, including (in the United States) furniture maker Gustav Stickley, glass designer Louis Tiffany, Los Angeles architects Greene and Greene, and the young Frank Lloyd Wright, were at least protomodernnist—*ante*-modernist—in terms of their formal innovations.[33] For example, in their fascination with what might be called the technological primitive, both Stickley and Greene and Greene produced designs that fetishized complex joinery and other traditional features of furniture and building craft. In using these elements of construction as ornament, these direct influences upon Wright created a style that, in its formal simplicity, departed from Victorian design and even looked ahead to the modernist emphasis on structure and function, so typical, for example, of the Bauhaus.

More importantly, however, it may be from the polemics of antimodernism that modernists developed their critical perspective on alienation and mass culture. The fin-de-siècle antimodernist William Morris, who imitated the guild-organized craft labor of the Middle Ages to critique the alienation of industrial labor in England, inspired a movement in the United States that, in addition to encouraging craftsmen and architects in innovative experiments in style, sought out and championed examples of what were perceived to be the authentic lifestyles in the strong craft traditions and folkways of certain immigrant groups, Appalachia, and the native tribes of the American Southwest. In these antimodernisms, the "simple" and "primitive" cultures being celebrated were seen to be reflective of the distant past of modern society, and the mirror opposite of its present. Admired or imagined in these "others" with a combination of nostalgic longing and solicitude were a connection to the land; ownership of the means of production through unalienated craft or agricultural labor; erotic frankness; and an unselfconscious relationship to the community, expressed in heartfelt custom and authentic ritual.[34] Many of these perceived traits would also be celebrated in the work of the more explicitly modernist artists later in the twentieth century.

Though rather different in terms of its aesthetics, antimodernism can also be seen to share some of the impulses and obsessions with the Orientalisms and primitivisms that have long been seen as significant features of continental modernism.[35] Providing, as Eliot put it, "The backward look behind the assurance / Of recorded history, the backward half-look / Over the shoulder, towards the primitive terror" ("The Dry Salvages," lines 106–8), modernist primitivism departed from its antimodern predecessor in its explicit, and of course racist, eroticism (the frisson implicit in "primitive terror"), and in its lack of interest in the political problem of labor's alienation. But like the American antimodernist fascinations with Indians or Appalachians, Matisse's *odalisques*, Picasso's African masks, Stravinsky's *Sacre du printemps*, D. H. Lawrence's *The Plumed Serpent* also offered a vision of modernity's other—or perhaps better, its "prehistorical" antithesis. The primitive represented a certain kind of timelessness, a conceptual space before the historical track that would lead to modernity itself.

If this was primitivism's fantasy, then its historical reality was one of registering the changing political *and* spatial relationship between an imperial Europe and its colonized territory—another phenomenon related, of course, to the ongoing process of global modernization. Jameson suggests that the discourse of imperialism itself changed in this period, so that the "axis of otherness" shifted from "the relationship of the various imperial subjects among each other" to the self-conscious focus on "the relationship between a generalized imperial subject . . . with its various others or objects."[36] Edward Said has suggested how easily this shift reflected itself in literary modernism, noting "by the beginning of the twentieth century, [tokens of empire] were used to convey an ironic sense of how vulnerable Europe was, and how—in Conrad's great phrase—'this also has been one of the dark places on the earth.' "[37]

Though the history of imperialism in the United States was different in some important respects from Europe's longer and more far-ranging colonial enterprises (for one thing, the United States contained some of its colonies within its borders), the effects of the changing relationship between colonizer and colonized territory were similar on both continents.[38] In a moment characterized by mass migrations to the industrial United States from the margins of Europe and the American South, the traditionally dominant groups of the United States articulated new concerns about their social position in relation to these very present others. *The Great Gatsby*, with its distortions of historical temporality and Tom Buchanan's anxious rantings about the supercession of the "white race," is, no less than *Heart of Darkness*, about having been (or perhaps better, *becoming*) "one of the dark places on the earth."[39] And certainly, an indigenous American primitivism can be found in the complex use and reception of African-American artists like Paul Robeson, as well as in the erotic cultural tourism of works like Carl Van Vechten's *Nigger Heaven* and Anderson's *Dark Laughter*, in Hemingway's Indian stories, and Oliver La Farge's Navajo romance *Laughing Boy*. But perhaps more so than in the European context, such instances of American primitivism—especially those addressing Native Americans—often intersected with strong antimodern impulses. Hence, modernist *salonnière* Mabel Dodge's eventual repudiation of New York for a cultural mission to New Mexico, to "[s]ave the Indians, their art-culture—reveal it to the world!"[40] Her mission (in which she was soon joined by D. H. Lawrence) was certainly shot through with primitivist fantasies about Indians as living examples of the prehistoric other and as possessors of an erotic Lawrentian life force. But unlike, say, Picasso's use of African masks, which served largely as inspiration for his formal aesthetic experiments, Southwestern Indian "art-culture" was *itself* a central focus of concern, valued both in antimodern terms as handicraft and artisanal labor and as a species of art.[41]

This interesting convergence of primitivism and antimodernism may perhaps be explained as an artifact of the peculiar historical position of the Native American in the Anglo-American settler-colonial imagination, as both the despised, displaced native other and the noble model of a landed national American identity. In a time and place deeply unsettled by the experience of modernization, it is unsurprising that the figure of the Indian would once again serve a dual purpose: on the one hand, mediating Americans' changed experience of empire (the West now pacified, the Indians have become tourist attractions), and on the other hand, reminding Americans of some other, preindustrial moment that they could attempt to appropriate as an alternative to their own. This Indian Southwest would be the common ground of both Dodge's modernist art colony and much of the pioneering work of American anthropology—an anthropology that may also be addressed in terms of its modernism.

The Modernism of "Culture"

There are a number of ways that one could delineate the relationship between anthropology in general and modernism in general, the most time-honored being the one modernist artists—notably, T. S. Eliot—themselves created, in their use of such works as Sir J. G. Frazer's *The Golden Bough* and Jessie Weston's *From Ritual to Romance*, as both models and sources for their own literary works. From there, one might turn to the academic literary criticism of the midcentury (itself a complexly modernist institution) to address the influence of myth critics including Richard Chase, Leslie Fiedler, and Northrop Frye, who, interestingly, also found theoretical inspiration in evolutionary comparativists such as Frazer and Weston. As Marc Manganaro has shown, the influence of these Victorian comparativists on modernist writers and myth critics represents a fascinating case of apparent historical a-synchrony between the two fields, in which major poets and critics of the period seem to have embraced an anthropology already outmoded in their own moment. Sharply distinct from the work of Frazer, the new anthropology that emerged by the 1920s and was virtually embodied in the figure of Bronislaw Malinowski, would be characterized by monographs on single cultures, based on information gathered by ethnographers acting as participant-observers. Moreover, this anthropology would pose a strong theoretical challenge to applications such as Frazer's of evolutionary theory to a study of human cultures.[42]

While this apparent historical a-synchrony poses a significant difficulty in delineating modernism as a historical period that would encompass both literary and anthropological practices, a more recent interdisciplinary conversation has emerged that shifts the direction of influence, and rearticulates the problem significantly. In the last decade or so, the unidirectional emphasis on anthropology's influence on literature has changed to a more reciprocal view, or perhaps even to a new emphasis on literature's theoretical and methodological influence on *anthropology*. This changing relationship was inspired by (among other things) the explicit "literariness" of anthropological works like Claude Lévi-Strauss's *Tristes Tropiques*; by studies like Edward Said's *Orientalism*, which revealed ideological connections between ethnography, aesthetics, and imperialism; and by a continued theoretical cross-fertilization of the disciplines from Lévi-Strauss's structuralism, to Clifford Geertz's "thick description," to a mutual indebtedness to poststructuralist theory. While this complex new interrelation between the fields has resulted in a few developments in literary critical practice—for example, in ethnographies of reading practices, and discussions of cultural identity in relation to literature—recent work in both disciplines has perhaps excessively emphasized the writing practices of anthropology.[43] This emphasis may be owing to the entrepreneurial spirit of literary scholars willing to claim their expertise as readers of all sorts of texts, but it is also the product of the recognition among anthropologists that the authorizing experience of fieldwork is mediated through the written ethnography. As interest in the rhetorical aspects of anthropology has grown, a textual history of the discipline has emerged, glossed in terms familiar to literary history; ethnography is now also occasionally categorized, as with works of literature, as "realist," "Victorian," "modernist," or "postmodernist."

Not surprisingly, the periodization of anthropological texts can experience the same kinds of pitfalls that are found in its parallel literary exercise. As with formalist discussions of literary modernism, the use of formal criteria for anthropological texts often leads to some odd conclusions. For example, a number of proponents of "reflexive" ethnography took an interest in the Bakhtinian concepts of "dialogism," and "polyphony" as useful tools for rethinking the complexities of intercultural exchange and authority in the ethnographic encounter. Occasionally, this recognition of the "dialogic" and "polyphonic" aspects of certain ethnographies led to periodizing gestures, in assertions that these experiments in ethnographic writing were either "modernist" in that they represent a reaction to "realist" ethnographies, or "postmodernist" because they are, and the ethnographer's voice is, "de-centered."[44] As with similar attempts in literary criticism to apply periodizing categories based on a work's conformity to a series of formal traits, these kinds of judgments resulted in some historical peculiarities. In what sense is textual "dialogism" and "polyphony" "postmodernist," given these terms' origin with the decidedly modernist theorist Mikhail Bakhtin (who elaborated them first in a study of Dostoevsky)? Then too, isn't there something ahistorical about describing ethnographies as "modernist" that were written a full generation, or more, after the publication of *Ulysses*? Here, one might almost be tempted to propose something of the inverse of the point that modernist literature borrowed from an outmoded anthropology, to observe that anthropology may have somehow lagged behind literature.[45]

The way out of this dilemma, of course, is to see modernism and anthropology—and literature, for that matter—as more than a set of textual practices. All involve a complex response to a set of changing conditions, an experience of modernity, unique to the decades surrounding the turn of the twentieth century. From this angle, we may begin to see how an ethnographic monograph of anthropology's "classical phase" emerged from the same complex milieu as the literature of "high" modernism.[46] Moreover, we may begin to see anthropology's role as an *agent* in some of the perceived changes of the moment.

We turn first to anthropology's function as the "factual" discourse of the "primitive." As I have argued, the "primitive" stood for modernists as part of a complex dialectic of past and present, modernity and premodernity, center and periphery. In its function as a bearer of the "truth" about the primitive, anthropology can thus be said to have served as a significant mediating discourse of this dialectic. However, the situation is still more complex, for anthropology as a field was also based upon, and partook of, this same dialectic, this fascination with the relationship between "primitive" past and "modern" present.

Tzvetan Todorov hinted at the ambivalent modernism of anthropology when, in *The Conquest of the Americas*, he described it as a phenomenon of the changing world order, as "at once the child of colonialism and the proof of its death throes."[47] In the United States, anthropology's origins coincided closely with the last days of U.S. continental expansion and with the height of its imperial adventures in the Pacific and the Caribbean. Roughly concurrent with the completion of the U.S. imperialist project in North America was the publication of the major works of Lewis Henry Morgan, the first American anthropologist whose work is still known and cited, and the establishment of the first major institutions of the discipline: important ethnographic museums, including the Smithsonian and the American Museum of Natural History, and federal agencies, including the Bureau of American Ethnology, charged with collecting and preserving the "salvages" of imperial adventure.[48] These "salvages" (about which I will say more in the next chapter) in turn had a Janus-faced ideological function: as artifacts of the "vanishing" past of native North America (and of a kind of racial childhood of all Americans), they also marked Euro-America's present and future as the agent of Manifest Destiny.

Yet by 1900, American anthropology was also beginning to change its relationship to this imperial past. Between 1900 and 1940, roughly the same years that modernist literature emerged and flourished, anthropology would be consolidated as a professional academic discipline, no longer tied to the ethnological museum, the field practice of "salvage" ethnography, or the ideological function of documenting American "progress." In their place would be a new institutional home in the university, an established fieldwork practice of participant observation—which necessarily acknowledged the contemporaneous existence of the "primitive"—and a more complex (and less self-congratulatory) understanding of human history. But for anthropologists working in these years, these transitions would not have been experienced in such a seamless fashion. They must have felt—and indeed in some sense were—poised on the border between the past of American conquest and a present that rather anxiously wondered about its relationship to that past and its future. Moreover, as we shall see in the next chapter, there was a significant, and often troubled, transition to be made from the institutional spaces of the museum and the university, from "amateur" to "professional" identities and practices, from artifact collection to participant-observer fieldwork. These basic experiences of, and crises in, the development of a professional identity are also significant features of the turn-of-the-century experience of modernity, one generally felt by intellectuals of the period.

Indeed, in a number of senses, twentieth-century anthropologists were delicately poised between social worlds. Julia Liss has convincingly argued that Boas and Malinowski's common experience of being aliens in their adoptive countries, an experience reinforced in fieldwork and resolved in their theoretical searches for cultural coherence and social functioning, is the central thread that makes both figures "cosmopolitan" participants in the "modernist sensibility."[49] This experience of being alien must have been shared by a significant number of Boas's foreign-born and second-generation students, but there is also a sense in which anthropologists in general courted alienation as a matter of their professional practice. While the fieldworker was never entirely absorbed into the culture of the other (not a positive thing, in any case, for these anthropologists, since that would entail losing one's capacity to explain and contextualize), the anthropologist also stood apart from his or her own context, as its critic and interpreter. It is in this sense of self-conscious estrangement and mediation that anthropology in the early twentieth century seems most characteristic of its moment. And, I believe, it is on the basis of this gesture of critique, and position of exteriority, that anthropologists are most easily comparable to other modernist intellectuals working in America at the same time.

As we shall see, professional anthropology in the United States would come to be associated with a refutation of traditional notions of progress and its corollaries, including hierarchical distinctions between the races. Also revised in this transition from amateur to professional anthropology were the primitivist views of the other as representing the prehistorical, the infantile, the feminine, the natural. Significantly, the rebuttal of these models of progress is also the site in which the discipline's central concept, *culture*, has been understood to operate. As we will see in the next chapter, the critique of racism engaged in by Boas only necessitated showing how race was not itself a limitation to full humanity. The idea of culture was thus a kind of corollary hypothesis, drawn on spatial-contextual lines, which was needed largely to offer some nonracial account of difference. But this spatial idea opened up a number of fascinating corollaries of its own, including the possibility of filling up one of these sites with descriptive content, as a way of organizing collective identity. It also implied the possibility of intercultural comparison, of checking one's own culture's time-honored habits and precepts with those of many others—including, crucially, those who seemed to have escaped modernity's grasp. I believe it is through the elaboration of these gestures that the central modernist project of the *critique* of modernity was explicitly, and often very influentially, enacted.

Thus, in their ethnographies of other cultural contexts, anthropologists often addressed the central questions of the time, including the antimodernist's problem of alienation and the role of the individual in an industrial, urban, and mass society. Margaret Mead's *Coming of Age in Samoa*, in which Samoan culture was held up as a positive antithesis to a sexually repressive West, is only the most familiar example of this project of critique. But no less crucial to this modernist estrangement of context was the project of attempting to imagine the culture one inhabited in full awareness of a world of other cultures. Suddenly the flaws, inconsistencies, hypocrisies, and "cultural lags" of one's own context come to the surface.[50] In other words, one's own experience of the uneven lurchings toward modernity suddenly become apparent.

2

Dry Salvages: Spatiality, Nationalism, and the Invention of an "Anthropological" Culture

HAVING, in the last chapter, discounted one modernist fable that would name anthropologist Franz Boas the creator of "culture," I must now reconstruct the case for a nearly indisputable point: that in a more complex way Boas was central to the creation of both the culture concept and the professional discipline of anthropology in America, and that he is an exemplary figure in the intellectual life of his moment. Moreover, I do see him as having instantiated a distinct conceptual break from previous views of human life, a break that enabled a wide variety of thinkers, including W. E. B. Du Bois, Horace Kallen, and Randolph Bourne (discussed at the end of this chapter) to reconceive racial, immigrant, national, and international identity in important new ways. However, I think it is something of a misreading to see Boas's contribution as being fundamentally antihierarchical or evaluatively relativist in nature; rather, his crucial intervention might be more properly described as a *spatial* reorganization of human differences.

To get at this point—and to stress the fundamentally *modernist* nature of this gesture—I will begin with what might seem to some like a detour, by invoking the idea of the "salvage," a concept that rhetorically links an anthropological practice of Boas's early career with modernist literature, via the work of T. S. Eliot. The connection of Eliot to Boas is intended to be provocative: though a famous citer of anthropological texts, Eliot's persona as modernism's "public face" was that of an often obscure elitist, whose own controversial contributions to the meaning of culture called for the (re-)empowerment of a cultural aristocracy.[1] Moreover, the anthropology he did champion was the very kind of work, evolutionary comparativism, that Boas is most commonly seen as having delegitimated. Thus doubly antithetical to many conceptions of the Boasian "cultural" legacy—a spokesman for both "high culture" and outmoded ethnological thinking—Eliot's work is, I will argue, similar to Boas's in one basic respect: namely, the common experience of a shift characteristic of modernism generally from conceptions of human history based on a vision of lineal, temporal advancement, to a more complex historical understanding that incorporates the possibility of *spatial* differences in humanity.

Dry Salvages

> The Dry Salvages—presumably *les trois sauvages*—
> is a small group of rocks, with a beacon, off the N.E.
> coast of Cape Ann, Massachusetts.
>   (*T.S. Eliot, prefatory note to "The Dry Salvages,"*
>   Four Quartets)

The pun in this title of the third poem of *Four Quartets* offers us an interesting way to think about the modernist obsession with the primitive and the regional, and about the connection between anthropology and modernist literature. After all, Eliot's islands, widely taken to be the best evidence of the poet's regional roots in New England, are also full of Indians.[2] There are *les trois sauvages* who give them their name, but also the "salvages" marked in the poem as "hints of earlier and other creation." These latter "salvages" are both of the natural world of "The starfish, the hermit crab, the whale's backbone," and the human jetsam of "the torn seine / the shattered lobsterpot, the broken oar / And the gear of foreign dead men" (lines 18–24). In the pun, the natural (sea and island) is elided with the human (the "savage" Indians); humans (both Indian and immigrant), with the works of their hands.

In this intricate elision, Eliot's "salvages" are not unrelated to the confused conceptions of the Indian presence in North America that undergirded the nineteenth-century project of "salvage ethnography." As in Eliot's figure, this project also complexly elided the categories of the natural, the human, and the technological, to suggest a way to read human history through the evidence of collected objects. Curtis Hinsley has argued that the foremost ideological function of this officially sanctioned activity of "salvaging" artifacts was that of "dehistoricization": as the Indian Wars drew to a close, evidences of the Native American presence (often produced by *living* artists and craftspeople at the behest of the collectors) were taken once and for all out of the drama of U.S. history and placed into the neatly organized glass cases of the ethnological museum.[3] But while dehistoricizing the Indian, salvage ethnography also served to bolster another narrative that reinforced the historical centrality of European-Americans. A central premise of the salvage endeavor of this period was that objects of Native American manufacture were both antitheses and progenitors of modern machinery and technology. Thus, Otis T. Mason, the first curator of ethnology for the Smithsonian's National Museum of Natural History, found a theoretical use for the objects his institution collected in his view that "the people of the world have left their history most fully recorded in the works of their hands." Charting the progress of humanity from savagery to civilization through the concept of "invention," or the successful technological manipulation of the environment, Mason could assert that the salvaged objects of Native American ways of life were windows into human history—specifically, into a triumphal American history of ever-increasing technological prowess.[4] The theoretical basis for much of this "salvage" work was thus social-evolutionary: because they were "primitive," the "savage" Native Americans would inevitably succumb to civilization.

By the 1920s, the moment George Stocking has identified as the "classical" period of American anthropology, the evolutionary theories of museum-based thinkers such as Mason—or of evolutionary-comparatists such as Eliot's favorite anthropologist, Sir James G. Frazer—were displaced by new theories and practices, which focused on the local features of a group of people as revealed by the participant-observer ethnographer.[5] But even after such teleological models of human history had come into disfavor among most anthropologists, and anthropological practice itself had undergone significant changes, a version of this salvage ethnography persisted. "Salvage" had become less a matter of collecting war trophies to take back to Washington than a nostalgic operation, recording ways of life that were seen to be dying out in the face of encroaching assimilation and modernization. As James Clifford has pointed out, the very structure of the classic ethnography is based on this newer idea of salvage, which both laments the inevitable loss of the other's "culture," and then reconstructs it as text.[6]

Though Eliot's own relationship to anthropology was complexly anachronistic, we can nevertheless see some ways in which his "salvages" overlap with the ones that concerned anthropologists. Marc Manganaro has shown how *The Waste Land* enacts the kind of salvage operation of lamentation and recuperation that Clifford described, on Eliot's own supposedly decaying Europe.[7] Similarly, in "The Dry Salvages" the islands-salvages are barren fragments of civilization's ruins, the recovered tokens of the moment before "worshippers of the machine" forgot the "strong brown god." Also, like the anthropologists of his day, Eliot is explicit in this poem in his rejection of a progressive direction to human history. Just as Eliot dismisses psychoanalysis by comparing it to fortune-telling, so, he preaches, such models of historical "development" are "a partial fallacy, / Encouraged by superficial notions of evolution, / Which becomes, in the popular mind, a means of disowning the past" (lines 87–89).[8] Though perhaps only a criticism of ("superficial") misapplications of evolutionary theory, Eliot does insist here upon a more complex experience of history, in which present and past are seen as thoroughly, intimately, interrelated. It is in this sense that his "salvages" take on a specific function: as existing emblems of the past's presence, they are confirmation of Eliot's suggestion that "the past has another pattern, and ceases to be a mere sequence."

Though we might look first to the terror of the London Blitz to explain Eliot's particular fascination in *Four Quartets* with time and history and the fate of Europe, there is also something both representatively Eliotic, and representatively modernist, in his desire to locate such tokens of temporal paradox. What has often been called the modernist fascination with temporality, identified as early as the mid-twenties by Wyndham Lewis in *Time and Western Man*, may first be understood as a rejection of the models of teleological progress—"development"—that undergirded the nineteenth-century idea of civilization.[9] And while it is a (dubious) cliché about modernism generally to say that the events of the early twentieth century eroded the steady optimism of that earlier period (the very existence of the Futurists remind us that not all modernists were Eliotic pessimists), there were good reasons for the modernists to question older models of social, biological, and historical progress. Even the pains of modernization aside, the modernist self-conception of rupture and departure from the sterile academicisms of the previous generation itself required a new model of historical thinking that did not foreground a relationship, developmental or otherwise, between modernist experimentation and the older forms and models of the genteel tradition. In this light, we may partially understand the modernists' attraction to revolutions, both aesthetic and, occasionally, political. The desire for historical rupture also accounts for the modernists' fascination with their present's relationship to the remote or even mythical past— a past that, as Eliot suggested, is newly available once "superficial notions of evolution" are put to rest.[10]

In this larger project of retiring superficial notions of evolution, and of rearticulating historicity itself, Boas and his students would be central figures. In the United States, Boasian anthropologists were prominent articulators, and popularizers, of anti-Spenserian views. As with Eliot, this antiteleological project was part of a larger re-articulation of historical time. In challenging the prevalent racist and evolutionist thinking of the late nineteenth and early twentieth centuries, Boas and many of his students would instead address differences in human populations by invoking the fundamentally historical processes of contact, exchange, adaptation, and migration. It would become a mantra of Boasian anthropology that specific conjunctions of "race," "culture," and language were matters of historical contingency, not biological or developmental necessity.[11] But even more broadly speaking, these anthropologists were also centrally involved in connecting their present to the ever less remote "primitive" past, and thus in the project of recording the contradictions and unevennesses in modernity itself. Once again, a new look at "salvages"—specifically, a thoroughgoing reconsideration of the historical meaning of salvaged artifacts—may be seen to have instantiated this centrally spatial reconception.

To explain this point, I must offer another, again slightly overdramatic, origin story of the professional discipline of anthropology in the United States.[12] Its protagonist is once again Boas, but the site of his challenge to evolution is not yet "culture." Rather, it is a far more institutionally located story, involving the museum-based ethnological establishment of the Smithsonian's National Museum of Natural History. Boas's challenge to the curators, including Otis T. Mason, and to the evolutionary theory that formed their guiding principles, involved the rather technical issue of the proper method of displaying ethnological artifacts. In the 1890s, the collected objects of Indian "salvage" were organized and displayed in museum cases on the basis of apparent similarity of function or degree of technological sophistication, as (Boas reported) "different species of throwing sticks, basketry, bows, etc."[13] Grouped together for the purpose of demonstrating hierarchies of technical mastery, the advance from the most primitive of implements to the most sophisticated, fish hooks and spear points were made to conform to a classification system that directly followed the schema of biological phylogeny. Just as the orders of a phylogeny are divided from each other by their presumed evolutionary distance (changes that were also seen to reflect stages of organismal development), the categories of material objects were thought to reflect the stages of the development of human civilization, as demonstrated by the complexity of the technical "invention" required to create each object.

Against this elaborate speciation of artifacts, Boas wrote a series of articles in the pages of *Science*, arguing that different types of objects should be displayed together, not according to function, but to their sites of origin. Under his organizational schema, a given object would be understood not in comparison with other objects used for the same purpose (a throwing stick compared to relatively more or less technologically sophisticated throwing sticks), but according to its relationship to other objects produced among the same group of people. In other words, for Boas, a given throwing stick should more properly be seen (and displayed) as part of a regionally-defined production of a diversity of objects that would also include, for example, baskets and fish hooks.

Boas's intervention—his parting of the cases, as it were—has been seen as both the rejection of the evolutionary biologism that undergirded the older curatorial practices, and as the creation of a new ordering principle based on what would eventually be thought of as "culture"—for, it is assumed, this is the unnamed concept which best makes sense of the whole that includes baskets, fish hooks, and spears from the same place.[14] If this is indeed the founding gesture in the creation of the "anthropological" culture concept, then it is important to recognize that its central intervention was one of changing the axis of categorization and differentiation from the evolutionary-teleological terms of comparative levels of technical mastery to the geographical-spatial considerations of the location in which the items were produced.

Later in the chapter, I will flesh out the details of this important transformation, but for now it should be sufficient to note the similarities between Boas's reconception of the significance of artifacts and Eliot's use of "salvages." Not only do both Eliot and Boas reject the simple teleology of evolutionary models, but they can be read in their own very different terms to be effacing the idea that it is primarily developmental distance that separates "us" from the other. In the logic of Eliot's pun, "a small group of rocks off the N.E. coast of Cape

Ann, Massachusetts" is one with "salvage" Indians and human debris: as such, they are both artifactual reminders of specific historical moments and as eternally present as the granite New England shore. However, they are also *spatially* distant, and indeed offer a navigating beacon for the seafaring traveler. In other words, it is their geographical location, rather than their place in some developmental history, that becomes the significant fact of these salvages' existence. Similarly, in Boas's conceptual reorganization of his own kind of salvages, it is now the physical site of origin of an artifact that gives it its significance, not its ability to connote the historical origins of modern technological achievements. In the context of the museum display, the physical distance of the other is now echoed in the physical separation of the cases—each, in effect, its own island, containing its own salvages.

With this in mind, we may now offer a more specific theoretical connection between the anthropological culture concept and modernism. Conveniently for the ethnographer or the modernist artist (living in an era of increasingly easy and efficient travel), such a spatial reconception of one's relationship to the past makes its objects, and its physical and human representatives, newly tangible, and finally appropriable. In this sense, Eliot's fragments and salvages were not unlike the exotica that drew Gaugin to Fiji, Picasso to African art, or, in the American context, that brought the colony of modernist painters and writers to the pueblos of northern New Mexico. This spatial relationship to the other— this "cultural" logic—is central, in other words, to the modernist primitivisms and regionalisms I addressed in the previous chapter. In this context, we may also consider the geographical organization of a book like Jean Toomer's *Cane*, which takes us from South to North, and again to the South, in search of some kind of ideal space for African-American culture, and, of course, Eliot's transcontinental wanderings in *Four Quartets* from East Coker to the Dry Salvages, and back again.[15]

The Parting of the Cases

We will thus provisionally hypothesize that the culture concept is modernist precisely in the way that it enables alterity of a number of different kinds to be reconceived in spatial terms, as part of a complex social geography. That said, however, a number of crucial qualifications must immediately be made. First, such a spatial reconsideration of difference in no way negates historical, or even evolutionary, thinking. Just as Eliot's thinking borrowed heavily from the work of evolutionary anthropology, so we shall see that Boas (especially in his early career) worked within an evolutionary paradigm. What the spatial turn may more properly be said to do is to question the teleological narrative of many evolutionary models, by insisting on the simultaneity of the "primitive" with (and within) the "civilized."[16] Moreover, though this spatial turn unsticks the teleological thinking of evolutionary models, it does not imply cultural relativism, or in any way preclude the possibility of making invidious comparisons between groups of people. Put another way: though I would contend that modernist primitivism is something very different from nineteenth-century teleological understandings of "the primitive" (as a stage on the way to civilization), it would be absurd to conclude from this that modernist primitivism was not racist and easily capable of accommodating views of the other as inferior. There is, in other words, nothing necessarily egalitarian, or antihierarchical, about the gesture of imagining the other as spatially separate from oneself. Indeed, as we will discover, hierarchy itself can be a kind of spatial organization.

On a rather different point, it should be noted that although Boas's parting of the cases offers us an interestingly tangible origin story of the elusive concept of "culture," it only does so with a certain amount of retrospective reconstruction, for, as Ira Jacknis points out, it was not for a number of years that the implications of his challenge to the Smithsonian curators were realized in Boas's own work.[17] Indeed, Boas's intervention represents a very early statement in an extremely long and diverse career that encompassed significant work in folklore as well as in linguistic, physical, and cultural anthropology. As a result, Boas's specific legacy is hard to specify, a problem compounded by the fact that he trained so many students, each possessing a view of Boas's "real" contribution, based on the moment when they happened to have encountered him. The work of Boas and his older students concentrated for many years on the necessity of "collecting" with as much detail as possible the objects, languages, kinship data, and so on, of native peoples. For this Boas and this generation of students, the emphasis would have been on elaborating cultural traits on the model of natural history. For a later generation of students, he would be remembered for his defense of the rationality of primitive systems of thought, and for still others Boas would connote an interest in exploring the psychological aspects of cultures.[18] To further complicate the picture, Boas is widely remembered for waging, at some cost to his career, a vehement and life-long campaign against racism, national bigotry, and other forms of clan-based hatred.[19]

Not surprisingly, then, locating Boas's unique contribution to the culture concept is an especially fraught business. In fact, the "culture" Boas most commonly invoked in his earlier work to refute the social-evolutionary categories of "nature" or "biology" was only distantly related to "culture" as it came to be widely understood by the end of Boas's career in the 1930s and 1940s, as a transhistorical social "configuration," or indeed as the "personality" of a collectivity of people. This subsequent understanding of "culture," often functionalist and stressing the integration of cultural elements into a reified whole, had a strong impact in both the academic humanities and social sciences, and, just as significantly, captured the popular imagination through works like Margaret Mead's *Coming of Age in Samoa* and Ruth Benedict's *Patterns of*

Culture (to be discussed in Chapter 4). It is a sign of Boas's own changing views on "culture" that, against the expectations of many, he wrote laudatory prefatory material for both of these books.[20]

Finally, the problem of locating the origins of "culture" in Boas's work is compounded by one further fact: Boas's investments in establishing and recording the particulars of the people he studied has been seen by some as an impediment to the formulation of theoretical generalizations within the field of anthropology. This feature of the Boasian legacy has frustrated a number of commentators over the years, including several of Boas's own students. For example, after suggesting that much of Boas's most important work was to be found in papers with titles like "A Study of Alaskan Needlecases," Edward Sapir wrote of his famous teacher: "It is clear that Dr. Boas' unconscious long ago decreed that scientific cathedrals are only for the future, that for the time being spires surmounted by the definitive cross are unseemly, if not indeed sinful, that only cornerstones, unfinished walls, or even an occasional isolated portal are strictly in the service of the Lord."[21] It is one of the central complexities of Boas's career that, though he is widely associated with the significant theoretical development of the modern culture concept, he said frustratingly little on the subject of the meaning of "culture" until well after his own students, notably Sapir and Alfred L. Kroeber, had written extensively on the topic. Indeed, the father of American anthropology, widely remembered for his connection to "cultural relativism," did not actually offer a definition of culture in print until 1930, at least a full decade after his students had begun to use the word as a technical term.[22]

What follows, then, is an admittedly partial account of Boas's work, which, in pursuit of the origins of the culture concept, intentionally highlights several of the more widely familiar, and public, events in this complex figure's career. These include not only Boas's conflict with the museum establishment, but also his crusade against scientific racism and his public position against U.S. entry into the First World War. In emphasizing these moments, I hope to show how the specifics of the anthropological discourse of "culture" were intertwined with public issues of the day. But in taking this route through Boas's career, I am also pursuing another issue. In his central role in enabling the creation of a "professional" identity for anthropology, Boas can be seen not only as the developer of the culture concept, but as exemplifying a number of crucial institutional and ideological changes typical of his historical moment, and indeed central to modernism.

First, we will return to the particulars of Boas's battle with the Smithsonian. Boas's specific complaint with the curatorial practices of the Smithsonian has been explained as a historicist criticism of orthogenesis, or the idea that all of human history necessarily followed a set of definable stages on a common evolutionary trajectory toward "civilization."[23] Boas recognized that Mason's method of displaying superficially similar objects from different parts of the world together was based on a presumption of a single motor of historical change: as Mason saw it, different contextual circumstances gave rise to similar cultural phenomena. Boas, on the other hand, insisted that humanity was too complex to impute some underlying unity to its diverse actions and creations, and he presented the possibility that occasionally, "unlike causes produce like effects."[24]

These "unlike causes" were the very stuff of history and the local specificities of human behavior, far more complex than Mason's monocausal emphasis on "invention": "The rattle, for instance, is not merely the outcome of the idea of making noise, and of the technical methods applied to reach this end: it is, besides this, the outcome of religious conceptions, as any noise may be applied to invoke or drive away spirits; or it may be the outcome of the pleasure children have in noise of any kind; and its form may be characteristic of the art of the people."[25] Technical innovation was thus for Boas not merely a sign of the successful solution to practical problems, but the product of a whole range of needs, impulses, and practices, including the religious and the aesthetic. Moreover, it was a historically contingent process, subject to the specific accidents and changes endured by a group of people. As a better way to account for how different peoples might share traits or languages or technologies, Boas invoked diffusionism, the theory that features of human activity (implements, technologies, beliefs, and so forth) spread from one context to another, presumably via intergroup contact. Implicitly, then, historically locatable phenomena—the establishment of trade routes and trading partnerships, conflicts over resources and territories—became motors of change, and the regions in which such contact had influenced local practices became the organizing principle for understanding humanity.

While this diffusionist view inserted historical thinking into the study of human artifacts, it was not necessarily an assault on evolutionary theory. In fact, diffusionism had been useful to adherents of orthogenesis for explaining what seemed to be anomalies in the regular order of progress out of the darkness; and Boas himself quotes Mason as citing diffusion as an alternative explanation for new inventions.[26] Even Boas's departure from the unitary model of humanity implicit in the orthogenetic view could be seen as an effort to patch up some of the holes in evolutionary thought. By limiting the scope of inquiry to discrete cultural contexts, the problem of "unlike causes produc[ing] like effects" could be resolved.[27] His new emphasis could, in other words, be seen as simply redirecting evolutionism from humanity as a whole to many smaller, more local sites. Indeed, Boas justified his emphasis on the local unit by reference to evolutionary theory: "It is only since the development of evolutional theory that it became clear that the object of study is the individual, not abstractions from the individual under observation."[28]

If there was a challenge here to evolution, per se (as opposed to a particular teleological version of evolutionary thinking), then it was couched in some fairly conciliatory language—perhaps necessarily so, since this recent German immigrant was, after all, confronting some of the most influential men in the anthropological establishment of the moment—to suggest, indeed, that his views were hardly a radical departure from the theoretical bases of the ethnology of his day. He wrote,

> Former events . . . leave their stamp on the present character of a people. I consider it one of the greatest achievements of Darwinism to have brought to light this fact, and thus to have made a physical treatment of biology and psychology possible. The fact may be expressed by the words, "the physiological and psychological state of an organism at a certain moment is a function of its whole history"; that is, the character and future development of a biological or ethnological phenomenon is not expressed by its appearance, by the state in which it *is*, but by its whole history.[29]

By this argument, Boas conceded the importance of the general framework of evolutionary theory, and thereby justified his own revision of it. But he also, subtly, suggested something else: that "Darwinism" (properly understood) was, in effect, a version of his own brand of historicism.

It is easy to see in some of Boas's phrasings the outlines of an emergent culture concept. In his quick references to the "character of a people," we see the beginnings of the idea of "culture" as it would later be defined by Boas's students: as a complex set of life ways of a given group of people. Also implicit in his emerging view is another piece of what we have subsequently come to associate with the culture concept: cultural relativism and its corollary, the critique of celebrations of nineteenth-century "civilization." As Boas put it in another article on curatorial practices of the same year, "civilization is not something absolute, but . . . it is relative, and . . . our ideas and assertions are true only so far as our civilization goes."[30] But it is worth remembering that Boas's critique of the curatorial practices at the Smithsonian might have gone another way. Just as Boas's historicism challenged a monocausal, teleological view of human destiny, so might a rigorous emphasis on the accidents and contingencies of history—contact, exchange, migration, conquest—have worked against the development of an easily reifiable and easily ahistorical conception of culture. Interestingly, for the full-blown, spatialized culture concept to emerge, it would be Boas's diffusionism, which emphasized contextual porosity and exchange, that would largely be abandoned. The next sections attempt to address why.

From Museum to University

Some of the significance of Boas's criticisms of the Smithsonian's ethnological displays is located outside of the theoretical issues it addressed, in its symbolic function as a direct critique of the practices of the anthropological establishment of his day. The impetus for writing his criticism of the Smithsonian came from Boas's own visit to the museum's collections in 1885, and his resulting impression that his research was hampered by Mason's display methods. His challenge was, in other words, not only to the theory behind the method of display, but to the utility of the displays as tools for the kind of scholarship he wished to pursue. Though curatorial practices would change—indeed, at the time of Boas's critique Mason had already begun, of his own accord, to organize his displays according to "culture areas"—Boas's challenge in this sense was more fundamentally to the museum as a site of serious anthropological research.[31] In this respect, Boas's early essays foreshadowed an important institutional change in his career and in the history of anthropology: the museum would eventually be replaced by the university as the central site of anthropological work. Of course, this change is also related to the development of the culture concept, in that each institutional site in effect implied an object of study: for the museum-based anthropologist, it would be the ethnological artifact; for the university-based anthropologist, it could be something as abstract as "culture."

The transition from museum to university, and from salvaged artifact to "culture," was gradual, and in fact a number of academic anthropology departments (including those at Harvard, Berkeley, Pennsylvania, and Boas's own Columbia) were formed around ethnological museums, which were important sources of both teaching materials and funding for fieldwork. Between 1895 and 1905, Boas himself held both an academic position at Columbia and a curatorial position at the nearby American Museum of Natural History. But, as Jacknis has argued, Boas's own rather troubled relationship with the American Museum was a portent of the separation between these institutions that was to become the norm. Though the museum funded much of Boas's fieldwork in the Pacific Northwest, Boas resigned his position as curator of the ethnographic displays because of basic conflicts with the museum directorship—again, over the question of the proper methods of displaying artifacts. Boas's displays, organized to illustrate technical points in ethnographic research, were regarded by the museum's directors as being overspecialized, confusing, and unattractive to the museum's patrons. As Boas himself would subsequently note, ethnological museums served the multiple functions of "entertainment, instruction, and research," but Boas was far more interested in stressing the last of these roles than were his superiors in the museum hierarchy.[32]

In this respect, Boas's disagreements with the administration of the American Museum were typical of the heated debates then brewing in curatorial circles that opposed populist goals of entertainment and education against more scholarly interests in collecting, studying, and preserving valued objects. In these battles, the evaluation and display of ethnologic artifacts was especially vexed. For the popularizers—a number of whom took the new department stores as their models for satisfying museum experiences—ethnologic specimens were both intrinsically interesting exotica and important elements in the pedagogy of consumerism, demonstrating (as in Mason's views) the primitive origins of modern technology, and naturalizing the consumption of various objects as common to the desires of humanity as a whole.[33]

For the scientists and antiquarians, however, this popular fascination with the primitive could seem debasingly close to such quasi-ethnological amusements as those found in P. T. Barnum's polyglot exhibits or in Buffalo Bill's Wild West Show. This anxiety is tellingly revealed in Paul DiMaggio's account of the early years of Boston's Museum of Fine Arts, in which he notes that many of the ethnological objects donated to the museum—a Philippine chain cutlass, Egyptian mummies, Zulu weapons—were simply discarded, not only because they seemed outside the purview of "art," but because they evoked a lesser kind of museum-going experience than the museum's Brahmin sponsors had envisioned.[34] In a moment obsessively concerned with establishing and maintaining hierarchies of taste and value (in the wake of the erosion of other traditional class standards), categories were in the process of being established that would eventually separate the art object from other types of displayable objects: the ethnologic specimen, the natural curiosity, the folk object, the bric-a-brac.[35]

In so classifying these types of objects, and in arranging them into displays, the Gilded Age producers and preservers of cultural capital were also defining the generic categories by which particular kinds of objects ought to be appreciated. Boas's critique of Mason's curatorial practices may, in other words, be seen as an intervention into the problem of defining the ethnologic object's proper function: as a sign of another culture's more or less profound alterity, rather than of humanity's common "primitive" past. However, Boas's conflict with the administrators of the American Museum of Natural History involved a still more immediate gesture in the struggle to name and preserve cultural value. It signified the rejection of the site of a relatively public pedagogy in favor of an institutional home more accommodating to the pursuit of independent scholarly inquiry.

Not surprisingly, this change had strong consequences for the practice of anthropology. Jacknis has persuasively argued that when the institutional site of ethnology relocated from the museum to the university, the very terms and objects of study changed.[36] The salvaged artifact, a trophy that could be put on display for the satisfaction of museum visitors and patrons, would eventually make way for less tangible objects of knowledge, including language-based data, complex rituals and performances, and eventually, that interesting conceptual object, "culture" itself. Of course, understanding these objects required highly specialized language skills, interpretive abilities, theoretical knowledge, and other kinds of laboriously acquired expertise. By comparison, the older practice of rounding up material artifacts seemed unskilled, the work of dilettantes. Boas himself was remembered as having said, "If a man finds a pot, he is an archaeologist; if two, a great archaeologist; three, a renowned archaeologist!"[37] Whatever this comment connoted in the way of Boas's feelings about archaeologists in particular, it was, more generally, also a disparagement of those who saw the collection of artifacts as in itself a serious intellectual pursuit.

The institutional transition from the museum to the university also brought on other, more obvious changes. The university enabled the codification of professional credentialing in the granting of degrees and the development of rites of passage, such as fieldwork, associated with the inculcation of professional identity. Eventually, a doctorate based on fieldwork would become the professional norm for practicing anthropologists. The university would also, eventually, be the site of the development of the theoretical apparatuses that would define the difference between "professional" knowledge and what would soon be disparagingly dubbed the "amateur" work of anthropologists such as Mason. In this respect, Boas can be seen not only as a direct counterpart of his fellow German-trained philologists who were simultaneously producing a specialized academic literary scholarship, but as an exemplary agent in a social phenomenon typical of the late nineteenth and early twentieth centuries: the creation and consolidation of professional identity.[38]

The professionalization of the discipline had a number of interesting consequences, not the least of which I have already mentioned: the opening up of its ranks from the gentlemen explorers and military men who comprised the ethnologists of the nineteenth century to a much more socially diverse group, including women and men whose origins were in the working class, or who came from immigrant families. But it also had significant ideological consequences for the meaning and social import of the discipline. Professional anthropology's emphasis on the specificities of cultures brought into question the moral basis of the nineteenth-century progressive project. For some "amateur" proponents of anthropology, the field was not only part of the project of human uplift and enlightenment, it was also particularly accessible. According to Mason, anthropology had "no priesthood and no laity, no sacred language" because of the simple fact that the field's object was humanity itself: everyone was already a potential investigator, informant, and object of study.[39] We may now see the Boasians' conceptual de-emphasis of the idea of one humanity with a common trajectory in favor of the idea of individual cultural contexts as both an intellectual intervention *and* a professional gesture, one that would resist the view that everyone had equal access to the object of study. Rather than sharing in a common experience of humanity, anthropology's "amateurs" could now only be impressed by the facts of cultural distance and strangeness brought back to them from afar via the institution of professional anthropological fieldwork. On the other hand, the newly professionalized anthropologists were not necessarily immune from the experience of distance and estrangement. Their own critical position left them no more comfortable with the concept of "humanity," and indeed, encouraged them to think in newly estranged ways about the condition of the so-called civilized world.

I would argue that it is on this multivalent ground—of the transition from museum to university, from "amateur" to "professional" identities and practices, from artifact collection to participant-observer fieldwork, from one "humanity" to multiple "cultures," from progressivism to estrangement—where we may properly locate a separation between Boas and his students and their Gilded Age predecessors. But I will go further, and also suggest that these basic institutional experiences of the move from the museum to the academy and the development of a professional identity are significant features of the turn-of-the-century experience of modernity—and hence, features of the historical conditions related to the emergence of modernism as a particular aesthetic and intellectual moment and practice. It is a point that parallels Raymond Williams's observation that literary modernism represented the avant-garde of the metropolitan bourgeoisie, expressing the emergent aspirations, frustrations, and class prerogatives of this newly expanded group.[40]

Significant among these changing interests of an expanding professional stratum of the middle class were those related to the protection, consolidation, and justification of professional prerogatives. This involved not only the political work of setting up what were in effect trusts of professional expertise in the form of self-regulating associations (the AMA, ABA, MLA, AAA, etc.) but several kinds of ideological work: the development of the idea of the professional as a disinterested expert to whom various interested parties could trust their affairs (be they medical, legal, administrative, pedagogical, etc.); the establishment of specific fields of professional expertise and the separation of them from each other and from lay practices;[41] and the work of justifying the social, cultural, and moral value of specific kinds of professional labor. However, these ideological projects were not advanced simultaneously by all professionals, and they could very easily be at odds with one another. While some professional groups stressed disinterestedness and autonomy (especially those who consolidated their professional identities first, and who tended to contract their services, such as doctors and lawyers), others (especially the employees of large private and public bureaucracies that were to emerge around the turn of the century) emphasized the wider social mission their labor helped to further. For some professionals, however, the ethos of the detached professional often directly contradicted the development of wider social justifications for a profession. This may have been especially true in the case of the professoriate, as academics tended to see themselves as autonomous intellectuals and yet were also workers within university bureaucracies. For example, in his discussion of professionalism and literary scholarship, Bruce Robbins has pointed out that the elaboration of special practices and theories of criticism has long been at cross-purposes with the wider social justification for literary study as purporting to preserve and transmit the humanistic values of literary "culture."[42]

In the years that saw the consolidation of anthropology as a profession, Boas and his students were similarly subject to the competing pulls of these divergent propositions about professionalism. Anthropological specialization and expertise was potentially in conflict with the older view of science as a basically moral, humanistic undertaking. Fascinatingly, however, Boasian anthropology eventually finessed this potential dilemma, to suggest that the supposedly moral and humanistic world of nineteenth-century science was both scientifically illegitimate *and* immoral. This may well have been one of the significant ideological effects of cultural relativism as a theory: it offered both an evaluatively neutral, professional, way to discuss "culture," the new "object" of the field, *and* it proposed a new moral position for anthropology that evoked a strongly ethical and humanistic respect for the complexity and integrity of cultural others. The professional and affective success of this gesture is perhaps best measured in the degree to which contemporary (professional) American anthropologists still strongly identify with this theoretical proposition as the core of their disciplinary identity.[43]

Of course, given the complexities of locating the origins of the culture concept in Boas's work, it must be remembered that cultural relativism did not emerge overnight as a field-defining theory. But there was another gesture which preceded the development of cultural relativism, which also served to resolve some of the contradictions between expert knowledge and social justification. Released from the burden of representing a coherent "humanity" and possessing a specialized knowledge of cultural *diversity*, Boas and his students became experts in the manipulation of cultural estrangement for the purposes of social critique. Indeed, it is a distinctive feature of Boasian anthropology that it turned a great deal of critical attention on contemporary American life. We see this feature of the Boasian project in some of its best-known texts: in Mead's *Coming of Age in Samoa*; in Benedict's *Patterns of Culture*; and in Boas's own popularizing texts, *The Mind of Primitive Man* and *Anthropology and Modern Life*.[44] In texts such as these, the anthropologists in effect advertised their professional expertise to society in terms of their ability to offer contrastive examples of other societies.

While the gesture of intercultural comparison would become a familiar critical tool, thanks in part to Boas, it is significant that much of Boas's most significant polemic, against scientific racism, was engaged in the more traditional register of "professional" expertise versus "amateur" pseudoscience. This may well have had to do with Boas's early role in the professionalization of the discipline, and it is a point that I think may clarify some ambiguities in Boas's reputation as an important figure in antiracist battles of the early twentieth century. Moreover, to get at Boas's contribution to the creation of the culture concept (and to his role in subsequent elaborations such as cultural pluralism), both of these features of his interesting career—his self-image as a wielder of expert knowledge and his desire to influence public debate—need to be reckoned with. Indeed, I would argue that they must be thought of together, since it is only under the pressure of the wider social debate that Boas seems to have committed to a theoretical principle. In other words, his "culture," like his influence, is a complex product of both science and politics.

Anthropology's Public Face

From a contemporary perspective, Boas's interventions into the evolutionary-biological paradigms of his day can seem a bit arcane. Nowhere is this more true than in a study he conducted in 1911 at the behest of the United States Immigration Commission, on the assimilability of the children of various immigrant groups. The commission's mandate was to address social and economic factors influencing the assimilability of the children of immigrants. Doubtless aware of the enormous political charge of such an inquiry (the premise of the study being that members of some groups were more capable of assimilation than others), Boas did something surprising: ignoring the study's mandate, he focused the entire study on the children's anatomical measurements.

The children whose bodies and craniums he measured were categorized as belonging to one of four somewhat fantastically differentiated "races": "Hebrews" (Jews of Eastern European origin), "Central Europeans" (Bohemians, Hungarians, Poles, and Slavs), "Sicilians," and "Neapolitans." In the resulting paper, entitled "Changes in the Bodily Form of Descendants of Immigrants," he concluded, unsurprisingly, that the "racial" origin of the children was a less significant determinant of their head shape or stature than the length of time the children and their parents had resided in the United States.[45] Thus, the central question Boas asked in his study was not the "cultural" one of why people do or do not assimilate, or the social and economic ones of the conditions by which assimilation was facilitated, but the "racial" one of whether or not assimilation was biologically possible.

The rediscovery of Gregor Mendel and the development of genetic theory would eventually delegitimate the scientific idea of distinct "racial" populations of humans. However, Boas's antiracist crusade was pregenetic, and thus relied on the same scientific principles and kinds of evidence as his theoretical opponents, the scientific racists. In other words, Boas's critique of racism was largely internal to that paradigm, showing how such factors as nutrition—or, later, "culture"—might influence otherwise self-evidently "racial" differences.[46] Working from within the paradigm of scientific racism—within which the very idea of distinct "Sicilian" and "Neapolitan" "races" was actually deemed significant—Boas engaged in an exercise in negative critique, to show the limits of such racial distinctions under the pressure of environmental factors.[47] Moreover, by not considering social or economic issues in his report, Boas explicitly forestalled the temptation to speculate on the relationship between race and social or economic attainments.

Given the widespread current understanding of race as a social and cultural construction (a view enabled by both genetics and the work of Boas and his students) Boas's insistence on this strict separation between "race" and "culture" may seem surprising. This separation is characteristic of much of his work on race throughout the 1900s and 1910s. Even a 1909 article on "Race Problems in America" avoids anything like a discussion of the various social issues related to race and racism, offering instead a technical explication of contemporary biological theories of race. Some commentators are tempted to see Boas's avoidance of the cultural or social in these contexts as either an inconsistency in his thinking or a flaw in his political vision. Hence, Leonard B. Glick sees the emphasis on physical data in the study of immigrant children as a significant departure for a scholar so interested in elaborating on the cultural minutiae of the Native Americans. He reads this emphasis as evidence of a blindness to the cultural uniqueness of the eastern European Jews, and a not-so tacit call for assimilation.[48] Glick then explains what he sees as Boas's inconsistency as an artifact of Boas's personal history, arguing that Boas, who was raised in a liberal, middle-class, German Jewish household, and who himself identified strongly with German culture, simply did not regard Jewishness itself as a cultural identity. He may have shared the prejudices of many educated and relatively well assimilated Jews of his day that the peasant Jewry fleeing the Russian pogroms into Germany and the United States were at best uncouth and old fashioned, and at worst harmful to their own chances for acceptance in the Gentile world. In line with German Jewish reformers of his day, Boas understood Judaism to be a faith, comparable to Protestantism or Catholicism, and thus an aspect of social identity that did not interfere with the primary allegiances of community or nation. In the United States, Boas joined many liberal Jewish Americans in becoming a member of Felix Adler's Ethical Culture Society, a secularized "religion" that emphasized humanist values.[49]

In partial agreement with Glick, I would suggest there is a problem in discerning how Boas marks his cultural map; he may very well not have considered Jews or American blacks to possess a unique culture along the lines of the Baffin Bay Eskimo or the Kwakiutl. And clearly, Boas was no opponent of assimilation. But on a more abstract level, what may seem like an inconsistency is in fact a conflict between Boas's historicism and a moral relativism that would hold that every culture is equally deserving of respect.[50] Rather than seeing eastern European Jews as not having a culture worth preserving, Boas's assimilationist views were quite consistent with a crucial theoretical point: that there is no necessary relationship between the "race," the language, and the culture of a people. Boas insisted that these were distinct features of a given people's existence which converged accidentally through the historical contingencies of migration, contact, and conquest. Assimilation too would have counted as one of the accidents of history, no more to be lamented than the Roman conquest of Gaul. Here, Boas's position as an assimilated German Jew is also relevant. It seems that Boas refused to concede a "racial" difference between Jewish and Gentile Germans,[51] but even were he to assent to such an idea, he would have refused to conceive of "culture" in such a way that Jews as an apparently different physical "type" could not be accommodated within a German culture.

In other words, Boas was advocating not so much assimilation as the antiracist point that assimilation was *possible* within the context of racial diversity. Nineteenth-century racist thought conflated race not only with the mental and moral characteristics of individuals, but with the characteristics of whole human societies. Boas's seemingly overtechnical intervention thus got at the heart of that view by attacking both these assumptions, the first by stressing the individual's unstable relationship to racial typology, and the second, by addressing race and culture as unrelated phenomena. Because Boas saw these categories of race and culture as arbitrarily related to one another, he imagined cultural traits traversing racial classifications, and racial groups crossing cultural boundaries. In other words, his insistence on the possibility of assimilation was not merely the outgrowth of an inconsistent liberalism, but a necessary corollary to his thinking.

What this also shows us is that Boas's commitment to a certain antiracist critique in some ways prevented his articulation of culture as much more than a spatial construction that cut across the logic of race. In other words, he did not (yet) have a conception of culture that was in any way describable in terms of its positive content. This was also evident in Boas's stirring 1906 Atlanta University commencement address, "The Outlook for the American Negro," which has been frequently cited for its paradigm-shifting effect on "racial" thinking among African-American intellectuals, notably, W. E. B. Du Bois, who was in attendance.

Speaking to the graduates of this all-black institution, Boas made his usual point about the lack of scientific validity to the category of "race": "The physical inferiority of the Negro race, if it exists at all, is insignificant when compared to the wide range of individual variability in each race."[52] But he also offered historical facts—heard by many for the first time—that would become key pieces of evidence for much subsequent thought in African-American cultural politics. In addition to detailing the "civilized" accomplishments of Africans—the political and military sophistication of African leaders, the existence of vital economic and judicial systems, and the admirable artistic accomplishments of Africa—Boas also cited African "cultural inventions" in agriculture and iron-smelting technology as crucial contributions to "the advancement of the human race."[53] However, this exciting gesture of historical recovery was offered in the service of a comparatively humble point about human potential:

> If, therefore, it is claimed that your race is doomed to economic inferiority, you may confidently look to the home of your ancestors and say, that you have set out to recover for the colored people the strength that was their own before they set foot on the shores of this continent. You may say that you go to work with bright hopes, and that you will not be discouraged by the slowness of your progress; for you have to recover not only what has been lost in transplanting the Negro race from its native soil to this continent, but you must reach higher levels than your ancestors had ever attained.[54]

In these comments, we again see Boas's investment in assimilation: the destiny Boas has in mind for African-Americans is in no way separate from the wider American context. It is now clear that, in keeping with his usual logical strategy of argument by way of the negative instance, Boas had used the new cultural information about the achievements of Africans largely to show that African-Americans were fully capable of becoming valued members of American society, *irrespective of* their race. However, in others' hands, this vision of Africa would become a crucial concept in the efforts of black intellectuals to transform African-American identity from a teleological racial concept, into a spatially-conceived cultural one.

Du Bois, for one, was attentive to Boas's argument in both its modest and its bolder claims. Later, Du Bois would replicate the very structure of Boas's argument in the pages of the *American Journal of Sociology* to insist not only that African-Americans were capable of full participation in American life, but that racial separation was a geographic, economic, and social impossibility.[55] But far more significantly for the direction of Du Bois's thinking on race and for the development of black political movements in the early decades of the century, Boas's comments about Africa inspired a transition in Du Bois's thought that would bring him from advocating a race-based "pan-Negroism," to a culturally based pan-Africanism. This transition is exemplified in the shift from his ideas in the 1897 paper "The Conservation of Races," which argues for a unique history and destiny for the "Negro" "race," to his 1915 book, *The Negro*, which makes the Boasian point of refuting concrete "racial" identity on the grounds of the historical interinfluence and interaction of peoples from Europe, Asia, and Africa, while providing an affirmative history of African cultural accomplishments.

Arnold Rampersad points out the significance of this latter work to the political tradition of "Ethiopianism," best represented by Marcus Garvey's rise to power in the 1920s.[56] But more generally, we must note the significance of this type of thinking to the development of the Harlem Renaissance, a movement of black intellectuals who took as a founding premise the idea that black Americans possessed a particular cultural heritage, identity, and destiny. As George Hutchinson points out, Boas was constantly cited in the pages of the *Crisis*, and alluded to in works by a number of important Harlem intellectuals, including Jessie Fauset, Wallace Thurman, George Schuyler, and Langston Hughes.[57]

It is useful for us to reflect on this phenomenon. Though Boas saw his role to be the fairly narrow one of challenging the premises of others who held themselves out as experts on "race," the very scientific authority that he produced as a result was taken up and circulated (as, to a lesser degree, it still circulates) as an important feature of an antiracist critique. Moreover, it gave credence to a significant de-emphasis on "race" as a biological category and a corresponding new interest in developing positive descriptions of what a specifically African-American "culture" might contain. While this incident offers us an example of one route by which Boas authored a certain kind of cultural politics even before he put pen to paper about "culture," it also exemplifies Boas's successful negotiation of competing ideologies of professionalism: by working strictly within the theoretically value-neutral terms of professional art, Boas was also able to engage in the socially valuable work of challenging racism. Unfortunately, Boas's careful negotiation of the roles of professional and public advocate was to be severely challenged by events surrounding the First World War.

Culture and Nationalism

It is only in the context of another challenge to his social and political views that Boas himself felt compelled to articulate a vision of "culture" that was somehow more than a counter-hypothesis to "race." While hints of the formulation of "culture" are certainly present in Boas's strictly disciplinary work, for example in his allusions to the "character of a people," the concept is especially evident in some of his most political public statements, which, in turn, belong to important social discourses of the period. Specifically, I believe it is on the grounds of public debate about questions of nationalism and national identity that we may best understand Boas's contribution to a fully spatial culture concept.

Just as social Darwinism had been subjected to serious scrutiny for decades by social reformers such as Henry George and Edward Bellamy, and many of the ideas broadly associated with cultural relativism (including the critique of objectivity and the cultural construction of knowledge) had already been elaborated by philosophical pragmatists such as William James and John Dewey, the idea of cultural wholes was also in the air when Boas was writing.[58] However, cultural relativism really came into the popular consciousness around the time of the United States entry into the First World War, when it fit into a constellation of questions, including the burning issue of nationalism, and the no less fraught issue of the apparently new and changing character of American society. Not surprisingly, this is also this moment when Boas felt compelled to invoke the idea of culture as a kind of synonym for the autonomous nation-state. In doing so, he joined the cultural criticism of other intellectuals of his time—not only that of Du Bois, but also the "cultural pluralism" of Horace Kallen, and the "transnationalism" of Randolph Bourne.

Certain new types of social description were necessitated by the onset of the European war in 1914. Though the United States was technically neutral until April 1917, most Americans had long been exposed to a discourse on German national character. From the start of hostilities, both Allied propagandists and the anti-German American press provided lurid accounts of the sinking of the *Lusitania* and of German atrocities committed in the invasion of Belgium, to paint Germany as a nation of savages and murderers. Among the university-educated elite, feelings about German belligerence were somewhat more conflicted, given a widespread esteem for German artistic, philosophical, and scientific heritage, and for the German academic institutions in which so many Americans had studied. However, this esteem was often countered by the fact that Germany had attacked *England*, felt by many to be America's true ancestral homeland. Because of this conflict of allegiances, German artistic and intellectual achievements themselves became subjects in the prewar debate. Thus, John Dewey argued in 1915 that Kantian idealism was to blame for German militarism, and high schools and colleges across the United States witnessed a backlash against German language instruction, heretofore the most widely studied foreign language after Latin. Boas, who strongly identified with German culture (he helped to found the Germanistic Society in New York), was particularly dismayed to find that orchestras could no longer play the works of his favorite German composers.[59]

Of course, these kinds of descriptions of Germany's national character, power, and military prestige were also derived from German propaganda itself, in which the fiction of a unified "German" history and destiny was advanced via the Herderian idea of *Kultur*.[60] In the American press, German *Kultur*, *Volkstum*, or *das Deutschtum* (the more extravagantly German-sounding the word, it seems, the more negative the connotation) were then taken up as particularly nationalist applications of Nietzschean philosophy (then enjoying a tremendous vogue), with the effect of showing how individuals could be subsumed under the State's terrible will to power.[61] Christian Gauss, a professor of modern languages at Princeton (President Wilson's former institution) offered up a representative sample of this rhetoric in his 1918 book *Why We Went to War*: "We are fighting *das Deutschtum*. And what is *das Deutschtum*? It is the mystic conception of the mission, the power, and the privileges of the

German people which is to be realized by the German state. It has no principles. It is above them."[62]

Boas vehemently opposed U.S. entry into the war. He spoke out early against American support of the Allies, describing U.S. material support to Great Britain and France as war profiteering, and arguing generally for tolerance and civil conduct between nations.[63] However, characterizations such as Gauss's of the German national *Kultur* required a somewhat different rhetoric. A scant fifteen months before the United States entered the war, Boas wrote in a letter to the editor of the *New York Times*:

> To claim as we often do, that our solution is the only democratic and the ideal one is a one-sided exaggeration of Americanism. I see no reason why we should not allow the Germans, Austrians, and Russians, or whoever else it may be, to solve their problems in their own ways, instead of demanding that they bestow upon themselves the benefactions of our régime. The very standpoint that we are right and they are wrong is opposed to the fundamental idea that nations have distinctive individualities, which are expressed in their modes of life, thought, and feeling.[64]

As an argument for U.S. neutrality, Boas's point had its limitations. Indeed, both his propositions, that states were autonomous wholes and that they worked by different standards and logics, seem to have been granted some credence on both sides of the debate about entry into the war. Instead, the debate turned on the question of whether or not there was something particularly vicious or disruptive of world order about the "distinctive individuality" of the German nation. However, Boas's argument is interesting as an uncharacteristically bold theoretical statement. Here, Boas applied to contemporary problems the fundamental tenet of his 1911 *The Mind of Primitive Man*, the morally relativist view that societies should not be judged by standards external to their own contexts. Moreover, he here alludes to something very like the "culture and personality" conception of cultures as coherent, autonomous totalities with their own "modes of life, thought, and feeling." In effect, Boas's recognition that something like the culture concept had already crept into the public debate required him to intervene in his professional capacity.

Boas concluded his letter to the editor of the *Times* by insisting on his own dual allegiance to the United States and Germany: "I believe this is the attitude of many German-Americans: To conform to the dictates of our conscience, to our loyalty to America, and to our love for the ideals of our youth."[65] As Boas and Gauss's presence in the American academy shows, German-Americans held positions of prominence in American society, and potentially represented a strong political bloc, as did the many Irish-Americans who, in the moment of the Irish independence struggle, also opposed U.S. military support of Great Britain. In turn, prewar nationalist feeling was not sympathetic to those who became known as "hyphenates," and their apparently divided allegiances. If the invocation of the concept of the "hyphenate" resembles that of the more explicitly derogatory catchword of the day, "mongrel," it serves to show that much of the anti-German hysteria had roots far deeper than the war. Henry F. May cites the *Saturday Evening Post*'s opinion that wartime vigilance might help clean out the "scum of the melting pot."[66]

The pieces were thus in place for an American nationalism based on a notion of pure cultural types. If Germans had a national *Kultur*, then so could Americans. Indeed, even the *New Republic*, the voice of reluctant pro-war liberalism, used this idea of an American *Kultur* (critically) to denounce an act of fanatic anti-German violence in which a German-American was lynched in Illinois by a mob of five hundred, who suspected him of being "disloyal" to the United States. This editorial of April 13, 1918, entitled "Lynching: An American Kultur?" found "Kultur," German or American, to be synonymous with racially justified, belligerent national chauvinism.[67]

For many Americans, the war suggested the definitive end of (European) civilization, and a nationalist American *Kultur* along German lines hardly seemed like much of an alternative. Many on the antiwar Left were prophetic in seeing a resemblance between the horrors attributed to the German state and the American nationalism that had been mobilized for the war and perpetuated for the decade afterwards. The witch-hunts for German sympathizers, the massive bureaucratic mobilization of propaganda efforts to control wartime opinion, the passage of the Espionage and Sedition Acts of 1917 and 1918: all suggested a climate of government repression in the name of nationalism, only culminating in the Red Scare of the 1920s and the trial and execution of Sacco and Vanzetti. But ironically, it is also out of this context of leftist antinationalism that some would feel compelled to argue for a vision of "culture" with the very different connotations of a positively conceived, inclusive, antinationalist national "community." Again, Boas is an interesting figure to consider in tracing this development from antinationalism to "culture."

Boas was furious over the repeal of civil liberties caused by the war hysteria, and because of this issue publicly endorsed the Socialist ticket in the 1918 election.[68] Meanwhile, at Columbia, he was embroiled in a celebrated case of academic witch-hunting, when he supported James McKean Cattell, his distinguished colleague and the editor of *Science*, who was fired from Columbia for "sedition and treason" after issuing a public statement against military conscription. The incident led the (pro-war) historian Charles Beard first to join Boas and John Dewey in support of Cattell, then to resign suddenly and dramatically from Columbia for what he saw as a gross infringement of academic freedom. Boas was retained at Columbia—probably because he stopped making his antiwar views public after the United States officially entered the conflict—but he remained active in the effort to limit the Columbia administration's control over the speech of the faculty and students. It is clear, however, that his relationship with the administration was permanently damaged over the incident. Alexander Goldenweiser, Boas's only other colleague in the an-

thropology department and his former student, was fired for his antiwar sentiments and joined Beard and many other former Columbia faculty members at
the newly created New School for Social Research. Boas, now a department
unto himself, was forced to rely on the munificence of his wealthy student
Elsie Clews Parsons to pay his secretary's salary.[69]

The consequences of Boas's wartime opinions also followed him into the
1920s. In 1919, he published an angry letter in the *Nation* claiming "incontro-
vertible proof" that several anthropologists working in Mexico were also spy-
ing for the U.S. government. He decried this compromise to scientific objectivity, and warned against a general climate of distrust which this practice might
foster against anthropologists in the field. This airing of professional dirty linen
soon produced a resolution of condemnation by the American Anthropological
Association. Thanks largely to the dissenting votes of his numerous former
students, the resolution was only narrowly passed, but Boas was removed from
the Council of the AAA and, tellingly, soon resigned as representative to the
National Research Council, the government body formed in 1916 to sponsor
scientific research.[70]

In exposing these spies, it is likely that Boas was passing public comment
on the wider wartime phenomenon of professional social scientists offering
their services in Washington in aid of the war effort. But this very public letter
to the community of anthropologists—his student Esther Goldfrank later called
it an "anthropological bombshell"—should also be read as an indicator of the
seriousness with which Boas took the concept of scholarly autonomy. Boas
clearly saw the practice of scientists working for government as corrupting the
appearance of professional impartiality he wished to maintain—an appearance
which he saw as an enabling condition for the kinds of public stands he wished
to take.

Meanwhile, as wartime IQ test data offered racists new pseudo-scientific
evidence for theories of "white superiority," and as the xenophobia of the war
period led to the strictest immigration laws ever passed in this country, Boas
must have been shaken in his faith that the dissemination of scientific facts
had any effect on the irrational prejudices of a racist and rabidly nationalist
world. Under the various pressures of this moment, Boas must have felt compelled to reconsider his agenda both as a professional and as a public figure.
Thus, in the pages of the *Dial,* he issued some extremely interesting public
statements on the position of the intellectual in modern society that not only
gave an account of why reason had seemed to him to have failed in the war
debates, but that also implied a new agenda for intellectuals based on a more
positive construction of national identity.

In "The Mental Attitude of the Educated Classes" Boas modified his position
on the importance of "scientific objectivity," rejecting outright the very idea
of "free thought." In the essay, he asserted not only that all ways of thinking
were embedded in a cultural context, but that, as a "privileged class," intellec-

tuals were bound to a thought-limiting "tradition" via the educational process, and naturally invested in advancing their class interests. In "Nationalism," he argued that this class interest was furthered by nationalist feeling, which was the ideological construction of intellectuals in the service of the state. In other words, rather than blaming intellectuals for participating in the war effort—an argument made more famously by Boas's French contemporaries Romain Rolland and Julien Benda, severe critics of their peers' wartime abandonment of the principle of intellectual autonomy—Boas viewed intellectuals' service to the state as an inevitable outcome of their own social inculcation as members of a professional class stratum.[71] More clearly than his French contemporaries, Boas registered the central paradox of the ethos of professionalism, brought into particular crisis by the Great War: professionals were impartial purveyors of expertise, and yet they were also (in ways they might often wish to conceal) *interested* in consolidating and furthering professional power and prestige.

Boas's solution to this problem was (inevitably) unsatisfying, but interesting nonetheless. After acknowledging that his own social group behaved in accordance with its own investments and interests, Boas identified another group—the thoroughly modern "masses"—as existing outside of class, and thus outside of the problem of both nationalist fervor and even interestedness. He argued that "the desires of the masses are in a wider sense [more] human than those of the classes"; their thinking is "freer" in that it is less traditional, and their inclination is to the "group solidarity" of "nationality," rather than to the predatory imperialism of nationalism. As a remedy to the shortcomings of intellectuals, Boas suggested in effect that they take a sympathetic cue from these masses, whose impulses were not only decent, but fundamentally humanist. Intellectuals' work should not only be an interrogation of the "traditions" that made their thought so unfree, but comprise "an intelligent understanding of our own life, of its merits, and of its defects," "balanced by an appreciative understanding of the reasons why other nations are equally devoted to their countries and to their ideals."[72]

Though this proposed program of what we might today call reflexive critique largely finessed the conflict between class interests and professional detachment, we may nonetheless see it as indicative both of the direction Boasian anthropology was to take in its "classical" moment in the 1920s and of another (I would say, central) feature of Boas's basic modernism. As the twenties progressed, Boas became somewhat less invested in the natural-history approach to ethnographic data, and more interested in the psychological aspects of the study of culture.[73] This change both conformed to and enabled the work of students such as Mead and Benedict, who would instantiate in their ethnographic work something like the approach Boas suggested here: a relativist appreciation of other cultures, combined with a critical eye turned toward the prejudices of their own social context. (However, as we shall see in Chapter 6, both significantly departed from their mentor's example in one major respect, in enthusiastically agreeing to work for the government during the next world war.) Moreover, in that we can see a similarity between Boas's usage of "nationality" and the culture concept, it becomes possible to imagine how, even for Boas, "culture" could imply something like "national character," at least insofar as it represented a bounded and relatively stable space of human thought, action, and fellow-feeling.

As various public intellectuals, including the Boasians, became interested in imagining national "cultures," other kinds of questions would come to the fore. For example, during the war period, it was widely recognized (by Gauss, among others) that the idea of distinct cultures hardly implied that all cultures are equally attractive, equally "good," equally worthy of tolera-tion.[74] This argument against the moral equivalency of cultures looked out-ward, of course, to German *Kultur*, but it also implied an interrogation of the particular culture of the United States, and, further inward, an evaluation of the "hyphenate" populations that seemed to present such a problem for the pro-war propagandists.

Given these tensions, it is unsurprising that the years surrounding the Great War represented an enormously fertile moment for reconceiving American identity: interrogations, largely, of the question of whether or not it was a good thing for immigrants to assimilate into an American version of *Kultur*. Specifically, the period spawned several important revisions of "melting-pot" ideology which very clearly employed a spatial model of culture to reimagine national and community belonging. However, as we shall see in the interven-tions of both Horace Kallen and Randolph Bourne, these spatial re-articula-tions in no way precluded the formation of new kinds of hierarchies, this time opposing certain kinds of "genuine" identity to that of the deracinated—and cultureless—masses.

Culture and Community

Many of those dedicated to joining hostilities in support of Great Britain had defined the American *Kultur* as the product of the English colonial heritage; for them, it was the (failed) responsibility of the "hyphenates" to conform to this Anglo-American cultural model in all its aspects. In some ways, this view competed with the common "melting-pot" rhetoric of assimilation, which had been championed by such notables as Theodore Roosevelt and Henry Ford, and exemplified in the work of immigrant writers such as Mary Antin, Jacob Riis, Israel Zangwill, and Edward Bok. Rather than portraying assimila-tion as a process of acceding to the ways of a dominant ethnicity, the melting-pot metaphor is alchemical, or perhaps (as in Emerson's "smelting pot") metal-lurgical: the United States is the crucible in which *all* the immigrant groups will be transformed into the new alloy of the nation (presumably stronger, sharper, less prone to corrosion than its European counterparts).[75] Of course, both Anglocentric and melting-pot models of assimilation are fundamentally progressive, emphasizing a process leading toward a common goal of national cohesion.

But with the onset of the European war and, I would argue, the concomitant changes in the discourse of "culture," significant challenges to these models began to appear. One of the more influential revisions of this rhetoric was Horace Kallen's two-part essay, "Democracy Versus the Melting-Pot."[76] A broad-ranging critique of both the Anglocentric and the melting-pot models of assimilation, Kallen's essay boldly argued that immigrant groups be allowed, and even encouraged, to maintain their linguistic, religious, and institutional autonomy. But rather than arguing for this position on the grounds of maintaining "racial" purity (as did so many segregationists and antimiscegenists) Kallen saw the ethnic enclaves, and specifically their cultural nationalisms, as bright spots of resistance to an encroaching threat: massification. Using language that (as we shall see in Chapter 5) became widespread among literary and social critics of the 1930s, Kallen saw the "standardization" brought about by the spread of mass entertainments, yellow journalism, and public schooling to be the enemy of democracy itself.

Kallen's argument, anticipating subsequent elaborations such as Constance Rourke's plea for regionalist feeling, was as much directed against the idea of class struggle as it was against assimilationism and xenophobia. Arguing that ethnic bonds superseded those of class, Kallen hinted that if the people become "standardized" through the loss of these bonds of ethnic kinship, they would start behaving like the proletarianized masses of Marxist rhetoric (194). It was only through "cultural pluralism," he argued, that Americans as a whole could avoid this threat to democracy. In the place of the melting pot, Kallen offered two models of this "cultural pluralism": that of the "federal republic," in which each ethnic enclave represents an internal nation within the larger body of the nation-state; and (more poetically) that of the orchestra, in which "each ethnic group is the natural instrument, its spirit and culture are its theme and melody, and the harmony and dissonances and discords of them all make the symphony of civilization" (220). Crucially, both models refused the developmental core of assimilationism, and posited a view of these plural cultures as spatially arrayed, as a federation of nations are arranged on a map, or as the instruments in the orchestra are divided into sections.

Among the admirers of Kallen's essay was Randolph Bourne, whose famous statement "Trans-National America" grafted many of Kallen's ideas onto a strenuously argued antiwar position, and offered yet another spatial metaphor for the place of the "hyphenate" in American society.[77] Bourne is perhaps best remembered for breaking sharply and publicly with his mentor John Dewey and his editors at the *New Republic*, when they decided to support U.S. involvement in the war. He subsequently joined the editorial staff of the lively little magazine *Seven Arts*, in the pages of which he not only chided his fellow intellectuals' cowardice for supporting Wilson's changed position on the European conflict, but held out for the necessity of an adversarial intellectual position:

> Is there no place left, then, for the intellectual who cannot yet crystallize, who does not dread suspense, and is not yet drugged with fatigue?. . . There must be some irreconcilables left who will not even accept the war with walrus tears. There must be some to call unceasingly for peace, and some to insist that the terms of settlement shall be not only liberal but democratic. There must be some intellectuals who are not willing to use the old discredited counters again and to support a peace which would leave all the old inflammable materials of armament lying about the world.[78]

This essay places Bourne along with Boas, in the midst of an impassioned international debate provoked by the war about the position of intellectuals in society. Like Boas, Bourne acknowledged the possibility of a specific "intellectual class," but while Boas (a university professor, not a largely freelance writer) addressed intellectuals' already compromised and conflicted position as interested parties in the state bureaucracy, Bourne attempted to imagine a group identity based upon the principle of *opposition* to mainstream American opinion and policy.[79]

It was this position that made Bourne such an important figure to subsequent generations of intellectuals searching for a committed position from which to oppose U.S. involvement in Vietnam. But as these later generations would also discover, Bourne's specific formula of a community of intellectuals based on the common commitment to principled critique was often a difficult one to enact. This was even true, it seems, in Bourne's personal life. An avid correspondent and a brilliant conversationalist, Bourne's critical edge may have deeply complicated his quest for a community of intellectual peers. Though his fellow members of the Greenwich Village literary clubs joined him in opposing the pieties and hypocrisies of genteel America, he found no real community there—and described the clubs as intellectually disappointing and riven with trivial squabbles. In a letter to Elsie Clews Parsons, the prominent feminist and anthropologist, and a fellow member of a club called the Heretics, he expressed his frustration over the literary clubs' unfulfilled ideal: "Wouldn't it be an important thing to do to get a dozen very serious people and deliberately set about learning how to discuss, agreeing on a vocabulary, on categories, practicing faithfully until the group was welded together into a real thinking nucleus?"[80]

Though realizing an intellectual community seems to have bedeviled Bourne, he had already found a conceptual model for such a community while on a traveling scholarship after his graduation from Columbia in 1913. He was deeply affected by France's new cultural nationalism, which seemed to him to have united intellectuals in a common purpose and a common identity. In 1915, he translated this vision to an American context, to argue in the pages of the *New Republic* that nationalism was natural and even desirable, so long as "political nationality" coincided with "cultural unity."[81] In the light of the European war, he argued further that an American understanding of the German concept of *Kultur* might overcome the American tendency to understand the war in terms of "personal wickedness." The next logical step was to apply the concept to the perpetual problem of *American* national unity—most recently threatened by the recent boom in immigration.[82] Later that same year, Bourne thus argued not only for the desirability of national cultures, but for the creation of a distinctly American culture—a controversial notion when the article is entitled, "American Use for German Ideals." Bourne's enthusiasm for German "ideals" (never quite specified in this essay) is perhaps rhetorical, but the salient fact is that these ideals were significantly different from those of the "civilizations" of England or France, the two countries on whose behalf the United States was likely to join the war. After suggesting that recent innovations in French art and architecture are "sadly spiteful degenerations of taste" brought on by the French rejection of all things German, he writes of America's own cultural future,

> In this severe enterprise [of building a national culture] we shall get little help from the Allies whose cause we find to be that of "civilization." Both England and France are fighting to conserve, rather than to create. Our ideal we can only find in our still pioneer, still struggling American spirit. It will not be found in any purported defence of present "democracy," "civilization," "humanity." The horrors of peace in industrial plutocracies will always make such terms very nebulous. It will have to be in terms of values which secure all the vital fruits of the German ideals, without the tragic costs. It must be just as daring, just as modern, just as realistic. It must set the same social ends, the realization of the individual through the beloved community.[83]

One can imagine the alarm Bourne must have caused his more moderate readers in this dramatic proposal for the creation of the "beloved community" along the lines of "German ideals"—to say nothing of his rejection of the hollow pieties of "democracy," "civilization," and "humanity." This irreverence was only matched by his disdain for most things English, an attitude that formed the core of much of his writing. Like a number of his contemporaries, Bourne was strongly influenced by the work of his colleague Van Wyck Brooks (discussed more fully in the next chapter), whose criticism had long associated the English colonial legacy of the "Puritans" with Americans' inability to produce a truly great arts tradition.[84] In Bourne's view, not only was Puritanism representative of the worst aspects of America (its mercantilism and moral conservatism), but it led to a cultural inferiority complex in which England, and English critics like Matthew Arnold (Bourne's particular *bête noire)* were excessively revered—to the detriment of the production of a unique "American" culture.[85] The following year, Bourne would write in the important essay

"Trans-National America," "The Anglo-Saxon was merely the first immigrant, the first to found a colony. He has never really ceased to be the descendant of immigrants, nor has he ever succeeded in transforming that colony into a real nation, with a tenacious, richly woven fabric of native culture" (252).

This statement criticized not only slavish Anglophilia, but also the kind of ethnic Anglocentrism that Kallen had attacked in his earlier essay: Bourne here accused Anglo-Americans of being precisely what they criticized the "hyphenates" for being, an insular ethnic enclave. But more importantly, Bourne took from Kallen the makings of a more positive vision of what a complex "native culture" might look like, writing, "America is already the world-federation in miniature, the continent where for the first time in history has been achieved that miracle of hope, the peaceful living side by side, with character substantially preserved, of the most heterogeneous peoples under the sun" (258). But Bourne added a cosmopolitan twist to Kallen's vision of peaceably coexisting ethnic enclaves: they were not subunits of America, but "threads" in a global tapestry. Recognizing the fact that immigration was often a two-way movement of people and resources between the United States and their countries of origin (it was especially common then for Greeks and Italians to repatriate either permanently or temporarily), Bourne offered an interesting dynamism to the usual descriptions of the United States and its "hyphenate" population: "America is coming to be, not a nationality but a trans-nationality, a weaving back and forth, with the other lands, of many threads of all sizes and colors" (262). In this vision, the immigrant "threads" not only produced the unique national pattern of the American "cloth," but also reached outward, cords of attachment from the shores of this country to their homelands.

This spatialized construction of identity offered Bourne a way to explain the complex allegiances of the "hyphenate" populations, and indeed, to see them as models for the proper position of a "transnational America" in the arena of world affairs. In his view, the apparently insular ethnic feeling of the "hyphenates" was rather the sign of their being simultaneously tied to the United States *and* to Germany or Ireland. This made the hyphenates themselves the representatives of a mediating position between the "beloved community" of America, and a wider internationalism. Moreover, these representatives of transnational America offered a dialectical model for the resolution of the European conflict:

> The war has shown America to be unable, though isolated geographically and politically from a European world-situation, to remain aloof and irresponsible. She is a wandering star in a sky dominated by two colossal constellations of states. Can she not work out some position of her own, some life of being in, yet not quite of, this seething and embroiled European world? This is her only hope and promise. A transnationality of all the nations, it is spiritually impossible for her to pass into the orbit of any one (263).

Both a "wandering star" and subtly bound to other nations by "threads" of "hyphenate" loyalty, the United States could, therefore, neither retreat from world affairs nor engage in an impassioned and falsely filial military defense of one group of belligerents against the other. America's proper role in the conflict, he suggested, would be that of exemplifying global citizenship, based on the model of its already global citizenry.

Clearly, this attractive vision has brought us an enormous distance from Boas's early attempts to wrest a new model of human difference from the artifact displays at the Smithsonian. Under the pressure of war and its aggressive chauvinisms, Bourne offers us a flexible model of human identity that both gives content to a positive American nationalism and conceptually links the individual to other nations and allegiances, including the totality of humankind. In this sense, it conforms closely to the central precepts of a fully articulated Boasian anthropology, which stressed both a morally relativist appreciation of the uniquely valuable contribution of every culture and every human being, and a humanist emphasis on the commonalities that unite people irrespective of context. Indeed, given Bourne's dynamic vision of cosmopolitanism and his sophisticated understanding of the actual circulation of populations through national borders, it is unsurprising that the idea of "transnationalism" is currently interesting to postmodern theorizers of identity.[86]

But as I have already suggested about Matthew Arnold, for whom "culture" offered a resolution to class struggle via the idea of "perfection," there is a strong quality of wish fulfillment in Bourne's essay. This rests not simply in the fact that "transnationalism" seems to slide from being an alternative model for understanding America into being a description of American society as it *actually exists*, but in the fact that the very resolution to the European conflict seems to emerge as the result of this imaginative construction. Despite its thrilling optimism and rousing rhetoric, Bourne's vastly influential essay is perhaps best looked at in reverse, so that its wish-fulfilling vision reveals a countervision—its negation, which is the threat of what will happen if the other hopeful possibility does not come to pass. We need, in other words, to ask, what is the opposite of Bourne's "culture"; what does it not contain?

Most immediately for Bourne, the opposite of the fulfillment of "transnational America" was something rather like Matthew Arnold's "anarchy," the terrifying state of war itself, and the domestic hatreds it would no doubt produce. But Bourne's other fear, representing another kind of anarchy, was related to his own private struggle to find a community: that perhaps the "richly woven fabric of native culture" that he hoped was produced by the conjoining of different national groups was also a chimera, and that, therefore, the multicultural nation did not cohere. In this respect too, Bourne's account built on Kallen, who worried about the particular threat to democracy that resulted from the loss of ethnic community. For Bourne, the fear was less articulated in political terms, than in the terms of a cultural, or even a spiritual alienation:

"Each national colony in this country seems to retain in its foreign press, its vernacular literature, its schools, its intellectual and patriotic leaders, a central cultural nucleus. From this nucleus the colony extends out by imperceptible gradations to a fringe where national characteristics are all but lost. Our cities are filled with these half-breeds who retain their foreign names but have lost the foreign savor" (254). In one sense, Bourne is here simply reversing the customary opinion that would value the assimilated immigrant over the immigrant who stays close to the "cultural nucleus." But—remembering that Bourne talked about his own frustrated quest for intellectual community as a search for a "real thinking nucleus"—it is clear that he possesses a real antipathy to those who remain on the "fringe" of their "colonies." In this light, it is less surprising that in addressing these fringes, Bourne winds up disgorging the otherwise repressed rhetoric of race (in which a cultural version of miscegenation produces cultural "half-breeds").

Indeed, he goes on in this vein, evoking animality and devolution among those relegated to the "fringes" of their cultures:

> A truer cultural sense would have told us that it is not the self-conscious cultural nuclei that sap at our American life, but these fringes. It is not the Jew who sticks proudly to the faith of his fathers and boasts of that venerable culture of his who is dangerous to America, but the Jew who has lost the Jewish fire and become a mere elementary, grasping animal. It is not the Bohemian who supports the Bohemian schools in Chicago whose influence is sinister, but the Bohemian who has made money and has got into ward politics. Just so surely as we tend to disintegrate these nuclei of nationalistic culture do we tend to create hordes of men and women without a spiritual country, cultural outlaws, without taste, without standards but those of the mob. We sentence them to live on the most rudimentary planes of American life. (254)

Here, we may begin to see the limitations, indeed, the inconsistencies, of Bourne's vision for America, a vision which also, once again, demonstrates the pervasiveness of hierarchical thinking in even strongly "anthropological" visions of culture. While Bourne is ready to see culture as existing in the multiple contexts of his many "nuclei," he here shows that community membership is a prerequisite for the possession of culture, meaning that multiple memberships (in "hyphenate" identity) must logically endow one with still *more* of it. Having a culture in this way is indeed so much like "being cultured" that Bourne compares transnationalism at one point to the broadening experience of attending a college with what has come to be stereotypically described in the catalogues as the "diverse" student body (259). In producing his elaborate model of cultural allegiances, Bourne thus verges on the very conception of culture that elsewhere he claims to spurn: the view of culture as an accumulation of knowledge and correct opinion.

While it would be easy to dismiss Bourne's thinking as a failure to theorize a tolerant and inclusive American identity, we can also see it as exemplifying a larger "cultural" dialectic that goes back to Boas's antiracist polemics. The critique of progressive, cumulative models of culture necessitated the elaboration of a spatial model of plural contexts. For these contexts to be understood as evaluatively equivalent, however, they had to be understood as whole, definable entities. But as the specter of World War I nationalism proved, the idea of cultures as conceptual wholes would not always imply cultural equivalence. Germany—or America—could both represent an autonomous cultural realm *and* claim cultural superiority over other such wholes. Bourne's solution, as elegant as any, was to argue that these autonomous cultures could overlap, both within and beyond national boundaries. While this solved two crucial problems—the theoretical one of how to envision a national culture that was not provincial, isolated, or chauvinistic, and the more concrete question of why some people could feel an emotional allegiance to two counties at once—it did not suggest anything very helpful to those who (caught between cultural wholes) did not seem, or even feel themselves to be, one thing or the other. Indeed, it brought the "cultural outlaws" right back to where they began in the racist thinking of an earlier day, in which the alien masses represented the uncultivated, the precultural. It is thus tempting to speculate that Boas's earlier emphasis on history—and hence on change, influence, instability, and permeability—in these otherwise reified cultural contexts might have broken down the culture concept into some more nuanced model. But the larger pressures, both of developing a concrete metadiscourse and of dealing with the pressing contemporary issue of nationalism, would shake Boas and anthropology from this cautious and pedantic course. Instead, this moment in the culture debate set firmly into place a view of cultures as occupiable places, as conceptual homelands, which contained within them specific, "authentic" attributes. This, in turn, set into play another regime of value, hinted at by Bourne, of the culturally *real*. This too was part of the spatialization of culture, in that now hierarchies of value were articulated in terms of insiders and outsiders, rather than in terms of the more or less civilized. Indeed, it is the Bourne who talks about the cultureless America of the "mob" and the "hordes" whom Dwight Macdonald would later approvingly quote in his elaboration of that phenomenon of alienated taste, the "masscult."[87]

And in this sense, Bourne also reveals a conceptual connection between his "cultural nuclei" and a vision of the unalienated, integrated *Gemeinschaft*. Indeed, for Macdonald, "high culture" is to the two degraded subcultural "cults" ("masscult" and "midcult") what "community" is to the "masses." This investment in the saving possibilities of community not only connects Bourne to Macdonald, but also to a range of other thinkers, including various "antimodernists"; the Agrarians and other romantic regionalists; and, more recently, communitarian thinkers like Christopher Lasch and Robert N. Bellah.[88] Indeed, the desire to find complete communion, or simply to ease the intensity of the competition of interests inherent to politics, seems to be a persistent strain in modern thought, expressing in its most fundamental form an anxiety about the changing relationship between the individual and his or her social context. What is new to this period is that the desire for resolving this tension would be articulated in the terms of "culture." The next chapter will take up this problem of the individual's place in culture in more detail, by addressing the work of Boas's student Edward Sapir, and Bourne's colleague Van Wyck Brooks.

Returning briefly to Eliot, we may also see how the larger trajectory of his "cultural" thinking also conforms to this point. In "Tradition and the Individual Talent," Eliot's famous early description of the poetic process, "tradition" was a counterweight to the excesses of individualism, a manifestation of social continuity, and a storehouse of forms and possibilities for creating the new. It was thus at heart a dialectical concept: a way of thinking about the relationship between past, present, and future. Thus, in some ways it prefigured the complex historical thinking of his much later, poetic work, *Four Quartets*. But elsewhere in Eliot's thought, it would also be possible to see "tradition," like "culture," as more simply a matter of spatial demarcation, pertaining to the valued characteristics of a bounded population of humans. Nowhere is this more true than in Eliot's most controversial essay, *After Strange Gods* (1933), where (after approving enthusiastically of the Southern Agrarian manifesto) he clarified, "What I mean by tradition involves all those habitual actions, habits and customs, from the most significant religious rite to our conventional way of greeting a stranger, which represent the blood kinship of 'the same people living in the same place.' "[89] While this invocation of "blood kinship" encouraged Eliot's critics in their suspicions of his *volkisch*, even racist, sentiments, this spatial definition of "tradition" also sounded a lot like what his contemporaries had for a while been calling, and what Eliot would soon call, "culture": the space where a group of people shared intimate ties of understanding, expressed in the quotidian language of custom.

3

The National Genius: Van Wyck Brooks, Edward Sapir, and the Problem of the Individual

Yet we cannot be sure of legends
   Coming from our wise
Grandfathers and grandmothers,
   Many of them are lies.
Our aching hearts can tell us that
   Many of them are lies.
   (Edward Sapir)

Behind every theory of culture lies a latent
psychology.
(Robert F. Murphy)

As WE SAW in the previous chapter, the emergence of a spatial culture concept—one usually linked to the nation, or more romantically, to the organic unity of the "beloved community"—opened up a new set of problems regarding the role of the individual in culture. In its most general outlines, the problem can be put this way: if, as was increasingly shown by the Boasians, diversity in human behavior could be explained "culturally" rather than in terms of biological differences, where did the individual fit in? Was culture all-determining of one's behavior, as some had held race to have been? How did one understand individual creativity, innovation, or "genius" within the cultural context? To what extent did individuals produce cultural changes? For Bourne, whose hopeful vision so relied on the freedom from alienation only found within the community, the individual who did not fit in was relegated to the space of loss or impurity outside the "cultural nucleus" of real belonging. But this problem could also be articulated in the reverse: that for the individual who feels alienated, exterior to the society in which he or she lives, the problem might be that there is something vitally wrong with that *society*.

In Chapter 4, I will show how this problem of alienation is in some sense resolved—or better, *displaced*—in the work of Ruth Benedict, Waldo Frank, Jean Toomer, Hart Crane, and Sherwood Anderson, by the articulation of a fully spatial conception of multiple, relatively equivalent social contexts, among which the individual is apparently free to choose. But here, I will discuss the work of literary critic Van Wyck Brooks and anthropologist Edward

Sapir, two writers who enabled that subsequent gesture by articulating their own sense of the inadequacy of American culture and their lack of a place in it from well within the dialectic of the individual and the social. In this sense, they are transitional figures in this account, mediating between the articulation of bounded cultural spaces and a fully spatial culture concept that implied a characterological study of groups of people.

They may be said to be transitional in other senses as well. Writing in a moment of dramatic cultural, social, and technological development, it was not hard for them to see the regional, racial, and class divisions, and the personal stresses, brought about, for example, by the mechanization of labor, the disruption of traditional communities, and the growth of complex urban centers. Typically modernist in their preoccupation with alienation, both Sapir and Brooks were, however, inclined to address the issue in terms reminiscent of antimodern critiques of the devaluation of craft and manual labor. This aspect of their work once again exemplifies the complex relationship between modernist and antimodern impulses in this period, in which it must have logically seemed that the pretechnological past held certain advantages over modern chaos.

Similarly, these writers could be seen to be invoking a rhetoric of culture that is also from an older moment of discourse. Brooks and Sapir, the two most Arnoldian thinkers among their respective peers, both described deep divisions in American life in the hierarchical language of the authentic and the alien, the "genuine" and the "spurious." Indeed, Brooks's use of racial and phrenological language in several of his analyses of American culture alludes to a way of thinking about human differences that both antedates, and is antithetical to, that of Boas and his students. This evocation of phrenology is most apparent in his famous articulation of the "highbrow" and "lowbrow" strands of American culture, which also takes up an issue seldom directly addressed in Boasian anthropology, except in the work of Sapir: the problem of aesthetic and social value. And yet the work of both Sapir and Brooks represents a logical complement to last chapter's discussion of Franz Boas and Randolph Bourne, in that these writers were trying to get at the implications of a spatial culture from a different perspective: the experiences of the individual.

United in working toward the common conceptual problem of articulating a spatial "culture," Brooks and Sapir also shared the same general social milieu as Boas and Bourne. A child of immigrant New York whose first language was Yiddish, Sapir studied Indo-Germanic philology at Columbia until he found his way to Boas's class on American Indian linguistics. From this linguistic initiation into the discipline, Sapir became a distinguished member of the first generation of students trained at Columbia by Boas. It was a generation committed to carrying out its mentor's project against racism, but unencumbered by the close filial relationships with "Papa Franz" that later generations of students seemed to both enjoy and labor under.[1] Sapir, by all accounts one of

Boas's most brilliant students, engaged in a lifelong relationship with his powerful teacher, characterized by admiration, envy, devotion, and defiance. Frustrated by Boas's reluctance to offer theoretical coherence, Sapir would be one of the Boasian students to beat his former teacher to print on the theorization of "culture."

Hand in hand with Sapir's interest in linguistics went an extended fascination with the arts, and with questions about the nature of creativity. A pianist and composer, he was also a respectably well-published poet. In addition to publishing a book of verse in 1917, his work appeared in the pages of the *Dial*, the *New Republic*, the *Nation*, the *Freeman*, and in several little magazines including the *Pagan* and Harriet Monroe's *Poetry*. For a few years overlapping with Randolph Bourne's most important moment of critical output in such venues as the *Dial* and the *New Republic*, Sapir was also a steady contributor of reviews and essays to these magazines, on topics—including the music of Percy Grainger and Richard Strauss; Romain Rolland's verse novel *Jean-Christophe*; the poetry of Rabindranath Tagore; a theory of realism in the novel; John Dewey's opinions on the assimilation of immigrants—that reveal strong convergences between his influences and ideas and those of Bourne. After Bourne's untimely death in the 1918 flu epidemic, Sapir eulogized his acquaintance and fellow contributor to the *Dial* as a "soul at once sensitive and remorselessly strong."[2]

Brooks was also a fixture of the literary circles in which Bourne traveled. Though somewhat more personally and politically conservative than Bourne (with whom he disagreed about U.S. entry into World War I), the two were close friends during the last three years of Bourne's life, and both were members of a small group of writers and critics who comprised one of the exuberant literary experiments of the prewar period: the journal the *Seven Arts*, founded in 1916 by the poet James Oppenheim and Waldo Frank, an aspiring novelist who had previously worked on the staff of H. L. Mencken's the *Smart Set*. Though this little magazine existed only two short years (folding, according to legend, for lack of a financial backer after it published Bourne's incendiary antiwar essays), it brought together in its pages an astonishing array of artists and critics, including Brooks, Bourne, Rolland, Dewey, Robert Frost, Kahlil Gibran, Leo Stein, Alfred Booth Kuttner (an early translator of Freud), D. H. Lawrence, Carl Sandburg, Eugene O'Neill, Theodore Dreiser, H. L. Mencken, John Reed, Floyd Dell, and Carl Van Vechten.[3]

Though its editors would later characterize the *Seven Arts* as a project antithetical to the "high modernisms" represented by Eliot, the Imagists, and little magazines like *Poetry* and the *Little Review*, they were in fact part and parcel of the same general modernist project. They published work by the Imagist Amy Lowell, and Ezra Pound apparently thought they were enough in his line to offer his services as the magazine's foreign editor (his offer was declined).[4] Though perhaps less invested in formal experimentation and more interested in social issues than some other modernist venues, the *Seven Arts* was nevertheless self-consciously vanguardist.

The writers and editors of the *Seven Arts* saw themselves as dedicated to the expression of "youth" (to use a catchword favored by Bourne and his colleagues) against the tired conventions and hypocrisies of the genteel tradition. Lewis Mumford, one of Brooks's closest critical heirs, would describe the position of *Seven Arts* writers Brooks, Bourne, Frank, and Paul Rosenfeld as follows:

> [These] men fiercely rejected the cherished idols of middle-class America, the very America that had sought to direct their footsteps from the storm-swept beach of contemporary life to the elevated boardwalk of respectability. They challenged the sordid, mechanistic, venal, hypocritical life that underlay the tepid spiritual manifestations of the genteel tradition. Despite their rejections they were, in the main, deeply affirmative personalities, full of generous hopes for the new American promise and the new American dream, a dream which both continued and denied the old one, for it demanded spiritual rather than physical adventure.[5]

By attributing to them both "deeply affirmative personalities" and an essentially "spiritual" quality to their artistic mission, Mumford contrasted these writers to the more deeply disillusioned "lost generation" of the postwar years. Though their optimism was, I think, far more sorely tested than Mumford acknowledges, they believed with religious fervor in Art, and artists, and in their power to transform an essentially corrupt society—a society dominated by a genteel middle class that Mumford suggests was alienated from the "storm-swept beach of contemporary life."

As Mumford's comment also makes clear, their critique of contemporary alienation entailed a commitment to the creation of native arts traditions. This was a project directly related to their rejection of their genteel predecessors who, they felt, were excessively captivated by European and classical models. And yet, in championing an American culture, their project cannot be reduced to the simple designation, "cultural nationalism." These writers' personal histories, political allegiances, and aesthetic interests all inclined them to cosmopolitanism and to a commitment to an international project that linked them to like-minded "youth" the world over. They saw themselves as engaging in what Waldo Frank would later describe as "the single recreative Task which, in this *fin de monde*, makes of our generation in all lands a Brotherhood."[6] Moreover, though they were interested in the *possibility* of an authentic artistic tradition rooted in America (and often wrote overblown hymns to its development) they were, generally speaking, strongly critical of American arts and letters as it was practiced in their moment. Indeed, as we shall see in the work of Van Wyck Brooks, these writers were often insistent on the *failure* of the nation to produce a hospitable creative environment, precisely because the very idea of the American nation was itself sadly incoherent.

This interesting combination of a critical cultural nationalism with the conscious internationalism of the avant-garde is strongly akin, conceptually, to Bourne's transnationalism. Just as Bourne's America was composed of distinct international threads within the whole cloth of the nation, the mission of the *Seven Arts* was to conceive of a world of related, but distinct, national cultures. Thus, the same journal that published "Young America," Brooks's manifesto for a native art tradition, would also print Seichi Neruse's "Young Japan," John Dos Passos's "Young Spain," and Padraic Colum's "Youngest Ireland."[7] But like so many other modernists who insisted on a political mission for art, they were also deeply interested in the problem of human agency in society. While this interest led them, as with many of their contemporaries, to psychoanalysis, it also brought them to more mystical assertions about the organic relationship of the individual to the inter-nesting wholes of transnation, nation, "race," and region. This emphasis led them to romantic assertions of mystical unity between nation and citizen, in which "America" was seen, in effect, to possess a personality—while the personality of its citizens was distinctly "American." In this respect, they anticipated the characterological turn in the work of some of Boas's students.

If Bourne thus provided a theoretical and political model for the magazine's internationalism, then it was surely Brooks who was the resident theorist of this characterological vision of American national culture and, crucially, of its failures. Already in 1908, in his first published essay, "The Wine of the Puritans," Brooks insisted that "good" (American) art be related to a specific (American) cultural scene, a view expressed in the racial language of this moment:

> It seems to me that an artist can produce great and lasting work only out of the materials which exist in him by instinct and which constitute racial fibre, the accretion of countless generations of ancestors, trained to one deep, local, indigenous attitude toward life. A man is more the product of his race than of his art, for a man may supremely express his race without being an artist, while he cannot be a supreme artist without expressing his race.[8]

Though clearly connected to a nineteenth-century racial discourse, his use here of "race" and "racial fibre" in conjunction with the idea of a "deep, local, indigenous attitude toward life," may be better contextualized in terms of his romantic organicism, which held that there existed a certain essential connection between the artist, the art, and the national or more local milieu. As Brooks would put it in 1920, "[T]he mind is a flower that has an organic connection with the soil it springs from."[9] By the time of his association with Randolph Bourne, the *Seven Arts*, and the U.S. entry into World War I, this organic conception of the relationship between individual and soil would be expressed in terms of "culture," and particularly, "national culture."[10]

However, in Brooks's writing, the bond he saw between the individual and the *patria* was troubled in all sorts of ways, not least in that he regarded the homeland in question as itself a site of loss and conflict. Brooks had already begun to explore this position in "Wine," which provided Bourne and many other contemporaries with a whole schema by which to think about America and its character. Using the archetypal figures of the "Puritans" and the "Pioneers," Brooks offered a genealogy of America's current woes, including, significantly, its failure to produce a vital contemporary literature and the failure of the community to ease the social and intellectual isolation of its members. Amounting to a symbolic displacement of the fathers, his historical reconstruction was an important, indeed perhaps psychologically necessary transition for a cultural movement that saw itself as belonging to a brotherhood of youth, and more generally to an age of profound cultural disjuncture. But as we shall see, Brooks's characterology, and his subsequent elaborations upon it, had a somewhat contradictory aim: while it posited the possibility of such a thing as a "national culture," it always seemed to fail to cohere.

The Divided Culture

In the generation before Brooks's writing, Frederick Jackson Turner's frontier thesis of American history had begun to transform the pioneers into important cultural heroes. They represented the spirit of adventure and entrepreneurship which had transformed the United States not only into a transcontinental power, but into a modern, industrialized nation. At the same time, the Puritans were due for a certain revival of reputation.[11] For popular midcentury writers such as Harriet Beecher Stowe, the Puritans had been antagonists in the literary explication of an important, and gendered, religious controversy, which imaginatively pitted an older, patriarchal, Calvinist theocracy against a newer, evangelical religion dependent on the impulses of the individual (and often womanly) heart.[12] In the 1890s, however, the Puritans were rescued from their role as perpetrators of a cruel and absolutist morality, to the new, though perhaps equally gendered, American context of unbridled capitalism and industrial expansion. Many began to regard the Puritans as the progenitors of the new America, through the heritage of the "Protestant ethic," which promoted the modern values of thrift and commercial energy.[13] This history often blended with narratives about the precapitalist Pioneers, to produce a historical mythology of American progress, technological might, and greed. As with symbolic deployments of this sort, however, those who were less sanguine about the condition of American modernity also manipulated these symbols to their own rhetorical ends. Some admired the Puritans as the utopian creators of a community *antithetical* to the grasping individualism of modern industrial America. Others, on similar grounds, but ultimately more sympathetic to the spirit of the Pioneer, rejected the Puritan past as both elitist and irrelevant to the modern, rational world of engineers and efficiency experts.

Brooks's innovation was to create from these complex cultural symbols an American version of Matthew Arnold's *Culture and Anarchy*.[14] Where Arnold described an intellectual "Hellenism" and a moralistic "Hebraism" as two competing tendencies in the English temperament, Brooks saw a rarefied, Emersonian Puritan strain competing with that of Pioneer practicality and entrepreneurial drive. The problem for Brooks, as it was for Arnold, was to blend these separate tendencies into a balanced whole.

For Arnold, the amalgamation of the two strains would produce "culture," the conjunction of "sweetness and light."[15] Arnold's "culture" connoted an inseparable individual and collective enterprise. Individuals aspired toward "perfection" by transcending their "ordinary selves" in favor of their classless "best selves." The collective "culture," in turn, would transcend political and class differences and act as a social glue to join distinct types, whether of "blood" or social class, into a (perfect) national whole: the "state." Of course, this assertion of "culture's" ameliorative possibilities represents a movement from politics to a cheery mysticism, Arnold's famous "secular religion" of "culture." Indeed, his vision of the unified nation contained a well-known logical circularity, in which it was unclear which was the precondition for the other, "culture" or the "state." While Arnold argued that the state, the body reflecting citizens' "best selves," or "culture," was the medium for social transformation, he also maintained that the state could not come into being until "culture" had been achieved.[16] Nevertheless the emotional mechanism behind this magical fusion is clear: its antithesis was political struggle—the Hyde Park riots and Irish resistance to English rule—or, as Arnold put it, "anarchy."

It will become clear that Brooks may also have fallen victim to his own version of wish fulfillment, but for him the fear was less of social unrest than of a permanent state of conceptual incoherence to American culture itself. Or (to put it closer to the metaphorics he commonly invoked for this frightening possibility) the organic entity of the national culture might never develop into a conscious being, but instead remain caught in the primordial ooze. Brooks's worst fear is that America is, and may remain, a "swarm," a "jungle of shoots": "America is like a vast Sargasso Sea—a prodigious welter of unconscious life, swept by ground-swells of half-conscious emotion. All manner of living things are drifting in it, phosphorescent, gayly colored, gathered into knots and clotted masses, gelatinous, unformed, flimsy, tangled."[17]

Brooks traced this problem to its roots in the transplantation of settlers from Europe to the New World. Using rather different metaphoric language, Brooks first articulated the problem as follows: "You put the old wine into new bottles, . . . and when the explosion results, one may say, the aroma passes into the air and the wine spills on the floor. The aroma, or the ideal, turns into transcendentalism, and the wine, or the real, becomes commercialism. In any case, one doesn't preserve a great deal of well-tempered, genial wine" ("Wine," 6).

Thus, from its first articulation, Brooks's origin story of American culture is one of permanent loss. It involves a literal fall—of wine to the floor—and thereafter the disastrous parting of the Puritan from the Pioneer, the spiritual from the material. Another feature of Brooks's historical narrative in "Wine" bears out this sense of loss. He argues that the Puritans arrived in this country in full possession of a culture (that of seventeenth-century England) which, according to Brooks, had already reached its "adulthood." Since the Puritans were supposedly America's founders, America was in effect a country deprived, by its dour parents, of a cultural "childhood," a moment that Brooks located in the European Middle Ages. Precocious America was thus left lacking a certain spontaneous creativity, a certain emotional savor, while the hardships the Puritans faced in the New World forced these cultural "adults" to value the apparently also adult qualities of "thrift and industry" to the exclusion of other pursuits—aesthetic, intellectual, and even religious ("Wine," 4). The Pioneers, hardly a positive alternative to the dusty legacy of the Puritans, were rather their culturally impoverished historical offshoot, Puritans uprooted in the pursuit of personal gain in the West. Driven through dire need to the betterment of their condition at any human cost, the Pioneers were the embodiment of an unprincipled, single-minded, and decidedly unlovely materialism.

In addition to furthering a picture of the aridity of the American character, this presentation of American "adulthood" is suggestive on a number of grounds. First, it directly analogizes the history of nations with the developmental trajectory of humans—especially their emotional and intellectual development. This fact makes clear the characterological nature of Brooks's project. Second, it suggests that, with the separation from Europe, America had been disastrously severed in some deeply emotional way from its roots. To lose contact with its proper "childhood" in the European Middle Ages is for America to have lost something like its race memory of traditional lore, superstition, and irrational custom—the things that Brooks saw as conducive to the creation of rich, authentic cultural traditions. Though Brooks ends this essay on a hopeful note, envisioning the creation of a new American culture, it is hard to imagine how, given this vision, such a thing will arise. It's as hard to recover a race memory you never had as it is to gather up wine once the bottle has "exploded."

One of the central differences between Brooks and Arnold is thus Brooks's basic pessimism. While Arnold could imagine, albeit circularly, how culture would reunite Hebraism with Hellenism and the impulses of the individual with the larger vision of society, Brooks is repeatedly at a loss for a similar resolution. In "Wine" he writes despairingly:

> The vague ideal of every soul that has a thought in every age is for that communion of citizens in some body, some city or state, some Utopia, if you will, which the Greeks meant in their word *politéia*. Those artificial communities—Brook Farms and East Auroras—are so pathetically suggestive of the situation we all are in! 'We get together' (what an American phrase that is!) because we *aren't* together, because each of us is a voice crying in the wilderness, individuals, one and all, to the end of the chapter, cast inward upon our own insufficient selves ("Wine," 55).

Already in this early moment in his career, Brooks articulated the pragmatist's skepticism of utopian longings, holding them to be both necessary and impossible to fulfill. And crucially, coming from a writer held to be a prominent cultural nationalist, he here already makes clear that America is not a nation, but a multitude of voices in the wilderness.

On the other hand, there is a sense in which the impossibility Brooks here laments is one of his own making—indeed, is nothing more than a pessimistic inversion of Arnold's utopian circularity. Brooks's organicism held that the character of a country was a human character writ large, at once producing the character of its citizens and shaped by them and their histories. But what if this character is somehow lacking? Can the individual, shaped by a national character, begin to change that national character? Brooks's longing here for a community is precisely an expression of his frustrated inability to crack open this problem. "Cast inward upon our own insufficient selves," we struggle with alienation represented on a larger scale by a culture divided against itself. Brooks imagines that if we could only get together, we could change things. But of course if we *could* get together, our culture wouldn't need fixing.

This problem clearly haunted Brooks. In a fascinating example of a repetition compulsion, Brooks's entire critical career is marked by the generation of new formulas for describing America's bifurcated soul. In "America's Coming-of-Age," Brooks provided his best-known, and perhaps most thorough, elaboration of his vision of the divided American culture, now articulated in terms of "highbrow" and "lowbrow" tendencies. Even more far-reaching than his Puritan-Pioneer opposition, Brooks divided all of American literature and much else into these two unrelated camps: in addition to the usual oppositions of the literate to the illiterate, the theoretical to the practical, the intellect to action, Brooks arrayed "political economy" in opposition to William Jennings Bryan, Good Government against Tammany Hall, Hawthorne against Poe, New England against New York, and "glassy, inflexible priggishness" against "humanity, flexibility, tangibility" ("America's," 83–86).

Brooks's application of the phrenological terminology, "highbrow" and "lowbrow," to all of these sites and objects has, of course, survived in the popular vernacular; the terms are widely familiar as denoting class-based hierarchies of taste. Certainly, some of this meaning was also present in Brooks's initial statement: "The 'Highbrow' is the superior person whose virtue is admitted but felt to be an inept unpalatable virtue; while the 'Lowbrow' is a good fellow one readily takes to, but with a certain scorn for him and all his works" ("America's," 83). But I think it is a mistake to see Brooks's point here as reducible to the subsequent understanding of the terms—just as it is a mistake to see Brooks's use of the idea of "Puritanism" as reducible to the Mencken-like attacks on the "puritan" sexual repression and moral hypocrisy of the "booboisie."[18] Unlike Mencken's impatient name-calling, which implied a sensible alternative to Puritanism in cosmopolitan broadmindedness, Brooks saw no such positive alternative—only the equally shabby legacy of the Pioneers. Similarly, the "highbrow" is not really superior (or inferior) to the "lowbrow." Nor, indeed, would the joining of "highbrow" and "lowbrow," result for Brooks (as Richard Chase asserted) in some third position midway between the two, a mediocre site of "middlebrow" culture.[19] Rather, Brooks lamented the absence of a "genial middle ground" between the two strains of American culture, which would, in any case, have been for him a kind of synthesis between the two tendencies, and a repair of the fragmentation of the whole. Indeed, Chase's assumption that the American culture that Brooks sought represented an intermediary tier of taste, "the middlebrow," is probably anachronistic. As we shall see in Chapters 5 and 6, the preoccupation with the "middlebrow" as a threat to culture was less one of Brooks's moment (the very term "middlebrow" did not exist in the time of Brooks's writing) than it was for Chase and his contemporaries after World War II.[20]

Indeed, with so many oppositions in play, it is apparent that Brooks's use of the terms "highbrow" and "lowbrow" could not in any simple way have connoted the hierarchy of taste in the way those words have since come to imply. Though these taste distinctions were certainly coming into being in such a way that access to the institutions of cultural authority was being limited to members of the privileged classes, it nevertheless seems clear that for Brooks (as for Arnold, in his distinction between Hebraism and Hellenism) the referent for *both* of these terms was, finally, situated with (the failures of) the rapidly expanding and increasingly politically powerful middle class.

This becomes evident by comparing Brooks's oppositions with Vernon Parrington's subsequent excoriation of the Puritan past in *Main Currents in American Thought*. In an argument very similar to Brooks's, Parrington distinguished between the "spontaneous" vernacular beauties of Bunyan's English, inherited from "medieval times," and the partial, incomplete, inorganic world of Puritan New England, which produced a culture both "prosaic and niggardly." This world was, as in Brooks's descriptions, divided by two competing tendencies, toward abstract idealism and mundane materialism, described in terms of the Puritan (embodied by John Cotton) and the Yankee (represented by Samuel Sewall). Unlike Brooks, however, Parrington saw in the "interweaving" of these two strains the basic pattern of life in colonial New England. And, more importantly, he was clear to point out the *middle-class* origins of both Puritan theology and Yankee ambitions.[21]

Similarly, Brooks is not equating the Puritan "highbrow" with the cultural elite, but with middle-class pretensions to a certain precious refinement. Nor, indeed, does the "lowbrow" correspond with those forms consumed by the lower strata of society; rather, the "lowbrow" tendency is a pragmatic resistance to the aesthetic and the spiritual. The binary logic of his model of the "highbrow" and "lowbrow" of American culture was, simply put, less a problem of good and bad, than of irreconcilable parts of a whole. As we shall see, his "genial middle ground" was less a gray mediocrity, than a mystical, impossible, *Arnoldian* fusion. Meanwhile, Parrington's identification of the specific site of these tendencies in the middle class may offer us a place to begin thinking about the historical specificities of Brooks's critique of American life: his anxieties about alienation, and about an America divided against itself.

Like most of his peers who wrote for the *Seven Arts*, Brooks was himself a child of the emergent professional and managerial strata of the middle class, which was created by the new bureaucratic needs of vast centralized fortunes and the concentration of urban workers in the post–Civil War industrial boom. While the *Seven Arts* editors Frank, Oppenheim, and Paul Rosenfeld were all the sons of prosperous German-Jewish businessmen from New York City, Bourne and Brooks were both the products of suburban New Jersey Protestant families that had failed to live up, economically, to the suburban ideal of gentility. Unusual for the time in its mix of Jewish and Gentile writers, the *Seven Arts*'s staff may have been united by a common sense of social liminality, all having grown up on the economic and ethnic fringes of the wealthy Protestant establishment.[22] Perhaps as a result of this sense of marginality, Bourne and Brooks were particularly stinging in their condemnation of the contradictions and hypocrisies of the class to which their parents aspired. In one of his angriest essays, Bourne described the "old tyrannies" of this world as centered on "the three sacred taboos of property, sex, and the State." He went on to suggest that the children of this world (implicitly including himself) were cosmic victims of their parents' circumstances, coming to consciousness of their environment "like a drugged girl who wakes up naked in a bed, not knowing how she got there."[23] Though there is perhaps much more to be said about this weird allusion to white slavery, the analogy of the drugged girl corresponds closely with Brooks's view that America as a nation was prematurely adult, coming to consciousness without knowing how or why it got where it is. It also reflects something of the nervousness of the turn-of-the-century bourgeoisie, which, as Bourne's essay suggests, was both prudishly averse to discussing sex and titillated by the affronts to chastity represented by the figure of the fallen woman.

Indeed, theirs was a culture in many respects divided against itself. While servicing interests centralized in the great cities, members of the managerial-professional middle class were the pioneers of that other late-nineteenth-century invention, the commuter suburb.[24] With this shift in the urban landscape, the place of urban office work was strongly differentiated from the home, from leisure, and from the feminine sphere. The creation of these distinct spheres of life represented a profound social change, and may have contributed to the epidemic of nervous complaints in this class of businessmen and professional workers. For some, the solution to these disorienting changes was a privatized application of Morrisite notions of unalienated labor; the basement workshop and the therapeutic "hobby" were both products of this application.[25] Another response to these changes was Theodore Roosevelt's more explicitly political cult of rugged masculinity, which called on Americans—but, obviously, *men*—to pursue "the life of strenuous endeavor" through sport, outdoors adventure, and military conquest. This call represented a reaction not only to the closing of that perceived social safety valve, the American frontier, but also to what were understood to be the "softening" effects of the modern lifestyle of so many middle-class Americans.[26] In its literary incarnations in writers like Jack London and Owen Wister, it described a world utterly alien from Wall Street, in which (an albeit excessively "virile") emotionalism still had a place—a fact noted, and denigrated, by Brooks, who labeled this rugged naturalism "the literature of apoplexy."[27] Hence the minor irony that, in a time when the social spheres of men and women of this class were more divided than ever, rugged masculinity attempted to cure men of their overdose of rationalism and commercialism (things which were already gendered masculine) by directing its critique at the "softening" influences of *women*.

Casey Blake has argued convincingly that the critique launched by Brooks and his circle of the genteel tradition and the class that embodied it involved an attempt to close this expanding chasm between the "masculine" world of work and the "feminine" world of the ideal, the aesthetic, and the domestic.[28] While their critique of American society was never explicitly gendered (Bourne's "drugged girl" being an interesting exception), several contemporaries influenced by Brooks and his colleagues would put just such a gendered spin on his argument about the cultural failure of genteel America. George Santayana's "The Genteel Tradition in American Philosophy" offers yet another elaboration of a Brooksian bifurcated culture, but for him it was split between the competing pressures of what he described as the masculine "American Intellect," and the feminine "American Will." The former is the profit-driven suburban commuter, while the latter is the home-bound middle class woman, responsible for maintaining Protestant morality and reverence for a listless genteel culture.[29]

Besides the separation of the gendered spheres of work and home, there were other social distinctions enabled by changes in genteel America that occupied the concerns of Brooks and his peers. The class into which these men were born was instrumental in the late-nineteenth-century creation of the differentiation of publics into elite and popular communities of taste. In the late-nineteenth century, the hereditary upper class and the increasingly affluent middle class supported and lent administrative expertise to the creation of the first nonprofit cultural corporations: symphonies, museums, opera companies, and other institutions that served to differentiate "legitimate" culture from "popular" culture.[30] The resulting genteel "high" culture, often exceedingly deferential to European works, performers, and opinions, was the subject of Bourne's derision when he criticized the Anglophilia of his fellow Americans. As an alternative, these critics argued for a robust culture that did not distinguish between high and low, that drew from its organic roots, achievable under the sign of a socially and culturally unified "America."

From this account, it should also be clear that the problems of a divided culture were also the problems of the divided selves of members of the middle class: domestic from public, feminine from masculine, "intellect" from "will," spiritual from pragmatic, elite from popular. Moreover, since society and personality seemed to Brooks inextricably linked, the simultaneously desired and impossible resolution to social division was also reflected on the level of the individual. The bifurcation of American society—between "highbrow" and "lowbrow," or between "Puritan" and "Pioneer"—that was both created by and resulted in the crippled and stunted personalities of the individuals who comprised it, seemed complete and irreconcilable.

In "America's Coming-of-Age," however, Brooks tried a new gambit to get out of this predicament: he imagined into existence a kind of super-individual, a transcendent artistic personality, who could offer to American life and letters "a certain density, weight, and richness, a certain poignancy" found in the literatures of other, more integrated, cultures ("America's," 127). There was only one such superhuman American writer—a "genius"—who would manage to Brooks's satisfaction to transcend his persistent dichotomies. That was Walt Whitman, who for Brooks, quite simply "precipitated the American character. All those things which had been separate, self-sufficient, incoördinate—action, theory, idealism, business—he cast into a crucible; and they emerged, harmonious and molten, in a fresh democratic ideal, which is based upon the whole personality" ("America's," 131).

Brooks argued that Whitman, of all the American writers, managed not only to literally embody American letters, giving it the vitality of emotion, humanity, and lived experience; he did this, in effect, by escaping history—or at least the historical context that first gave rise to the terrible dichotomy of Puritan and Pioneer:

> Whitman was the Antaeus of this tradition who touched the earth with it and gave it hands and feet. For having all the ideas of New England, being himself saturated with Emersonianism, he came up from the other side with everything New England

did not possess: quantities of rude emotion and a faculty of gathering humane experience almost as great as that of the hero of the Odyssey. Living habitually among
world ideas, world emotions, world impulses and having experienced life on a truly
grand scale, this extraordinary person, innocent as a pioneer of what is called urban-
ity, became nevertheless a man of the world in a sense in which ambassadors are
not; and there is every reason to suppose that he would have been perfectly at home
in the company of Achilles, or Erasmus, or Louis XIV. ("America's," 128–29)

But finally (after all this histrionic prose), Brooks must concede that even
Whitman presents less a reconciliation of the divisions of American life than
yet another confirmation of its utter irresolvability. As his analogy between
Whitman and the earthbound Antaeus suggests, Whitman too is finally caught
on the earthly side of Brooks's dichotomies: "Perfectly right in all his instincts,
perfectly right so long as he kept to the plane of instinct, he was lost on the
plane of ideas" ("America's," 133). What Brooks describes as the rash statements, the clumsy, enthusiastic affirmations of the later Whitman provide
further evidence for the poet's failure to transcend the American cultural
gaps and lacks. In effect, Brooks seems to also have returned the transcendent
Whitman to history, for it is clear that what Brooks saw as the inadequacy of
the later Whitman was also historically convergent with the moment of the
genteel tradition.

Nevertheless, the search here set the pattern for Brooks's subsequent criticism, in which he persisted in the search for an American literary super-person-
ality—a genius—only to repeatedly rediscover its absence. The next part of
his career was devoted to the writing of literary biographies, the subjects of
which seem to have been chosen not because they were the transcendent personalities in American letters, but rather because they ultimately confirmed
Brooks's theory of a hopelessly bifurcated American culture; he sought out
writers who represented to him the social and spiritual poverty of their late-
nineteenth-century milieu. Hence, the two books immediately following
"America's Coming-of-Age"—*The Ordeal of Mark Twain* (1920) and *The Pilgrimage of Henry James* (1925)—attempted to show how each of these writers
could have been greater but for the fact that they were victims of an irreparably
fragmented social world. Twain's bitter humor, Brooks argued, was the product
of an insufficiently developed personality, and James allowed his art (especially the late work, for which Brooks had no patience) to suffer from his exile
from his native soil.[31]

Risking a vulgar psychologism, I would suggest that Brooks's obsession
with the divided society of genteel America, and the divided personalities it
produced, was an anguished revelation of his own sense of alienation from an
inhospitable society. Shortly after the publication of the book on James, Brooks
became suicidally depressed. By Brooks's own account, the "season in hell"
precipitated by his breakdown was also an intellectual turning point.[32] No
doubt emotionally unable to continue exploring the literary and personal

chasms of a divided American culture, Brooks's criticism turned instead toward an unearthing of those moments in the American past when the culture seemed organically complete. This nostalgic search for a "usable past" (mirrored strongly by his close colleague Lewis Mumford's quest for America's literary "Golden Day") ended in Emerson and in what Brooks took to be Emerson's organic milieu of preindustrial New England.[33] Perhaps this moment would take the place of that medieval childhood lost to Americans upon the spilling of the wine.

Brooks's new direction mixed oddly with some of his older views. While it fit rather easily with his older cultural nationalism—indeed, it represented the achievement, in history, of what he had earlier held out to be America's *promise*—he became increasingly dubious about the social value of contemporary letters. Few indeed among Brooks's contemporaries could, or wanted to, live up to the model of Emerson, who addressed a very different world in hopeful and "life-affirming" terms. Unfortunately, Brooks saw his contemporaries' failure of optimism as the fault of the writers, not of the troubled times in which they lived. By the 1940s, Brooks began to publicly express his dislike of the high modernists—particularly the expatriates Stein, Pound, and Eliot— not only because they were "dilettantish" technical innovators, and their preoccupations "adolescent," but because they were "decadent" "defeatists," preservers of the late-nineteenth-century fin-de-siècle "death-drive."[34] On the eve of the Second World War, this argument (much more fully discussed in Chapter 6) contributed to the belief among a new generation of critics that Brooks had not only betrayed his early iconoclasm, but that his pronouncements on the social obligations of the literati represented an American version of cultural totalitarianism: "Kulturbolschewismus."[35] Not coincidentally, this new view of Brooks as an icon of a debased, or even dangerous, literary sensibility coincided with the remarkable popularity of his books, a highly dubious sign of value to the literary intelligentsia of the postwar. To them, Brooks had indeed finally fallen into a not-so-genial middle ground that a new moment had decisively labeled "middlebrow."[36]

Nevertheless, one feature of Brooks's criticism remained constant: he would continue to argue about American life and literature through the invocation of complex dichotomies—a remnant of his earlier insistence on America's divided soul. Just as "Pioneer" and "Puritan" made way for "highbrow" and "lowbrow," so later did he tend to invoke Jung's "introvert" and "extrovert"— a schema of psychological types which also influenced those anthropologists, including Edward Sapir, Margaret Mead, and Ruth Benedict, who were becoming interested in psychology. While these dichotomies were still being used by Brooks to represent halves of wholes that needed to be (re)united, Brooks would also increasingly make use of other distinctions that simply connoted the good and the bad. Hence, in addition to opposing Eliot's "defeatism" to Robert Frost's "idealism," he set up most modernist writers and critics as creators of "coterie literature," against the "primary literature" of great literary figures of the past. Still later, Brooks would return to his attempt to find cultural divisions and resolutions, when he described modern artists as engaged with their cultural world either as "optimists" or as "pessimists."[37] In his view, many of the same people who were "defeatists" and part of the "coterie" were also pessimists. Those in this group who chose not to abandon "tradition" altogether followed T. S. Eliot's erudite style, or created their own nostalgic "usable pasts" in such locales as the agrarian Confederacy. The optimists, on the other hand, were embattled, hopeless "utopians": the shell-shocked Cummings of *The Enormous Room*; the suicidal Hart Crane; the Ezra Pound who, according to Brooks, "retained his American desire to improve things," despite the apparently shaky grasp of reality that led him to Fascism. Though his own cultural strategy had largely been one of cultivating a usable past, there was, surely, something about him (innate hopefulness? his own bout with madness?) that also identified with, and insisted upon, the "optimistic" impulses of these poets. In the end, Brooks could do nothing more than invoke Pascal, in an "American wager," in which "faith" in America's possibilities—and the possibilities of its people—seemed, if unreasonable, then at least more desirable than "doubt."

Culture and Personality

While Brooks's meditation on the place of the individual in culture began with the assumption of an organic unity, the reverse might be said of those members of the first generation of Boasian anthropologists who created the first fully articulated versions of the culture concept. For them, the starting point was the Boasian imperative that the hereditary and biological makeup of a group of people had nothing but a coincidental, historical, relationship to where and how they lived or the language they spoke. From this rather negative principle, Alfred L. Kroeber and Edward Sapir stepped bravely into the business of generalizing about a central—perhaps *the* central—concept of their discipline, "culture" itself. These two may in fact vie for the honor of first articulating the concept in a context more concrete and more fully developed than Boas's more public arguments for the existence of an autonomous German *Kultur*. They both arrived, moreover, at their versions of culture from the perspective of linguistics, where the study of morphology, of pattern and order, may have presented a kind of structural metaphor for culture.[38]

In 1917, Kroeber made his bid to be the first to articulate an anthropological culture concept with a paper in the *American Anthropologist* entitled "The Superorganic." Here, Kroeber clearly saw himself as defining "culture," a term which, in the opening paragraph of his essay, he distinguished from the "organic," as "soul" was distinguished from "body," and the "mental" from the "physical."[39] Indeed, Kroeber would later claim that he intended his concept of the "superorganic" to be synonymous with "culture"—a term rejected for the title of his essay only because, in the shadow of the First World War, the German-American Kroeber "feared to be misunderstood outside of anthropology if he used the word."[40]

In line with Boas's public and scholarly battle against scientific racism, Kroeber's definition of "culture" was (he reflected in 1952) an effort to correct "a diffused public opinion, a body of unaware assumptions" that in 1917 too easily applied biological principles such as evolutionary theory to social issues. "What the essay really protests is the blind and bland shuttling back and forth between an equivocal 'race' and an equivocal 'civilization.' "[41] Thus, in defining "culture," Kroeber identified a "superorganic" realm of human activity that was independent of the human organism's genetic makeup. "Culture" or one of its cognates (the essay freely interchanges "civilization," the "social," and "tradition" with "culture") thus became that realm of behavior that was not biologically inherited, but learned and transmitted through contact with other persons: skills, techniques, styles, belief systems, languages, refinements of talents. Culture was, in other words, by definition collective; not the "mental action" of lone individuals, but a collective "body or stream of products of mental exercise."[42] Indeed, in Kroeber's view the superorganic could not be the product of, or even significantly influenced by, exceptional cultural actors, because individual mentalities were inherited, hence organic traits. Kroeber argued forcefully that it was precisely a casual slippage from individual mental attributes to assumptions about cultural mentalities that caused so many faulty assumptions about the applicability of biological theories to society. To reinforce his point that "civilization, as such, begins only where the individual ends," he offered numerous examples of instances in which great cultural inventions were not the product of one genius, but had been arrived at more or less congruently by many thinkers (for example, both Charles Darwin and Alfred Russel Wallace were working contemporaneously toward a theory of evolution).[43]

As an extension of the Boasian separation of culture and language from race, and even as a description of that uniquely human realm of behavior we could call "culture," Kroeber's essay worked tolerably well, and in these respects Kroeber was right, in 1952, to assert that his essay's "contentions have largely passed into [his fellow anthropologists'] common body of assumptions."[44] However, already in 1917, a number of problems with Kroeber's description were immediately apparent, particularly regarding the issues of agency and determination. If individuals were not significant cultural agents, and if culture was autonomous from the organic facts of the species, then how did culture operate on and in human history?[45] More particularly, a number of Kroeber's critics took sharp exception to his discounting of the role of the individual in culture.

One of these was Edward Sapir. Though Sapir seemed gratified that Kroeber had "taken up the cudgel for a rigidly historical and anti-biological interpretation of culture," he also asserted that "Dr. Kroeber greatly overshoots the mark in his complete elimination of the peculiar influence of individuals on the course of history."[46] Sapir suggested that this feature of Kroeber's theory resulted from his exaggerated emphasis on examples from technical "inventions and scientific theories." Sapir commented, "Had he occupied himself more with the religious, philosophic, aesthetic, and crudely volitional activities and tendencies of man, I believe that Dr. Kroeber's case for the non-cultural significance of the individual would have been a far more difficult one to make." He continued, "With all due reverence for social science, I would not even hesitate to say that many a momentous cultural development or tendency, particularly in the religious and aesthetic spheres, is at last analysis a partial function or remote consequence of the temperamental peculiarities of a significant personality."[47] Not surprisingly, then, Sapir also rejected the implicit antipsychologism of Kroeber's essay, refusing to discount out of hand the development of a responsible "social psychology."[48]

Kroeber's antipsychological position is somewhat ironic, in light of the fact that Kroeber was himself a pioneer among American anthropologists in the exploration of psychoanalysis. During a period of personal distress, Kroeber underwent analysis by a member of Freud's circle. The experience led to a brief correspondence with Freud himself, and to Kroeber's practicing for several years as a lay analyst.[49] His influential article on *Totem and Taboo*—by some accounts the first essay on psychoanalysis in an American journal of anthropology—suggested a particular interest in Freud's claim that there were distinct parallels between certain features of "primitive" ritual, and neurosis. Anticipating Freud's elaboration of this idea in *Civilization and its Discontents*, Kroeber argued that the prevalence of neurosis seemed to go hand in hand with the decadence of mythic traditions, and a corresponding cultural emphasis on rationalism. Further, he noted that his own experience in the field not only confirmed that "primitives" were on the whole less neurotic than members of "civilized" societies, but that neurotic tendencies in primitive society seemed to find appropriate channels for expression through ritual, or ritual roles for those who—like the "homosexual" Berdache of some American Indian groups—would be considered neurotic or abnormal in his "civilized" world.[50]

However, just as many Boasians justified their aversion to Marxist theory by citing Marx and Engels's use of the outmoded ethnology of Lewis Henry Morgan, so did they hold Freud suspect on the grounds of his reliance on cultural evolutionists like Edward B. Tylor and Sir James Frazer. Kroeber's careful refutation of the ethnological assumptions of *Totem and Taboo* likely discouraged many of his colleagues from seriously considering the application of psychoanalysis to anthropological work.[51] Indeed, despite his intense involvement with psychoanalysis, Kroeber himself never explicitly attempted to integrate its theory or practice with his own work in anthropology.

On the other hand, there is a way in which a certain reading of the Freudian paradigm could actually have supported Kroeber's de-emphasis on individual agency in cultural change. Though he rejected the ethnographic core of *Totem and Taboo*, his interest in the connection between primitive ritual and neurosis (however questionable this connection may now seem) suggests that he re-mained committed to certain central concepts of Freudian theory. It suggests, for example, that Kroeber entertained the possibility that there existed psychic events common to humanity as a whole, and that behavior—neurotic or nor-mal—was linked to unconscious processes. Like Lévi-Strauss's structuralism, Kroeber's concept of the superorganic may have discounted the role of the *conscious* individual actor in favor of a view of culture that emphasized largely unconscious patterns. At least, this seems to have been the speculation of some of Kroeber's colleagues at the time. In a 1919 address before a joint meeting of the American Psychological Association and the American Anthropological Association, Clark Wissler hinted at the relationship between psychoanalysis and Kroeber's "superorganic," commenting, "the psychologists may have taken some casual interest in the heralding of a new onslaught against scientific tradition under a banner labeled the superorganic. Perhaps when we get a clear view of this new anthropological doctrine and tear away the camouflage, we shall find under it the poor old discarded soul of the psychologists."[52]

Nevertheless, rather than Kroeber it was to be Sapir, who maintained a more iconoclastic (or at least less strictly Freudian) approach to psychology, who significantly influenced the development of a psychological approach in the discipline of anthropology. His seminar on "Culture and Personality" at Yale in 1931 inaugurated an entire subdiscipline of anthropological study and helped to shape the thought of a whole generation of psychologically oriented anthropologists, including Weston LaBarre. Sapir also maintained a long friendship with pioneering psychiatrist Harry Stack Sullivan, a relationship that led to a number of professional liaisons with members of the American psychoanalytic establishment, and eventually to Sapir's appointment in 1935 as a trustee of Sullivan's prestigious William Allanson White Institute.[53]

By 1917, Sapir had already written a number of articles on psychoanalysis, including one in which he argued that the theory of the unconscious was the "invaluable kernel" of the discipline.[54] However, a review in the *Dial* of Freud's *Delusion and Dream* (subtitled, "An Interpretation in the Light of Psy-choanalysis of 'Gradiva,' a Novel, by Wilhelm Jensen") suggests that Sapir might not have entirely accepted the key Freudian concept of the uncon-scious—for much the same reason that he rejected Kroeber's "superorganic." Though Sapir expresses his admiration for Freud, it is clear that he is uncon-vinced by Freud's argument that the novelist Wilhelm Jensen (whom Sapir describes as a writer of "very moderate artistic ability") is capable of revealing in his work the complex psychological phenomena Freud attributes to it.[55] Suggesting that it might be otherwise if the literary work under analysis were the product of "a Shakespeare, a Balzac, or a Dostoevsky," Sapir holds out for a fairly traditional vision of artistic genius. He also fails to accept the central Freudian idea that artistic expression itself is the result of unconscious processes, and that the work of art reflects these processes regardless of the talent of its creator.

Sapir had certain interests in preserving the concept of "genius." He was a man of both remarkable talent and personal ambition, and he very likely believed in "genius" both in the abstract, and as it related to *him*. Sapir seemed to find most personal interest in psychological theories which fortified this self-image. Hence, despite his confessed frustration with C. G. Jung's cultural speculations, Sapir seems to have been especially intrigued by what he described as Jung's "uncanny" theory of "introvert" and "extravert" personalities.[56] Finding some personal satisfaction in understanding himself as a sensitive "introvert," he also relished using these terms in informal analyses of his friends and colleagues—occasionally to their dismay.[57] These terms were, however, more than the basis for a slightly malicious parlor game; they formed for him—and for his close associates Mead and Benedict—a potential model for cultural patterning, based on the psychological propensities of groups of people.[58]

However, it was in *Language*, his popularizing work on linguistics, where Sapir would first elaborate on a definition of "culture." Here, Sapir would refute the existence of set *cultural* patterns implicit in Kroeber's "superorganic," but this time in the service of suggesting that *language* was instead the bearer of such basic form: "Culture may be defined as *what* a society does and thinks. Language is a particular *how* of thought."[59] Once again, Sapir advanced this argument to the classically Boasian end of discounting any natural or innate relationship between race, culture, and language. Following his mentor, Sapir argued that the linguistic, cultural, and racial makeup of any one group of people were the independent artifacts of historical drift. However, in distinguishing "language" from "culture" as the "how" versus the "what" of human thought, Sapir also opened up the possibility of identifying what might later have been called "deep structures" within human speech itself. Indeed, he argued, "language and our thought-grooves are inextricably interwoven, are, in a sense, one and the same," and that "linguistic morphology is nothing more or less than a collective *art* of thought, an art denuded of the irrelevancies of individual sentiment."[60] By thus privileging language as formative of the most basic of human activities, Sapir suggested far more than his humble conclusion that "language can no more flow from race as such than can the sonnet form"; in fact, he laid the conceptual framework for the ideas of his student, Benjamin Lee Whorf, whose controversial studies of Hopi and Shoshone linguistics led him to claim a strong, indeed arguably *determinate*, relationship between linguistic structure and human cognition.[61]

Though immortalized by what has occasionally come to be known as the "Sapir-Whorf hypothesis," it is unknown exactly to what extent Sapir in fact supported his student's much-debated work—work proposed in full, indeed, well after Sapir's death.[62] (And given Sapir's comments about the implicit "social determinism" of Kroeber's theory, it seems unlikely that he would have found Whorf's linguistic determinism more palatable.) Rather, it seems that Sapir would become less impressed with the distinction he had drawn earlier between language and culture, and increasingly interested in the idea that, as with linguistic morphology, certain arbitrary *cultural* rules might exist which provided strictures on thought and action. Thus, Richard Handler has profitably argued that Sapir's work on literary theory—itself on the cusp of linguistic and cultural theory—is most revealing of his developing thoughts on the culture concept.[63]

To this point, we might add some account of Sapir the poet. Sapir was hardly in the avant-garde of poetic form. He wrote free verse reminiscent of the Imagists; rhymed verse like Ruth Benedict's lyricist poems; poetry indebted to various folk forms; and even pieces derivative of Keats and Arnold.[64] Despite this diversity of formal interests, it is clear that Sapir was centrally invested in his poetry—and its publication—as an act of public self-expression. Indeed, he chided his fellow poet-anthropologist Ruth Benedict for avoiding personal pronouns in her poetry, and for what Sapir described as the "dissociation of personality" suggested by her insistence on publishing under the pseudonym Anne Singleton.[65] (This poetic commitment to "honest" personal revelation did not, however, impress the reviewer for *Poetry*, who commented on Sapir's 1917 volume of verse, *Dreams and Gibes*, "[T]he lack of loveliness in the book is, to a certain extent, the aspect of the author's own soul."[66]) Sapir was, nonetheless, a member of the literary community of the late teens and twenties, and this, as well as his apparent interest in form, led to an intervention in the raging debate of the time over the merit of free verse, or—as Max Eastman famously called it—"lazy verse."[67]

On the surface, Sapir's essay "The Twilight of Rhyme" seems to argue that measured, rhyming verse has outlived its cultural moment. Sapir marshals ethnographic evidence to disprove Eastman's Spencerian claim that technical complexity is related to social advancement, pointing out that "primitive" societies probably engage in more customary, ritualistic, and formal behavior than do their "advanced" counterparts. "Progress," Sapir writes, "if it means anything at all, may be ideally defined as the infinite multiplication of things one may profitably do, think, and enjoy, coupled with the gradual elimination of all things one must not do."[68] It would thus appear that the modern way is toward a loosening of the rules of versification.

However, this point is confused by a curious anecdote Sapir offers at the opening of the essay about his experience at an Ottawa debating club. There, an overly zealous British pro-war orator (the year is 1917) brings his jingoistic exhortations to a close with a few patriotic lines from Walter Scott ("This is my own, my native land!"). Not only unmoved by the performance, Sapir feels compelled to speak in rebuttal of the speaker's call for U.S. involvement in the war. But the subject of the essay is versification, not contemporary politics, and the point of the anecdote is to offer some comment about the rhetorical effectiveness of the speaker's invocation of "some of Scott's old doggerel": "Had he but called in the aid of measured blank verse or, preferably, free verse, he might have succeeded in producing a truly climactic effect. But what had such inane jingles as dead—said, shed—bed, Ted—Fred, to do with the expression of heightened feeling? What concern had we, stirred to the patriotism that dealt and suffered death, to do with pretty boudoir tricks and rococo curtseys?"[69] Sapir's construction here is highly ironic. Clearly, we are not meant here to take seriously his contention that free verse is somehow a *better* medium for pro-war oratory than rhymed verse. Sapir was never predisposed to be swept away with pro-war fervor—either by the content of the orator's argument, or by the lines from Walter Scott—and thus, jingoistic exhortations would have been just as annoying to him, whether in couplets or in free verse. On the other hand, his example of the debating-club speaker also suggests that rhymed verse is precisely the stuff of jingoistic exhortation. While this may make the orator's usage of "doggerel" a matter of questionable taste (he reminds us, archly, "Only the cultured élite can resist mere eloquence"[70]), it does not exactly suggest that we have reached the "twilight of rhyme." Rather, it suggests that certain subjects are appropriate to rhyme, just as others are to free verse; as he puts it later in the essay, "[T]here is no absolute standard by which to measure the validity of a formal aesthetic device."[71] In fact, Sapir comes very close to conceding an important point to Eastman's argument for rhyme, namely, that

> Rhyme sets definite technical limitations that tax the poet's ingenuity. He has to solve technical problems, and in their solution he is braced to the utmost limit of his powers of concentration, of clarity of vision, of self-expression. A chastening halt is put to a too easily satisfied, a too glibly facile flow of expression. The aesthetic product, which must of course appear perfectly natural and unhampered, is all the more refined and potent for the painful struggle that has preceded its birth. The dynamic value of the overcoming of conflict in aesthetic production is by no means to be lightly set aside.[72]

Sapir's poetic output also offers some confimation of his sympathy with this view; the majority of his poetry was written in rhymed verses.[73]

It is not hard to imagine how a theory of formal constraints in poetics might lend itself to a conception of "culture" as a similar set of historically contingent constraints upon behavior, thought, and creativity. Yet perhaps because Sapir was himself a creative artist—and clearly interested, personally and intellectually, in the idea of the creative "genius"—he was especially invested in the question of how creative individuals might negotiate and transform these cultural conventions. These interests—in convention as a kind of cultural form, and in the role of the creator as a cultural agent—were fully articulated together in his extremely interesting essay, "Culture, Genuine and Spurious." The article, published in its entirety in 1924, made its first appearance in 1919 in the pages of the *Dial*, and, fittingly for this venue, united the literary and anthropological interests of its writer in a work strongly evocative of both Brooks and Matthew Arnold. Like Brooks, Sapir focused on the problem of alienation and division—the failure of the social body to fully cohere or allow its participants to feel a sense of common purpose.

Sapir began by drawing the customary distinction between the two common uses of the word "culture"—the first derived from Boas's cultural history to mean a collection of social facts, and the second drawn from the standard reading of Matthew Arnold, to mean taste and refinement. In a three-part structure similar to that employed in Brooks's cultural criticism, Sapir then proposed an intermediary third definition of culture, poised between what he described as the absolute binary of the ethnographic and the aesthetic, the staunchly nonevaluative and the rigidly hierarchical. This new definition of culture was concerned, like the ethnographic definition, with the life of the social group, but Sapir claimed that, like its aesthetic counterpart, this new definition acknowledged the relative significance of certain types of human behavior and thought: behaviors and ways of thinking that seemed to *best* characterize the social group. Hence, "we may perhaps come nearest the mark by saying that the cultural conception we are now trying to grasp aims to embrace in a single term those general attitudes, views of life, and specific manifestations of civilization that give a particular people its distinctive place in the world."[74] Sapir concluded, "Culture, then, may be briefly defined as civilization in so far as it embodies the national genius" (311).

In producing the phrase "national genius" to describe "culture," Sapir complexly encapsulated questions about the place of the individual in culture that bedeviled both the *Seven Arts* writers and his anthropological contemporaries. "Culture" was a special combination of the individual "genius" and the national whole—indeed, it was the embodiment of that genius *in* the national whole. But given Sapir's basic adherence to Boasian views, this model of the relationship between the individual and culture was not reducible to the simple romantic organicism of Brooks and his peers. Rather, for Sapir "culture" was a kind of formal constraint that dialectically shapes and is shaped by the active cultural producer. As in his discussion of poetic form in "The Twilight of Rhyme," the individual (genius) both works within and is limited by the forms and traditions of the culture. Simultaneously, this cultural actor molds cultural forms to new social and personal needs—thereby transforming the shape of the culture itself. "Creation is a bending of form to one's will, not a manufacture of form *ex nihilo*. If the passive perpetuator of a cultural tradition gives us merely a manner, the shell of a life that once was, the creator from out of a cultural waste gives us hardly more than a gesture or a yawp, the strident promise of a vision raised by our desires" (321).

Sapir's dynamic vision of cultural processes was thus potentially extremely sophisticated—a significant revision and recombination of both Brooks's reliance on the power of transcendent geniuses like Whitman to transform culture, and of Kroeber's superorganicism which posited a culture independent of human agency. Unlike Kroeber, Sapir not only acknowledged that people—particularly artists—could change society, but that the cultural climate insisted that they become cultural and social actors. But unlike Brooks, Sapir would hardly have looked to the iconoclastic Whitman (the poet who proudly sounded his "barbaric yawp over the roofs of the world") as an adequate agent of cultural change. But under precisely which conditions could this delicate dialectic take place?

As with Brooks, Bourne, and the Boasians generally, Sapir also attempted to articulate a conception of national cultures that avoided the creation of invidious distinctions. "Primitive" cultures in his view could stand on morally equivalent terms with the "civilized." However, Sapir offered one proviso to this basic moral relativism: that certain attitudes and lifestyles were maintained in some cultures—whether "primitive" or "civilized"—that made these cultures "inherently harmonious, balanced, self-satisfactory" (314). Such cultures, which he called "genuine"—as opposed to disharmonious, hypocritical, "spurious" cultures—were ones in which its members felt a sense of natural spiritual satisfaction, of purpose and fulfillment: an unoccluded expression of "national genius." "Genuine" cultures could, of course, be understood as relatively comparable to one another, but "spurious" cultures were another matter.

Sapir considered his own milieu an example of a "spurious" culture, in which the dialectic of the culture and the individual agent had failed. He argued that the contemporary cultural scene was dominated by pretentious consumption of tradition on the one hand, and by unrestrained, historically ungrounded expression on the other. In other words, he saw something very like what Brooks suggested in his description of the incommensurate heritages of the "Puritans" and the "Pioneers." By contrast to this mess, "genuine" culture abhorred hypocrisy:

> It is not a spiritual hybrid of contradictory patches, of water-tight compartments of consciousness that avoid participation in a harmonious synthesis. If the culture necessitates slavery, it frankly admits it; if it abhors slavery, it feels its way to an economic adjustment that obviates the necessity of its employment. It does not make

a great show in its ethical ideals of an uncompromising opposition to slavery, only to introduce what amounts to a slave system into certain portions of its industrial mechanism. (315)

Sapir's negative comparison of his own "spurious" culture to a society that "frankly admits" its basis in slavery is extremely revealing. It allows him to argue eloquently for the "appalling sacrifice made to civilization" each time a "telephone girl" becomes engaged in boring, mechanized, and unfulfilling work—a theme that he would also develop in his poem, "The Stenographer."[75] But the overstatement of the case—ought we really to admire a society whose "harmonious synthesis" is based upon slavery?—also shows the extent to which he is willing to push the relative moral equivalency of all "genuine" cultures to make a point about the value of internal coherence.

In Sapir's preference for cultures with a "harmonious synthesis," we may also again dimly see the hand of Arnold, for whom culture was, centrally, the vehicle for the resolution of social and spiritual disharmony. Here, Sapir too offers a vision of culture that is above all harmonious, irrespective of the actual practices that are its norms. It is thus unsurprising that Sapir invokes the same—easily refutable—examples of "genuine culture" (of social harmony!) from which Arnold—and T. S. Eliot—drew solace: Periclean Athens and Elizabethan England (315). Clearly, "genuine" culture represents less an actual cultural site than a horizon of utopian possibility. And just as clearly, it would not be a society based on slavery, for such a society could hardly conform to Sapir's vision of "genuine" spiritual fulfillment.

Let us return to Sapir's telephone girl. In a somewhat romanticized version of the Marxist critique of alienation, Sapir observed that the specialized work of industrialized societies deprives most workers of the self-fulfillment which comes with satisfying essential human needs, and suggested that interest and energy should thus naturally and logically be transferred to spheres of what he called "nonessential" work, including the pursuit of knowledge and the creation of art. Like Brooks, he believed in the personally and socially transformative power of art, but perhaps even more clearsightedly than Brooks, he recognized that unalienated production itself was being devalued in the wake of a newly emerging economic order:

Here lies the grimmest joke of our present American civilization. The vast majority of us, deprived of any but an insignificant and culturally abortive share in the satisfaction of the immediate wants of mankind, are further deprived of both opportunity and stimulation to share in the production of non-utilitarian values. Part of the time we are dray-horses; the rest of the time we are listless consumers of goods which have received no least impress of our personality. In other words, our spiritual selves go hungry, for the most part, pretty much all of the time. (321)

In such a spurious culture, individuals can only be cultured in a spurious way: they can acquire refined tastes and manners, they can gain knowledge of their cultural traditions, but they cannot engage their milieu in a creative, self-fulfilling manner. Individuals can, in other words, consume cultural values, but they cannot participate in their production.

But with this observation we return, distressingly, to the problem with which Brooks wrestled in vain: if individuals in "spurious" cultures are cut off from meaningful cultural production, then how is the culture repaired, made "genuine"? Thus we can see how Sapir's normative categories of "genuine" and "spurious" cultures finally work to undercut his dialectical theory of cultural change. While certain societies—genuine societies—operate through such a dialectic, the rest, it is supposed, simply grope for ways to once again become cultural producers. And, as with Brooks, Sapir seems to have been frustrated in imagining that the collective or the community could be a viable agent of such a transformation.

Indeed, like both Bourne and Brooks before him, Sapir seems to have suffered from the absence of even a collectivity of intellectual peers. In 1929 he wrote to Ruth Benedict (who, as we shall see, would extend his views in important new directions): "This is an age of perfectly terrifying loneliness and no wonder we run to the deceptive anodynes of the mob. I am content to be as lonely as my nature demands and as much more lonely as a profound distrust of the temper of intellectual America condemns me to being. . . . I am too old to learn to be different, too young to be indulgently or wisely indifferent."[76] We might thus forgive Sapir, caught in such a context, for being limited in his own creativity; for having produced, in his poetry, so much that seems derivative and "traditional"—*not* (as he would have had it) a new context created out of the dialectic of genius and ("genuine") cultural context. For indeed, just as Brooks's divided culture offers no coherency to the idea of the American nation, so Sapir's spurious culture offers no possibility of genius.

Given this apparent failure of the individual *and* the collective, Sapir's final, tentative, proposal for producing genuine cultures was again not unlike a turn subsequently to be made by Brooks. While Brooks would seek a usable past in American history, Sapir advocated undertaking something like an archaeological dig of the American psyche, to find the buried, "genuine," fragments of cultures, to shore against the ruins of our spurious existence:

> Sooner or later we shall have to get down to the humble task of exploring the depths of our consciousness and dragging to the light what sincere bits of reflected experience we can find. These bits will not always be beautiful, they will not always be pleasing, but they will be genuine. And then we can build. In time, in plenty of time—for we must have patience—a genuine culture—better yet, a series of linked autonomous cultures—will grace our lives. (331)

As we shall see in the following two chapters, Sapir here predicts the direction of the cultural criticism of subsequent decades, much of which was engaged in just such a search for "genuine" cultures through the reconstruction of folk memory and regional "autonomous cultures." For many of his contemporaries, such locally distinct cultures would come to be seen as alternatives to the homogenizing influence of what Sapir described as the "canned culture" of consumer society, and thus a way out of modern alienation. But, as we will see in the next chapter, this search was predicated on ignoring the complex dynamic relationship of individual and collective suggested by Sapir, in favor of a more basic view that the individual psyche is a storehouse of cultural memory, and (reciprocally) that cultures are "personalities writ large."

4

Terrains of Culture: Ruth Benedict, Waldo Frank, and the Spatialization of the Culture Concept

You know I like [primitive cultures to be] scandalous,
and the possibilities you touch on are endless,
aren't they?
  (Ruth Benedict to Reo Fortune, February 10, 1933)

IN TRYING TO OVERCOME the problem of the relationship between the individual and society, Brooks and Sapir could both be said to have succumbed to an updated version of the paradox that also haunted Matthew Arnold's vision of culture. The problem they both recognized, the alienation of the individual in modern society, couldn't, in their view, be tackled by the alienated individual alone. Recognizing on some level that the problem was part of the wider structural changes of industrial capitalism in the early twentieth century, they saw that the separation of the individual from the social could only be addressed socially, or at least by the smaller "nuclei" of community that Bourne had in mind. In other words, it took some kind of collective to change society, but of course, the absence of that kind of integrated collective was the problem to begin with. The only way out of this bind was either a "faith" that was deeply pessimistic at its core, or a search for some collective outside of modern alienation itself: a search for what Waldo Frank would call "buried cultures."

It is nearly a truism of American intellectual history that the period after World War I is characterized by cultural despair, a deep frustration, especially among urban intellectuals, over the seemingly unstoppable encroachments of such abominations as the Klan, the Red Scare, and the bad taste of the Babbitry and the "booboisie." And certainly, everything I have said about Brooks and Sapir can be read as exemplifying this attitude. But, as a number of others have shown, this postwar pessimism was only part of the story. For those sympathetic to the production of indigenous culture, there was also something exhilarating about Europe's catastrophic state: Americans, many thought, were finally freed of European culture to build something new on native grounds. Indeed, it was thought that the New World might even be in a position to save the Old from its own decadence.[1] Thus, in direct response to criticisms of American life such as Brooks's influential characterization of the divided American soul, some would find in "buried cultures" a highly optimistic, and even mystical, vision for America's future.

Using the very formulae—highbrow/lowbrow, Puritan/Pioneer, genuine/spurious—that Sapir and Brooks devised to talk about the problem of alienation, some of their closer associates worked out a resolution to this lack of an integrated organic culture by hypothesizing a diversity of cultures, each with its own "personality." Rejecting Brooks's historical turn, in which the Emersonian past served as a "usable" locus outside of modernity and its problems, these others, including writers Waldo Frank, Jean Toomer, Hart Crane, Sherwood Anderson, and the anthropologist Ruth Benedict, imagined the different cultures as spatially diverse, as if arrayed on a map of cultural possibilities. In a manner again reminiscent of Bourne's "transnational America," these different, autonomous cultural sites would then form a kind of loose federalism, creating a homeland for every cultural—and personality—type. Like so much cultural theory, this resolution of the problem of alienation in "culture" was on the one hand utopian, and on the other, nostalgic. The spaces of the "buried cultures" were geographically remote from urban America, and thus, their recovery could also be characterized as an opting out of the very sites associated with a troublesome modernity. In this respect, this search for the authentic cultural space was in effect a search for a "usable past" without reference to history. We will see in the next chapter how these disparate sites are reified into a full-blown political and aesthetic theory of regionalism. Meanwhile, however, by way of introducing Ruth Benedict's important theorization of a spatial "culture and personality" in *Patterns of Culture*, I will turn to her relationship with Sapir and their very different struggles to come to terms with the changing roles of women in modern society.

The Individual and Society

Nowhere is Sapir's basic conservatism—his final reliance on cultural forms and norms for their own sake—more evident than in his attitudes towards women's changing social roles. A prominent figure in a discipline that was remarkably open to women, Sapir is notable for publicly describing women's suffrage (in 1916) as "deplorably inevitable."[2] In some ways, however, Sapir's conservatism regarding gender issues and his own relationships with women were typical of the Greenwich Village milieu around which his life revolved. Like many of his peers within and on the periphery of bohemia, Sapir simultaneously resented the demands of the New Woman and craved the intellectual and emotional satisfaction of companionate relationships with women who were his equals.[3] Hence, during the time of his first wife's long illness and after her death, Sapir developed important relationships with two—feminist—women colleagues: Margaret Mead and Ruth Benedict. Though Benedict was of Sapir's generation (Mead was seventeen years younger than Sapir), both women were his junior professionally, and they regarded him as something of a mentor in anthropology. However, Benedict was clearly the most gifted of the three in their other shared endeavor of writing poetry. Together, they cultivated their mutual creative interests in poetry, and their scientific interests in psychology and in cultural configurations. Mead would later single out Sapir and Benedict, along with Boas, as comprising her most significant formative intellectual relationships.[4]

In her biography of Benedict, Margaret M. Caffrey has suggested that Benedict and Mead were for a short time lovers. It is clear, however, that their bond of lifelong mutual devotion, outlasting other partnerships, involved a great deal more than physical attraction. It was Benedict, who clearly thought of the younger woman as both a student and a daughter, who kindled Mead's interest in anthropology. Mead, in turn, introduced Benedict to Greenwich Village feminism, and to her friends Léonie Adams and Louise Bogan, two young Lyricist poets who would strongly influence Benedict's development as an artist.[5] After Benedict's death in 1948, it was Mead more than any other who kept Benedict's work before the public.[6] Sapir and Benedict, in turn, carried out a long and avid correspondence in which, in addition to discussing their mutual interest in poetry, they saw each other through Sapir's difficult years in Canada, the death of Sapir's wife, and the slow dissolution of Benedict's marriage.

By contrast, Mead's brief relationship with Sapir had deeply divisive effects on this complex little community, alienating not only Sapir and Mead, but Sapir and Benedict as well. Mead was preparing to begin her fieldwork in Samoa when Sapir asked her to leave her husband and marry him. Though Mead refused his offer of marriage, Sapir attempted to intervene with Boas to prevent Mead from leaving the country.[7] "Papa Franz" could be an autocrat with his students (it was he who directed Mead to study feminine adolescence in Samoa) but he apparently saw himself as too enlightened to forbid her plans at Sapir's behest. Nonetheless, Mead deeply resented Sapir's interference, later suggesting that his professed concern for her well-being was exaggerated, and indeed simply a ruse to keep her in her place, as a replacement mother for his children.[8] Sapir was also embittered by the failure of their romance, which he seems to have attributed to Mead's selfish, and probably unwomanly, ambition.

In 1928, the same year as the publication of *Coming of Age in Samoa*, Sapir published a paper in the *American Journal of Psychiatry* called "Observations on the Sex Problem in America," in which he criticized the idea, popularly supported by Mead's account of Samoa, that "primitives" were less sexually repressed than "moderns." He argued that, like eating, sexuality was a culturally defined and controlled act, and that sexual "freedom," generally regarded in psychiatric circles as a "healthy" lack of inhibition, might in fact be a cultural *mal*adjustment. Rejecting the dialectical model of culture in "Culture, Genuine and Spurious," in which individuals acted both within and *against* their culture, Sapir argued that culturally determined inhibitions related to sex were transcultural and above all "normal"; that romantic love (as opposed to mere erotic attraction) was a universal human truth derived from the universally applicable Freudian concept of sublimation; and that sexual jealousy was this love's most supreme expression. Along the way, he castigated the "modern woman" who engaged in "free love" as "a safe, and therefore a dishonest, prostitute," and described her (contradictorily) as both sexually frigid and narcissistically invested in her own pleasure. He argued, moreover, that homosexuality was the inevitable—"unnatural"—outcome of the new amoralities of feminism and "free love."[9] Though it seems clear that these comments were directed at Mead if at anyone, it was Ruth Benedict—soon to separate from her estranged husband and to begin the first of several long-term relationships with women—who took his words to heart.[10]

Benedict's *Patterns of Culture*, her most popular and probably most enduring work, may thus be multiply indebted to Edward Sapir.[11] There is little doubt that his description of formal cultural configurations, derived from an analogy to language, helped form Benedict's thoughts on culture. And yet, some of Benedict's major departures from earlier articulations of the cultural configurations idea seem to have been motivated by opinions such as Sapir's on homosexuality and the New Woman. Moreover, her version of the cultural configurations idea as it emerged in *Patterns of Culture* would directly refute some of the basic themes of Sapir's "Culture—Genuine and Spurious."

In answer to Sapir's intervention into psychiatric practice in "Observations on the Sex Problem in America," Benedict wrote a thoroughgoing critique of normative views of sexuality entitled "Anthropology and Abnormality," and published it, as had Sapir his "Observations," in a professional journal of psychology. There, she argued that the cultural acceptance of homosexuality is comparable to different cultural reactions to people who fall into trances or have fits of catalepsy: in some cultures it is reviled; in others, it is regarded as unexceptional; and in still others it is given special regard as socially or spiritually meaningful behavior. For her audience of psychologists she concluded, "In this matter of mental ailments, we must face the fact that even our normality is man-made, and is of our own seeking."[12]

Though intended for a much broader audience than "Anthropology and Abnormality," *Patterns of Culture* concludes with a similar discussion of the social construction of normality. In what Clifford Geertz describes as one of Benedict's typical "onward and upward sermons" on cultural relativism, she addresses the existential crisis that relativism seems to produce, and offers good cheer.[13] "As soon as the new opinion is embraced as customary belief, it will be another trusted bulwark of the good life."[14] Implicitly, this new opinion—whether about homosexuality or catalepsy—will be embraced through the discursive mechanism of books such as hers, which show that if it is in the range of the humanly, culturally, possible, it cannot, in the absolute sense, be considered "abnormal."

However, it is in some ways remarkable that *Patterns of Culture* is regarded as a popularly influential treatise on cultural relativism. Benedict's use of intercultural information is, in the broadest sense, an extended application of Boas's method of refutation though the use of the negative instance. But in her attack on normative descriptions of human behavior, Benedict stretches the Boasian negative instance to the breaking point, relying upon her choice of intercultural examples to turn a literally foreign idea into a "trusted bulwark of the good life." In this sense, her commitment to cultural relativism seems seriously limited. Her real goal is, of course, not to prove that a given belief or practice is not "abnormal" in an absolute sense, but to show that social acceptance of that belief or practice is not itself *unreasonable*. Proving that something is not "abnormal" is not, however, the same thing as proving that it *is* acceptable or desirable in a given social context. In other words, her arguments about the different cultural attitudes toward homosexuality and catalepsy might serve to convince her readers *not* that these practices could be a "bulwark of the good life," but that, while appropriate for Plains Indians and Siberian shamans, these practices are not right for "us."

Indeed, the configurations approach to culture, which Benedict helped to popularize under the banner of "culture and personality," would itself seem to encourage such conclusions through its implicit construction of fairly rigid cultural boundaries. Benedict insisted in *Patterns of Culture* that "it would be absurd to cut every culture down to the Procrustean bed of some catchword characterization" (228). However, her model of cultural personality types, captured in her famous dictum that culture is "personality writ large," at the very least led many others toward just such reductive thinking about culture.[15] Moreover, the "culture and personality" approach to culture posits a new set of norms, a new prescriptive relationship, that obtains between the individual and his or her culture. For example, if one lives in a culture that is essentially "paranoiac" (as Benedict would suggest of the Melanesian Dobu), then paranoid behavior is both "normal" (in its context) and expressive of one's relationship to the social body. Conversely, acts of fellow feeling and open friendliness in such a context are not only "abnormal," but culturally *deviant*.

The ethnographies that make up the body of *Patterns of Culture* make an equally ambivalent case for either cultural relativism or intercultural tolerance. Benedict is remembered for advising her students to "read ethnographies with empathy, to project ourselves into the culture being described, and to imagine what life must be like."[16] In two of the book's three ethnographies in particular, such empathetic reading is indeed a significant challenge. Of the New Mexican Zuñi, the Melanesian Dobu, and the Kwakiutl of the Northwest Coast, only the Zuñi are described as people among whom one could imagine living—and even they seem to take the expression of mildness and self-effacement to a fault.

On the other hand, in her portrayal of the Dobu, they are not only malicious and paranoid, but the absolute inverse of the stereotype of the contented South Sea islander, as described in a study like *Coming of Age in Samoa*. Benedict makes the incredible seem matter-of-fact, stating of these "hostile," "suspicion-ridden" people, "the social forms which obtain in Dobu put a premium upon ill-will and treachery and make them the recognized virtues of their society" (131,135,138). Alfred Kroeber, noting that Benedict derived her account of the Dobu solely from an ethnography by Reo Fortune (then Mead's husband), suggested that as a people they came off far worse in *Patterns of Culture* than they did in the original study; indeed, that here they were "pathological to the point of repellence."[17]

Clearly, Benedict's characterization of the Dobu departs from the protocols of social-scientific "objectivity." But to what end? First, following Geertz, I think we may see a strong parodic impulse revealed in Benedict's portrayal of the Dobu.[18] In this reading, her description of the Dobu (and of the Kwakiutl and Zuñi) is less a bad, reductive summary of others' ethnographic work, than a pointed caricature, directed, as many commentators upon *Patterns of Culture* have noted, at her own cultural context. Indeed, perhaps she is working more in the tradition of Thorstein Veblen than in that of Boas.

But there is another way to read Benedict's weird ethnographies. The example of the Dobu, as she presents it, provides evidence for one of the central theoretical points of the book, a point that she states and restates in the final chapter, that "society and the individual are not antagonists"—or, to put it another way, there is no such thing as Sapir's proposed "spurious" culture (251). This proposition, applied to the Dobu, suggests that their behavior is organically related to their society as a whole; despite appearances, they are not antisocial, or abnormal, but very much integrated into their cultural configuration. But somewhat more radically, I also think her example of the Dobu is conceived with an eye toward those hostile paranoiacs among her own milieu who would seem to be exemplars of the antagonism between the individual and the community; in effect she is suggesting that they too have a homeland out there, where their behavior, "abnormal" as it is, may in fact be a "bulwark of the good life."

It may now seem that we have moved from anthropology to fantasy; and indeed, in a sense we have. In my reading of Benedict, I will suggest that her project contains a strongly utopian element, showing not only that "society and the individual are not antagonists" (this despite her own plausible alienation as a lesbian in a sexist and homophobic world), but that for everyone there is a "genuine" culture, an imaginary homeland, of perfect integration beyond alienation. In this sense, her book moves beyond critical parody of American society, and into something rather more radical.

The Imaginary Homeland

Though during World War II Benedict engaged in numerous studies of modern cultures (notably of Japan, in *The Chrysanthemum and the Sword*), at the time of the writing of *Patterns of Culture* she joined many of her fellow anthropologists in hesitating to engage in ethnographic generalizations about complex industrialized societies. Thus, it is difficult to ascertain in *Patterns of Culture* whether or not she thinks contemporary American society is also describable by a specific cultural configuration. In what is likely a further refutation of Sapir's lament about the lack of "integration" in contemporary society, Benedict argues that ease of travel, social stratification, and the multiplicity of voluntary social groups (she cites the Rotary Clubs and bohemian Greenwich Village as examples) only give one the *impression* of disharmony in comparison with a geographically isolated village (229–30). Though this characterization of modern society would suggest that different, more nuanced conceptions of culture would be necessary to describe "American culture," Benedict elsewhere alludes to "the will to power so conspicuous in modern life"—as a basis for its comparison with the cultural patterns of the Zuñi and the Kwakiutl (241). Indeed, I would argue that Benedict forms her critique of the American context in and *between* her ethnographic chapters, through a range of comparisons between the three cultural sites of the Zuñi, Kwakiutl, and Dobu.

As James A. Boon has noted, there is a whole "field of contrasts" working throughout the three ethnographies, which tend to work toward a number of different theoretical points both within and outside the discipline of anthropology. In many of these contrasts, the Dobu often figure as a bizarre third term, mediating between, or opposed to, less "scandalous" cultural possibilities. Thus, with a view to addressing contemporary attitudes toward women's "natural" social roles, Benedict emphasizes sharp contrasts in the social construction of gender: the Zuñi are matrilineal and matrilocal; the Kwakiutl are patrilineal and patrilocal; the Dobu take up residence in alternating years at the wife's and then the husband's village. To address the issue of contact and cultural drift, Benedict contrasts the Zuñi with the neighboring Apache, and the Dobu with their neighbors, the Trobriands (where they again come off as almost comically terrible: "In the centre of the [Dobu] village a graveyard takes the place of the open communal dance plaza of the Trobriands" (133). To address the longer historical narrative of tribal diversification, Benedict compares the Zuñi and the Kwakiutl. [19]

In this last comparison, Benedict concludes that the Zuñi cultural configuration is unique among all other American Indian groups: "The Zuñi are a ceremonious people, a people who value sobriety and inoffensiveness above all other virtues" (59). They are mild tempered, and they value order and harmony in their daily life. They are self-effacing, and seek consensus in all things. Their unique configuration, to which she applies the Nietzschean label "Apollonian," is, she claims, in strong contradistinction to most of the rest of the North American Indians, whose cultural patterns tend to be "Dionysian." Exemplary of this latter configuration are the Kwakiutl, who, Benedict tells us, are given not only to ecstatic rituals, but to the profligate destruction of private property in the potlatch—all for the sake of personal glorification.

This language of the Apollonian-Dionysian distinction is probably the best known, and most thoroughly critiqued, of the theoretical points of the book. Benedict's Nietzschean dichotomy first appeared in a 1932 article, largely on the Zuñi, entitled "Configurations of Culture in North America."[20] Because her chapter on the Zuñi in *Patterns of Culture* retained much of this language, and because the Zuñi were the best studied of the three groups she discussed in the book, Benedict's description of them as an "Apollonian" society has come under special scrutiny. Over the years numerous anthropologists have nibbled away at her claim (yet again enacting the Boasian strategy of refutation by the negative instance) by citing copious instances of arrogance, disharmony, and violence among the group Benedict described as "incorrigibly mild."[21] Caffrey suggests that many anthropologists objected to the Nietzschean opposition as an unscientific importation into the field. She argues further, "disproving the Apollonian-Dionysian contrast became the key symbolic activity for disproving or disparaging the historical approach and reaffirming the primacy of science in anthropology."[22]

While Benedict's Nietzschean taxonomy is evidently problematic on several grounds, there is some textual evidence that Benedict herself was not especially interested in its elaboration by the time of the writing of *Patterns of Culture*. Excepting the chapter on Zuñi, which was partially based on her 1932 article and other material she had already written, the Apollonian-Dionysian opposition is far less prominent as a structuring principle of the book than her critics' preoccupations would suggest. The chapter on the Kwakiutl, which begins with an account of their "Dionysian" religious practices, switches midway from discussing this feature that Benedict says unites them with most North American Indians, to focus on "the pattern of culture which was peculiar to them"; namely, the Kwakiutl "megalomania," expressed particularly in the profligacy of the potlatch (182).

In fact, if one brackets the Apollonian-Dionysian contrast, it becomes clear that the ethnographies distinguish the Zuñi from the Kwakiutl not so much on the grounds that one culture is sober and the other is ecstatic, but that one is communal and the other is individualistic. This difference is evident in the way Benedict explains the two cultures' approaches to death. The Kwakiutl, Benedict tells us, saw the death of a loved one as a personal affront, and as a potential source of shame for the survivor—often ameliorated only through the violent taking of another life. The Zuñi, by contrast, confront death with a minimum of grief and loss. In general, compared to the "megalomaniac" Kwakiutl, "the Zuñi people . . . devote themselves to the constituted forms of their society. They sink individuality in them. They do not think of office, and possession of priestly bundles, as steps in the upward path of ambition" (104). On the other hand, Benedict's description of the Kwakiutl, who build potlatch bonfires of canoes and other valued objects for their social glorification, is explicitly parodic of American conspicuous consumption, to the extent that their customs are compared to the behavior of the residents of the American city "Middletown," the subject of Robert Lynd and Helen Merrell Lynd's famous 1929 community study of that name (discussed at greater length in Chapter 5):

> It is an unattractive picture. In Kwakiutl life the rivalry is carried out in such a way that all success must be built upon the ruin of rivals; in *Middletown* in such a way that individual choices and direct satisfactions are reduced to a minimum and conformity is sought beyond all other human gratifications. In both cases it is clear that wealth is not sought and valued for its direct satisfaction of human needs but as a series of counters in the game of rivalry. If the will to victory were eliminated from the economic life, as it is in Zuñi, distribution and consumption of wealth would follow quite different "laws." (247–48)

From this last sentence, we might be ready to see the Zuñi as exemplifying a cultural pattern in some significant respects "better" than that of the Kwakiutl. But Benedict is careful to stress that the Kwakiutls' opposite, the communal Zuñi, do not enjoy their individual humanity to its fullest, and thus, Zuñi culture is "far from utopian":

> [It] has no place, for instance, for dispositions we are accustomed to value highly, such as force of will or personal initiative or the disposition to take up arms against a sea of troubles. It is incorrigibly mild. The group activity that fills existence in Zuñi is out of touch with human life—with birth, love, death, success, failure, and prestige. A ritual pageant serves their purpose and minimizes more human interests. The freedom from any forms of social exploitation or of social sadism appears on the other side of the coin as endless ceremonialism not designed to serve major ends of human existence. It is the old inescapable fact that every upper has its lower, every right side its left. (246)

Rather than offering a better alternative to the Kwakiutl configuration, the Zuñi are shown to exemplify a pattern that takes the opposite tendency, communalism, to extremes. By now, Benedict's distinction between the Zuñi and the Kwakiutl should sound like a familiar one in the context of this narrative. It is, in fact, similar to Brooks's distinction between the Puritan and Pioneer tendencies in American culture, in which the Kwakiutl play the part of the grasping, mercenary Pioneers, and the Zuñi are the bloodless, "highbrow" Puritans. There is, however, one crucial distinction between Brooks's social criticism and Benedict's new construction of the dichotomy. Brooks—and Sapir—envisioned the different tendencies in American life as rooted in specific historical contexts, and handed down to contemporary Americans despite the fact that they were no longer relevant to present conditions. This was Sapir's "spurious" culture, the product of what the social science of this period so often referred to as "cultural lag." For Brooks, the new American society that might emerge out of the fragmented present would be built on the appropriation of a "usable past" to contemporary ends. Though Benedict's cultures clearly serve as object lessons of a sort for her contemporary American society, they are not part of some historical narrative of a larger American culture which must be healed or restored. Indeed, if anything, it is the individual cultures that are endangered and subject to the depredations of historical change—hence, her use of the slightly elegiac past tense throughout her chapter on the Kwakiutl. Rather, the connection between an American culture and these other cultural sites of the Kwakiutl and the Zuñi is an essentially analogical one, in which each of the cultures she describes is a distinctive space of belief and behavior. This spatial conception of cultural possibilities seems to me also to be the central significance of Benedict's famous allegory of culture, which also serves as the book's invocation. Of Ramon, her "Digger" Indian informant, she writes: "One day, without transition, Ramon broke in upon his descriptions of grinding mesquite and preparing acorn soup. 'In the beginning,' he said, 'God gave to every people a cup, a cup of clay, and from this cup they drank their life.' ... 'They all dipped in the water,' he continued, 'but their cups were different. Our cup is broken now. It has passed away' " (21–22).

But then where do the "paranoiac" Dobu fit into her story? They could of course simply be a third "cup of clay," and a startling example of her point about the cultural contextuality of normality and deviance. But I think there is something more at work here, that makes the Dobu less a third example, less of an "odd culture out," as Boon puts it, than a negative *synthesis* of the cultural traits of the Zuñi and the Kwakiutl.[23] The Dobu are, after all, both communal and individualistic, after a fashion: communal to the extent that they look to their village as a safe haven from the harmful magic of other villages, *and* individualistic to the extent that they constantly assume that they are the objects of malicious intent. Dobu culture acknowledges the terrible power of both the community and the individual, and organizes social life in such a way as to balance out the malignant force of one with the other. In this sense, Dobu culture suggests the worst of communal constraint and self-aggrandizement, expressing this "paranoiac" combination in its unusual social arrangements.

If such a synthesis of the *worst* possible features of a society exists (albeit, safely offshore in Melanesia), then surely a *better* one may also be possible. In making the Dobu into a negative synthesis of Zuñi and Kwakiutl patterns, I see Benedict as also figuratively opening up the space for a "good" society, constructed as a melding of the best of her two polar opposite contexts: a new combination of the social and economic generosity of the Zuñi combined with the self-gratification that the Kwakiutl pattern affords. However, this combination would not result in a rearrangement of familiar social forms but in some altogether different arrangement, which is therefore unnameable and unrepresentable. In this sense, one detects the presence of a fourth ethnography in her text—the last one unwritten.

In this reading, Benedict can be seen as less interested in cultural relativism for the purposes of social reform (indeed, we will see in Chapter 6 that her commitment to cultural relativism is historically limited), than in holding out the possibility of a radically new, other place, as accepting and tolerant of human individuality as the Dobu were hostile and paranoid. And, of course, because every individual is different, the individual is also offered the specter of a *choice* of cups of clay, of cultural possibilities. This hopeful vision of an end to social alienation stands in stark contrast with Sapir, who—to extend the conceit—saw the individual as an entity swimming in the "water of life," *within* the cultural cup, or indeed (to use Benedict's phrase), "submerged in an overpowering ocean" of custom (251). Benedict's construction offers a dramatically different possibility. Standing before a map of cultures, a terrain of potential configurations, it is for the individual who sees herself as working outside of the conventions of her current context to imagine a perfect space that is wholly hers.

"Buried Cultures"

Benedict's arguments about race, heredity, homosexuality, and cultural relativism all had significant, and remarkably long-lived, popular impact. More than a decade after its original publication, a paperback twenty-five cent edition of *Patterns of Culture* sold ten thousand copies in one year.[24] Works in the same "culture and personality" vein—by Mead, Benedict, and Erik Erikson in particular—captured the popular imagination as few other social-scientific books have before or since, enabling general readers to think about national and social identity in a basically new way, in which citizens of the United States imagined that they thought and behaved and lived in the context of a distinctly "American" cultural pattern. And yet, as Alfred Kroeber noted in his "official" review of *Patterns of Culture* in *American Anthropologist*, many of the issues that Benedict addressed were by 1935 "somewhat thread-bare" to her colleagues in anthropology. Indeed, what may have been most influential about Benedict's work (besides the vividness and accessibility of her prose) was the social scientific imprimatur it gave to ideas that already had some currency in the wider social discourse.[25]

In literary circles of the postwar period, Brooks and his colleagues encouraged a strain of modernist writing that was both formally experimental and rooted in what D. H. Lawrence would call "the spirit of place."[26] As represented in the work of William Carlos Williams, Sherwood Anderson, Hart Crane, and many of the writers of the Harlem Renaissance, this literature was both rooted in American contexts and cosmopolitan; indeed, many of its authors kept strong ties to the international modernist scenes and institutions of Europe. Notable for producing this new sense of place was *Our America*, written immediately after the war by Waldo Frank, Brooks's young colleague at the *Seven Arts*. Though Frank's odd, exhortative prose style (a feature of what Edward Sapir correctly identified as Frank's " 'vatic' pose") is a significant impediment to contemporary readers, *Our America* was widely influential in its moment.[27] Like Benedict's book (which it preceded by fifteen years), it reworked Brooks's schemas in such a way as to transfer American identity from the historical to the spatial axis, and it offered up a schema of spatial sites, both real and hypothetical, for imagining the transformation of American culture— from one of alienation and incompleteness to something approximating completion and organic integrity: what Frank himself liked to refer to as a "Whole."

   Though, as I will show, his final pattern of cultures is less elegant and consistent than Benedict's, Frank, too, was working his way through the problem of alienation that also preoccupied Benedict. Though an extremely successful man of letters at a very early age (he was thirty when he published *Our America*, to significant acclaim), he was also a restless spirit, lamenting in his posthumously published memoirs that he was "a Jew without Judaism, an American without America." In his passion to understand the mystical "Whole" that united him with the cosmos, he would become close with such religious thinkers as Reinhold Niebuhr and the Spinoza scholar Adolph Oko. Frank also physically crisscrossed the cultural landscape throughout the first half of this century—an attempt, one senses, to understand his other religion, "America." Along with his strong ties to the New York and Paris modernist scenes, Frank knew (through his friend Charlie Chaplin) the Hollywood of Douglas Fairbanks, Mary Pickford, and Hearst's San Simeon. Like Bourne, Frank also acted upon his strong social and political commitments. In the 1920s, Frank worked as an organizer and writer for an agrarian populist group in Kansas, and, to experience Jim Crow firsthand, he traveled through the South with his friend Jean Toomer posing as a black man. In the 1930s, he became a prominent figure in the literary Popular Front, and was for a brief time a minor celebrity after being beaten up by antilabor goons while trying to deliver a shipment of food to starving miners' families in Harlan County, Kentucky. Later, extending his quest for "America" to the Southern Hemisphere, he would travel extensively through Central and South America, eventually becoming an important interpreter of Latin American culture.[28] Though his cultural criticism would ultimately be remembered better in Latin America than in his own country, Frank's first book-length essay was extremely influential to a generation of young artists and writers in the postwar period, notably to the several artists whose careers he championed, including Toomer, Anderson, and Crane. I will end this chapter with a discussion of their work, to show how Frank's criticism offered its own kind of map for modernist writers working on the task of building something both indigenous and new.

Again complicating the view that this period was characterized by a general cultural pessimism, Frank's book sounded the more optimistic notes of his predecessors Bourne and Brooks about youth and its cultural mission, and put it together with a more hopeful description of America's possibilities. As with the criticism of the *Seven Arts* circle generally, Frank's long essay was not simply a work of cultural nationalism. Widely read in Europe and Latin America, *Our America* was written at the behest of Gaston Gallimard and Jacques Copeau of the *Nouvelle revue française*. The book was thus conceived, and read, as a work of intercultural explanation: to "create channels" between "Young America" and "Young France."[29] To that end, *Our America* was a kind of guidebook to what he perceived to be the important cultural sites, and actors, in the United States. Thus, he takes his reader to Chicago, and introduces the important writers of the "Chicago Renaissance," including Anderson, Theodore Dreiser, Edgar Lee Masters, and Carl Sandburg, and to New York, where he celebrates the achievements and qualities of many of his close associates, including Brooks, Bourne, Paul Rosenfeld, James Oppenheim, and Alfred Stieglitz.

But just as important to his analysis are such distant locales as the Indian and Hispanic Southwest and the immigrant ghettos of the urban Northeast. For him, as for a number of other writers in the twentieth century (including Nathanael West, whose work is discussed in the next chapter), the central, antithetical, figures in the construction of schemas of American identity appear to be the Indian and the immigrant Jew.[30] Also, in a fashion reminiscent of Brooks, his essay seems to resolve in a vision of the Promethean poet Walt Whitman, who, containing multitudes, therefore resolves this complex array of sites into a mystical unity, not only in "America," but beyond: "To draw Walt Whitman straight would bring us upon visions of a world in God whose boundaries converge with the vision of the Hindus, join the dominions of Isaiah and David" (203–4). Thus, as with Benedict, Frank's cultural sites were a complex blend of actual locales and speculative spaces of possibility. But the spiritual goal of the book was to find a "Whole" uniting these spaces; as he would later confess, *Our America* was "not an objective portrait of a real land, but an appeal to it *to be*."[31]

Following Brooks, Frank couched much of his criticism of contemporary American life in terms of the mythic-historical figures of the Puritans and the Pioneers. But predictably, given the cultural obsessions of the twenties and thirties, Frank turned his attention from the alienation and hypocrisy of the genteel tradition and toward the degradations and reifications of mass culture. The same logic of an ossified division between the material and the ideal would work here too. As Frank put it in the very first sentence of his long essay, "No American can hope to run a journal, win public office, successfully advertise a soap or write a popular novel who does not insist on the idealistic basis of his country" (13). In other words, an essentially commercialized culture can cynically employ the withered pieties of the Puritan ideal every bit as much as genteel America hypocritically wielded Puritan morality. In both cases, the resulting fusion of these impulses leads to a withered, incomplete, even "perverse," culture, in which (here is the psychoanalytic influence) there is no room for a natural expression of "desire" (45).

While Frank thus retained the basic critical and characterological structure of Brooks's arguments, he also altered Brooks's description of America's bifurcated culture in some important ways, arguing that, although the opportunist Pioneers had effectively cut a cultural swath across the continent destroying all that was charming and indigenous, America was still a "land of buried cultures," in which little geographic pockets of real, organic culture emerged from under, or perhaps in spite of, the burden of American history (93). Just as *Patterns of Culture* refused the historicity of Sapir's "genuine" and "spurious" sites to describe cultures as a range of spatially arrayed possibilities, so thus did *Our America* diverge from Brooks's historicism, to describe the coexistence of Puritans, Pioneers, and still others, as physically existing in specific geographical regions.

In this emended and more hopeful view of Brooks's America, even the vestiges of the Pioneer and the Puritan pasts begin to suggest distinct local charms. The Puritan traces found in the sermons of the itinerant evangelist Billy Sunday, or the pioneering exuberance of Chicago can also seem interesting and culturally significant (98–101). Of Chicago he waxes especially eloquent: "Chicago is a symbol. A splendid one, not subtle and hidden away but brutal like itself, and naked clear" (118). In his enthusiastic description of Chicago's grubby, muscular industrialism it becomes evident that Frank's judgment of the cultural significance of the sites he describes is in no way dependent on the terms of Brooks's critique. While for Brooks the Pioneers were one half of a general cultural malaise, Frank now distinguishes between the cultural sites of "good" and "bad" Pioneers, their value determined it seems by the authenticity of their relationship to the pioneering spirit. Thus, Chicago, situated at the edge of the prairie, is a city whose pioneering spirit is alive and well, in strong contrast to another land, of *moribund* pioneers, which Frank locates at the far reaches of the American continent:

> A preservative air is that of Southern California. And in it, like the corpse of some vast animal, the pioneer lies supine but in good condition: isolated from all hostile agents, a pretty specimen for the social student. His one activity, the hewing of roads beyond the hills, is gone. Behold his spirit in repose. . . .
> It is sterile. (104)

This latter characterization of California is replete with turn-of-the-century anxieties about the consequences of manifest destiny's fulfillment, of the Pioneer in "repose" becoming "sterile." On the other hand, we see that under the right conditions (in which, for example, the Pioneer is still living out his destiny of conquest over nature) even the rapacious culture of the Pioneers can still hold some value—not because it is inherently charming, but because it is authentic, integrated, or, in Sapir's words, "genuine." In other words, Frank's usage of Brooks both relativizes and spatializes the concepts of "Puritan" and "Pioneer."

Having thus rewritten the drama of Puritan and Pioneer in these spatial terms, Frank is then compelled to find replacements that might speak more clearly to the present and the future. Thus, he attempts to find conceptual alternatives to this historical opposition, and in doing so, he sets into play a new series of comparisons structurally very similar to the kind of work Benedict would subsequently do in *Patterns of Culture*. Of course, Frank's diverse cultural sites were not derived, as were Benedict's, from the ethnographic work of professional anthropologists. But they were ethnographies after a fashion, rooted in the cultural imagination of his New York–based intellectual milieu. The convergence of these two worlds—bohemian and anthropological—is once again demonstrated in the fact that, as with Benedict, his important sites included the putatively mystical Western realms of the Southwestern American Indian. But as a more dramatic counterpoint than even Benedict's Zuñi-Kwakiutl opposition, Frank offered the cosmopolitan Eastern seaboard world of that most recent of American success stories, the Jewish immigrants. To his Pueblos, the Jews of the Lower East Side were his Kwakiutl.

Frank was one of many of his New York milieu to have firsthand contact with the "buried cultures" of the American Indians, a common site in this period in the production of cultural alternatives. For Frank, as for other members of New York's bohemia, "Indian culture" meant specifically those of the Indians of the American Southwest. This was no doubt thanks in part to the connections between Greenwich Village and Columbia anthropologists like Elsie Clews Parsons and Ruth Benedict, who did their fieldwork in the Southwest. The connection between these milieus was also fostered by Mabel Dodge, a childhood friend of Ruth Benedict's and a ubiquitous presence in the avant-garde art worlds of prewar Europe and America. When Dodge exchanged her famous New York salon for a ranch in Taos, New Mexico, the Rio Grande basin became in the twenties Greenwich Village's western adjunct. Among the modernist visual artists, writers, and patrons who joined Dodge in her celebration of the region were John Sloan, Marsden Hartley, Andrew Dasburg, John Marin, Georgia O'Keeffe, Mary Austin, Willa Cather, Yvor Winters, D. H. Lawrence, and Jean Toomer. These artists, in turn, were joined by an assortment of anthropologists, entrepreneurs, patrons, and free spirits who (like Dodge) had found a new cause in the preservation of the art and culture of the Indians of the region. Dodge herself was drawn to New Mexico by her then husband, the painter Maurice Sterne, who urged her in a letter from Santa Fe in 1917 to consider taking up the cause of Indian art as others of their bohemian milieu were beginning to do for black artists: "Do you want an object in life? Save the Indians, their art-culture—reveal it to the world!"[32]

For Dodge and D. H. Lawrence, her most famous initiate into this emerging southwestern bohemia, the Indians had a mystical attraction: as "primitives," they were accessible living embodiments of the "life force." (Dodge would later extend her commitment both to the region and to this "life force" by marrying a local Indian, Tony Lujan.) In a comparably mystifying vein, many of the others attracted to the Pueblo Indians understood them to possess a uniquely "American" cultural and artistic tradition by which to be inspired, and from which to borrow. The eastern Pueblo Indians of the Rio Grande basin lived in scenic permanent villages that were accessible to tourists, and in which they held relatively open and colorful religious dances and festivals. Also, they were understood to be historically connected to the ancient Anasazi, the ruins of whose towns were of intense archaeological and aesthetic interest.[33] Indeed, as Benedict suggested in the Zuñi chapter of *Patterns of Culture*, the Anasazi ruins hinted at a romantic history, and, in their grand antiquity, even offered a plausible historical substitute for Europe's Middle Ages, that moment of cultural "childhood" which, Brooks had argued, America otherwise lacked.

The attraction of Pueblo culture for members of the Taos and Santa Fe artists' colonies also lay in a refined handicraft tradition of beautiful pottery. Neighboring tribes including the Navajo, Zuñi, and Hopi also produced rugs, jewelry, and ceremonial kachina dolls. Many of the new residents of Taos and Santa Fe collected Indian artwork, and others, including the painter Andrew Dasburg, became dealers in Indian art.[34] But the appeal of the locale for the New York avant-garde also lay in the fact that the Indians and their pueblos were also scenic—that they could serve as the appropriate subjects of a modern American art. The 1913 Armory Show, which Mabel Dodge had helped to produce, was vastly influential among the artists of her circle, but it also opened those who would be influenced by cubism and other European artistic movements to the charge of "derivativeness," a criticism deeply related to the organicist notion that there ought to exist an "American" content to the art of Americans. The painters who came to the Taos-Santa Fe region, including Dasburg, Marin, and Hartley, thus found the solution to this dilemma by applying cubist, fauvist, or expressionist approaches to new Southwestern subjects, including representations of the Indians themselves.[35] Thus admired both for their own geometrical artwork and for the (often modernist) artwork of which they were subjects, the Pueblo Indians had *already been* created for Frank by the artistic community that summered in the Southwest. These Indians were, in effect,

New York Indians, already immersed in, and processed by, the theoretical and artistic tenets of Frank's New York milieu of artistic modernism.

Frank was mildly ambivalent about the artist colonies' relationship to the "buried culture" of the Pueblos, fearing that, rather than seeing "Indian culture as a native fact from which vast spiritual wealth might still be mined," many of the artists saw only their superficially "picturesque" qualities (116). Frank, on the other hand, situated the Pueblos' refined crafts traditions within a description of an authentic and fully integrated way of life: "The Indian art is classic, if any art is classic. Its dynamics are reserved for the inward meaning. Its surface has the polish of ancient custom. Its content is the pure emotional experience of a people who have for ages sublimated their desire above the possessive into the creative realm. The uncorrupted Indian knows no individual poverty or wealth" (114). Frank's "uncorrupted" Indians, unalienated producers of beautiful geometric pottery, rugs, and jewelry, were thus both in touch with "ancient custom" and (as Lewis Mumford would later ahistorically conclude of *Moby Dick* and "cubist" patchwork quilts) "distinctly modern."[36] Moreover, in terms somewhat anticipating Benedict's description of the "incorrigibly mild" and communal Zuñi, Frank also understood their culture to offer an integration of art with life comparable to any Morrisite utopia.

In this sense, Frank's particular appropriation of Pueblo culture might have provided a conceptual resolution to the chasm separating not only the Puritan ideal and the Pioneering spirit of enterprise, but also the national and the international, the folk and the cosmopolitan, tradition and modernist experimentation. He could, in other words, have concluded, as D. H. Lawrence did in 1920, "As Venice wedded the Adriatic, let America embrace the great dusky continent of the Red Man."[37] Lawrence himself would follow his own injunction, in *The Plumed Serpent*, to "start from Montezuma," as would a number of American expatriates who moved to Mexico in the twenties and thirties, to participate there in a lively international artists' colony. Indeed, Frank would also eventually turn in this direction; his increasing interest in Latin America was clearly related to just such a fascination with indigeneity.[38]

But interestingly, Frank rejected this course in 1919, seemingly unable to conceive of this "buried culture" as a sufficient base for sustaining an American renewal. Speaking in increasingly epic tones, Frank suggests somewhat ominously that the Indian "had one fatal weakness: he knew not iron" (109). Succumbing thus to the classic logic of the Noble Savage, this "weakness" "before the iron march of the Caucasian" was both the sign of the Indians' cultural doom, *and* the sign of their cultural purity, of their lack of access to the corrupting elements of modernity (115). However, it made them both the ideal, and the *impossible* resolution to the central dichotomy of American life—indeed analogous, I would argue, to that unnamed utopian space in Benedict's vision that would be the inverse of the grotesque Dobu.

   Though these modernist Indians thus fail (or are not allowed) to provide a resolution to the cultural gap between materialism and idealism, Frank offers another potential cultural site that is, by contrast, somewhat *too* successful— too full of those traits which he described in connection with both the Puritans *and* the Pioneers. According to Frank, *Jews* are both (like the Puritans) "the chosen people," and (like the Pioneers) stereotypically given to "material aggression" (78–80). The irresolvable poles of Puritan and Pioneer in American culture are thus strikingly similar to what Frank identifies as the "Jewish paradox": "Always [the Jew] has been moved by these seemingly antagonistic motives: the will-to-power, the need of mystical abnegation, the desire for comfort on the sensuous and mental planes" (79). This very combination of elements which Frank identifies in a "Jewish" character, instead of replicating the hollow center of American culture, provided the very recipe for the survival and success of the Jewish immigrant:

> The stiff-necked Jew was actually the most flexible man that the world had ever known. He needed power, comfort, the sense of being lost in a greater Whole. Inordinate needs, and yet, above his brethren, he was able to attain them. He had the genius for *transferring* them, when they encountered obstacles in life, to some other but still *real* plane. And I say *real*, because the Jew never lost the objective balance, never leaped up in the transcendental escape. The plane to which he lifted his needs was ever one upon which his emotions, instincts, experience, and activity of life could remain in play. If he was persecuted and despised, he found his sense of power in his religious mission. If he was forced to live in an evil Ghetto, physically tortured, he found his comfort in the joys of suffering and denial. If he was rich and great in the world, his synagogue brought him back to the sweet misery of mystical humiliation. (80–81)

This paradox, Frank says, quickly adapted itself to modern rationality, resulting in a creeping tendency towards the pioneering side of the Jewish cultural makeup. And thus we have a different kind of fissure in Jewish cultural life, between the "Jews of Genius" (including "the masters of the Old Testament," Moses Maimonides, and Spinoza) who truly transcend the Puritan-Pioneer distinction on the one hand, and the "majority of Jews," on the other, who have succumbed to unrelieved rationalism and materialism. These latter, Pioneer-Jews would, he suggests, have "doubtless deemed Moses a scatter-brain and preferred Egypt" (83).
   Important among Frank's "Jews of genius" is Alfred Stieglitz, the noted photographer of the modern landscape, and, just as importantly to Frank, the owner of the famous "291" gallery which introduced America to the paintings of the French modernists, and to some of the more promising American painters of the period, including John Marin, Marsden Hartley, and Georgia O'Keeffe (indeed, some of the very figures who were colonizing the Southwest). It is in Stieglitz's gallery that Frank finds his temple:

"291" is a religious fact: like all such, a miracle. It is an altar where talk was often loud, heads never bared, but where no lie and no compromise could live. A little altar at which life was worshiped above the noise of a dead city. Here was refuge, certain and solitary, from the tearing grip of industrial disorder. When you were heartsick with all the dominance of death, you came to "291" and you found life. No place could be so holy as this place, for no place could be less holy than the world around it. New York was a lying and destroying storm: "291" was a candle that did not go out, since it alone was the truth. (184)

Stieglitz is thus joined to the "the masters of the Old Testament" as a rabbi—but of a distinctly American modernist art.

As a "Jew without Judaism" raised in a liberal, middle-class, German Jewish milieu strongly influenced by the secularized Judaism of Felix Adler's "ethical culture," Frank was socially far removed from the poor, crowded eastern European Jewish East Side of New York.[39] But as a member of New York's intellectual circles, he was certainly well acquainted with it. Among his friends would have been the "fashionable slummers" whom Abraham Cahan (a prominent East Side journalist and later novelist) would describe in *The Rise of David Levinsky*:

The East Side was a place upon which one descended in quest of esoteric types and "local color," as well as for the purposes of philanthropy and "uplift" work. To spend an evening in some East Side café was regarded as something like spending a few hours at the Louvre; so much so that one such café, in the depth of East Houston Street, was making a fortune by purveying expensive wine dinners to people from up-town who came there ostensibly to see "how the other half lived," but who saw only one another eat and drink in freedom from the restraint of manners.[40]

Despite this patronizing cultural tourism—a feature linking the East Side with New York and, later, Harlem—there were also commonalties between the Greenwich Village intellectuals and their East Side neighbors. Just as many artists felt they shared an aesthetic vision with the Pueblo Indians, or the Harlemites, bohemian New Yorkers recognized common interests with the ghetto's thriving community of intellectuals, who like them embraced radical political ideas and were familiar with the works of European artistic avant-gardes.

Already in 1902, Hutchins Hapgood (who would later become a fixture of Mabel Dodge's—pre–New Mexico—New York salon) sang the praises of the East Side's artistic and intellectual life in *The Spirit of the Ghetto*.[41] Of particular interest to Hapgood was the ghetto artists' bent for "realism," by which he meant not only an enthusiasm for the technical novelties of literary realism and dramatic naturalism, but an interest among these artists in "realistically" portraying the life and problems of their community.[42] Hapgood's preference for this sort of "realism" reflects yet another manifestation of the desire to reconcile the individual creator with the community, a problem which Hap-

good identified as one of rapid assimilation. Orthodox Jewish culture, represented by "The Old Man," was pitted against "American" culture, in the figure
of "The Boy."[43] In terms strikingly similar both to Frank's view of Jewish
culture and to his peers' general complaints about the alienation of modern
society, Hapgood wrote,

> It is easy to see that the ghetto boy's growing Americanism will be easily triumphant
> at once over the old traditions and the new socialism. Whether or not he will be
> able to retain his moral earnestness and native idealism will depend not so much
> upon him as upon the development of American life as a whole. What we need at
> present time more than anything else is a spiritual unity such as, perhaps, will only
> be the distant result of our present special activities. We need something similar to
> the spirit and unity underlying the national and religious unity of the Orthodox Jewish
> culture.[44]

Like Bourne's schema to recreate America through transnationalism, Hapgood's appeal for spiritual community in America as a whole thus started from
his anxieties about the (over-) assimilation of immigrants. The recurrence of
this problem of assimilation in the cultural criticism of the early twentieth
century is clearly not accidental, and indeed suggests that the various conceptual oppositions of ideal and material, highbrow and lowbrow, so intricately
connected to the concept of culture in this period, are also bound up with the
changing ethnic composition of America.

While we have seen that assimilation is often anxiously connected to the
idea of a mongrel, "hyphenate" America, recalling the hysterical language of
racial miscegenation, it is also possible to see in these descriptions an important
strain of social critique. The prewar period is the moment of Henry Ford's
English School, which put on pageants representing immigrants emerging out
of huge melting pots, transformed into Ford's perfect standardized workers,
and of Theodore Roosevelt's arguments for universal military conscription
as a way to speed up the process of "Americanization."[45] Antiassimilationist
perspectives, in stressing the loss of traditional customs and communities, presented important counterpoints to various ills associated with contemporary
society, from militarism to Fordism to Hapgood's perceived lack of a "national
and religious unity." More generally, however, the problem of assimilation
probably seemed an extreme version of the "cultural lag" facing the country
as a whole. As with immigration, various features of modernization, not to
mention widespread migration to urban areas within the United States, produced a populace that, the critics informed us, felt out of touch with its own
cultural roots. The culturally rooted Orthodox Jews and Pueblo Indians may
indeed have seemed to Hapgood, Frank, and others especially blessed. One
consequence of this logic was that, to stay important to these thinkers as points
of critique, the representatives of East Side or Pueblo culture had to stay culturally "pure." As such, Frank's "Jews of Genius" were also in effect Noble Sav-

ages, as culturally uncontaminated and as vulnerable "before the iron march of the Caucasian" as his modernist Pueblo Indians. Indeed, even the "buried cultures" he found most interesting tended to reflect this interest in pure types, Chicago being a better representative of the pioneering spirit than "supine" Los Angeles. And thus we return to the problem of hierarchy, articulated, as with Bourne, in terms of cultural authenticity.

In the end, Frank's deployment of the Indian and the Jew as spatial-cultural types thus seems little more than a replacement for the historical Puritan and the Pioneer dichotomy described by Brooks. The difference, however, is that the terms of the dichotomy have shifted to something similar to what we saw in Benedict's complex arrangement. As with Benedict's Zuñi, Frank's modernist Indians represent a total lack of individuality; they are ciphers for their cultures—a fact reflected, indeed, by the anonymous way in which individual Indian subjects were portrayed in the paintings of the Santa Fe and Taos modernists. The Jews' cultural value, on the other hand, rests with their personal decision to pursue lives of "genius" (pure, individuated personality)—or else to succumb to the impulses of the grasping masses, and hence to engage in a life of antiart. But where Benedict left it to the reader to imagine what a unification of these two tendencies would look like in an ideal society, Frank can be seen to leap right in, and to offer a geographical resolution that is, in fact, geographically midway between Taos and Hester Street: Chicago.

Thus, Frank thus describes Chicago as the distilled and unreflective "hope" of the Pioneer's frontier, but it is also no coincidence that it is at the country's geographical and commercial midpoint: a physical crossroads of East and West, and (as the great American processing center for agricultural products) the meeting place of Eastern industrialism and Western agrarianism. In placing this special emphasis on the Midwest as a special locale for cultural renewal, Frank joined Randolph Bourne, who somewhat earlier had identified the Midwest as "the apotheosis of American civilization."[46]

Chicago

Though one senses a measure of hyperbole in Bourne's particular characterization, it is true that a number of his peers in the New York scene also felt that the Midwest best defined American culture.[47] The "Chicago Renaissance," created in large part by the local presence of Harriet Monroe's little magazine *Poetry* and the innovative writers who gathered around it, was of course well known and admired in Frank's set. Floyd Dell, editor of the *Masses*, and James Oppenheim, Frank's cofounder of the *Seven Arts*, both developed their skills as poets and critics in the Midwest. Midwesterners Anderson and Dreiser were the two undisputed literary heroes of the *Seven Arts*. Thus, when Frank announced that in Chicago "new gods come out of the corn: and shoulder their way across the iron streets" (147), he was referring first to Dreiser, Anderson, Edgar Lee Masters, and Carl Sandburg. Leaving behind him the intricate play of cultural oppositions, Frank locates the future of American culture with these writers.

By Frank's description, Masters and Dreiser are the most typical products of pioneering Chicago. Their genius lies in the fact that they have identified the "bankruptcy of pioneering"; their failure as artists, however, is in their inability to transcend it (130). However, in Sandburg, and especially in Anderson, Frank does find a transcendent ability to create "life" out of the "despair" of American culture. While Sandburg's gift lies with some (doubtless Whitmanesque) quality of his poetry, Anderson seems to achieve his special place of artistic merit by means approaching the Christological. For Frank, it is Anderson's mythologized biography as a former businessman and manufacturer who renounced wealth, position, and Chicago, for art and village life in Elyria, Ohio which makes him significant: "So the rich man died, and slowly from his sacrifice the artist rose" (139). The superiority of Anderson's craft seems simply to follow from this happy union of art with life, of East with West. Thus, it is with Sherwood Anderson that we find Frank's practical resolution to *Our America*'s "recreative Task." In 1926, Frank still kept the faith, writing of Anderson, "For his tales are a testimony; and they testify to the still infantile revelation of Our America."[48]

Given Frank's epic sensibilities, Anderson and his work seems like an odd foundation upon which to create the renewed American vision. Indeed, a number of critics have wondered about the basis of Anderson's widespread acceptance among writers of the modernist avant-garde generally, suggesting that his vision of small-town life offers a species of antiprovincial criticism especially appealing to urban sophisticates and pseudo-sophisticates alike.[49] While this point seems true of a writer like Sinclair Lewis, it rather badly misses the source of his interest for at least some members of the avant-garde: Anderson is less a moralist or polemicist than a sociologist, interested in portraying the human experiences and crises peculiar to the historical transition from agrarianism to industrialism—a transition, as Frank's biographical point emphasizes, in which Anderson himself had once participated. In this sense, Anderson's work is not only an "infantile revelation of Our America," but a historically specific portrait of an "infantile" future—an America yet to be. Yet it is this fact, the very historical particularity of his work, that makes Anderson somehow insufficient to Frank's more mythic task of presenting a new vision of America. Thus, Frank's final word on Anderson is that though his stories may be "testimonies," "Scripture they are not."[50]

Frank thus goes off in search of a more historically transcendent spokesman for the new America. Following Brooks, he is finally compelled to look to the (usable) past, to find in Walt Whitman "the raw materials of a racial norm."[51] Unlike Brooks, who felt that Whitman and Emerson had both somehow failed to put their "impulses" into a program for America's spiritual rejuvenation, Frank sees in Whitman the ultimate resolution to the original problem of the fissure between the Puritan ideal and the Pioneer's enterprising materialism. Not only does he opine that "*Democratic Vistas* is quite as clearly our greatest book of social criticism as *Leaves of Grass* is our greatest poem," he sees Whitman as the boundless god of Genesis:

> For the song of Whitman's vision was the orchestra of life. The Word of Whitman's vision was a perfect sea, and in the sea a world, and in the world all men. To cavil at his form is simply to fall short of his ultimate vision, to fail of being caught in the sweeping rhythm of his consciousness.
>
> The critics, therefore, who interpret Whitman as "father of social revolution," "father of free verse," "father of the American tongue," "propagandist of American cultural liberation" dangerously reduce him. He was all these things. But he was far more. To call him American in the sense of explanation is to reduce him also. Little men and little groups hack at the mighty figure and take their chip and cry: "Behold our poet!" Let us not do likewise. (203)

Frank uses "the multitudes in Whitman" to figure for the reconfigured America of the future. But if Whitman the transcendent being was degraded by "little men," Frank's Whitmanesque America would retain that being's transcendent unfathomability. "I contain multitudes" would thus mean something both less, and intangibly *more*, than what it later came to represent in the post–civil rights era's liberal rhetoric of multiculturalism: a "multitude" of variously ethnicized autonomous entities which are all part of that great "cultural mosaic" of America.[52]

Frank's vision of Whitman conforms well to the spatial metaphor of America which Bourne suggested in "Trans-National America." America's cultural symbolism is no longer an epic historical struggle of Puritan and Pioneer fathers; it is a map of coexisting hues and varieties. In the East, there are the Jews, in the West there are the Indians, and in the middle, there is Chicago and Winesburg, Ohio—all of which are, in some respects, *really* about the cosmopolitan world of New York. However, the instant Frank imposed a new god, Whitman, over this conceptual cultural terrain, yet another spatial dimension was added. As he put it in the very first sentence of his chapter on Whitman, "The one true hierarchy of values in the world is the hierarchy of Consciousness" (202). Enter the priesthood. Certain people—initiates to the cult of Whitman—were required to survey the democratic vistas from on high: "They partake of this global, three-dimensioned world, but know it too for a mere moving surface, moving beyond itself into dimensions that are truer, and that cease from motion as they become more true" (202).

In this vision of "truer dimensions," we may read the existence of a cultural destiny, Frank's injunction for America "to be." It is the fully spatial vision of America: motion stilled, each region takes on its own unique characteristics, its own timeless pattern, as seen from above. This is also perspective of human flight—a perspective, as Hart Crane would remind us, that is common to both the glorious freedom of the first flight at Kitty Hawk and the violent heroics of World War I. Or, as John Dos Passos would later point out at the end of his *U.S.A.* trilogy, it is the perspective that allows the lonely figure of the Vag to recede into nothingness, while the airplane passenger who is allowed to survey the world from such Olympian heights, such undemocratic vistas, sickens from vertigo and excess.[53] It is, in other words, an ambivalent cultural logic, some of the political consequences of which will be discussed at length in the next chapter. For now, however, we may chart some of its ambivalences by considering the work of the "captains" whom Frank recruited to undertake the "recreative Task."[54]

The Turning of the Soil

In 1922, Jean Toomer commented to his friend Frank that the absence of a discussion of southern black life represented a flaw in *Our America*'s portrayal of the country and its cultural possibilities, a point which Frank conceded, and attempted to address in his book *Holiday*, a product of his trip south with Toomer.[55] But a more important result of that same trip was Toomer's own exploration of this "buried culture" and its relationship to a displaced black intellectual milieu, in his astonishing and innovative work, *Cane*, which both marked a starting point and helped to create a kind of thematic map for the cultural efflorescence known as the Harlem Renaissance.[56]

As with *Our America*, *Cane* would be a field of spatially organized contrasts, opposing a feminine, erotic, primitivist southern black life in the first section with the sterility and alienation of the northern urban black experience in the second. A final section (dedicated to Waldo Frank) suggests a synthesis, in which a northern intellectual, Kabnis, returns to rural Georgia, and asks himself, "Whats beautiful there?" in the hopes of someday being able to represent the truth of the black South. Of course, Kabnis is in some sense Toomer himself, and the book a product of Toomer's attempt to resolve his own geographically articulated alienation from his creative cultural source: "hills and valleys, heaving with folk-songs, so close to me that I cannot reach them."[57]

Toomer's book was very consciously invested in the project of imagining Frank's idea of the Whole: he employed a graphic element of a semicircle at the beginning of the first two sections, while the third section is represented with a figure suggesting the joining of these semicircles into a circle, with the gaps between the semicircles remaining. But aside even from the presence of these telling gaps, there are several hints that Toomer's Whole does not cohere. Surrounded by broken and discarded wheels in the blacksmith shop where he finds employment, Kabnis spends a night of drinking in the shop's basement, the home of a blind and speechless old man, "Dead blind father of a muted folk who feel their way upward to a life that crushes or absorbs them" (105). The basement (a prefiguration of the Invisible Man's retreat) is called, tellingly, the "Hole." Thus the pattern only tentatively resolves itself with "Kabnis," if at all, a view that Toomer also apparently had when he wrote to Frank, "From the point of view of the spiritual entity behind the work, the curve really starts with 'Bona and Paul' (awakening) . . . and ends (pauses) in 'Harvest Song.' "[58] Though the particular curve Toomer offers here alludes to the natural cycles (of the day and of agricultural seasons) that are important to the design of the book, Toomer also suggests that both its beginning and its end are to be found in the second section of the book, which addresses the distortions of humanity produced by the urban experience. In his reading, the poem thus not only begins where it began in Toomer's own alienated urban context, but, indeed, ends on a note, in "Harvest Song," of hunger, fatigue, fear, and loneliness (69).

It is well known that something like an inability to find the Whole—or, indeed, to contain multitudes—also overtook Toomer's personal life and his subsequent career as an African-American artist. Far more daunting than imagining some middle ground in a play of mythical historical opposites such as the Puritan and the Pioneer, Toomer would take on the most recalcitrant binary in American society, represented by the fixity of the color line. Caught as a man of mixed race in a society that saw only the unbridgable binary of black and white, Toomer would later insist on another "American" identity that was a synthesis of three races and multiple nationalities. Claiming a complexly mixed heritage, Toomer saw himself as "growing towards the universal Human Being," in something like a Whitmanesque transcendence of race.[59] But conceiving a resolution to binaries is sometimes not as simple as enacting it, and he seems to have retreated from the project of synthesis in the end, claiming later in life that he had no black ancestry, and (tellingly) that it was Waldo Frank who misconstrued and misrepresented Toomer's racial heritage.[60]

Similar spatial arrangements, and ambivalences, also emerge in the long poem *The Bridge*, the best-known work of another Frank protégé and a friend of Toomer's, Hart Crane. In conceiving of the Bridge, both symbol and poem, as a parabolic joining of past and present ("And of the curveship lend a myth to God" [2]), Crane's overall design echoed Toomer's structuring half circles.[61] One also sees traces of Toomer's work in the "Three Songs" section of *The Bridge*, which explicitly links the historical Americas to the modern one (and earlier parts of the poem to later ones): the naked Pocahontas to the stripper of "National Winter Garden," Columbus's "Ave Maria" to "Saturday Mary, Mine!"[62] As with Toomer, Crane would use the image of the woman to figure for the transition from a nurturing nature to the degraded, mechanized present.

Also like Toomer, Crane had expressed some frustration with *Our America*, writing to Gorham Munson that, though he appreciated Frank's generous treatment of Sherwood Anderson, "I cannot make myself think that these men like

Dreiser, Anderson, Frost, etc., could have gone so far creatively had they read this book in their early days. After all, has not their success been achieved more through natural unconsciousness combined with great sensitiveness than with a mind so thoroughly logical or propagandistic (is the word right?) as Frank's?"[63] Crane suggests, in effect, that these writers might have become trapped in Frank's structures in the process of trying to create the new, mystical unity. Ironically, something like this may have happened to Crane himself, in the process of composing *The Bridge*. Margaret Dickie has argued that Crane had a very clear idea of the final synthesis his long poem would achieve; in terms very similar to Frank's, he conceived of his poem as elucidating the "Myth of America."[64] Beginning thus with this image of completeness, Crane also began writing at the end, with "Atlantis." The composition process thenceforth was a painful one of struggling with this artificially imposed closure. It is my view, however, that the outcome of this composition process resulted in a work that was both faithful to, and critical of the implications of, the structures that Frank established in *Our America*.

Walt Whitman figures centrally in this poem too, but as a bridge between past and present—not, as in Frank, as a culmination. He figures centrally in the poem "Cape Hatteras," which physically separates the historical sections of *The Bridge* from those dealing with modern life. Appropriately, for a poem marking a transition from past to present, "Cape Hatteras" meditates on an idea encouraged by the theory of relativity, that modern perception of space and time is fundamentally different from previous experiences.[65] Beginning with an allusion to the difference between the geological time of the "mammoth saurian" and the much more recent human time, Crane contemplates the Wright Brothers' flight, which transformed the experience of space-time itself. As if in answer to Frank's vision of the "truer dimensions" of the spatial perspective, Crane muses, "Walt, tell me, Walt Whitman, if infinity / Be still the same as when you walked the beach" (40–41). It is only after rejecting the air, now become violent with "Skygak" and "Falcon-Ace," and once again taking to "The Open Road," that Crane can proclaim of Whitman, "[T]hy vision is reclaimed!" (43, 46). Feet firmly on the ground, Crane can now embrace a more corporeal Whitman, "My hand / in yours, / Walt Whitman— / so—" (47).

Having thus qualified Frank's effusions about Whitman, it is in his usage of Frank's other figures that we see the shape of Crane's own transformative project. In the long section "Powhattan's Daughter," which deals most explicitly with American history, the Pioneers (in "Indiana") completely reverse their historical trajectory, turning eastward again, and then (as also in "Cutty Sark") going out to sea. However, what Frank would have called the "buried cultures" of the Indians remain, not only in the figure of the westward-moving "squaw" who passes the returning Pioneers, but in the "mythical"—here, meaning eternal—Indians of "The Dance." To the sachem Maquokeeta he commands, "[D]ance us back the tribal morn!" (24). Fittingly, then, it is the recurring Aztec symbol of "the serpent with the eagle" that ends the "curve-ship" of the poem (76).

Crane also deploys the other figures in *Our America*, the Puritan and the Jew, in a slightly different way than Frank used them. "Quaker Hill" speaks once again to the end of the Pioneer's destiny, and sees it culminating in the bovine tedium of settlement. This is the land, now, of the contaminated and the ersatz: of "old Mizzentop," a hotel in the shape of a ship, whose "central cupola" reveals not the grand vistas of maritime adventure, but "Weekenders," "the Czars / Of golf" (59–60). He notes tartly, "This was the Promised Land, and still it is / To the persuasive suburban land agent." In this land of the Pioneer in repose, we also see the obliteration of the Puritans. Crane mourns, "Where are my kinsmen and the patriarch race?" (61). The answer, apparently, is that, like the promised land, they have been consumed, in two senses of the word:

> The woodlouse mortgages the ancient deal
> Table that Powitzky buys for only nine-
> Ty-five at Adams' auction,—eats the seal,
> The spinster polish of antiquity. (60)

Here, the idea of a person with a Jewish surname buying up the spinsterish remains of the Puritan Adams represents a process of decay and consumption paralleled to the pest working on the table's "polish." As with Crane's annoyance with the cows (herding animals), this image is as much about anxieties about massification as it is anti-Semitic. Asking "What eats the pattern with ubiquity?" (61), Crane sees the specific "pattern" of "the patriarch race" being lost in the "ubiquity," the homogeneity, of the (foreign) masses.

Yet, rather than remain "resigned" to this "ubiquity" in massification, Crane imagines a new cultural destiny that transcends both the "spinster polish" of the Puritan heritage and a (coded Jewish) massification.

> But I must ask slain Iroquois to guide
> Me farther than scalped Yankees knew to go:
> Shoulder the curse of sundered parentage,
> Wait for the postman driving from Birch Hill
> With birthright by blackmail, the arrant page
> That unfolds a new destiny to fulfill. (61)

This new destiny, embarrassed by its "sundered parentage," avoids the exalted perspective from on high, and sticks to a vision much closer to the soil: "So, must we from the hawk's far stemming view, / Must we descend as worm's eye to construe / Our love of all we touch, and take it to the Gate. . . ?" This "humble" perspective, rejecting (Kitty) "hawk's far stemming view" is that of Whitman's reclaimed, earthbound, vision at the end of "Cape Hattaras." Grounded in soil, in place, it is fitting that its other "guide" is the Iroquois. Finally, uniting these figures, this also becomes the vision of *The Bridge* itself, the "arrant page / That unfolds a new destiny to fulfill" and a sacrament— indeed, a communion wafer—leading to the transsubstantiation of mythic America into reality: "[Y]es, take this sheaf of dust upon your tongue!" The next poem, "The Tunnel," thus becomes the womb that leads to the birth of the ecstatic new America, in *The Bridge*'s final pages, in "Atlantis."

In this way, *The Bridge* enacts a stunningly sly commentary on Frank's "recreative Task." Rather than ending, with Frank, in contemplating the god-like Whitman viewing the world from on high, Crane imagines the "turning of the soil" in the rather more literal terms of the earthworm's alimentary tilling. Perhaps even more astutely, he sees that any Frank-like project that imagines the resolution of competing sites within the American landscape re-lies on a presumption of authenticity, on a metaphysics of pure types. Thus, any conjoining of these types will represent a kind of cultural miscegenation, a "sundered parentage," and its birth announcement will be the "arrant page" of a blackmail letter.[66] In the end, Crane envisions a much more complexly messy and interesting American culture—that could, nevertheless only have been imagined with Frank's architecture as a model.

Poor White

Though the fruitfulness and influence of Frank's protoregional vision should by now be evident, I will end this chapter with a final example of the deploy-ment of this spatial logic, from a figure extremely important to Frank: Sher-wood Anderson. Cecilia Tichi has read Anderson's novel *Poor White* as an antitechnological and nostalgic work about the machine-made destruction of agrarian America.[67] While I agree fundamentally with this view, I would qual-ify it slightly, to suggest that the machine itself is less the central problem of the book than the sign of the transformation in *work* that is taking place in the narrative, from agricultural and craft labor to an alienated, proletarianized industrial labor. I believe this transition is articulated in the novel in terms of the spatial schema described in *Our America*, so that the spatially imagined figures of the Puritan and the Pioneer both establish, and then resolve, the concretely articulated problem of alienation in the locale of a nostalgically conceived Midwest. In Anderson's specification of the site of this resolution, he anticipates a further development in the spatialized culture concept, the logic of thirties regionalism. Thus, he offers a bridge between the utopian spatial logics discussed in this chapter, and its concrete regionalist manifesta-tion, which is the topic of the next.

Like *Winesburg, Ohio, Poor White* is set at the turn of the century, in a fictional town in the gas and oil belt that extends through northern Indiana and northwestern Ohio. Far more explicitly than *Winesburg, Ohio*, however, this novel connects Anderson's interest in the grotesque human products of social alienation with the industrialization of rural America. The hero, Hugh McVey, is a "dreamy" "poor white" boy from the Pioneer land of Missouri who— under the tutelage of a stern New England woman—engages in a regimen of "self-improvement" to rid himself of his dreaminess. However, this training, an attempt to fuse the Puritan and the Pioneer, is somehow unnatural, and Hugh becomes in the process something like the walking embodiment of alienation. Not only estranged from his drunkard father, he is also pathologically shy, incapable of engaging in normal human relationships. Far more comfortable with machines, he becomes a telegraph operator, spending his nonworking hours teaching himself mechanics and creating mathematical problems for himself to solve. Nevertheless, he does have some impulses toward human contact. In the still-bucolic town of Bidwell, Ohio, where Hugh settles, he spies enviously on his neighbors, particularly on courting couples, and on the farmers as they engage in the back-breaking work of planting cabbage seedlings.

Here, Anderson implicitly equates the "normal" expression of sexual desires with the cabbage farmers' grueling but unalienated agricultural labor. Unselfconscious expressions of sexuality and farm work, together with craft labor, are components of the happy, integrated, simple life—the "buried culture"— of the Bidwell which is about to disappear. Hugh, a voyeur in this world, is a socially maladjusted monster: a Pioneering technician, warped by the Puritan will. He is also the catalyst which will change Bidwell from its happy preindustrial idyll into an industrial town controlled by a ruthless capitalist elite. His tool is that perverted fetish of modernity, the machine, which is, of course, also the sign of his alienation from "normal" human life. Hugh allows his dreaminess (which, we are told, might in another environment have been the raw material for the production of "art and beauty") to resurface sufficiently to turn his sublimated energies to the invention of labor-saving farm equipment—the first being a seedling planter for the cabbage farmers (133). His good intentions are soon twisted by the desires of grasping (Pioneer) businessmen. When Hugh's seedling planter proves unworkable, his financial backers take the opportunity to gain complete control of their new factory and all of Hugh's future inventions, causing the more humble Bidwell investors to lose their money. As the people who once labored on farms around Bidwell are transformed into pieceworkers in the factory, other social changes emerge. Craftsmen, like the harness maker Joe Wainsworth, are distressed to find not only that factory-made goods are threatening to replace their wares, but also that the craftsmen themselves are being superseded socially, and even in their own shops, by salesmen and money handlers, like Joe's own employee, Jim

Gibson. Bidwell grows, however: factories and warehouses line what were once country roads, the roads are paved, sewers are laid, cabbage fields become sites for flimsy workers' housing.

Though Hugh and his machines provoke these changes, he nevertheless remains painfully outside of the social life of the town. This is true even after he marries Clara, the daughter of a farmer who has become a factory owner. Clara feels as estranged from Bidwell as Hugh. While attending college in Columbus, she was introduced by her friend Kate Chanceller (a daughter, clearly, of Henry James's Olive Chancellor, in *The Bostonians*) to progressive ideas, and even to lesbian romance. Clara understands, however, that she wants a "man . . . in order that she might fulfill herself," and so returns to Bidwell and to her father, made corpulent and "vulgar" with his new extreme wealth (250). "Touched by the idea of the romance of industry," her attraction to Hugh was instantaneous: "Hugh was what she wanted to be. He was a creative force. In his hands dead inanimate things became creative forces. He was what she wanted not herself but perhaps a son, to be" (252, 253). The confusion here, about what Clara "wanted to be," and how it is related to her attraction to Hugh, is indicative of the larger problem of these two characters' sexual incompatibility. As Hugh understands their problem, the salient differences between him and Clara are ones of class: she is a "lady," and he is "poor white" (259). But their problems can also be articulated in terms of a Puritan-Pioneer dichotomy. Hugh represents for her the practical vigor of the industrial Pioneer, while Hugh perceives Clara as an unapproachable embodiment of physical and moral refinement: the Puritan ideal. Thus fundamentally incompatible with one another (as Brooks would have it), their marriage remains unconsummated for weeks.

Hugh and Clara's marital differences are mirrored by deep conflicts emerging in their community, a breakdown in its organic integrity. Workers, angered by conditions at the factory, begin to strike, and labor organizers arrive in the town. The harness maker Joe Wainsworth, forced by his profit-oriented employee Jim Gibson to buy factory-made goods to sell in his shop, murders Jim with his harness-maker's knife, and in a frenzy shreds the factory-made harnesses (342–43). Clara, accidentally involved in Joe's capture, initially has pity on the man: "In her mind the harness maker had come to stand for all the men and women in the world who were in secret revolt against the absorption of the age in machines and the products of machines. He had stood as a protesting figure against what her father had become and what she thought her husband had become" (354–5). Clara's pity turns to rage, however, when the crazed harness maker attacks her husband: "And then the past rose up to strike. It struck with claws and teeth, and the claws and teeth sank into Hugh's flesh, into the flesh of the man whose seed was already alive within her" (368). Clara, who pulls the harness maker off Hugh, realizes at this moment both that her husband needs her, and that the older order of craft labor is obsolete. The physical and spiritual union between the Puritan Clara and the Pioneer Hugh can now be completed—and of course, physically embodied in the child Clara is carrying.

What we have in this marriage between Puritan and Pioneer is a twentieth-century rendering of a fairly typical type of national allegory, figured in terms of sexual reproduction. Just as an earlier moment offered up narratives of the union of (a progressive, civilized, European) John Smith with (the traditional, natural, North American) Pocahontas to create suture in the uneasy concept of "America," now Anderson offers us a similarly ideological wedding fable. Its ideological nature should be immediately evident in Anderson's insistence on this moment as one of the restoration of "normal" sexuality, which comes to Clara through motherhood and through her realization that *Hugh* is a kind of childlike victim of the new industrial age. By saving Hugh, she discovers both her maternal instincts and a certain Pioneering aggressiveness; "the woman who had been a thinker stopped thinking" (368). Hugh, on the other hand, begins to suffer from "the [Puritan] disease of thinking," gains some of Clara's more critical insights about the industrial order, and begins to make ethical decisions about his inventions, and his own role as a laborer:

> Unconsciously and quite without intent he had come to a new level of thought and action. He had been an unconscious worker, a doer, and was now becoming something else. The time of the comparatively simple struggle with definite things, with iron and steel, had passed. He fought to accept himself, to understand himself, to relate himself with the life about him. The poor white, son of the defeated dreamer by the river, who had forced himself in advance of his fellows along the road of mechanical development, was still in advance of his fellows in the growing Ohio towns. The struggle he was making was the struggle his fellows of another generation would one and all have to make. (364)

What we have here, in other words, is the enactment of the very thing that Brooks thought to be impossible: the melding together of opposed tendencies of the American character, Puritan and Pioneer, into a more perfect union. As with Frank's vision, which placed such an emphasis on Chicago as the physical site for such a resolution of tendencies, this one too is located in a town in the symbolically significant Midwest. But it is also important to notice what this fable fails to resolve. While things seem nicer for Clara and Hugh, it is far from clear how this happy partnership will have any impact on the very crisis that the novel establishes as central: the problem of alienation that caused the harness maker to go mad with fury, and that subsequently precipitates the consummation of their bond. All Anderson gives us in this regard is the rather obscure promise of Hugh and Clara's unborn baby, the literal product of the happy commingling of Puritan and Pioneer tendencies, and the representative of "another generation" which might more successfully deal with the stresses and strains of modernization. Still more problematic is the hint in the passage above that *Hugh*, "in advance of his fellows," might actually begin to resolve the problem of alienation for the Joe Wainsworths and the factory workers of Bidwell. If this is in any way a possibility, it is clear that a modern, technical solution is not what Anderson has in mind for Hugh. Having tried to alleviate some of the drudgery of labor with his cabbage-seedling planter, and having only inadvertently created more drudgery of a different kind (plus a few new problems), Hugh's new kind of thinking seems to disincline him from pursuing his inventions at all. In this new mood of idleness and lack of interest in business competition, Anderson suggests, "there was unconscious defiance of a whole civilization" (365).

With this vaguely anarchic gesture, we see finally that Anderson comes very close indeed to advocating a refusal of modernity—and hence, a kind of turning back to the agrarian past that Bidwell once exemplified. Instead of a resolution to modern alienation, what Anderson largely leaves us with (besides the allegorical family of Clara, Hugh, and unborn baby), is the nostalgically drawn location of the Midwest. Indeed, when we begin to think of the locale itself as yet another (non-)resolution to the central conflicts Anderson puts into play, we begin to see that the Midwest as a region contains multitudes. Bidwell even manages to encompass Frank's dichotomy of Jews and Indians. Hugh McVey appears at night to some farmers working in the cabbage fields as a ghost from an Indian burial ground—the specter, perhaps, of an economic order still older than that of the cabbage farmers. While the Indians are thus represented as ethereal remnants of this older order, we get hints that figures very like the stereotypical Jews of the anti-Semitic imagination are looming in the future. They are the capitalists, swindlers, and immigrant laborers who arrive from New York, the "strange-talking, dark-skinned men who had come with the coming of the factories," or the anarchist and socialist labor organizers, "foreigners" with "strange doctrines" (289, 337). But the important point here is that however this drama of crisis and change is articulated, it could be enacted and resolved in the transitional social order of one Ohio town.

Forget, or—as Anderson may be accused of doing in *Poor White*—gloss over the struggles implicit in this transition, and you have the makings of sentimentality. Just as Anderson seemed to wish away the prospect of unions and anarchists, bosses and strike breakers, so eventually would he lose interest in representing the complex realities of places like Winesburg and Bidwell, which before had so clearly represented to him both the benefits of community *and* the oppressive closeness of provincialism. Elmer Cowley's paranoid fantasies about being trapped under the watchful eye of his neighbors, and George Willard's longing to experience life more widely than in the confines of Winesburg, Ohio, finally become, in Anderson's 1940 documentary book, *Home Town*, "the necessity of nowadays staying put," and "thinking small," in comfortable, homogeneous, small-town America.[68] In this respect, the Anderson who was a modernist icon for the writers of the *Seven Arts* showed the way toward the more conservative regionalisms and agrarianisms of the 1930s. As we shall see in the next chapter, this physical and symbolic locale became, through the concept of "regionalism," a crucial site for a new phase in the struggle over "culture."

5

The Culture of the Middle: Class, Taste, and Region in the 1930s Politics of Art

Art in America is an affectation of caste.
(Thomas Craven)

You never hear now of Greenwich Village, which
used to be a haven for the exiles from Alabama and
Kansas, the West and the South; and the reason you
never hear of it is that the exiles have all gone back
to Alabama and Kansas.
(Van Wyck Brooks)

IN 1940, Stuart Chase, a well-known writer of popular social science, offered
the following anecdote at a banquet honoring First Lady, Eleanor Roosevelt:

> The story goes that an American tourist was being shown the new subway in Mos-
> cow. His guide pointed out the frescoes on the walls, the ticket-choppers' booths, the
> turnstiles for passengers. After admiring all these, the tourist inquired: "What about
> the trains?"
>
> Then the guide showed him the new washrooms, more turnstiles, and more fres-
> coes. "What about the trains?" the tourist asked again.
>
> "What about the trains?" the guide repeated angrily. "What about the trains? What
> about the share-croppers in Alabama?"[1]

The story, though offered as a bit of light after-dinner patter, presents an interesting retrospective summary of some of the more common concerns of American intellectual life throughout the decade of the thirties. It reminds us, first,
that a hesitant tolerance of, and even interest in, Soviet communism in the face
of capitalism's Depression-era crisis was sufficiently widespread to unite in
common discourse a fellow traveler like Chase with the First Lady of the New
Deal. Second, it brings the idea of the sharecropper, that most enduring icon
of the period's cultural politics, into this general left-liberal political framework. But it is also an interesting example of a central—I would be tempted
to say, defining—feature of the culture concept in its fully domesticated form:
the comparative gesture, in which one culture is held up to scrutiny in the light
of the patterns of another.

Joining writers like Mead and Benedict in this widespread project of inter-cultural comparison, Chase himself had begun the decade by writing *Mexico: A Study of Two Americas*, in which he compared the isolated "organic" culture of Tepoztlan, Mexico, to that of the same medium-sized industrializing city in the American Midwest that Benedict had also found a useful point of reference: "Middletown." In Chase's comparison, Middle America once again fared rather badly; Chase worried that the "parasites" of capitalism were poised to "plague, if not ultimately to kill, the vast sprawling body of mechanical civilization. In this body, Middletown is but a single cell, while Tepoztlan is aloof and unincorporated, an organic, breathing entity."[2] Cultural comparison—full though it was of these reified organic wholes mysteriously surviving outside the processes of change—was fundamentally a project of cultural critique.

The same is also true of Chase's anecdote about the Muscovite and the tourist, even if the Muscovite's comparison between the absence of trains and the existence of Alabama sharecroppers is meant to seem a bit dogmatic. For, as with all good intercultural comparisons, his comment reveals a basic truth about the similarities and differences between the two countries: the Soviets' lack of heavy industrial commodities like subway trains and the existence in the United States of oppressed and impoverished sharecroppers are both signs of their respective countries' priorities in the face of their *common* failure at complete modernization.

The meaning of the anecdote is thus relevant to the larger message of Chase's speech, which urged an increased commitment to Roosevelt's New Deal. For indeed, the New Deal did represent a vast modernization project, dedicated to eradicating the kinds of problems represented by the image of the sharecropper. This is most obviously the case with the programs directed at developing infrastructure (notably the Rural Electrification Program and the Tennessee Valley Association), which addressed some of the most egregious symptoms of uneven development in the United States. But even the "cultural" programs of New Deal agencies such as the Federal Writers' Project, the Federal Artists' Project, and those of the Farm Securities Administration were involved in this modernization effort. While mural projects and the like represented a kind of cultural uplift, the documentation of such problems as rural poverty and labor conditions offered the ideological justification for the New Deal's modernization projects. Other efforts, such as the Works Progress Administration guides and a number of the documentary projects, performed the crucial service of mapping the cultural terrain, thus opening up the heretofore remote parts of the country to view by the nation as a whole. In "salvaging" the otherwise "buried cultures" of the American landscape—including the folk, ethnic, and regional "cultures" of Hoosiers, Idahoans, former slaves, "Georgia Coastal Negroes," "The Italians of New York," "The Armenians of Massachusetts," and "The Swedes and Finns of New Jersey"[3]—these agents of modernization helped produce the sense of an overarching "America," a new perception of national coherence that Warren Susman described as the "domestication" of culture.[4]

While Susman saw anthropological ideas such as those found in Benedict's *Patterns of Culture* to be central to this development, I would suggest that this new vision also required the changes brought about by the modernization projects of the period—just as before, in the work of Brooks and Sapir, America did not have an "organic" culture, or even a "genuine" culture, because of the social, technological, and ideological "lags" in the pattern of American modernization itself. Though writers like Benedict and Frank offered a new spatial vision of American culture drawn on much more hopeful lines, it was only when the problem of gaps and inconsistencies in the project of modernization was sufficiently addressed that Americans as a whole could come to believe that theirs was a more or less unified "culture."

Not surprisingly, in this moment of widespread consensus over "culture," the period also witnessed a culmination in the convergence between anthropological thinking and the more aesthetic tradition of cultural theory represented by writers like Bourne, Brooks, and Frank. In these years the folklorist Constance Rourke connected her mentor Brooks's organicism and her friend Ruth Benedict's conception of cultural configurations to launch anew the argument that America had a unique art tradition—this time, to be found in its living, local "folk" heritages.[5] This is also the moment when Zora Neale Hurston assimilated her anthropological studies of the folk culture of rural African Americans to aesthetic ends. Most obviously, however, the efflorescence of the documentary form itself, that strange hybrid of ethnography, social realism, and the Movietone News, is the most ubiquitous sign of this convergence, turning a remarkable range of people—writers, photographers, social crusaders, bureaucrats—into ethnographers, all working on the premise that there were "cultures" out there to be revealed. As George E. Marcus and Michael M. J. Fischer put it, "American cultural criticism in the 1930s became ethnographic with a vengeance."[6]

But if there was a certain broad popular consensus as to what "culture" was and even some agreement as to the methodology for describing it, there was a good deal of dissension in this period over what constituted "American culture." A widespread perception of something identifiable as an "American Way of Life" did not necessarily lead to widespread nationalist feeling, or even to agreement that this way of life was all that *good*. There was also a certain conceptual tension between this more inclusive American Way of Life and the smaller "cultures" in the process of being unearthed. Put another way, the impulse to go out and document the lives of tenant farmers or Hoosiers usually went beyond wanting to propagandize for the New Deal, or even to provide a calmly accurate social-scientific report. It extended into sentiment, nostalgia, and the kinds of critical and political impulses that made Chase want to compare Mexican villagers with the denizens of an industrializing Midwest.[7] Because "culture" in this moment was largely understood to connote an operation of comparison, exploring these smaller contexts could be a way to celebrate the autonomy of groups or regions, mourn the loss of older patterns of culture, or point out the shortcomings of the rapidly modernizing and massifying present. As such, this new cultural vision emphasized both the internal coherence of cultures and differences between cultures.

This, in turn, is a central point for understanding another feature of the cultural discourse of the thirties: the emergence of new logics that emphasized crucial divisions and hierarchies within the American Way of Life. Not only does regional identity begin in this period to have strong political and aesthetic connotations, but this is also a moment of increasing awareness of class and status differences in cultural taste. Just as "culture" became "domesticated," so, in fact did the terms "highbrow," "lowbrow," and "middlebrow" also enter the general discourse. In other words, if the thirties represented a moment of widespread acceptance of a national identity articulated in terms of "culture," the same concept would also be deployed in the same period to suggest ways in which Americans were different from each other.

The Logic of Regionalism

The work of Constance Rourke work offers an instructive example of how "culture" in this period often tended to produce theoretical elaborations of smaller subunits of cultural demarcation. As Joan Shelley Rubin has suggested, Rourke's interest in American folk traditions was at least implicitly a critique of Brooks's description of a hierarchically bifurcated American culture.[8] Rourke asserted that an appreciation of the folk influences of writers like Twain and Melville could both dignify folk culture and show how Brooks's distinction between "highbrow" and "lowbrow" was already transcended in the full existence of an organic, unified, and distinctly American culture. While this attention to folk roots thus helped both to resolve the Brooksian problem by imagining America as complete and undivided, it also suggested the existence of distinctive local cultures, each with their own folk traditions and lores. Each of these local cultures, in turn, could suggest new ways in which the nation did not cohere.

Indeed, Rourke's emphasis on folk tradition, typical of many of the cultural debates of the 1930s, was also related to a burgeoning interest in regionalism. One of the earliest and clearest examples of this phenomenon is the Southern Agrarians' manifesto of regional cultural autonomy, *I'll Take My Stand.*[9] Central to their argument that the South should be allowed to pursue its own social, political, and cultural destiny was the assertion that the South as a coherent region possessed a culture distinct from that of the rest of the United States. They argued that while the nation as a whole suffered from various evils resulting from industrialism, the South's cultural pattern (to use Benedict's term) was essentially, fundamentally, agrarian. Hence, they insisted that Southerners should not be expected to create a modernized "New South" in the alien pattern of the country as a whole.

Like so many deployments of the idea of cultural locales, this conception of regions assumed a natural and essential relationship between geography and social destiny. Historians and social scientists, who were also beginning in this period to think of geographic regions as manageable sites to study specific culture patterns, also picked up on this organicism. In a 1938 volume, significantly titled *American Regionalism: A Cultural-Historical Approach to National Integration*, Howard W. Odum and Harry Estill Moore articulated this quality as follows:

> In the generic sense, [regionalism] magnifies the meaning of the local group in relation to the whole and features the folk-regional society as basic to the growth of cultures. It emphasizes the new realism of the people as the scientific as well as symbolic basic element in modern civilization. From a more practical viewpoint, namely, that of the inventory and planning of modern society, regionalism emerges as an equally definitive economy of balance and equilibrium between conflicting forces. It goes further; it offers a medium and technique of decentralization and redistribution in an age now being characterized as moving toward over-centralization, urbanism, and totalitarianism.[10]

Regionalism thus served multiple political and ideological ends. Not only did it offer "folk" roots to complex social issues and indeed to social-scientific inquiry itself, regionalism also represented a model of political and social organization which, because it divided the totality of the nation into regions, seemed inherently antitotalitarian. Significantly, the centralized, federal (and, some thought, "totalitarian") New Deal that did so much to reveal America to itself may have also helped inspire the regional reaction to this vision. In dedicating themselves to describing the various regional cultures of the United States, the workers in the "cultural" New Deal programs also helped cement the relationship between regionalism and "the new realism of the people as the . . . basic element in modern civilization."

Though Odum and Moore did not specify the "conflicting forces" to which they claimed regionalism provided a "definitive economy of balance and equilibrium," much of the ideological force of regionalism (certainly as represented in *I'll Take My Stand*) was that social problems could be addressed as either incidental, uncharacteristic, or the product of interregional politics. In the "Agrarian" section of his humorous poem "Period Pieces from the Mid-Thirties," James Agee nicely addressed the conservative underside of regionalism:

When the world swings back to sense
(But the world is *so* damned dense)
An indisputably Aryan
Jeffersonian Agrarian
Will be settin' on the ole rail fence,

Swaying slightly with a hot cawn bun,
Quoting Horace and the late John Donne,
He will keep the annual figures
Safe from the prying eyes of niggers,
And back his Culture up with whip and gun.[11]

Descriptions of regional uniqueness, dressed up with lots of local charm, served as an effective discourse for obscuring the significant racial and class tensions of the Depression era. As such, regionalism would become an important counterdiscourse to the class-based politics which—in the thirties more than possibly any other moment in American history—were mainstream.

Indeed, the same logic that extended American "culture" into a proliferation of regional cultures could also be used to suggest the possibility of distinct and competing *class* cultures. James Gilbert describes the 1930s politics of class-based cultures as follows:

> The young radical sought a cultural revival in which to play a central role. The radical literary movement promised him a renaissance and a political revolution—old and worthy goals—and a literary movement which would produce a new Jack London or Walt Whitman. It promised a continuation of old traditions in America set to new purposes, and it asserted that the production of radical literature was work for a great future. The search for a new America during the 1930s ended in the vision of a society transformed by the proletariat and the intellectuals.[12]

In many respects, this vanguardist vision was a continuation of the project of Brooks, Bourne, Frank, and their circle, who also sought "a continuation of old traditions in America set to new purposes." Not surprisingly, this older generation of bohemian intellectuals quickly found places in the thirties as elder statesmen in the new cultural organs of leftist intellectual and literary life.[13] However, this new program for American culture clearly contained one element that was only occasionally present in the thought of the older group: an explicit political belief in the historical centrality of the proletariat and of the radical intellectuals' (in other words, their own) position at the vanguard of change.[14] This alliance would manifest itself not only in a critical championing of "proletarian" art, but in many radicals' interest in popular culture, particularly Hollywood film and sports. It was, in other words, an interesting moment of possibility for the rejection of the distinction between "highbrow" and "lowbrow" cultural interests—even as these terms were coming to explicitly connote class-based strata of taste and cultural production. Nevertheless,

even for those attempting to reconstruct the cultural landscape on newly democratic grounds, a new descriptor of taste was increasingly coming into use, to
describe the cultural position occupied by the reactionary bourgeoisie, those
on the outside of radical political change: the "middlebrow."[15]

While this new model of a transformative culture resulting from the alliance
of intellectuals and the proletariat took the "middlebrow" culture of the bourgeoisie to be its antithesis, the very idea of class-based differences was often
seen as a competing proposition to the assertion of *regional* cultural difference.
Key terms in this opposition included the question of "totalitarianism," and
the nature of that mysterious collective, "the people." To this lexicon of fighting words we might also add "standardization," feared by more conservative
voices of the period because it was imagined that the Taylorized subjects who
comprised the massified proletariat no longer possessed the idealized individualism that enabled them to participate in a democracy.[16] Thus, in 1933 Constance Rourke felt compelled to refute the Marxist critic V. F. Calverton's claim
that industrialism had created a homogeneous working class in America. She
questioned the extent to which America had in fact become "standardized,"
writing, "So far as social coherences have developed among us, these seem to
have appeared mainly in geographic sections; and they have been shown for
the most part in that class with which the Marxian is most concerned. Call this
the folk or the proletariat as you like: the two have been pretty consistently
identified in most countries."[17] Of course, as far as Marxists like Calverton
were concerned, the "folk" and the "proletariat" were *not* identical. Calverton
would certainly have read Rourke's conflation of the two as an attempt to
obscure class relations existing within regions, in favor of portraying a largely
nostalgic "social coherence." Moreover, while the "standardization" of
America likely raised for Rourke the specter of totalitarianism (much as "over-
centralization" did for Odum and Moore), the "folk" would come to be equally
tainted by totalitarianism in radical circles, where it was associated with the
rhetoric of German fascism, much as "culture" had once been associated with
the Kaiser.

Thus, from the "domesticated" concept of culture there emerged two competing maps of cultural difference: one, based on regional difference, and the
other based on class difference. Both represented idealistic attempts to make
"culture" coextensive with, and a product of, "the (real) people." Both were
also antitotalitarian in principle, and both held over the other's head the charge
of totalitarianism. Both also managed to exclude certain concepts and terms
from the others' rhetorical arsenal. While this meant that the regionalists could
never argue *for* "standardization," it also (far more significantly) deprived
Marxists of the capacity to talk about the "folk"—or indeed, "the people."

Nowhere was this opposition more clear than in the proceedings of the first
American Writers' Congress. The congress, which was held in New York in
1935 shortly before the creation of the Popular Front, was convened by the

John Reed clubs to create a broader-based organization for writers with radical and progressive leanings. This first Writers' Congress, in turn, became the founding point of the new Popular Front League of American Writers, in which Brooks and Frank were chosen for positions of leadership—Frank, as the League's first chairman, and Brooks as a member of the National Council.[18] On the second day of the congress, Kenneth Burke provoked a heated discussion with his paper, "Revolutionary Symbolism in America," in which he addressed what he called the "propaganda" function of the writer. Burke suggested that revolutionary writers should attempt to recoup for their political purposes the term "the people," because it held more ideological force with most Americans than did its more revolutionary alternative, "the worker."[19] This suggestion was roundly denounced by the delegates. The angry audience was quick to offer examples of situations in which the workers' political goals had been rhetorically arrayed against those of "the people" by Hitler, and by the American fascist Father Coughlin.[20] Though Burke, in his response to these criticisms, was right to defend his proposal as a *strategy* in the furtherance of "propaganda," and hence as an attempt to engage in precisely these rhetorical battles with the forces of fascism, he may have failed to acknowledge his audience's perception that this particular rhetorical battle was already lost. Those whom they perceived to be their opponents in art and politics had already succeeded in making the idea of "the people" a singularly "bourgeois"— or even fascist—concept.

This issue would follow Frank to Paris the following year, where, as chairman of the League of American Writers, he spoke before the Soviet-sponsored International Congress for the Defense of Culture. Malcolm Cowley, in his *New Republic* account of the congress, reported "a curious unanimity in regard to the most important subjects under discussion. In the first place, nobody spoke in favor of abandoning 'bourgeois culture' for the sake of a 'proletarian culture' still to be created. All writers of whatever political complexion agreed that the old masterpieces should not only be preserved but should be rendered available to a much wider audience."[21] Though this "unanimity" may have been created at the price of some rather heavy-handed censorship by the congress organizers, it is clear that a significant issue of the congress was the question of *whose* (class-defined) culture was in need of "defense." This discussion may, moreover, have involved rather more controversy had André Breton not been excluded from the proceedings—either (as Breton himself claimed) for failing to toe the Soviet line, or (as the congress organizers maintained) because Breton assaulted a Soviet delegate. However, in comments presented to the congress by Paul Éluard, and in a subsequent pamphlet, Breton made clear his "defiance" of the congress, and of the politics of the Popular Front in general. In addition to excoriating the Soviet organizers for demanding political and aesthetic conformity, Breton objected to the Soviet Union's creeping nationalism in the name of antifascism, and, most generally, to their understanding of "culture." He argued, essentially, that the "culture" that the congress wished to defend was the reactionary culture of the bourgeoisie. In Breton's case, this bourgeois culture may have been seen as less perilous to the proletariat than antithetical to his own frankly elitist surrealism. But this distinction is almost beside the point: whether one's allegiances were to the high, the low, or some synthesis of the two, the enemy was seen as residing somewhere in the middle.[22]

Middle West, Middlebrow, *Middletown*

Out of this moment's highly politicized cultural landscape, an interesting convergence of the two competing narratives of cultural difference began to emerge. In effect, the class-based version of difference would be lined up with the regionalist account in such a way that one region, the Midwest, became synonymous with the middle (bourgeois) stratum of cultural taste. As we shall see, this convergence had a certain political power on both sides of the cultural debate, and from both sides of the geographic divide. While elites in the urban centers were thus justified in maintaining their traditional disdain of the provincial (nicely summed up by *New Yorker* editor Harold Ross's slogan for his sophisticated urban magazine: "Not for the old lady in Dubuque"), Midwesterners too found a kind of comfort in the association. Turning the negative stereotype into a more positive sign of identity, some would embrace the "middlebrow" label as a sign of its antielitist American authenticity. Like their heir, Garrison Keillor, regionalist cultural boosters of the Midwest would murmur back a defensive, "We like it here." Before addressing the Midwestern response to this interesting convergence between images of the Midwest and the idea of middlebrow taste, the link must first be explained in terms of both historical conditions and the cultural imagination of the period.

Pierre Bourdieu reminds us that "highbrow" and "middlebrow" tastes are both indigenous to the dominant classes, but that they are derived from different portions of the bourgeoisie. The first ("legitimate" culture) belongs to people secure in both their economic and cultural capital, while the other (*culture moyenne*) belongs to members of a still-ascending fraction of the middle class, who are, hence, insecurely reverential of a high culture to which they still have limited access. As with the distinctions between high and low culture generally, the difference between highbrow and middlebrow tastes is a question of social distance from the centers of cultural production. Thus, to Bourdieu, the quintessential products of middlebrow taste are "cultural intermediaries" such as film adaptations of works of "legitimate" literature and symphonic "pops" concerts, which fill the gap, as it were, in the social-cultural hierarchy.[23]

In the 1930s United States, such cultural intermediaries abounded, reflecting the social aspirations of many middle-class Americans. But their ubiquity also reflects the uneven national distribution of cultural resources. As with the Sears catalogue for the prairie farmer, it is easy to see how much more important cultural outlets such as the Book-of-the-Month Club, the Chautauqua and Lyceum lecture circuits, or the CBS Radio Orchestra would have been to cultural consumers living outside of major cities.[24] And even among cities, there were few that could support an active community of artists whose livelihoods did not depend on providing such "cultural intermediaries." Though Chicago had been an important market hub since before the turn of the century, and in the 1920s had a thriving arts scene, even the artists of the "Chicago Renaissance" eventually made their bid for national prominence in New York, the location of most of the supporting institutions which they required: galleries, critics, collectors, publishing houses, and little magazines. Thus, there is a way in which the social distance between classes and class tastes was also reflected in *physical* distances from the centers of cultural production; in this sense, a connection between an entire geographical region and a class taste is not implausible.

Meanwhile, a number of the Midwest's literary sons were quick to understand the complexities of their, and their region's, provincialism, and to in effect mythologize it as a regional trait. While Southern writers cherished their own myths of cultural autonomy, their unique "agrarian" identity, or even their gothic-tinged history, writers like Theodore Dreiser, F. Scott Fitzgerald, Sinclair Lewis, and Sherwood Anderson tended to emphasize the dynamics of modernization, placing the Midwest in a relational drama of rural and urban, East and Midwest. In doing so, they often portrayed the Midwest's Gopher Prairies in a way that walked a tense line between tragedy and satire: emphasizing loss, banality, petty corruption, hypocrisy, alienation, and frustration. Even Sherwood Anderson (a writer probably incapable of satire) helped to cement a view of the region as narrow, backward, and seething with sexual repression.

In 1929, literature and social science converged on the point of Midwestern identity, when Robert S. Lynd and Helen Merrell Lynd published *Middletown*, their best-selling anthropological study of a small, anonymous city (Muncie, Indiana) located in the same Midwestern gas and oil belt as Anderson's Bidwell, Ohio. Quoting from *Poor White* to describe how Middletown might have looked in the 1890s, the Lynds not only took Anderson's portrayal of Bidwell at face value, but expanded on Anderson's basic theme: namely, the destruction of the theoretically organic communities of the rural Midwest by the introduction of modern industry and its products.[25] The fundamental arguments of *Middletown* were then organized in terms of a comparison between the period portrayed in the opening pages of *Poor White*, and the period (1924–25) in which the Lynds and their team conducted their fieldwork in Muncie. Since the 1890s, they argued, the growth of business and industry, the invention of the private automobile, and the expansion of consumer credit were among the catalysts of a number of significant social changes, including the reinforcement of class divisions, the dissolution of family ties among the work-ing class, new habits of conformity and materialist pursuits of status among the more affluent, and a general weakening of religious faith and observance (this latter point being key both to Robert Lynd, a Presbyterian minister, and to his sponsors, the Rockefeller-funded Institute of Social and Religious Re-search).[26] Chosen carefully both to illustrate "a plentiful assortment of the growing pains accompanying contemporary social change" and to be as "mid-dle-of-the-road" as possible—medium-sized, racially and ethnically homoge-neous, in a temperate climate—"Middletown" was to become an American sociological baseline.[27]

Though the Lynds no doubt found distressing many of the changes they described, their portrayal of the people of Middletown, particularly the la-boring classes, was in the tradition of the participant-observer; their views were presented as rational, nonjudgmental, and often sympathetic. For example, the Lynds chided reformers concerned about "juvenile delinquency" for failing to acknowledge the stresses that sixty-hour work weeks and frequent night shifts placed on working class families. Though they were harder on the communi-ty's newly acquired habits of conspicuous consumption, they were careful to place even this development within the context of a general breakdown in older forms of social distinction, including those formerly important differ-ences between apprentices, journeymen, and master craftsmen. Indeed, the Lynds portrayed a community which was itself deeply uncomfortable with many of the changes brought about by modernity, but insufficiently capable of adjusting its institutions, traditions, and values to the new social pressures. The result of this "cultural lag" was a certain desperate hypocrisy, in which the people of Middletown conformed to the forms and strictures of social institu-tions even after they no longer believed in their efficacy. Though Middletown-ers still attended church regularly, few still read the Bible daily or engaged in family prayer; parishioners were regarded by their ministers to be generally uninterested in the topics of sermons; and newcomers were more likely to select the denomination of the church they attended for business and social reasons than for doctrinal considerations. Similarly, the great majority of the upper classes of Middletown supported the Republican Party (closely associ-ated in Indiana politics of the time with the Ku Klux Klan)—less on the basis of political beliefs than because it was considered "good business" to be a Republican.[28] This case of cultural lag directly addressed the personal and social effects of the process of modernization itself. In the face of rapid social and technological changes, the Lynds suggested, the Middletowners had not adapted, had not acquired habits "genuine" (as Sapir would say) to their new, more modern context.

Of course, the Lynds were hardly implying that Middletown was unique in this respect. Robert Lynd would later make it clear in his polemical book *Knowledge for What?* that, besides social scientists, *most* Americans were sty-mied by the complexities of modern society. On that basis, Lynd would advocate a new role for the social sciences as offering an elite technocratic cadre of bureaucratic leaders—an idea that, as we shall see in the next chapter, was widely embraced in the war and postwar years.[29] Nevertheless, much of the popular press was content to assume that its readers were a bit more advanced than these Midwestern Babbitts.

For many reviewers and subsequent commentators, the most impressive and frightening feature of the Middletown study was the Lynds' portrayal of the more prosperous Middletowners' quick, but also somehow *aberrant*, adaptation to consumer culture, represented by a strong inclination to conspicuous consumption on the one hand, and by an equally strong propensity to social conformity on the other. Not yet fully capable of expressing themselves correctly through the use of consumer items, these new consumers instead became themselves akin to the mass-produced products they coveted. They were, in other words, "standardized," and as such, could be seen as representing a threat to democracy itself. H. L. Mencken took this line, when he wrote of the typical resident of the Lynds' "city in Moronia" as

> a man of almost unbelievable stupidities. Well-fed, well-dressed, complacent and cocksure, he yet remains almost destitute of ideas. The things he admires are mainly mean things, and the things he thinks he knows are nearly all untrue. The government he lives under is ignorant and corrupt, the industrial system he is part of is inefficient and cruel, and the ideals that inspire him are puerile and ignominious. His principal effort in this world is to appear as much as possible like his fellows—to act like them in all situations, and to think like them whenever his powers of thought are challenged.[30]

Thus, while others saw in regionalism a counterweight to conformity and totalitarianism, it was easy for many (who also knew of the presence of the Klan in Indiana and of the fascist radio preacher Father Coughlin in Michigan) to see these archetypal Midwesterners as themselves harboring tendencies toward fascism, in their apparent stupidity, gullibility, and tendency toward conformity in thought and action.

In this way, we can construct something of a metonymic chain between the concept of "the people" and "fascism," through the concept of the "middlebrow": these Midwestern "people" (or at least the ones the reviewers seemed to notice) belonged not to an organic "culture," but to a liminal—middle—space in transition to full modernity, too replete with the goodies of a massified consumer culture. This precarious position provided the right environment for a propensity toward conformity, and hence toward fascism. This set of connections not only helps to further explain why the "people" was an impossible symbol for the revolutionary delegates at the Congress of American Writers, but also helps contextualize the terms for many of the cultural debates of the 1930s. In this period, political radicalism and artistic modernism were arrayed against political and artistic conservatism and, somewhat more ambivalently, against regionalism.

"We Common Americans"; or, The Midwest Strikes Back

Few reviewers outside of Muncie itself doubted the veracity of *Middletown*'s portrayals of life in the Midwest. However, those (like the reviewer for the *Saturday Review of Literature*) who identified most strongly with the reflection in the book's "mirror"-like image of America, also seemed to feel that *Middletown* condescended: "[I]f only [we could read *Middletown*] without becoming not only highbrows but highbrow investigators."[31] Putting, thus, a decidedly negative turn on the "highbrow," the reviewer wished to be knowledgeable about America, but not to appear elitist about it. Neither highbrow nor lowbrow, he might have wished (to use a phrase redolent of homey, Will Rogers–like wisdom) to "know an ass and the dust of his kicking."

This was the folksy phrase that appeared on the December 24, 1934, cover of *Time* magazine to caption a self-portrait of the painter, Thomas Hart Benton. The accompanying article—complete with lavish full-color reproductions of art works including Grant Wood's famous *American Gothic*, John Steuart Curry's *The Tornado*, and Benton's *The Ballad of the Jealous Lover of Lone Green Valley*—served to launch Benton and fellow artists Curry, Wood, Charles Burchfield, and Reginald Marsh into national prominence under the misleading collective banner of "regionalism."[32] While the *Time* article was pivotal in the careers of these artists, it is also an important document in the creation of a canon of middlebrow painting, and in the elaboration of an *oppositional* middlebrow aesthetic: antielitist, antimodernist, decentralized, and politically and socially conservative.[33]

The *Time* article created a history of contemporary American art, in which regionalism became the triumphal moment in an epic struggle between French modernism and good old American common sense. Inverting the French and American roles of the victim and the rescuer in World War I, the *Time* article argued:

> In 1913 France conquered the U.S. art world. At the famed Manhattan Armory show arranged by the late Arthur B. Davies, the U.S. public got its first big dose of the arbitrary distortions and screaming colors which were making France's crop of artists the most spectacular in the world. The War took the public's mind temporarily off art but at its end French artists were sitting on top of the world. U.S. painters, unable to sell at home or abroad, tried copying the French, turned out a profusion of spurious Matisses and Picassos, cheerfully joined the crazy parade of Cubism, Futurism, Dadaism, Surrealism. Painting became so deliberately unintelligible that it was no longer news when a picture was hung upside down.
>
> In the U.S. opposition to such outlandish art first took root in the Midwest.[34]

On this last point, the article was not entirely accurate. All of the painters featured in the *Time* article but Burchfield had studied art in Paris; Benton (whose father was a congressman from Missouri) spent much of his youth in

Washington, D.C., and much of his adult life in New York; only Grant Wood had lived the majority of his working life in his native Iowa. Reginald Marsh—born in Paris, raised in New Jersey, and committed to painting the life of New York City in a manner inspired by the Old Masters—was not connected to the Midwest *at all*, and neither considered himself, nor has subsequently been regarded, a "regionalist" painter. *Time*'s purpose for grouping these painters together thus had less to do with a shared subject matter rooted in the Midwest, than with a common commitment among the artists to representationalism and an outspoken hostility to modernist abstraction.

Nevertheless (with the exception of Marsh) there was a significant *ideological* connection between the Midwest and these painters. This connection had something to do with the problem of the middlebrow, and something to do, once again, with Sherwood Anderson. Burchfield, whom the *Time* article identifies as having "the honor of being a pioneer in the [regionalist] movement" claimed that reading Anderson's *Winesburg, Ohio* saved him from an artistic "degeneracy" similar to the "vagaries of the Da-da school."[35] Anderson's works, so ambiguous in their portrayal of the sad, emotionally thwarted Midwestern townspeople, helped legitimate as "artistic" treatments of the Midwest such as Burchfield's, which (at least in theory) maintained a careful balance between sympathy and parody. Burchfield was representative of the regionalists when he wrote of his Midwestern subjects, "If I presented them in all their garish and crude primitiveness and unlovely decay, it was merely through a desire to be honest about them."[36] For these artists, sympathy for the Midwest and its people reflected a concern for social issues and a love for things American. A certain critical disdain for them proved one's sophistication, and preserved one's reputation for producing "art."

Thus, what connects these regionalist painters is a common bent for playing with this precarious balance that made them both critics and celebrators of Midwestern life. Before the *Time* article, Benton, Curry, and Wood (the regionalist Big Three) had all had trouble getting their paintings accepted with the very folks they later claimed to represent, often because they were seen as caricaturing Midwestern life. Kansans were worried that Curry's *The Tornado* would give the world the wrong meteorological impression of the state; Benton encountered strenuous resistance to images (of the Klan) that he wanted to include in his *Social History of Indiana* murals; and Grant Wood received angry letters from farmers about *American Gothic*.[37]

The *Time* article, however, significantly changed the popular perception of the Regionalist painters. Now oppositional heroes in the struggle between representationalist common sense and foreign abstraction, the artists gained an instant constituency in the Midwest. This meant not only that their portrayals of the Midwest were regarded less suspiciously, but that the artists themselves also began to direct their interests, and their views on art, toward the regional audience. This was especially true of Benton, who found in the *Time* article, and in his new identity as a professional Midwesterner, a new avenue for artistic success. Indeed, we see in his case how the regionalist rhetoric of antitotalitarian decentralization could have significant practical implications, for the *Time* feature offered Benton, never a very popular figure among the New York art elites, a means by which to circumvent their centralized authority.[38] Attempting to break free of the galleries, critics, and collectors of the New York art world, Benton would use the relatively new vehicles of mass media and corporate sponsorship to build his reputation and his audience.[39]

This story of the repudiation of the New York art world's hegemony is, of course, not directly conveyed in the *Time* article, but rather, indirectly narrated in the more nationalist terms of the artists' rejection of French abstraction in favor of American representationalism. The account of these artists' works and lives is thus redolent with conversion experiences, in which, like Burchfield's encounter with *Winesburg, Ohio*, events led the artists to reject modernist notions about what made art "serious" or "good." Benton's story is perhaps most remarkable in this respect, since it also fits neatly with *Time*'s martial narrative of American artistic revolt against an obscure French modernism. Benton began, according to the article, as a young Missourian fleeing to Paris to copy French "fads." Happily, however, "Six Wartime months in the U.S. Navy knocked French impressionism out of him," and Benton began to paint "realistic water-colors of War activities around Norfolk, Va." This release from faddism led Benton naturally back to his roots in southwestern Missouri and to an interest in painting "recognizable observations," including "such typical Americana as revivalists, bootleggers, stevedores, politicians, soda clerks." The appeal of his art, and its political and moral justification, is that his "recognizable" portrayals of "typical Americana" are essentially democratic in a way that the "vagaries" of modern art are not. Indeed, Benton seems quite the champion of the common folk:

> To critics who have complained that his murals were loud and disturbing, Artist
> Benton answers: "They represent the U.S. which is also loud and 'not in good taste.' "
> "I have not found," he explains, "the U.S. a standardized mortuary and consequently
> have no sympathy with that school of detractors whose experience has been limited
> to first class hotels and the paved highways. At the same time I am no sentimentalist.
> I know an ass and the dust of his kicking when I come across it."[40]

Against the "loud" aesthetic sensibilities of the common man, Benton thus pits his "school of detractors," a monolithic taste elite who would presume standardization where none exists.

Benton's rather disingenuous characterization of his critics plays on "highbrow" stereotypes of both "low-" and "middlebrow" taste. His detractors have a "standardized" view of America, which is associated with a certain degree of privilege ("first class hotels") and with prissily genteel aesthetic sensibilities (they find Benton's murals "loud and disturbing"). While claiming to represent the common folk, Benton thus also takes care, through this Mencken-like characterization of the "booboisie," to describe himself as *above* that. His assurances that his art was neither "standardized" nor genteel both refuted a highbrow characterization of the taste of his potential supporters, and allayed their fears about the cultural inferiority of his art.

If such a "school" of Benton detractors in fact existed, it would thus not have been found with supporters of the Muncie Chautauqua, but rather in the decidedly "highbrow" circles of the New York art world. For Benton, it was Alfred Stieglitz in particular who personified this world and its gatekeeping function in the American art scene. Benton and Stieglitz first met in 1914, when Stieglitz was one of the most prominent figures in American visual art, and when Benton—twenty-five years Stieglitz's junior—was still a struggling and unrecognized proponent of synchromism (an American version of Delaunay's cubist Orphism). Stieglitz, it seems, never bestowed upon Benton the support that might have made him an important American modernist, though it is unclear whether the reason was personal, or a judgment of his work. Benton, for his part, once described Stieglitz as "picturesque, consciously and effectively so. He has a mania for self-aggrandizement, and his mouth is never shut."[41] Clearly, he resented the enormous power Stieglitz wielded in the New York art world. In the twenty years that followed their meeting, Benton, whose regionalist work had made him something of a force himself, began a polemic against his own past as a nonrepresentational modernist painter who once courted Stieglitz's favor, and as a communist sympathizer. For him, too, a set of associations emerged, roughly antithetical to that which connected "the people" with standardization, the middlebrow, the Midwest, and fascism. For Benton, modernism, communism, and (largely through Stieglitz) highbrow cosmopolitan Jewish foreignness were also inextricably linked.

In Benton's new incarnation as the theoretician of regionalism, nonrepresentational modernism was overly European, elitist, and confused by obfuscatory theory. However, in keeping with the generally leftward inclination of so much of thirties politics, Benton's repudiation of communism was rather less dramatic than his disenchantment with modernism. In a 1935 interview in the hostile *Art Front*, Benton stated his political views concisely: "I believe in the collective control of essential productive means and resources, but as a pragmatist, I believe actual, not theoretical, interests do check and test the field of social change."[42] Communism, besides being (like modernist painting) excessively theoretical, was largely synonymous for Benton with Earl Browder's Stalin-controlled Communist Party, and was thus understood to be at base totalitarian. More startlingly, Benton also manipulated one of the Left's standard arguments against regionalism, contending that the Communist Party was also "provincial": "It is a dependent, a province of certain kinds of thought, and it is set in a region where the sort of social behavior and instrumentation which actually objectifies that thought is checked and frustrated."[43] For my purposes, however, Benton's most significant break with communism was his rejection of the theoretical centrality of the industrial proletariat. This argument was central to his articulation of the relationship between regionalism and "the people."

In an extended reply to an essay by Diego Rivera, Benton took exception to the Marxist emphasis on the proletariat to implicitly define his own constituency, as follows:

> In spite of the fact that industrial development has not increased the numbers of the proletariat—the essential revolutionary element of the Marxist scheme—in any relative scale, but has tended, particularly in the industrial countries, to increase the so-called middle class—a class of skills and small ownership stakes—Marxists still adhere to the master's conception of the major position of the proletariat in the struggle to put an end to the crude exploitation of human energies for profit. This middle class which, in spite of the efforts of Marxists to classify it, is neither bourgeois nor proletarian, occupies today the strategic position in the world. The lever of mass power is in its hands.[44]

Subsequently, Benton would turn what can only be described as this revolutionary middle class into "the people"—a concept he would wield with far greater success than did Kenneth Burke. These "people," authentically connected with America, and likely with an American region, were, in a classic formulation of cultural nationalism, the basis upon which to build real art. From this, the political and aesthetic project of isolating both art and "the people" from foreign influence logically followed. While Benton characterized himself and his constituency as "the common man," and as essentially "American," he thus opposed his vision of "the people," their interests, and their needs, to those he found to be intrinsically un-American: immigrants, communists, and Jews—a trio which Matthew Baigell suggests were for Benton largely synonymous. Hence, Benton would write of Stieglitz, "He never laughs at himself as we common Americans do."[45]

Benton's rejection of both modernist aesthetics and communism thus had a distinctly ugly cast. This was only exacerbated by Benton's close connection with the art critic Thomas Craven, possibly one of the most hated men in the art world of his time. Craven began his career as a critic, and Benton's all-but-official publicist, in the pages of the sedate *Dial* and Mencken's slightly less sedate *American Mercury*, where, paralleling Benton's own story of development, he maintained a cautious enthusiasm for modernism. In the late 1920s, however, he was hired as art critic for Hearst's jingoistic New York *American*, where he allowed his talent for invective to blossom, and began writing articles with titles like "The Curse of French Culture."[46] One of Craven's popular books, *Modern Art* (which devoted a full, adoring chapter to Benton), described Picasso as "rude and illiterate," and compared Matisse to a "canny shopkeeper," and a "shrewd . . . Polish Jew," vending a questionable bill of goods to "unsuspecting and snobbish business men."[47] In this latter vein, both anti-Semitic and xenophobic, Craven famously described Stieglitz as "a Hoboken Jew without knowledge of, or interest in, the historical American background [and] . . . hardly equipped for the leadership of a genuine American expression."[48] Similarly, he commented upon the American modernists' critique of genteel culture as follows:

> What fine old American families were represented in this assault on the fortresses of academic culture! Benn, Bouché, Bluemner, Dasburg, Halpert, Kuhn, Kuniyoshi, Lachaise, Stella, Sterne, Weber, Walkowitz, Zorach,—scions of our colonial aristocracy! There were other painters of true American lineage—Benton, Burchfield, Chapin, Coleman, Demuth, Dickinson, Hartley, Marin, McFee, O'Keeffe, Sheeler, Wright and Yarrow, but most of them at this time, thanks to Stieglitz and the French, were alien in method and in point of view.[49]

Craven's nativist slurs are especially outrageous because these facts of birth and heritage are, finally, the only way he could manage to distinguish his own professed project of promoting an American art from the Stieglitz group's similar, and older, commitment to a basically identical agenda. This commitment was, of course, reflected in Waldo Frank's cultural criticism, and more recently in that group's choice of a name for a volume of essays in celebration of Stieglitz's seventieth birthday—*America and Alfred Stieglitz*—which appeared in 1934, the same year as both the *Time* article and Craven's *Modern Art*.[50] Benton's review of this volume (pronouncing Stieglitz's influence "dead," and comparing his influence to that of Father Divine and Aimee Semple McPherson) was entitled, "America and/or Alfred Stieglitz."[51]

While Benton and Craven thus pitched their regionalist polemic against modernism as a battle against foreignness, elitism, and charlatanism (they would eventually add homosexuality into the mix), Stieglitz's supporters and others found it easy to connect Benton, Craven, and regionalism as a whole to fascism.[52] Stuart Davis, the cubist painter and radical organizer of the 1936 American Artists' Congress, was quick to make an analogy between Benton and Craven's opinion that modern art was "decadent" and Hitler's own pronouncements about the degeneracy of abstract art.[53] Moreover, as a theory of art, regionalism was not significantly different from *Blut und Boden*—and indeed, by the time the United States declared war against Germany, it was already something of a commonplace of art criticism to consider regionalism fascist.[54] Benton responded to these attacks by arguing (characteristically) that his views were more "democratic" (hence, more "American") than those of cubist-communists like Davis. Significantly, however, several prominent artists who had been variously associated with regionalism—including Burchfield, Marsh, and Edward Hopper—all vehemently distanced themselves from regionalism because of its political connotations.[55]

Even while regionalism seemed thus to be on the political defensive, it nevertheless preserved the important high ground of claiming to represent "the people." Regarding Benton's painting, this point was a difficult one for his opponents to refute, because his subjects so often converged with those of the artists of the Popular Front—including the lives of the rural poor, southern blacks, and industrial workers. Benton's critics thus turned their attention to how Benton portrayed these subjects: to what many saw as his propensity for caricature, condescension, or even mean-spiritedness in his portrayals of human subjects. Benton's 1932 *Arts of Life in America*, a series of murals painted for the reading room of the Whitney Museum, was regarded as particularly offensive for its portrayal of rural blacks. One panel, entitled *Political Business and Intellectual Ballyhoo*, contained anti-Semitic caricatures of intellectuals, holding copies of the *New Masses*, the *Nation*, and the *New Republic*, uttering (with the aid of cartoonlike dialogue-balloons) such puffed-up phrases as, "really merely quantitative," and "the hour is at hand."[56] In a particularly scathing review of *Arts of Life in America*, Paul Rosenfeld (an ardent admirer of Stieglitz) wrote,

> Benton has exhibited the ugliness of his human subjects in an ugly fashion. To begin with: his thesis is that the arts of life in America are thoroughly crude, gross and ungracious. And to illustrate it, he has presented us with dancing, carousing, murdering types drawn from the primitive fringe of American life from among Indians, city racketeers, and burlesque-show entertainers, hill-billies and cornfield Negroes; and exhibited them now humorously, now nastily, violently, hysterically expressing the national insensibility. This in itself is an unfriendly exaggeration. Many of the arts of life in America, particularly the folk-arts, are charming and gracious; nor are the more primitive types of people and their expressions the centrally, dominantly, American. The under-expressive, timorous, conventional rotarian type is far more characteristic of us. In any case, a real feeling for things would have made Benton contrast the two classes.[57]

Rosenfeld was not alone in taking offense at the murals' depictions of blacks and the laboring classes; a petition was circulated (allegedly by Stuart Davis) calling for the murals' removal, and the controversy caused Benton to lose all of his black, and many of his Jewish, students.[58] But Rosenfeld's criticism of the murals goes beyond questions either of the veracity of his portrayals or his affection for his subjects. In fact, Rosenfeld seems to acknowledge Benton's attitude of critical distance towards his subjects, and to argue instead that the subjects he chose were not *truly* representative of the "arts of life in America." Instead of caricaturing "hill-billies and cornfield Negroes," in other words, he should have leveled his mean-spirited brush on the "timorous, conventional rotarian type," who was, in fact, "the centrally, dominantly, American." At the least, Rosenfeld's argument was for representational parity between the classes; at most, it suggested bad faith on Benton's part. Significantly, however, Rosenfeld conceded one crucial ideological point: that Benton's apparent constituency, the *middle* (-class, -brow, etc.), was centrally representative of American culture—and, of course, that was not such a good thing.

Naturally, the *Time* article utterly ignored this controversy when it elaborated on Benton's 100 percent American image. Without a trace of irony, *Time* suggests that Benton's illustrious family background—the son of Congressman Maecenas Eason Benton, and the great-nephew and namesake of the famous populist senator from Missouri—gave him a unique familiarity with the United States and with the humble subjects he painted. This logic may, finally, be at the heart of the notion of the middlebrow. Just as his paintings are both perceptibly "modern" in style *and* representational, Benton also managed to be both a close descendent of an important historical figure *and* a democrat, a denizen of the New York and Paris art worlds, *and* a wartime veteran of the U.S. Navy. These pairings of facts, which helped to legitimate Benton in the middlebrow-taste community which read *Time*, are the inverses of the opinions that pitted him against Stieglitz and the modernists: Benton was not unartistic, and yet he was not obscure; he was neither "common" nor un-American, yet he was not a snob; he was not without learning and culture, yet he was not a sissy, incapable of performing masculine duties.[59] In other words, the middlebrow's own self-presentation was that it was neither lowbrow nor highbrow. In this light, Rosenfeld's suggestion that the Whitney murals might have been less offensive had they also portrayed "the under-expressive, timorous, conventional rotarian type" takes on a new significance. Benton's omission of caricatures of stereotypical patrons of the middlebrow simply follows the logic in which the middlebrow is essentially constructed in terms of what it is *not*: not black, not "foreign," not snobbish, not intellectual, and so on. As Benton himself said of his revolutionary middle class, the middlebrow is "neither bourgeois nor proletarian."

Despite Benton's refusal to see the "middlebrow" as "bourgeois," the logic of this middlebrow self-construction as a negation of a series of other identities and cultural positions in fact conforms rather well to the process of bourgeois self-creation of two centuries earlier, in which, as Janice Radway puts it, "the rational bourgeois was distinguished not vertically from his social inferiors, but horizontally from all those who did not exhibit the appropriate, highly moralized traits of rationality, decorum, and discretion."[60] Like the middlebrow in the 1930s, the bourgeoisie defined itself against the behaviors, tastes, and morality of others. But whereas the bourgeoisie labored to produce "discretion" against the wild proclivities of the mob, the middlebrow position operated centrally against "foreignness"—a quality that could be variously inhabited by, for example, blacks, Jews, and intellectuals.

Thus, finally, we begin to see some of the contradictions within typical descriptions of the thirties, a decade often associated with an aesthetic interest in the lives and struggles of "the common folk"; an interest, in turn, often connected to the anticapitalist politics of the Depression era. That Benton, one of the most important public artists of the thirties, partook of this period's documentary impulse—a fact reflected in the very names of his major mural projects: *America Today* (1930), *Arts of Life in America* (1932), *A Social History of Indiana* (1933), and *A Social History of Missouri* (1936)—should remind us of the political complexities of what has subsequently been taken to be a more or less univocal leftist and populist form of expression. The case of Benton also shows that the metonymic relationship between "the people" and fascism, created on the left, would be much less enduring in the end than the association between communism, standardization, and totalitarianism, created by more conservative elements. Benton's version of the American "people" was, I have argued, explicitly Midwestern, and implicitly white, middle-class, and middlebrow. Because these people, *his* people, would prove in the coming war to be ready to fight Hitler, they would largely succeed in shaking the association with fascism.[61] Indeed, though Benton's star fell somewhat in the postwar years along with representational painting in general, he may never-theless be said to have won two ideological victories: first, in the idea that modernism was somehow opposed to the art of the "people," and second, in his populist claim to be representing "America."

As always, however, his victory was inadvertently aided by the New York modernist Left. As the decade ended, a new theory of modernism would emerge that would detach both art and intellectual life in general from political engagement, thereby confirming as never before Benton's fundamental argu-ment about the elitism and antipopulism of modernist aesthetics. This new, antipolitical, high-mandarin aesthetic (to be discussed further in Chapter 6) was the product of the emergence of factions between intellectuals allied with the Popular Front in the wake of such events as the Moscow show trials, the Hitler-Stalin pact, and the war itself. Among these divisions, an influential new anti-totalitarian left-liberal position would emerge, represented by the post–Popular Front *Partisan Review*. In its pages, New York intellectual writers like Clement Greenberg and Dwight Macdonald would articulate a new set of associations—between totalitarianism, standardization, and the tastes of "the masses" (meaning both the proletariat *and* Benton's people)—to produce a vision of modernist aesthetics that was explicitly antipopular and anti-representational. As their influence grew during the postwar period, Benton (now ensconced in Missouri) would remain excluded from New York art cir-cles, this time for doing work that was too representational and too political; in short, for painting (to use Greenberg's famous word) "kitsch."[62] However, it is a well-known irony of art history that the painter anointed as the pre-eminent artist of abstract expressionism, the new postwar modernist movement championed by Greenberg, would be Benton's former student and friend, Jackson Pollock.[63]

*

Before turning my attention to Nathanael West, one last figure whose work I will discuss to get at the complexity of "culture" in the thirties, I should con-cede that in describing the final years of that decade as devolving into an elitist high modernism, I run the risk of recapitulating the old nostalgic stories, so typical among the postleftist New York intellectuals, about the thirties as a strange cultural and political anomaly in the longer history of the United States: a lost moment of unique political and cultural opportunity, or (more commonly) a moment of equally unique self-deception and bad taste. Rather, I am generally ready to revise these views; to accede, for example, to the power of Michael Denning's recent account of the "cultural front," which argues that the heart of the Popular Front, a broad coalition of working-class immigrant communities, survived into the postwar years to significantly alter American culture and politics.[64] Indeed, I see other continuities that could be emphasized between the thirties and its adjoining decades, not the least of which being the older, and perhaps occasionally ongoing, tradition of intellectual vanguardism, which emphasized the connection between culture and politics in the first place. But, in telling this story about "culture," I am inevitably drawn toward a narrative that would emphasize the distinctive features of these years, for, as I have argued, without the achievement of a certain uniform degree of modernization, Americans would not have conceived of themselves as actually possessing a national "culture." Nor, indeed, would Americans have articulated class and regional tensions in terms of that concept without similarly historically specific perceptions of difference. Though ideologies of regional difference have of course persisted, and been exacerbated by such internally divisive events as the Civil Rights movement and the Vietnam War, the events of World War II and its aftermath, including the unprecedented internal migrations from the countryside to the wartime munitions plants and the postwar establishment of a high-Fordist consumer society, would do much to complete the nationalizing work that the New Deal had already done. These events would also do much to change Americans' perceptions of class and class relations. In short, after the thirties, the discourses of taste and class would never again converge so neatly with accounts of regional distinctiveness. This strange convergence—a realization not only of the domestication of culture, but of a popular appropriation of the fully spatial culture concept—is the one anomaly of the thirties for which my account will hold out.

The Whorehouse of Culture

Nathanael West represents a final figure in my discussion of the thirties, for the way his work reflects back, critically, on the political and cultural preoccupations I have traced thus far. Unlike Greenberg and Macdonald, West is not exactly antipopulist, nor is he antipolitical, though he does offer a vision that suggests why these views could have emerged from the populism and cultural vanguardism of the thirties. West's work offers satires of the transformational politics of thirties radicalism and even of the *Seven Arts* crowd's earlier urgings for a national culture from fully within these contexts. Moreover, he traces the end of the possibility of certain kinds of conceptions of cultural difference in the face of an encroaching consumer culture, fully realized in the United States in the postwar years.[65] His contribution to the discourse of the thirties is, in other words, to trace out a moment of pure negativity, which is also poised on the verge of another view of culture, a product of the postwar. Thus, far from being the anomaly of thirties literature that he is often taken to be, I see West as both charting the territory of culture in the thirties and delimiting its possibilities.

While West was of precisely that generation of writers and artists who flocked to the Popular Front in the thirties, his life also resembles Waldo Frank's in several respects. Thirteen years younger than Frank, West, born Nathan Weinstein, was also the son of wealthy, largely agnostic Jewish New Yorkers. Though West's parents were Lithuanian immigrants, they identified strongly with German culture, spoke German in the house and, like Frank's family, employed German servants. Both Frank and West attended New York City's De Witt Clinton High School. Both were active in leftist causes and organizations, but not party members.[66] They were both Francophiles. Frank experienced those movements, scenes, and experiments that would become important early influences for West: international modernist art and literature; the radical politics and Russian romanticism of New York Jewish intellectual circles; the influential shows at Stieglitz's galleries; and Hollywood.[67] More generally, West was immersed in modernist discourses on American culture which were, by the 1930s, greatly influenced by the criticism of Frank and his circle.

In spite of these similarities in background and influence, however, their differences in outlook could not have been greater. It is not simply that Frank was a stellar student, athlete, and amateur musician, while West's deficiencies in these areas apparently helped him develop his famously caustic wit. Nor is it simply a matter of West's being influenced by the pose of cynicism that marked some of his immediate artistic predecessors in the Lost Generation. In the space of these few years between Frank and West, it is, rather, that "American culture" was no longer simply an idea with strongly utopian overtones, but a widely held ideology of national specificity, with its own accumulated share of complex social and political connotations. A few short years younger than Frank, West could thus create a nightmare negation of Frank's vision, in which he would not only satirize Frank's cultural typologies and his optimism about cultural change, but even suggest some sinister political implications of Frank's vision of transformation through a lyrical cultural nationalism.

Throughout West's last two novellas, *A Cool Million* (1934) and *The Day of The Locust* (1939), there is a constant, almost harping, concentration on the corrupt, the ersatz, and the culturally impure. West's is a world in which "[p]aper had been made to look like wood, wood like rubber, rubber like steel, steel like cheese, cheese like glass, and, finally, glass like paper."[68] Whereas

Frank gave us a map of authentic "buried cultures" from which to create a wholesome cultural future—the Indian Southwest, the Jewish Lower East Side—West presents us with a world in which Indians like "Chief Kiss-My-Towkus" in *The Day of the Locust* utter the tag lines ("Vas you dere, Sharley?") of Yiddish-accented radio comedians.[69] The "Chief" (a close relative of Mel Brooks's Yiddish-speaking Indian in his 1974 spoof of the Westerns, *Blazing Saddles*), who wears "a bead strap around his forehead" and a sandwich board advertising the "GENUINE RELICS OF THE OLD WEST" of Tuttle's Trading Post, is, needless to say, not a "real" Indian, but a human hybrid of popular cultural icons, and a walking example of the vortex of the culturally impure (*DOL*, 404–05). The fact that we recognize this comical corruption of pure types in the Jewish Indian as an identifiable joke serves as evidence for the cognitive power of Frank's original ("pure") archetypes. However, it also suggests the extent to which West is ready to see the difficulty, indeed the impossibility, in Frank's search for "buried cultures." In an America where Tuttle's Trading Post exists, Frank's vision for a transformation of culture through the embrace of little pockets of indigeneity may just be obsolete.

We also get hints of this possibility in West's earlier treatment of the Jewish Indian gag, in his satirical novella *A Cool Million*, where the "Indian" in question, the Harvard-educated Israel Satinpenny, speaks in a hodgepodge of street slang and hortatory rhetoric:

> 'When the paleface controlled the things he manufactured, we red men could only wonder at and praise his ability to hide his vomit. But now all the secret places of the earth are full. Now even the Grand Canyon will no longer hold razor blades. Now the dam, O warriors, has broken and he is up to his neck in the articles of his manufacture.
>
> He has loused the continent up good. But is he trying to de-louse it? No, all his efforts go to keep on lousing up the joint. All that worries him is how he can go on making little painted boxes for pins, watch fobs, leatherette satchels.
>
> Don't mistake me, Indians, I'm no Rousseauistic philosopher. I know that you can't put the clock back. But there is one thing you can do. You can stop that clock. You can smash that clock. (*CM*, 233)

Here too, West insists that "all the secret places of the earth are full" with the "surfeit of shoddy" produced by the "paleface's" modern civilization. But despite Satinpenny's call to arms to reverse this situation, West offers nothing in the place of Frank's transformative vision. Satinpenny (another Jewish Indian) already embodies the culturally corrupt, and the revolution his speech foments is also similarly incoherent. His Indians, riding off to their new war cry of "Smash that clock!" discover *A Cool Million*'s eternally luckless hero, Lemuel Pitkin, scalp him, and steal his false teeth and his glass eye. It seems that even these antimodern "Indians" still want the most pathetic (and, of course, *false*) "articles of [paleface] manufacture."

Indeed, all that is "real" about Satinpenny's revolution is the enemy, which includes not only watch fobs and leatherette satchels, but an American fascist movement. As in the common leftist thinking of the period, the standardized products of mass manufacture are thus associated with fascism, which is, in turn, associated with the consuming middle class. To Nathan "Shagpoke" Whipple, ex-President of the United States and leader of the National Revolutionary Party ("popularly known as the 'Leather Shirts' "), this Jewish Indian is part of a cabal (which also includes "the Jewish international bankers" and the "Bolshevik labor unions") against the "revolutionary middle class" (*CM*, 186–88). Their conspiracy also includes the poet Sylvanus Snodgrasse, who at the end of the novella creates what is described as Bolshevik propaganda in a medicine show called the "Chamber of American Horrors, Animate and Inanimate Hideosities." The "inanimate" portion of the show contains a "large number of manufactured articles of the kind detested so heartily by Chief Satinpenny," including "a Venus de Milo with a clock in her abdomen, a copy of Power's 'Greek Slave' with elastic bandages on all her joints, A Hercules wearing a small, compact truss" (*CM*, 238–39). Snodgrasse's job in his show is to connect these artifacts of the "surfeit of shoddy" with such "hideosities" of American culture as the branding of the Quakers, the cheating of the Indians, and the enslavement of the Africans.

Through the character of Snodgrasse, West parodically anticipates the trajectory of modernist Left intellectual thinking in the United States from figures like Brooks, Frank, and Bourne to the highbrow cultural politics of postwar figures like Clement Greenberg and Dwight Macdonald—figures who would soon be similarly involved in the project of explicating a relationship between kitsch and the "hideosities" of the twentieth century. But Snodgrasse began his career elsewhere. Driven, the narrator informs us, to the dissemination of this "propaganda of the most subversive nature" out of "revenge" for his failure as a poet, Snodgrasse first appeared in the novel as a Brooksian spokesman for literary nationalism. After the Vermont country-boy hero Lemuel Pitkin injures his eye saving a man and his daughter from a runaway carriage (in the Horatio Alger vein), the Windsor tie-wearing poet asks Lem if he may write an ode to his heroic act: "Poor Boy, Flying Team, Banker's Daughter . . . it's in the real American tradition and perfectly fitted to my native lyre. Fie on your sickly Prousts, U.S. poets must write about the U.S." (*CM*, 183). Just as Israel Satinpenny seems somewhat other than a noble savage (especially in relation to the other Indian character in the novella, Jake Raven, who speaks in the stereotypical Tonto *patois*), this troubadour of the "native" poetic voice has "Latin" mannerisms, and, it turns out, holds forth in this manner as a diversion from the pickpockets who are busily working the crowd. His potential as a spokesman for an aesthetic movement is thus as ridiculous and hollow as his later "propaganda."

The representatives of revolution thus revealed to be false prophets, those characters and things that represent the purely "American" seem, if anything, still *more* sinister. Most are connected with Shagpoke Whipple and his brand of American fascism. Whipple, himself a cracker-barrel Vermont politician, who solemnly invokes "Andy Jackson and Abe Lincoln," attracts other all-American stereotypes like the hero Lem, Lem's boyhood sweetheart Betty Prail, and the Indian chief Jake Raven. The novel begins with a struggle over an "authentic" American commodity, Lem's boyhood home. This New England cottage is about to be sold to the ("un-American") New York decorator Asa Goldstein, who will in turn incorporate its pieces into the ingenious decor of a whorehouse owned by the (equally "un-American") white-slaver, Wu Fong. Wu Fong's is a "House of All Nations" in which, along with French and Spanish prostitutes, he keeps a "genuine American"—the captured Betty Prail—who entertains her clients in an "authentic" atmosphere ("antimacassars, ships in bottles, carved whalebone, hooked rugs"), serves them colonial New England cuisine, and dresses in appropriate period costume (*CM*, 169–70).

The fact that it is a whorehouse aside, Betty's quaint place of bondage cleverly partakes of a number of trends that swept the country in the 1920s and 30s: for early American home decor, and for the recreation of authentic period structures and rooms. Henry Ford, for one, lavishly restored a number of historic buildings, including his own boyhood home and several colonial inns, where period authenticity extended (as in Wu Fong's whorehouse) to the food guests were served. Like Asa Goldstein (a comparison the anti-Semitic Ford would have disliked), Ford had entire buildings moved across the country to Dearborn, Michigan, to become featured attractions in his jumbled American recreation, Greenfield Village.[70] Still more grand and more historically "authentic," however, was colonial Williamsburg, which opened as a tourist attraction in 1932, two years before the publication of *A Cool Million*. In Williamsburg, the generous funding of John D. Rockefeller Jr. turned a small Virginia college town into an open-air museum of colonial Americana—a simulacrum of period authenticity enhanced by park employees' costumed performances of daily life.[71]

As "a very shrewd man and a student of fashions," Wu Fong is alert to these, and other, developments: "He saw that the trend was in the direction of home industry and home talent, and when the Hearst papers began their 'Buy American' campaign he decided to get rid of all the foreigners in his employ and turn his establishment into an hundred percentum American place" (*CM*, 202). Though a foreigner himself—indeed, a grotesque stereotype of the evil Oriental white-slaver—Woo Fong is able to change his "House of All Nations" into "an hundred percentum American place" through a strategic deployment of interior decoration. Rooms once decorated in meticulous Louis XIV and Directoire styles are transformed into "Pennsylvania Dutch, Old South, Log Cabin Pioneer, Victorian New York, Western Cattle Days, California Monterey, Indian, and Modern Girl" (*CM*, 202). Interestingly, his prostitutes are rendered almost incidental. Less the reason for a visit to his establishment, they are instead props in his recreated authentic scenes; they are the whorehouse equivalents of colonial Williamsburg's costumed employees.

Woo Fong's redecoration can also be considered allegorical of a change charted in the pages of this book: the transformation of the desire for national culture as one among many in the "House of All Nations," to the proliferation of subnational, regional cultures, as represented by the rooms of the "an hundred percentum American place." But what is new and startling here is West's suggestion that these regional and national cultural identities are already *false*: at worst, whorehouses, sites of exploitation and degradation; at best, empty categories, the effects of which can be cobbled together—*bought*, rather than inherited—with the right combination of painted pine furniture, spatter ware, and gingham. The success of Wu Fong's establishment is based on the premise that even the most meticulous cultural purity is no less (and indeed perhaps *more*) susceptible to commodification than the allegedly "impure" cultural product. Hence, the narrator informs us that Wu Fong anticipated great success for his regionalist prostitutes, because "many of his clients were from non-Aryan countries and would appreciate the services of a genuine American. Apropos of this, it is lamentable but a fact, nevertheless, that the inferior races greatly desire the women of their superiors. This is why the Negroes rape so many white women in our southern states" (*CM*, 169).

Though Wu Fong is, in some senses, very like Israel Satinpenny (besides his "artistic" taste in interior design, this Chinatown white-slaver speaks fluent Italian and is a graduate of "the Yale University in Shanghai"), he is more obviously connected with that other purveyor of the 100 percent American, Shagpoke Whipple. Like Wu Fong, Whipple's fascist vision is utterly implicated in the marketplace, and hence also in the "inanimate hideosities" of Snodgrasse's "Chamber of American Horrors." As he drums up new recruits, Shagpoke hands out business cards reading:

EZRA SILVERBLATT
Official Tailor
to the
NATIONAL REVOLUTIONARY PARTY

Coonskin hats with extra long tails,
deerskin shirts with or without fringes,
blue jeans, moccasins, squirrel rifles,
everything for the American Fascist at
rock bottom prices. 30% off for cash.
(*CM*, 189)

Similarly, Whipple's hesitation about admitting into the party the (culturally "pure") Indian chief Jake Raven (owing to his "suspicious . . . complexion") is easily overcome when Jake promises that he "Gotum gold mine, oil well" (*CM*, 189). To West, fascism is thus not only connected with racism and the essentially empty ideology of Americanness, it is associated with greed and with the culturally shoddy—be they mass-produced watch fobs and leatherette satchels, or Asa Goldstein's meticulous interiors of reproduced American authenticity. Both the politics and the cultural detritus are the products of the undiscerning *people*. It is they, however, who have succeeded in justifying their politics and their habits of cultural consumption by invoking the category of the "American." The failed revolutionaries Satinpenny and Snodgrasse, of course, also made their bid to invoke the "American," but failed. West sees only one "revolutionary" outcome to this situation, an outcome reflected in the resolution of both *A Cool Million* and *The Day of the Locust*: the volatile and violent mass culture of the "revolutionary middle class" will inevitably give free rein to its baser impulses of racism, hatred, and greed—ironically, at the expense of archetypal, stereotypical American victims, including the Indian Jake Raven, lynched by a southern mob who thought he was black; "the American Boy" Lemuel Pitkin, made into a Horst Wessel–like martyr to Whipple's new party; or, in *The Day of the Locust*, the catatonic Midwesterner Homer Simpson.

In addition to West's implicit equation of cultural nationalism with a pernicious political nationalism, West's creeping antipopulism stands in contrast to Frank, who (at least through his admiration for Whitman) mouthed the rhetoric of the power of Everyman to participate in Art.[72] Instead, West's association of mass culture with fascism points forward, to the end of the thirties, when cultural critics like the Frankfurt School refugees, Clement Greenberg, and Dwight Macdonald would make the connection between fascism and mass culture a familiar one. In rejecting the revolutionary possibility of the project of cultural transformation, West thus also participated in solidifying the more current meanings of Brooks's "highbrow" and "lowbrow" distinction, to distinguish between an embattled high culture capable of producing art and an all-too-prevalent "mass culture," which produces . . . "leatherette satchels." Also anticipating what Andrew Ross has identified as the Cold War cultural critics' "germophobic" anxieties about mass culture, West phrases the distinction through that (inauthentic) voice of authentic culture, Israel Satinpenny: "In return for the loss of [our natural, indigenous culture], we accepted the white man's civilization, syphilis and the radio, tuberculosis and the cinema."[73] In his portrayal of the decorator Asa Goldstein and the cultured white-slaver Wu Fong, West also anticipated Macdonald's later identification of that other taste fraction, the middlebrow (Macdonald's "midcult").[74] In their snobby concern for regional accuracy (imitative, for example, of the New Mexico artist colony's taste for locally inspired interior decoration), Asa Goldstein and Wu Fong are clearly uninterested in mass-produced and -consumed articles such as watch fobs and leatherette satchels. On the other hand, their decorated whorehouse *is* rather like that commercial "hideosity" of the statue of Hercules wearing a truss: it is the comically literalized corruption of highbrow taste by the whorehouse marketplace—and hence (as Macdonald suggests of midcult) represented as the more significant danger to (highbrow) art.

But in anticipating these developments of the Cold War intellectual scene, West is nevertheless a creature of the thirties in several crucial respects. Where (as we shall see in the next chapter) the postwar critics would come to regard aesthetic formalism as a safe haven from both mass culture and the "kitsch" of political art, mass culture's "hideosities" were the very stuff of West's writing, and of his political commentary. This is as true of his last novella, *The Day of the Locust*, as it was of *A Cool Million*. In the five years between the publication of the two works, West turned his anger and frustration at the encroachments of both fascism and consumer society into a more subtly tragic portrayal of the midwestern, middlebrow, "people" as souls hopelessly overwhelmed by a homogeneously mass-cultural world. *The Day of the Locust* also makes West a notable literary contributor to what Mike Davis has called the "dystopianization of Los Angeles"—a genre to which Frank may also be said to be an early contributor.[75] West located this vision of American cultural defeat in Southern California, where he graphically confirmed what Frank had earlier suspected about its cultural potential. By 1939, Los Angeles had been transformed from Frank's land of the "Pioneer in repose" (the geographical and spiritual terminus of America, the site of the last gasp of Manifest Destiny) into the undisputed home of the popular-culture industry: fellow screenwriter F. Scott Fitzgerald's "mining town in lotus land"; West's "dream dump" (*DOL*, 353).

In fact, West envisions Los Angeles as a kind of middlebrow recapitulation of the art wrought by the culture of the Pioneers. Whereas the architectural schools of the genteel tradition once gave the middle classes the European-derived neogothic, neo-Romanesque, beaux arts, and Victorian eclectic styles, West's Los Angeles has *again* become the nightmarish spectacle of the bourgeoisie's architectural fantasies, fashioned somewhat too easily on foreign models. Reflecting the fact that this new bourgeoisie is the vastly expanded middle class of 1930s consumer society, these new middlebrow monstrosities offer the flimsy illusion of cultural roots, and are even made from the second-rate, if infinitely mutable, materials of "plaster, lath and paper." With a lust for destruction that pervades this book, West writes, "Only dynamite would be of any use against the Mexican ranch houses, Samoan huts, Mediterranean villas, Egyptian and Japanese temples, Swiss chalets, Tudor cottages, and every possible combination of these styles that lined the slopes of the canyon" (*DOL*, 262). In this city of the movie set, the architecture mimics the back lots, where we are offered the specter of "the skeleton of a Zeppelin, a bamboo stockade, an adobe fort, the wooden horse of Troy, a flight of baroque palace stairs . . . part of the Fourteenth Street elevated station, a Dutch windmill, the bones of a dinosaur, the upper half of the Merrimac, a corner of a Mayan Temple" (*DOL*, 352). Here, Napoleonic cuirassiers again charge heroically up Mont St.

Jean to their defeat—not at the hands of the British, but of the movie studios' carpenters, painters, and technicians, who let the hill of lath and painted canvas (the very same materials that made the fanciful bungalows) collapse beneath their weight (355–56).

In West's Los Angeles, what Horkheimer and Adorno would soon call the "culture industry" is thus rather obviously pitted against Culture—and, simultaneously, against *all cultures*, Samoan, Trojan, Dutch, Mayan, and so forth.[76] The builders of this Los Angeles do not create, as Frank would have had them do, out of the "buried cultures" of their region, nor do they create under the guidance of any (modernist) aesthetic priesthood. Moreover, the technologies of industrial modernity, which futurists had thought might be used profitably in the service of an artistic ideal, are here *too* versatile, too full of possibility; they are used by these builders to serve the shadow—or, perhaps, the caricature—of an ideal.

But culture is not the culture industry's only victim. In fact, the novel offers us a kind of a Southern Californian sociology of victimization. These victims range from the female tennis champion whose speech is infected by the witty rhetorical reversals of stereotypical socialite chitchat in thirties movies ("Are you talking smut?" she asked. "I adore smut."), to Harry Greener, a vaudeville clown, who (like Lem Pitkin in *A Cool Million*) spent a career receiving comedic blows on the head and kicks in the pants (*DOL*, 273). West's viewpoint character, Tod Hackett (a studio scenery painter, hired directly from college) is also a victim, hopelessly fascinated by Harry Greener's daughter Faye, a talentless movie extra and occasional prostitute.

In between two social extremes, which are also highbrow and lowbrow— the artist-intellectuals and (parodic) socialites on one hand, and the exploited workers in the culture industry on the other—is, of course, a middle. This middle is ostensibly comprised of the bungalow builders, who also seem deserving of sympathy for their own misguidance at the hands of the culture industry. Though we are obviously to disapprove of their Samoan huts and Rhine castles, West musters sufficient pathos to suggest, "It is hard to laugh at the need for beauty and romance, no matter how tasteless, even horrible, the results of that need are. But it is easy to sigh. Few things are sadder than the truly monstrous" (*DOL*, 262).

Tod mentally identifies these bungalow builders, the subjects of *The Burning of Los Angeles*, the Goya-influenced masterpiece he plans to paint, both as "the people who stared," and as "the people who had come to California to die" (*DOL*, 261, 282, 420). As Tod's first designation suggests, they are comprised of the largely passive consumers of the shoddy products created in Hollywood by highbrow writers and artists (like Tod and his sellout writer friend Claude Estee), and lowbrow producers and actors, including Harry and Faye Greener. While the second, equally significant, description of Los Angeles's middle class reflects West's *noir*ish sensibilities, it was also reflective of a

demographic reality. Beginning in the 1880s, Los Angeles was heavily promoted as an attractive destination for, often elderly, health and sunshine seek-
ers. Mike Davis (providing an excellent example of the currency of the association between the Midwest and the middlebrow), describes these immigrants as
comprised mostly of the "restless but affluent babbitry of the Middle West."[77]

Typical in almost every way of those who came to California to die is Homer
Simpson, a transplanted Midwesterner who, after a bout of pneumonia, used
his savings from his job as a bookkeeper in an Iowa hotel to retire in Southern
California. If he is not quite like the others of this class which so fascinates
Tod, it is because Homer is pathetically, pathologically shy. Moreover, his
longings are so deep and frightening that if they were actually fulfilled, they
would destroy him. In some ways, thus, a grotesque portrait of his entire class
of Midwestern immigrants, he is also a caricature of a Sherwood Anderson
character, especially Wing Biddlebaum in *Winesburg, Ohio*. In the earlier
work, Wing Biddlebaum is a man living a secret life: once a teacher, he was
accused of pedophilia and driven out of town. Relocated in Winesburg, Ohio,
Wing's strangely mobile hands are the signs, simultaneously, of his frustrated
sexual desires, and of his related, and hence tragic, transcendent love for humanity. Homer's hands are similarly, erotically, restless: "Their fingers twined
like a tangle of thighs in miniature" (*DOL*, 313). Creating Homer thus in
Wing's distorted image, West in a sense completes a circle, in which Anderson,
once held as the exemplar of a new, indigenous American modernist aesthetic,
becomes the source of a grotesque representation of the frustrated desires of
the middlebrow.

Most of the action of the novel is devoted to Tod's pursuit of the unattainable
Faye. Conscious that his own internal language is contaminated by the dialogue of film *noir*, Tod reflects on his obsession:

> Her invitation wasn't to pleasure, but to struggle, hard and sharp, closer to murder
> than to love. If you threw yourself on her, it would be like throwing yourself from
> the parapet of a skyscraper. You would do it with a scream. You couldn't expect
> to rise again. Your teeth would be driven into your skull like nails into a pine board
> and your back would be broken. You wouldn't even have time to sweat or close
> your eyes.
>
> He managed to laugh at his language, but it wasn't a real laugh, and nothing was
> destroyed by it. (*DOL*, 271)

Like the *noir* genre itself, Tod's pursuit of Faye is the highbrow's attempted
marriage of interests with the lowbrow. Faye, however, rejects Tod and joins
forces with (middlebrow) Homer Simpson—not in a love relationship, but in
a dubious "business arrangement," analogous to that of the film industry in
general. As the writer Claude Estee, discussing the subject matter of Hollywood movies, tells Tod, "What the barber wants is amour and glamour" (*DOL*,
277). Homer, the sponsor of Faye's dubious acting career, now gets his share

of "amour and glamour" in a kind of sham marriage, in which, in return for her mere presence in his drab life, he provides her with a home, clothes, food, and a servant (Homer himself). When she finally leaves him, however, Homer is utterly destroyed.

Like Homer's "business arrangement" with Faye, the movies and bungalows that the middle classes consume in their desperate search for "beauty and romance" are finally insufficient to contain their desires:

> Their boredom becomes more and more terrible. They realize that they've been tricked and burn with resentment. Every day of their lives they read the newspapers and went to the movies. Both fed them on lynchings, murder, sex crimes, explosions, wrecks, love nests, fires, miracles, revolutions, war. This daily diet made sophisticates of them. The sun is a joke. Oranges can't titillate their jaded palates. Nothing can ever be violent enough to make taut their slack minds and bodies. They have been cheated and betrayed. They have slaved and saved for nothing. (*DOL*, 412)

Inevitably, this disillusionment comes to a head in an orgy of violence, precipitated in part by the hapless figure of Homer Simpson. Walking around in a daze after the loss of Faye, he encounters a restless crowd waiting for the stars to appear before a preview at "Kahn's Persian Palace Theater." Taunted by a bratty child actor named Adore Loomis, he attacks the child and (again echoing Wing Biddlebaum) he is labeled a "pervert" and thrown to the mercy of the mob (*DOL*, 408–18). Anderson's hauntingly tragic portrayals of unfulfilled desire in the Midwest succumb, thus, to the transplanted Midwesterners' violent desires to escape boredom. The terror of this mob (of which Tod Hackett finds himself both a part and an observer) is complete, in that it is also self-consuming. Through Tod Hackett's imaginative association of the scene with his painting-in-progress, *The Burning of Los Angeles*, it is the very mob that inhabits these monstrous houses who light the "great bonfire of architectural styles" which destroys them.

This riot is the effective inverse of Frank's "recreative Task": instead of joyous production of an integrated culture, joyless consumers destroy the artificial products handed down to them by a cynical and mediocre culture industry. It is the mob's *annoyance*, their irresolvable frustration of desire, and not a vision of transformation, that will cause West's revolution. As a gesture of pure refusal of the processes of change, it has a certain libidinal appeal. However, as the forties began, and as a new consensus was mobilized for a new war effort, such refusals of history were, of course, rendered impossible. Meanwhile, it is the specter of this very mob—middle class, middlebrow, Middle Western—that has come (through the aversions of the highbrow antipopulists, and the assertions of the champions of the middlebrow) to best represent the American "people." In this view, "the American way of life" was already seen to have been replaced by a degraded "Kulchur" of the mob. As we will see in the next chapter, this would become a central theme of "highbrow" cultural criticism for the next twenty years.

6

"Beyond Relativity": James Agee and Others, Toward the Cold War

IN MY DISCUSSION of the "cultural" moment of the thirties, I addressed the double-sided consequences of the domestication of culture: while it offered a way to articulate national coherence conforming to the country's increased political, economic, and social centralization, it could also be used to express a certain resistance to that centralization (associated with both massification and totalitarianism) through the idea of regionalism, on the one hand, and through a class-based cultural politics, on the other. As we saw, the regionalist idea would be especially powerful for the way that it mobilized a populist antiurbanism and contributed to the formation of a new, positively conceived category of taste: the middlebrow. However, this development produced its own reactions, including an emergent "highbrow" anxiety about mass culture and populist politics.

Here, I turn to the moment of mobilization for World War II and its aftermath in the Cold War, which would put new ideological pressures on these usages of "culture." While the fear of totalitarianism (first fascist and communist, and later Soviet) remained a more or less constant feature of American politics from the thirties onward, the cultural responses to this threat proved inadequate in the face of the war. Indeed, both regionalist and radical understandings of culture produced in the thirties were increasingly seen as ideologically dangerous for their divisiveness and for their potential to encourage "isolationism," an issue of particular concern as policy makers tried to preempt the kind of antiwar sentiment that had arisen during World War I. In the ideological battle against isolationism, moral applications of cultural relativism also became a target. For, as we saw in Chapter 2, relativist deployments of "culture" such as those by Randolph Bourne and Franz Boas were part and parcel of arguments for military neutrality, suggesting both that nations had shapes and destinies unique to themselves, and that (thus) there was no moral justification for interfering in other nations' affairs. In the face of the new national emergency, such sentiments would clearly require revision.

This revision of "culture," from a basically comparatist one to a normative and hierarchical one, affected the two groups represented in this narrative in rather different ways. As we saw in the last chapter, elements once affiliated with the cultural Left, newly suspicious of the political impulses of the "people," were transformed into the relatively marginalized "highbrow" antipopulists of the postwar period. For them, a rewriting of culture enabled a new emphasis on the necessity of preserving the modernist aesthetic culture of the avant-garde against the onslaughts of mass culture, and reinforced their belief in the moral necessity of political and intellectual detachment. Meanwhile, anthropologists were becoming more *attached* than ever before, as they were quickly assimilated into the government-academic partnership that saw its first complete expression in World War II. While this new professional role of government service increased both their prestige and their institutional authority in the postwar academy, it also involved some significant compromises to the Boasian tradition. My narrative here will show how the lineage from Boas to Kroeber and Sapir, to Benedict and Mead, would eventually come to serve Cold War political interests through its relationship to new institutions such as Area Studies. I will also show how these ideological and institutional changes necessitated the separation of the anthropological and literary strains of thinking about "culture," resulting in (and indeed institutionalizing) the familiar bifurcated map of "culture" that we commonly invoke today, one addressing the purely aesthetic issues of "highbrow" culture, the other associated with anthropological and other social-scientific discourses.

After addressing the changes facing the anthropologists and literary figures in this moment, I will once again turn to a literary text of the period, in this case, James Agee and Walker Evans's famously complex documentary book, *Let Us Now Praise Famous Men*. The work seems appropriate for addressing the issues of this historical juncture for several reasons. Long seen as the crowning achievement of the documentary book genre of the thirties, it also looks ahead to the preoccupations and concerns of the Cold War, when *Praise* was "rediscovered" and placed in its current position as a canonical work of American literary modernism. For Cold War aesthetes, *Praise* redirected the documentary project from its roots in the New Deal modernization program, to a depoliticized act of moral introspection and aesthetic play. For our purposes, it can also be seen as representing the terminus of the kinds of "cultural" concerns represented by its earlier counterparts—indeed, as challenging, from the perspective of high art, the political and moral value of representing the cultural other at all.

Mobilization and "Culture"

The centrality of the idea of "American culture" itself to the ideological mobilization for war can be seen in a "symposium," "The American Culture," published in the *Kenyon Review* in spring 1941. Sandwiched between essays by Rushton Coulborn and John Peale Bishop, Harvard anthropologist Clyde Kluckhohn weighed in on the state of "the [American] way of life." Like Sapir and Benedict, Kluckhohn emphasized the lags, inconsistencies, and hypocrisies of American culture, but insisted that America nevertheless possessed a discrete and intelligible "way of life," a pattern or "configuration," derived (as many historians of this period also asserted) from its frontier past. This basic assumption about the existence of a coherent if internally riven American culture was shared by all three contributors to the symposium, who drew from it the same clear political message: America, strong and vital precisely *because* of its heterogeneity (both Kluckhohn and Bishop remind us of the benefits accrued to Rome by its welcoming of refugees from a fallen Byzantium) would take up its new Manifest Destiny as the agent of world order. In strikingly similar language, all three essayists traced a historical trajectory from the Pax Romana to the Pax Britannica to the coming postwar "Pax Americana."[1] Nor would this new world order simply be political; Bishop asserted, "The center of western culture is no longer in Europe. It is in America. It is we who are the arbiters of its future and its immense responsibilities are ours."[2]

This flattering vision of American imperial destiny—a less jingoistic version of Henry Luce's famous assertion of "the American Century," written in the same year—would both encourage entry into the war (to save Europe) and, later, provide an important ideological basis for the development of the United States's identity as a "superpower" in the Cold War.[3] Moreover, because the United States was asserted to be the arbiter of the future of Western culture, "American culture" and Western culture would soon become synonymous, a fact made manifest by the ubiquity of "Western Civ" courses on postwar college campuses.[4] However, it is clear that this rewriting of American culture is also an implicit critique of the kind of moral relativism that Boas, for one, had offered as an intellectual justification for noninvolvement during World War I. In insisting upon an imperial American destiny, these writers offered a discourse of culture that made moral and teleological claims for American (or Western) superiority, and for the (consequent) necessity of military involvement in the Second World War.

If relativism was an ideological problem in the mobilization for war, then so was the potential presence of intellectuals who might feel inclined to espouse it. This problem of intellectuals' passivity in the face of the war effort was addressed in direct relation to cultural relativity in one of the more notorious pro-involvement salvos of the prewar period. The 1940 essay "The Irresponsibles," by the poet Archibald MacLeish (the librarian of congress and a familiar of the Roosevelt White House), connected the "cultural crisis" of fascism, which he saw as a kind of anticulture, to the failure of intellectuals to actively defend the eternal principles of the "culture of the West."[5] As we shall see, much of the literary intelligentsia reacted with horror to MacLeish's call for the mobilization of art and literature, but a great many others strongly supported his denunciation of scholarly detachment. Among them were Franz Boas and Van Wyck Brooks, who joined a host of other prominent intellectual figures including Albert Einstein, Enrico Fermi, and Paul Tillich to support the convening of the "Conference on Science, Philosophy, and Religion in Their Relation to a Democratic Way of Life." The purpose of the conference was to address just the kinds of questions MacLeish had raised: the fascist threat to America's "democratic way of life," and the responsibility of intellectuals in addressing this threat.[6] It was also a conspicuous example of what a later generation of academics would call "interdisciplinarity." The project of bringing together intellectuals from diverse fields was in part a response to MacLeish, whose essay reviled scholarly overspecialization, while also expressing a palpable desire for a master discourse that would both unify "science, philosophy, and religion" and offer an alternative to the "pseudo-philosophies"—especially Marxism and fascist appropriations of Nietzsche—that seemed to give philosophical foundations to totalitarian regimes.[7] Not surprisingly, a constant theme of this conference and the ones that ensued over the following decade was the bankruptcy of a rather broadly construed cultural relativism, which was seen as the root cause of academic skepticism, overspecialization, political detachment, and the general decay of both intellectual inquiry and public morality.[8]

Though Brooks was unique, in that he was one of the few participants who did not have an academic position, it is not hard to understand why he was attracted to the project of the conference. Brooks was a public admirer of MacLeish's essay, and both he and MacLeish held similar political views as visible, but relatively conservative, figures in the literary Popular Front.[9] Brooks apparently saw MacLeish's call to action as coinciding with his own emerging views on the decadence of high-modernist literature. His major contributions to the first two conferences would be elaborations on this theme, castigating modernist writers not only for their political quietism, but for their fascination with the "death-drive."[10] Also, the conference's general topic of a threatened "democratic way of life" allowed Brooks to return to some of the themes of his earliest work. In terms strongly reminiscent of his lament for the divided nature of American culture, Brooks accounted for the "instability of our culture" by decrying excessive individualism, the fetishization of technology, and a "lack of historical perspective."[11]

Boas never participated formally in the three conferences that were held before his death in 1942 (at the age of eighty-four). However, his formal support of the conference as one of its convokers requires more explanation than does Brooks's presence, given its fairly explicit antirelativist and anti-isolationist agenda. In keeping with his pacifism during World War I and with his experience of the oppression and bigotry which can be caused by wartime nationalism, Boas did not formally support U.S. involvement in the Second World War until the Japanese attack at Pearl Harbor. Nevertheless, throughout the 1930s, he had been both an impassioned public critic of German fascism (proposing, in print, that Hitler belonged in an "insane asylum") and a tenacious debunker of Nazi "master-race" theory. Though his books were officially burned in Germany, several of his works from this period circulated in the antifascist underground. Boas was infuriated by the abridgment of intellectual freedom wrought by fascism, and he devoted the last years of his life securing academic positions for scholars displaced by the Nazi and Vichy regimes. At a luncheon honoring one of these scholars, the anthropologist Paul Rivet, Boas suddenly died while in the middle of a comment about the necessity of combating racism at every turn.[12] It is likely, then, that Boas's enthusiasm for the conference rested both in the organizers' stated belief that democracy was a necessary precondition for free intellectual inquiry, and in its explicit articulation of his own principled views about the social obligations of the scholar.

One wonders, however, how he felt about his student Margaret Mead using the occasion of the second "Science, Philosophy, and Religion" conference to refute a central critical gesture of Boasian anthropology. In the name of refining the anthropological meaning of cultural relativism, Mead wrote:

> Historically, those who are desirous of breaking down some particular traditional value for our society have arrayed a miscellaneous assortment of divergent practices, showing that this or that other people, or indeed ourselves at some other period in history, regarded a given practice in a different moral light, arguing that, therefore, all moral practices are limited in time and place and therefore lack any ultimate validity. This mischievous and uninformed use of cultural material is often mistakenly called cultural relativity, but that is exactly what it is not, for cultural relativity demands that every item of cultural behavior be seen as relative to the culture of which it is a part, and in that systematic setting every item has positive or negative meaning and value.[13]

Here, Mead helpfully identified what may be seen as the real anxiety about relativism, in a moment when the term seemed to cover so many things. Clearly, the moral relativism that Boas invoked during World War I to argue for the sovereignty of nations ("The very standpoint that we are right and they are wrong is opposed to the fundamental idea that nations have distinctive individualities, which are expressed in their modes of life, thought, and feeling."[14]) was not persuasive in the context of Nazi aggression. Nevertheless, Mead's statement shows that it was not so much this rather impoverished relativism that was being dismantled, but the critical gesture of using other cultural contexts as bases for critical reflection on one's own society. In other words, what was being shut down in the name of relativism was *critical distanciation* and the project of cultural comparison that was typical of the thirties. Of course, Mead's characterization of this project of critique as "mischievous" is deeply ironic in the context of her own work and that of her closest associates, including Ruth Benedict. What was Benedict doing but invoking "divergent practices" for the purposes of "breaking down some particular traditional value" when, for example, she challenged the categorization of homosexuality as "abnormal" by suggesting that in other contexts it was accepted, or even embraced, behavior? Indeed, what was the purpose of the last two chapters of Mead's most famous book (one of which was entitled, "Our Educational Problems in the Light of Samoan Contrasts") if not to engage in a similar critical distanciation of familiar practices and beliefs?[15] Not surprisingly, several of the respondents to Mead's paper, including Clyde Kluckhohn and her close colleague Geoffrey Gorer, hesitated to embrace Mead's criticism of this practice, Kluckhohn arguing cautiously for the value of the comparison of cultural details for "providing some persons with some detachment from the conscious and unconscious emotional values of their culture."[16]

On the other hand, *Benedict* strongly assented to Mead's point about "the mischievous and uninformed use of cultural material," and to her restriction of the meaning of cultural relativity.[17] In fact, in an unpublished manuscript written at about the same time as the conference, Benedict had come to largely the same conclusion about relativism, asking, "As anthropologists must we, in this conflict of value systems [between German fascism and American democracy], take a professional stand of relativity, and no matter how we are involved as citizens write ourselves down as skeptics?"[18] Her answer to this vexing question about the apparent ill fit between anthropological theory and political practice followed the lines of Mead's argument. Asserting that public ignorance of the technical meaning of cultural relativity had led to a caricature of the anthropological position, Benedict modified the common definition into a fairly toothless reminder that no one social form (whether "democracy" or "bride price") *necessarily* created the desired good of "social cohesion." Here, she only minutely altered Mead's point about the malicious use of intercultural comparison, to suggest that *some* cultural habits and traits could be criticized, if they did not serve the maintenance of the cultural whole. She tentatively proposed a new, functionalist anthropology, *"beyond relativity,"* whose task was to "study . . . aspects of society which *do* correlate with social cohesion and so with minimizing individual aggression and frustration."[19] As with Mead's revision, there was very little room for critique in this new program for anthropology.

Rather, the goal for the new anthropology that both Mead and Benedict had in mind was to describe the cultural whole whose each trait was an otherwise indecipherable part, and to identify the principles of internal "cohesion" that made the parts work together. Cultural relativity was confined to the proviso that no one trait within a culture, and no one "way of life," *necessarily* produced the social good. It was thus still possible to identify and criticize the "cultural lags" and a-functionalities within American "democracy," but it was not possible to look to some other context, to say that *they* did things better than *us*. On the other hand, it was pretty clear that some ways of life—like German fascism, or Benedict's gothic rendering of the cultural "pattern" of Melanesian Dobu—were simply unacceptable, even if they *did*, in their own ways, manage to create "social cohesion." Thus, as we already saw in Benedict's *Patterns of Culture*, it was possible to see some cultures as "bad" by some fixed standard of values, the way the Dobu might be seen as a "bad" culture, or indeed the way *persons* might be seen as "bad." For, of course, the cultural patterns that Mead and Benedict were interested in elucidating were modeled on the idea of ("coherent") individual personalities. Thus, Mead wrote, "Comparison of different cultures demonstrates that man may set his spiritual goal low or high, that he may cast himself a cheap or a heroic role, and that as he casts himself, so will he live, and his children after him."[20] Given the widespread belief that this war was different from others precisely because of the starkly defined ideological differences between combatants, it is not hard to see how this new approach to the study of culture could conform excellently to the needs of war mobilization. German culture, the newly anointed other to Western "democracy," "freedom," and so on, was not comparable to the West; like its leader, it was *insane*.

On the other hand, understanding the particular insanity of both the leader and the country he led had clear, pragmatic possibilities for such areas as intelligence, psychological warfare, and diplomacy. Mead herself was especially quick to understand the practical applications of this kind of "culture and personality" research. Even before the war, she went so far as to write to Eleanor Roosevelt to persuade her (and, of course, her husband) of the value of a thoroughgoing anthropological study of Hitler's "peculiar psychological make-up."[21] Though nothing ever came of this particular proposal, Mead, Benedict, and a host of other anthropologists sharing their general culture-and-personality approach were soon swept up into war work. While Mead devised anthropologically informed policy for dealing with rationing and food shortages with the Committee for National Morale, Benedict, Gorer, and Kluckhohn worked for the Office of War Information.[22]

The participation of anthropologists in the war effort was a culmination of a trend that had begun during the Depression, when the Roosevelt administration introduced cadres of "experts" to Washington to manage its New Deal programs. However, it was the war that really offered new opportunities for social scientists to influence policy and gain access to financial support through government service. Remembered by historians of the social sciences as a "godsend," and the beginning of "the years that were fat," World War II signaled the beginning of the revolving door between university and government service perhaps most visible in the Kennedy and Johnson administrations.[23] During the war, anthropologists recognized that government service presented a significant opportunity for advancing their authority and visibility in a society that increasingly valued technical expertise. In this way, Mead, Benedict, and their colleagues would both be at the vanguard of the new technocratic elitism, and its corollary development, the newly strengthened partnership between government and academia.

Of course, this participation in government-sponsored research and service was every bit as much of an abandonment of the Boasian legacy as the theoretical emendations Mead, Benedict, and others made to the idea of cultural relativism. At the end of the last world war, Boas had powerfully denounced the idea of anthropologists working in government service, not only for its potential to compromise anthropologists' access to militarily sensitive areas, but because it was offensive to his commitment to the principle of free intellectual inquiry. He believed, moreover, that anthropologists could best maintain their unique authority on matters of cultural change if they preserved the appearance of political autonomy.[24] Indeed, the sinister side of this new government-academic partnership would become clear by the Vietnam era, when the complicity of intellectuals in the United State's conduct of the Cold War came under intense and justified scrutiny.[25] By then it was well known that anthropologists had been involved in government-sponsored counterinsurgency projects throughout the globe, and (in Mead's own anthropological back yard) were employed by the navy in Micronesia in preparation for its use as a demonstration site for the United States's nuclear prowess.[26] As Boas had maintained, both intellectual freedom and the anthropologists' traditional role as advocates for cultural others had been severely compromised.

This was even true of some of the more interesting anthropological works of this moment, such as Benedict's *The Chrysanthemum and the Sword*, a study of Japan published shortly after the war. Unable to speak Japanese or, during wartime, to visit Japan, Benedict relied largely on Japanese-American informants for her information about the culture that was the subject of her book. The complexity of the resulting portrait of Japan is, therefore, all the more astonishing, as is the degree of empathy she manages to convey for the United States' recently vanquished enemies. Though hardly returning to the critical intercultural comparisons of *Patterns of Culture*, Benedict here also makes a number of interesting comparative observations about American and Japanese customs, tastes and habits of mind (e.g., that the Japanese are better sleepers than Americans).[27] Nevertheless, the beginning and ending chapters of *The Chrysanthemum and the Sword*, on Japanese behavior during the war, and on postwar Japanese-American relations, convey a clear pragmatic message about the military and diplomatic utility of knowing about such things as Japanese child-rearing practices and their reactions to shame. Even more popularly successful than *Patterns of Culture*, *The Chrysanthemum and the Sword* did much to legitimate national-culture studies of fully industrialized societies—especially in circles outside anthropology, hungry for useful information about other nations. As Mead trenchantly observed, "It was the kind of book that colonels could mention to generals and captains to admirals without fear of producing an explosion against 'jargon.' "[28]

While *The Chrysanthemum and the Sword* has its felicities, most of the culture-and-personality work conducted during the war now seems irremediably suspect. Though Geoffrey Gorer's pioneering study of Japan (an important source for Benedict) directly influenced military policy in its conclusion that the emperor himself not become a military target, it was also packed with outrageous psychological generalizations—which lived on in the form of grotesque propaganda—about the consequences of rigid toilet training practices on the Japanese national character.[29] Indeed, many of the policy recommendations derived from this practical anthropology work now seem ridiculously naive, as in, for example, the suggestion (enthusiastically cited by Mead) that during sensitive negotiations with the United States Great Britain should employ Scottish liaisons, because English mannerisms were "particularly irritating to Americans."[30]

Even the United States itself did not escape this particular brand of scrutiny. Mead's *And Keep Your Powder Dry* (1942), written around the time of her appearance at the Conference on Science, Philosophy and Religion, was very much in keeping with the conference agenda to find a unifying foundation to "our democratic way of life." In fact, Mead asserted that it was an abstract "democracy" itself that was the unifying cultural trait of the United States. Helping Mead in her identification of this national culture pattern was her decision to exclude from mention most of the obvious possible factors which would tend to complicate a picture of clear national unity, including regional conflict (the South is not discussed), and racial and ethnic diversity and prejudice. Clearly an artifact of the exigencies of maintaining wartime morale—why emphasize deep internal animosities in a time of national crisis?—Mead's method was also in keeping with the limited theoretical agenda of national-character studies generally. As Mead would put it later, "We narrowed the idea of cultural character to cover those aspects of personality that could be referred to national institutions that transcended regional, class, or ethnic subdivisions within a nation-state."[31]

Given the evident theoretical limitations of so much of this work—its reductiveness, its tendency to impressionistic and ahistorical generalizations, its crude view of the relationship between individual and group psychology—it is not surprising that, after the war, national-character scholarship lost its position on the cutting edge of theoretical movements within the field of anthropology. Singled out for specific criticism—indeed, ridicule—by the theoretical opponents of national-character studies was an argument advanced in the postwar years, especially by Geoffrey Gorer, that the Russian practice of tightly swaddling infants had explanatory relevance to Stalin's totalitarianism and to the "Russian character" generally.[32] In some ways, the swaddling hypothesis itself was simply an exotic version of the Freudian pop-psychology obsessions of the period with the psychological consequences of other child-rearing practices, such as toilet training and breast feeding.[33] Indeed, in retrospect, far more appalling than this weird theory were the conclusions the study derived from its general observations of Russian character—with their clear practical implications for the conduct of the Cold War ("Great Russians . . . will expand their boundaries like a flooded lake, and this flood will only be contained by the political equivalent of a firm and solid dyke." [34]). Nevertheless, caricatured as "diaperology" the Russian swaddling hypothesis did much to discredit the culture-and-personality approach in academic circles. In retrospective accounts, the psychological approach to culture associated with Mead, Benedict, and Boas (and, in another vein, by Sapir) would be seen as less influential to subsequent anthropology than Julian Steward and Leslie A. White's cultural ecology.[35]

This work had several theoretical and institutional advantages over the culture-and-personality approach. While Mead, Benedict, and Gorer's studies tended to suggest the existences of ahistorical cultural essences, the evolutionists could address cultures in terms of dynamic processes of change. Also, while culture-and-personality de-emphasized cultural comparison in favor of reified cultural wholes, applications of evolutionary theory to culture offered, as Steward put it, an analysis of "similarities and parallels." [36] Cultural ecology could suggest macrological descriptions of processes across cultural contexts. Of course, the emphasis on macrological description was not out of keeping with American political ambitions of the Cold War period: just as "American culture" made way for "Western civilization," so too would the theoretical focus on discrete cultures make way for more global forms of social analysis, including development theory.

Meanwhile, the institutional advantages of cultural ecology were also clear. It was a theoretical apparatus that united anthropologists, since it seemed widely relevant, not only to scholars working in diverse areas of cultural anthropology, but to physical anthropologists and archaeologists. Moreover, cultural ecology conformed to the discourse of science in a moment when science's social prestige was extremely high. In the not so covertly gendered terms by which intellectual approaches are differentiated, cultural ecology was "hard" theory and social science, while culture-and-personality (which often addressed such "feminine" issues as child-rearing practices—"diaperology") was viewed as "soft," impressionistic, and popularizing. In one respect, however, there was a strong continuity between the two theoretical moments. In the cultural ecologists' thoroughgoing rejection of cultural relativity—in their view, cultures *could* be compared as qualitatively different, insofar as they represented different evolutionary "stages"—these anthropologists were only extending a weakening of cultural relativism already considerably advanced by members of the culture-and-personality crowd.[37]

While the particular "cultural" genealogy I have traced, of Boas to Sapir, to Benedict and Mead, was thus somewhat marginalized as a theoretical lineage within professional anthropology, it is important to emphasize that both its institutional structures and its guiding philosophical assumptions survived and even flourished in the Cold War academy. Besides those anthropologists who had engaged in national-culture studies for the government, others had been employed during the war to train soldiers in exotic, and now militarily useful, languages, often using techniques developed by Sapir and Boas. The government connections of anthropologists associated with both national character work and this language training occasionally paid off in the receipt of government-sponsored grants to research militarily sensitive nations. These included large multinational studies such as Benedict's own navy-sponsored Research on Contemporary Cultures project, on which she was working when she died in 1948. Doubtless of particular interest to the government for having developed techniques for studying "cultures at a distance" in her work on Japan, Benedict and her colleagues (including Gorer and Mead) would now turn much of their attention to the often equally impenetrable countries of the communist block.[38]

Another, more long-lived institutional outgrowth of these practical, culture-and-personality applications of anthropology during wartime was the establishment in the postwar years of Area Studies programs, which emphasized interdisciplinary research on single countries, focusing especially on the Soviet Union. This history of the shift from wartime culture-and-personality work to Area Studies can be clearly seen in the career trajectory of Clyde Kluckhohn, who began as an academic specialist on the Navajo, turned during the war to government-sponsored national character research in the Office of War Information, then became the first director of Harvard's new Russian Research Center in the first years of the Cold War.[39]

Thus, we can see both ideological and institutional connections between culture-and-personality studies and the ideologies of the Cold War. Indeed, as Carl Pletsch has argued, Area Studies comprised a crucial piece in the social-scientific justification of American imperial ambitions. The Cold War social-scientific "three worlds" paradigm, which parsed the globe into a schema of self (the rational, developed, "free," first world); other (the ideological, communist, second world); and those over whom self and other struggle (the developing, prerational, preideological, third world), was predicated on the hierarchical understanding of American society as coextensive both with the "first world," and with the "real," unideological, aspirations of the "third world." This binary of self and other was then reinforced by Area Studies, which became the preferred site for engaging in research on communist-block countries.[40] The somewhat impoverished status of theory in Area Studies was thus part, in effect, of this othering operation, in which the Soviet Union and its allies were held to be unique and outside of the processes of "rational" development that would eventually lead to American global hegemony. On the other hand, Area Studies of "developing" countries such as Japan, a favorite test site for modernization theory, performed the crucial task of explaining why their desire to become developed, like "us," was not a product of ideology, but a natural outgrowth of deep-seated cultural patterns. In other words, Area Studies offered the specific context for normalizing the rigid hierarchy implicit in modernization theory. This naturalizing function was sufficiently thorough that, for years after the war, the work of Benedict and Gorer would remain a theoretical model both for U.S. *and Japanese* scholarship on Japan and its culture.[41]

Not surprisingly, a similar naturalizing function would also be performed on the United States, in American Studies, a site similar to Area Studies both in terms of its institutional structure (as an interdisciplinary academic program emphasizing one national culture) and in its theoretical indebtedness to culture-and-personality anthropology.[42] Like Area Studies work on Japan or the Soviet Union, American Studies emphasized the unique, transhistorical character of the American culture, very much along the lines of Mead's *And Keep Your Powder Dry*. Also like contemporary studies of Japan, the direct ideological function of such work was fairly clear: to show why the United States had "naturally" progressed to the apex of freedom, rationality, and modernity, and why it would, naturally, stay that way. Here, Mead's book is again exemplary. In its emphasis on an abstract "democracy" as the unifying feature of the American experience, combined with an intentional avoidance of issues and events that had caused internal conflict, Mead's work not only suggested that the United States was free of the kinds of stresses and dissensions that might provoke an inclination toward revolutionary violence, but offered a theoretical model for the natural, consensual relationship between the (American, democratic) individual and the (American, democratic) state. This position clearly anticipated another discourse that would also become influential in American Studies throughout the 1950s and 1960s, the "consensus" model of American culture offered by such Cold War historians as Richard Hofstadter and Daniel Boorstin.[43]

Returning, then, to the issue of the meaning of "American culture" in the wartime and postwar years, we can see that it actually had two facets. On the one hand, it suggested an imperial American culture quickly transforming itself into an unbounded Western, or even global, civilization. On the other hand, "American culture" suggested something that was both a counter-hypothesis and a corollary to this unbounded America: a coherent, consensual, transhistorical national character. Clearly, this latter idea held a strong attraction both for academics and the public at large. Perhaps it kept Americans from feeling too much like members of a body every bit as "totalitarian" in its own way as the Soviet Union. Perhaps, in a moment rife with paranoia of space invasions and schemes to engage in mind control through fluoridation, the perceived menace was not only global communist domination, but (a survival, in a sense, of the thirties) the threat of the *success* of American imperialism, resulting in global massification and the end of national identity and autonomy. It is significant in this respect that *And Keep Your Powder Dry* spawned a genre of popular social science preoccupied not only with the nature of the American character on its related individual and collective levels, but with the threat posed to it by the encroachments of mass society. This genre would include such best-selling national-character studies as David Riesman and others' *The Lonely*

Crowd: A Study of the Changing American Character (1950); William Whyte's *The Organization Man* (1956); Charles Reich's *The Greening of America* (1970); Christopher Lasch's *The Culture of Narcissism* (1979); and Robert Bellah and others' *Habits of the Heart* (1985).[44] It is one of the central antinomies of Cold War culture (right up there with the constant emphasis on "freedom" in one of the U.S.'s more politically repressive moments) that, in the context of the height of American power, American national character was apparently in a constant state of siege.

This sense of embattlement in the context of imperial triumph may, in turn, be helpful for understanding another "cultural" phenomenon of the forties and fifties: the deep anxiety about cultural loss on the part of intellectuals concerned with literature and the arts. Some of this sense of loss also goes back to the transformative experience of World War II. Just as it was common in the social sciences to refer to the experience of the war to explain the obsolescence of the gesture of intercultural comparison (an anthropologist reviewing a paperback edition of Benedict's *Patterns of Culture* asserted, "the Gold Star Mother (for instance) is going to be reluctant about granting significance to Hitler's culture"[45]), George Steiner would argue, famously, that the presence of death camps in the land of Bach and Goethe made the saving values of high culture similarly obsolete.[46] The ultimate effect of this oft-repeated formula was not so much to show that culture did not save, but to suggest that culture had no political effect one way or another, thus legitimating an antipoliticism directly analogous to the anthropologists' retreat from the critical project of intercultural comparison. Not surprisingly, however, this sense of the political ineffectiveness of culture allowed some intellectuals to give in to a wistful nostalgia for another moment of political engagement. Hence, the proliferation in this moment of what Bruce Robbins has identified as the "familiar narrative which presents the professionalization of literary criticism as the Fall of the freelance intellectual from the heights of Culture."[47] In the work of the New York intellectuals, among others, the familiar anxiety over the (ir-)responsibility of intellectuals (for fleeing into the academy) combined with an almost nationalist sense of a mythical golden moment, when culture (with an aesthetic emphasis) was complete, powerful, authentic, and important. This golden time was the moment of high modernism, when the intellectual was seen to have operated as a critically distanced, but engaged, commentator on society. What had since been lost was both an object, "high culture," and a particularly engaged social role for the intellectual.

We need only remember the anguished longings for a genuine community of committed intellectuals, expressed by Bourne, Brooks, Sapir, and others, to know that this golden time for intellectuals probably never existed. But in another sense, this perception of loss is directly analogous to wider anxieties of the moment about the erosion of national character. In its own way, the increasing globalization of "American culture" also suggested the increasing difficulty of locating a position for the intellectual to inhabit that was critically exterior to the (global) social whole; for, how could one locate critical distance in the context of spatial and ideological totality? In other words, intellectuals' perception of the failure of modernist critical distanciation may in fact have been a way of registering the foreclosure of the idea (heretofore spatially conceived) of critical and ideological difference. In this sense, the crisis of modernist critical distanciation was not mere mythology. Moreover, it seems logical (especially given the Cold War obsession with "containment") that the intellectual crisis was perceived in the terms that it was, as a "co-optation" or "captivity" of intellectuals by the larger systems of academia, government, or an increasingly homogeneous and normative "mass" culture.

In addressing this sense of crisis, literary intellectuals resorted to a time-tested strategy for dealing with cultural or national instabilities. Namely, they located an internal enemy: the "middlebrow." In effect the cultural manifestation of the totalitarian threat, the middlebrow infected what remained of their high culture with the creeping pollutants of mass culture. We may turn, once again, to Archibald MacLeish and Van Wyck Brooks's wartime efforts, to understand this shift in project among literary intellectuals.

The (Cold) War Against the Middlebrow

Brooks's speech at the Conference on Science, Philosophy and Religion was only one of a number of public pronouncements he made in the early war years on the decadence of modernism. In these speeches, and in the pages of his book *The Opinions of Oliver Allston*, he criticized high-modernist literature for its fatalism, passivity, and fascination with the death drive, and saw its emphasis on formal play as self-serving, adolescent, and amoral. Citing with horror the "Oxen in the Sun" section of Joyce's *Ulysses*, Brooks saw modernist literature as bent on destroying the very "tradition" critics like Eliot claimed to revere. Brooks also accused the modernists of having perverse tastes (Pound, for Rimbaud and Corbière; Eliot, for the metaphysical poets) and compared them to "Little Jack Horners," selecting from the pie of literary history

the particular plums that please themselves, and they regard these plums as the big plums; they even insist that their plums are big, for, if these turned out to be little, what might this not throw on their own dimensions? Meantime they forget that they are in a corner, while the center of the room is occupied by someone else. But the someone in the center sits in the place of humanity, and he has the final word.[48]

This "someone" who figures for "humanity" was, obviously, not the narrow "coterie" of Eliotic modernists, but the broad public that Brooks three decades previously had believed could be created in America through the synthesis of highbrow and lowbrow, and to whom Brooks still felt an allegiance. Castigating modernist writers for their elitism, he refuted the modernist tenet that experimental artists represented an aesthetic vanguard, both culturally in advance of, and opposed to, the masses of the cultureless:

> I note that various writers, following James Joyce and others, have taken to speaking of "the rabble." This is the time to say that there is no such thing as an American rabble. When Alexander Hamilton said, "The people is a great beast," he backed himself out of the American door. There is one categorical imperative in American life, that one must respect man as such. Whoever does not respect man as such is, in America, a traitor.[49]

In the context of the politically tense climate of the war, such accusations of treason were, no doubt, extreme. Indeed, many of the comments and judgments made by Brooks while pursuing this generally populist line of argument were decidedly not to his credit. If they were intended as wartime propaganda, they are propaganda of a rather shallow sort. More likely, they reflect Brooks's uncharacteristically visceral hatred of Eliot, as a poet, a critic, and a person.[50] But every bit as bizarre as the vehement and prescriptive tone of Brooks's views was the response it generated in the pages of the "Trotskyite" (meaning the anti-Stalinist culturally Left-leaning) *Partisan Review*. This began with a scathing condemnation of Brooks by Dwight Macdonald, entitled "Kulturbolschewismus is Here," which was followed in several subsequent issues by responses from writers, including Eliot himself, to Macdonald's rather selective representation of Brooks's argument.[51] As John Crowe Ransom astutely pointed out, "There would be an irony if the writers whom Mr. Brooks has abused should find in *Partisan Review*'s invitation the occasion to form a chorus and—abuse Mr. Brooks. They would be supporting his charge that theirs is a coterie mentality."[52]

It is easy to imagine that the highbrow crowd at the *Partisan Review* might simply have dismissed Brooks's attacks on modernism as the ravings of a middlebrow populist, an argument quickly launched, as we saw in Chapter 5, against celebrations, such as his, of the centrality of the "people." Indeed, Macdonald did see Brooks's insistence that "primary" literature reflect a more hopeful vision of the age as an endorsement of the "positive, optimistic, constructive, popular" values offered by the "worthless" and "profoundly antihuman" literature found in the *Saturday Evening Post*.[53] Following the same chain of associations, it is similarly unsurprising that he would see Brooks's "defense of bourgeois-Philistine values" as totalitarian. In calling it "Kulturbolschewismus," Macdonald managed to rhetorically connect Brooks's position on literature and culture with both villains of the moment: Hitler, who had denounced expressionism as "Kulturbolschewismus," and Stalin, whose socialist realism presumed that "culture" and "bolshevism" could be made to go together. The argument could, in other words, be boiled down to a simple tit for tat: where Brooks saw the modernists and their critical supporters as somehow aiding fascism through their elitist fatalism, Macdonald, on the other hand, rejoined that Brooks's criticism revealed his own fascist tendencies.

In other words, in criticizing Brooks's cultural and political values, Macdonald never really refuted Brooks's central assertions that modernism was elitist and (a more refutable charge) apolitical. His silence on these topics is only more notable for the fact that Macdonald concerns himself at length with the question of whether or not modernism is representative of its historical moment, arguing—rightly—that what Brooks saw as reflective only of the perversities of a "coterie" might in fact have been complex responses to the conditions of the interwar years. But to say that literature is characteristic of its time is not to say that it is not quietist, fatalistic, or elitist. Finally, the vehemence of the attack on Brooks may be accounted for by the fact that high modernism's attraction for the *Partisan Review* crowd lay in exactly what Brooks condemned: its apparent disengagement from the fray.

In this respect, Macdonald was following his fellow *Partisan Review* editor, Clement Greenberg, who, two years previously, had taken a major step in the revision of the modernist concept of the avant-garde, a concept that had connoted a role of related aesthetic and political leadership. For Greenberg, the avant-garde artist's detachment from commercial (or official Soviet) culture was no longer a sign of critical distanciation, but of a necessary political *disengagement*. This rewriting helped Greenberg to explain, by antithesis, what was wrong with the politico-aesthetic theories of those two huge "philistines," Hitler and Stalin: to propose a political function for art was both to engage in antiart ("kitsch") and to have totalitarian political leanings.[54] The proper role for the intellectual, including the artist and the critic, was now defined as the implicitly antitotalitarian (but, as Macdonald himself conceded, ultimately "rear-guard") one of preserving for a better moment the works of the modernist avant-garde, in the face of the encroachment of politics-kitsch. This position, in turn, produced a new set of criteria by which new works of the avant-garde could be identified. Art would be known by its very political autonomy, signaled, according to Greenberg, by the fact that it was nonrepresentational, and all "about" aesthetic form. This, of course, became the theory to the practice of abstract expressionism, the preeminent American art movement of the postwar period, of which Greenberg was an important champion.[55] Meanwhile, this new emphasis on formalism was also being felt in literary circles; the New Criticism, a highly formalist school of literary interpretation, would soon dominate the Cold War academy.[56] This tradition would reduce Brooks's own brand of historical and biographical criticism to a series of "fallacies" and "heresies," in favor of a rigorous analysis of the literary object alone. The literary object, in turn, was likely to gain admission to the canon (including the developing canon of modernist literature) on the basis of its conformity to the qualities emphasized by these theoretical perspectives: formal complexity, psychological subtlety, and political disengagement.[57]

But in a sense, the real significance of Greenberg's revision of the idea of the avant-garde lay in what it implied for intellectual work. Not only was it important to be politically detached, but to be otherwise was implicitly to be *totalitarian*, hence a political threat. On the other hand, the critic's role was all the more central, for he or she had the task of determining what was truly representative of the vestigial avant-garde, and therefore aesthetically and politically acceptable. In this sense, the "Kulturbolschewismus" controversy was a crucial struggle for Macdonald and Greenberg's view of art. Unless the critic was also politically detached (and Brooks and MacLeish clearly weren't), he couldn't find his way to art as they understood it. Of course, the controversy also amply demonstrates how the vestiges of the class-based political engagements of the thirties could be transmuted into the far narrower question of the extent and degree of the political and institutional role of intellectuals themselves.

Though the academically based New Critics were less invested in these issues of intellectual praxis than their New York intellectual counterparts, we may also see vestiges of similar concerns in John Crowe Ransom's response to the "Brooks-MacLeish Thesis." For the New Critics, historically connected to the deeply conservative—but certainly *political*—Southern Agrarians, a trace of the modernist vanguards' assumption of a connection between the political and the aesthetic spheres still existed. Thus, in his comparatively gracious response to the "Brooks-MacLeish Thesis," Ransom agreed in some basic respect with Brooks's contention that art and criticism are both political. Identifying the sad state of their present "Age of Machines" as centrally connected to a "crisis of language and expression," Ransom saw both poetry and the New Criticism he would champion as efforts to rescue a language that had become "factitious and technical": "There are now many men of good will attempting in the name of criticism to analyse the logical or linguistic element in poetry, a study which is nothing if it is not intensive; believing that perhaps the obscure fate of literature itself may depend on the issue which they are trying to isolate."[58] For Ransom, the former Agrarian, the "Age of the Machine" with its "factitious and technical" language was the centralized, bureaucratized society of post–New Deal America. His flight, and the flight of the New Criticism generally, into poetry itself as a kind of vehicle for rescuing humanistic values was thus another version of Macdonald's "rear-guard" action, undertaken against something very much like modernity itself. Of course, in focusing on language as the site of resistance to the new hegemony, the New Critics established their own view of a technically specialized elite, comparable to the *Partisan Review* critic, who would ferret out and preserve that which was resistant.

In this rejection of the centralized, technocratic culture of the day, the conservative New Critics were very like the New York intellectuals (though the latter often made a self-congratulatory practice of seeing the academy itself as one of the sites of culture's homogenization). For example, William Barrett, an editorial staff member of the *Partisan Review* from 1945 to 1955 (before he joined the New York University philosophy department), would rail against the "fantastic bureaucracy" of the postwar years, which had contributed to the flattening of culture and the deadening of literary innovation.[59] For these writers and critics, however, cultural hegemony was less represented by a totalizing bureaucracy or "institutionalization" than it was by that more traditional enemy of both the political Left and the avant-garde: mass culture. Yet for the *Partisan Review*, the political critique associated with this idea, which went to the heart of industrial capitalism, was abandoned for a moral crusade, not dissimilar to the New Critics' protection of humanistic values. Moreover, just as the New Critics pursued the mysteries of poetic form, the crowd at the *Partisan Review* took up Macdonald's "rear-guard" action of identifying and protecting those aesthetic objects, ideas, and practices somehow still untainted by the marketplace. As Barrett recollected, "the highest calling left seemed to be to denounce the fake, to keep a steady eye on the high and serious even if the period could not quite produce these itself—in short, the dreary war upon the middlebrow."[60]

The "middlebrow" of the postwar years was not the same creature as it was in the thirties. Denuded of much of its political and regional connotations, it was, most simply, a highbrow synonym for a "fake," which (as Dwight Macdonald would later explain) "exploits the discoveries of the avant-garde" for the purposes of market-related considerations, such as the pursuit of profit or conspicuous display.[61] In that it often masqueraded as the genuine highbrow object, the middlebrow was, for Macdonald, if anything *more* dangerous to high culture than mass culture proper; or, "masscult," as he would have it, the false pleasures offered for the entertainment of the masses by the "culture industry."

In his horror of the contaminating effects of the middlebrow, and in his vestigially leftist view that "masscult" represented a phony alternative to the development of a genuine proletarian culture, Macdonald differentiated himself from more conservative voices of the moment such as José Ortega y Gassett and T. S. Eliot, who called for the restoration of feudal hierarchies to combat the encroachments of mass culture.[62] Nevertheless, in arguing for the need "to restore the cultural distinctions that have become increasingly blurred since the industrial revolution," Macdonald and many of his New York intellectual contemporaries often approximated their frank elitism (229). Moreover, though suspicious of the bureaucratic centralization of the moment that brought so many academics into the fold of expert culture, those more autonomous writers at the little magazines nevertheless shared in the antipopulist cult of expertise. In the "dreary war upon the middlebrow," "culture's" boundaries would be policed by vigilant critics, whose job was to know a "fake" from the real thing. The chief weapon in this war was the deployment of that ineffable faculty, taste. Insofar as this faculty was seen as something God-given and unteachable, their partisanship on behalf of "culture" was every bit as much a class war as that waged by Eliot and Ortega y Gassett.

Yet this was also a war the highbrows could not win. Though the postwar class mobility that likely animated Macdonald's anxieties in the first place would largely end by the 1980s, the dramatic expansion of consumer society would make the boundaries between art and the market increasingly irrelevant. These would eventually collapse altogether, when the vestiges of Macdonald's avant-garde would embrace first pop art, and then a more generalized postmodernism, which deliberately transgressed both the taboo of the commercial and the taste categories this ban produced.[63] Similarly, theoretical developments such as structuralism and semiotics (once again uniting anthropology and literary criticism, in another way) also flattened the distinction between high and low forms, so that Roland Barthes, for example, would soon write influentially about toys and wrestling with the intensity and seriousness once reserved for "high" cultural objects.[64] As a result, the categories of highbrow, lowbrow, and middlebrow, once understood with all the gravity of sociological fact, have by now come to seem more like amusing descriptors of diverse lifestyle choices.[65] Nevertheless, the fallout of this "war" remains with us, in the persistent belief in the mystifying faculty of taste, in critical pieties that simplistically oppose art to commerce, and in a canon of "Heroes/Victims," as Macdonald put it, who earned their status by seeming to preserve an already selective memory of an autonomous avant-garde.

The Documentary Book to End All Documentary Books

One of Macdonald's own "Hero/Victims" was James Agee, a writer Macdonald unequivocally christened "the most broadly gifted writer of [their] generation" (144). Not coincidentally, Agee's views on art and politics closely conformed to those of the writers at the *Partisan Review*, a fact revealed in Agee's response to a questionnaire sent by the magazine in 1939 to selected American writers, and fully reprinted by Agee in the pages of his monumental work, *Let Us now Praise Famous Men*.[66] Though Agee writes that the questionnaire "happened succinctly to represent a good deal that made me angry" (as we shall see, this emotion was not unfamiliar to him), his answers were largely in conformity with the fully formed opinions of his friend Macdonald, as well as Greenberg and others. Agee opined that Brooks's idea of a "usable past" was not particularly interesting; that "a good artist is a deadly enemy of society"; that communism was a good idea in theory, but not in practice; that he had a "violent enmity and contempt toward all factions and all joiners"; that (on MacLeish's "Irresponsibles") his "responsibility" as a writer was largely to write (Agee, 350–57).

To Macdonald, however, Agee was remembered, and mythologized, not as someone who helped form a critical orthodoxy, but as a tragic figure "spectacularly born in the wrong time and place" (Macdonald, 153). His friend's dismissal of other intellectuals' political commitments seemed to Macdonald both remarkably hard-headed and "not at all the thing for the post-Eliot thirties." In the place of trendy political passion, Agee would offer, and Macdonald would admiringly accept, the more abstract values of "reverence and feeling" (Macdonald, 154,163). Equally important to the formation of the "Agee cult," however, was the view that Agee's talent was tragically wasted, both by his own self-destructive behavior and by his employment in venues that were simply beneath him. Agee's aspirations as a writer for Hollywood and his long involvement with mass-media journalism as an employee of Henry Luce's *Fortune* magazine were examples both of a talent that could not be confined to the "specialization" demanded of the modern artist and of the waste of time these commercial endeavors represented for the production of art. For similar reasons, it was also important to the highbrow critics that his best-known work, the antidocumentary *Let Us Now Praise Famous Men*, be remembered as a commercial flop.[67] In failing to succeed in an increasingly commercialized world, Agee's story both confirmed the highbrows in their narrative of the perils of commercial antiart, and, reciprocally, offered them a victim/hero who represented the last vestige of the dying avant-garde. He was important to them, in other words, precisely because his failure confirmed their own nostalgic view that they were preserving the dying embers of a better, purer past.

The purpose of the reading that follows will be to suggest precisely the opposite point: that Agee and his work were, in fact, very much of their time, representing the transitional moment in visions of culture from the thirties to the wartime and Cold War years—years which, moreover, consolidated a cultural orthodoxy. Indeed, features of Agee's own biography suggest how much a man of these years he was. In the late thirties, Agee shared an office with Whittaker Chambers, soon to become famous as America's foremost "commie fink"; in 1945, he wrote *Time* magazine's cover story on the dropping of the atomic bomb.[68] However, Agee's literary reputation was largely a product of the fifties, made after his death in 1955 through the hagiographic efforts of two friends, Macdonald and Robert Fitzgerald, and by his posthumous award in 1957 of the Pulitzer Prize for the novel *A Death in the Family*. In this sense, Agee very clearly spans the gap between his own moment and a later one, where he was often seen to represent the "serious" literary ancestor of the sixties radicals—as opposed to the younger, still less political Jack Kerouac, whose romantic persona Agee's in many respects resembles (both were darkly handsome, fascinating figures; both vehemently antibourgeois bohemians; both occasionally obsessed Catholics; both gifted, prolific writers in a vein often described as "Whitmanesque"; both alcoholics; both dead before the age of fifty). While the antibourgeois freedoms of Beat bohemia in *On the Road* suggested hippie counterculture, *Praise* was, legendarily, a book that young college students took south with them during the Freedom Summer of 1961.[69] This fact, in turn, has its ironies, for *Praise* was clearly not a call to action; rather, its power lay in a highly moralized, but fundamentally antipolitical, outrage at the lot of the sharecroppers and at the hypocrisies of bourgeois society.

However, it is the specific form of *Praise* that signals its centrality to a literary historical transition, for *Praise* is an explicit rewriting of, and comment on, that archetypal aesthetic and social-scientific form of the thirties, the documentary book. Warren Susman concluded his essay "The Culture of the Thirties" with the observation that *Praise* "may be the decade's great classic." However, I think it clear that *Praise* suggests another kind of limit to the "domestication of culture" that Susman found to operate in that decade.[70] Rather than assenting to the new idea that all of humanity was understandable by reference to the existence of unique yet definable "cultures," Agee and Evans used a form associated with this view to suggest something rather different: that, as individuals, even the humblest of us were both full of "human divinity" and essentially *unknowable* (Agee, xlvi). Insofar as the documentary form is one of the clearest manifestations of the ethnographic and literary convergence of the thirties, *Praise*'s position as, in Alfred Kazin's words, the "documentary book written to end all documentary books" thus marks a closure of the possibilities of that joint project.[71]

The book offers three epigraphs, which Agee suggests are also analogous to musical "themes" running through the book as a whole (Agee, li). However, these "themes" are less organizing principles than representative perspectives on the problem of southern rural poverty that will largely be *undercut* over the course of the narrative. The first, from *King Lear*, advocates humility in the face of others' suffering and charity for the "[p]oor naked wretches." In the context of the book as a whole, which, as we shall see, focuses intensely on the problem of Agee and Evans's own relationship to the tenant farmers, this anodyne of charity appears both condescending and insufficient. The second epigraph, the famous final lines of the *Communist Manifesto*, is similarly undercut by the narrative's multiple criticisms of "da dialectic" specifically, and organized political activism, generally (385). Indeed, the epigraph from Marx is itself footnoted, to insist that the words of the passage were not invoked with the intention of advocating Marxism.

The third epigraph, of particular relevance to Agee's revision of the documentary's project of spatial mapping, is a page taken from a children's geography textbook. It asserts that "The Great Ball on Which We Live" is also home to other children, "some of whom live in far-away lands. They are our world brothers and sisters." The page goes on to suggest that this common humanity is expressed in, among other things, needs for "Food, Shelter, and Clothing," satisfied in different ways (lii). This view, that the basic unity of humankind is divisible into comparable and relatively equivalent "cultures" is, of course, a distillation of the central premise of Boasian anthropology, and the underlying premise of the various ethnographic and documentary projects that this anthropology influenced. However, thus reduced to the children's vernacular, this premise too is cast into doubt. Agee writes about education, "Adults writing to or teaching children: in nearly every word within these textbooks, for instance, there is a flagrant mistake of some kind. The commonest is this: that they simplify their own ear, without nearly enough skepticism as to the accuracy of the simplification" (311). In other words, the problem with this simple message is that it is both banally true and a complex kind of lie, told condescendingly to children who likely know that the world is not a "ball" and that all humans are not, in fact, "brothers." *Praise* casts the entire project of the thirties documentary in a similar light, as being both condescendingly simplistic and somehow fundamentally untruthful as to the real relations between different people. As we shall see, it also suggests that the project of detailing the lives of others for the purpose of cultural comparison, of knowing the details of how others negotiate the necessities of "food, shelter, and clothing," is the wrong project, is somehow obsolete.

However, like the most recent war to end all wars (the United States had just joined hostilities when *Praise* was published), the documentary book to end all documentary books also signaled the emergence of something like a new order. Certainly, in the context of the war, and the emerging new global vision of an American destiny, the narrow frame of the lives of Alabama tenant farmers may well have seemed a bit irrelevant. On the other hand, just as the new visions of American imperial destiny required the specific articulations of American (and Russian and Japanese) national character, *Praise* also invents a new use for the tenant farmers. In the context of literary intellectuals' anxieties about the limits of critical distanciation, combined with the highly moralizing crusade against the middlebrow, this project is one of reflecting content back upon the middle-class intellectual himself, without acknowledging the obvious fact: that he is a member of the same social stratum that also produced the middlebrow.

The reader gets a hint of this complex agenda of self-representation through the other upon examining the very first image in the book. It is an uncaptioned Walker Evans photograph of a middle-aged man, standing in a rumpled and ill-fitting summer weight jacket, staring forthrightly, but slightly downward, into the camera. This man, whose medium-shot image takes up almost the whole frame of the photo, is not a member of one of the three tenant-farmers' families that are the ostensible subject of the book; he is Chester Boles, the landlord of the tenant farmer George Gudger.

This picture is the first of many violations of the reader's expectations for a documentary book on southern tenant farmers. It introduces us to the famous spare style of the photographer Walker Evans, whose aesthetic is deliberately poised against that of other documentary photographers—including that of Margaret Bourke-White, and Evans's fellow photographers of the Farm Securities Administration, including Dorothea Lange, Russell Lee, and Arthur Rothstein. These other photographers followed more closely the injunction of turn-of-the-century documentary photographer Lewis Hine, that social photography be a kind of advertisement for a particular way of understanding people and their problems.[72] Compared to the more dramatic—and, some would say, manipulative—style of these other documentary photographers of the period, Evans's photos are insistently simple: the camera angle and lighting is direct and obvious, the subject appears to have posed himself, conscious that he is being photographed. Yet in this picture, there is also the trademark Evans ambiguity. Despite the rumpled suit and what may even be a slight smile on his face, Chester Boles looks a little angry or disapproving. As William Stott says of this photo, "This person was capable of successful deception; he had the power to mislead. Significantly, he was of the middle class."[73]

Stott's reading, that the "middle class" Chester Boles had a greater capacity for deceiving the camera than did the tenant farmers, is both odd and extremely revealing. It is now well known that the tenant farmers didn't particularly want to be portrayed looking dirty, careworn, and earnest; reasonably, they preferred images of themselves smiling and scrubbed, wearing their Sunday best.[74] We can easily imagine a similar preference on the part of Boles. In other words, if there is the smirk of "deception" on Boles's face, it is there, at the front of the book, because Agee and Evans—and Stott—wanted it there; similarly, if the tenant farmers look more sincere, it is also the product of what one might call a sincerity-*effect*. That Stott could find other portraits, such as those of George and Annie Mae Gudger, any less ambiguous shows in part how overdetermined the meanings of thirties photos of "sharecroppers" have become, thanks in part to the efforts of Bourke-White, Lange, Lee, Rothstein, and Evans himself. It is as if (condescendingly) the thirties rural poor are by definition the subject matter of honest imagery.

However, read as a conscious decision, the placement of this enigmatic image of Boles at the front of the photos reveals a lot about the complex intentions behind this notoriously difficult book. The counterpoising of this image of white, southern, middle-class authority and privilege to the subsequent images of the tenant farmers has, of course, a political dimension. But it cannot unqualifiedly be described as the expected thirties political fable about misery caused by the evils of the land-owning class. Though perhaps having the power to "mislead," the rumpled Boles doesn't even look like a terribly successful capitalist, much less the incarnation of evil. Indeed, if his portrait invites mistrust, it also invites a certain condescending superiority on the part of the viewer, for he is not really all that much.

Rather, I would argue that Chester Boles's image is central to the book as a whole for two reasons. Its combination of ambiguity, deceptiveness, and a certain availability to condescension introduces the book's central theme of the problems and ambiguities of representation. Meanwhile, the middle-class Chester Boles is also the enigmatic figure for what the book is both about, and not allowed to be about: the middle class that includes Boles, Agee, Evans, and the book's presumed readership among its members. As we shall see, this middle class occupies an important position in *Praise* as a special kind of antithesis to the lot of the tenant farmers. But this image of a somewhat miserable middle class is also directly related to *Praise*'s unique status, as an auto-critique of the documentary form. In short, Agee seems to locate a particular moral problem in the documentary itself, and this evil is associated in turn with the pretensions, blindness, and hypocrisies of the middle class.[75] In this sense, *Praise* offers another example of the phenomenon explored in the previous chapter, in which representations of the "people," such as those in the documentary, came to be seen as themselves politically and aesthetically suspect.

But the emerging antipopulism of the late thirties is not alone sufficient for understanding the narrative and visual complexity that is *Praise*. Rather, at its heart is a larger shift that happened in the thirties, involving the end of the project of modernization. As the decade closed, the desire to survey the rural periphery of a rapidly unified nation no longer seemed quite so urgent. In the case of Agee and Evans, this obsolescence was a crucial factor in the development of the project, in that they had been beaten to publication by the documentary work of two far better-known figures, the novelist Erskine Caldwell and the famous "girl-photographer" Margaret Bourke-White. In 1936, the same year that Agee and Evans were in Alabama, Bourke-White and Caldwell were also in the South working on what would become *You Have Seen Their Faces*, a book popular and influential enough to be fairly described as the *"Uncle Tom's Cabin* of tenant farming."[76] Its publication and success, Agee must have felt, made their project obsolete—until, that is, Agee hit upon the device of making *Praise* itself a self-reflective critique of the documentary form.

Praise directly responded to both *You Have Seen Their Faces* and the other documentary projects of the time, such as those sponsored by the federal New Deal agencies. Like other successful political calls to action such as *Uncle Tom's Cabin*, Caldwell and Bourke-White's documentary book was not above either sentimentality or dramatic excess to make its point. Bourke-White's photos were all captioned to heighten the images' drama and pathos. But (a disclaimer at the beginning of the book tells us) the quoted words next to the pictures were not those of the people represented. Rather, to "avoid unnecessary individualization," the captions reflected "the authors' own conceptions of the sentiments of the individuals portrayed."

By contrast to Caldwell and Bourke-White's book, however, many of the other documentaries against which Agee wrote were calmly social scientific, factually accurate, and politically tame, partaking of the new languages of professional expertise and bureaucracy. This was especially true of the many documentary projects sponsored by or related to federal-government programs, which, if they had a political slant at all, tended to promote New Deal reforms. For example, writers for the 1939 Federal Writers' Project collection of informant narratives, *These Are Our Lives*, were explicitly directed to "avoid the expression of judgment," and to relate the stories of their informants "in the words of the persons who are consulted."[77] These writers were, moreover, required to follow an "Outline of Life Histories"—appended to the finished book—that detailed specific categories of information to be elicited by the writers from their informants: "Family," "Education," "Income," "Attitudes Toward Occupation and Kind of Life" (of which the first subheading is "Pride or Shame in Work"), "Politics" (focusing on voting habits), "Religion and Morals," "Medical Needs," "Diet," "Miscellaneous Observations" (mostly about the size and cleanliness of the subject's dwelling), and "Use of Time" (focusing on the subject's daily routine).[78]

The structure of *Praise* critiques both the sentimental representations of poverty found in documentaries such as *You Have Seen their Faces*, and the more social-scientific pretensions of the soberly "objective" versions of the form. In response to Caldwell and Bourke-White's practice of devising captions for the photos, Agee not only insisted on leaving Evans's intentionally undramatic images uncaptioned, but repeatedly insisted in the text of the book that the images spoke a profounder truth than words. For him, the captioning was clearly a species of fakery, and in his case "truth" was only to be had by some kind of immediate relationship to the photos. His interest in "truth," in other words, was not simply a matter of factual detail.

Indeed, Agee also criticizes the obsessive need to get at the "facts," as exhibited in such books as *These Are Our Lives*, by parodying its rigid structuring of information. In *Praise*, the "Design of Book Two" (in lieu of a table of contents) offers such basic headings as "Money," "Shelter," "Clothing," "Education," and "Work"; and we are also given an outline for the section on "Shelter" that is itself a vaguely nonsensical poetic rendering of these categories. It reads, in part:

NOTES

> Beauty
> Relations and averages
> Further comments on relations and averages
> Age
> General habitability
> Sanitation and lighting

> · · ·

RECESSIONAL AND VORTEX
(126)

The excessively social-scientific language of "relations and averages" spoofs the scientific pretenses of documentary projects, while its juxtaposition with the intriguing "recessional and vortex" quickly suggests other descriptive possibilities outside the frankly realistic social-scientific range of traditional documentary reportage. Indeed, Agee insists that there are "less sociological and more attractive things about [the tenant farmers]; though these in turn are more difficult to define, or even to understand, and would be merely tiresome to those whose intelligence is set entirely on Improving the Sharecropper, and who feel there's no time to waste on petty detail" (215).

The range and plasticity of Agee's anger at the emotional detachment of the social scientist and the condescension of the social do-gooder is typical of much of the prose of this book. In a remarkable run of invective, Agee at one point identifies a "corruptive odor of inverted snobbery, marxian, journalistic, jewish, and liberal logomachia, emotional blackmail, negrophilia, belated transference, penis-envy, gynecological flurry and fairly good will" that has infected the representation of poor white southerners (455–56). Though he covers a lot of territory here, his identification of the twin evils of "penis-envy" and "gynecological flurry" probably refer most directly to fellow documentarist Margaret Bourke-White, whom he renames "maggie berkwitz." Also included in the text of *Praise* is a New York *Post* "women's page"–style interview with Bourke-White, detailing her "superior red coat," her tango dancing, and her horseback riding. Against the rest of the content of *Praise*, or even against Bourke-White's own condescending pronouncements about the subjects she photographed in *You Have Seen Their Faces*, these observations do make her appear vulgarly bourgeois (450–54). (Of course, this nasty dig at Bourke-White also represents a revenge against Agee's most important competitor in the documentation of southern rural poverty.[79]) Indeed, Agee's wrath would seem to encompass anyone who seems somehow to have falsified the sharecroppers, by reducing their lives to something less than a fundamentally ineffable humanity, what he elsewhere calls their "human divinity" (79). The documentary form has apparently failed, and, equally clearly, the participants in this form have revealed themselves to be somehow immoral.

Agee's central problem thus becomes one of adequately representing the tenant farmers' "human divinity," and thereby rescuing himself from the immorality of misrepresentation. The impossibility of this task, and the resulting self-disgust of the author, is acutely represented in the often agonized pages of *Praise*. Even after the book's publication, Agee wrote to his mentor Father Flye that he thought it "a sinful book at least in all degrees of 'falling short of the mark' and I think in more corrupt ways as well."[80] Yet he also resolves this representational problem to some degree simply by asserting that the "divinity" he is seeking is there to be found. He hints, in other words, at the possibility of grace.

This possibility is in some sense implicit in the phrase, "recessional and vortex," one word suggesting religious ritual, and the other evocative of Poundian modernist aesthetics. These two sites, in turn, correspond to the dual role of the cultural-religious elite that T. S. Eliot advocated in his *Notes toward the Definition of Culture*. In *Praise*, Agee in effect takes up the Eliotic cultural and religious priesthood, the first in the formal innovation of his book, and the second in his repeated assertions that his is an encounter with sublimity, a grappling with "those problems which stand thickly forth like light from all matter, triviality, chance, intention, and record in the body, of being, of truth, of conscience, of hope, of hatred, of beauty, of indignation, of guilt, of betrayal, of innocence, of forgiveness, of vengeance, of guardianship, of an indenominable fate, predicament, destination, and God" (10).

Here, we may begin to see how closely Agee's rejection of the documentary comes to dovetail with the cultural criticism of the *Partisan Review*, particularly in relation to its obsession with the proper role of the intellectual. The traditional documentary book fails for Agee in precisely the same way that representational art fails for Greenberg. Its contents are literally captionable: reducible to easy sentiments and categories, and therefore it is both antiart and politically suspect. Moreover, like those who would promote any kind of politics/kitsch, his fellow documentarists are fundamentally morally culpable for trying to reduce complexity in this way. They are, in effect, middlebrow: interpreters, translators, captioners of the "truth." The truth he understands, on the other hand, is fundamentally unsayable; like taste or religion, it can only be perceived by the chosen: "For in the immediate world, everything is to be discerned, *for him who can discern it*, and centrally and simply, without either dissection into science, or digestion into art, but with the whole of consciousness, seeking to perceive it as it stands" (11; emphasis mine).

In identifying both "art" and "science" as the antitheses of this creative process, Agee is clearly opposing himself to both middlebrow aesthetics (which merely "pretty up") and the "science" of both New Deal bureaucratism and classical Marxist aesthetic and political theory. However, it also reveals Agee's relationship to the tenant farmers—for, clearly, he sees his role in their relationship as one in which *he* understands *their* truth. Thus, Agee quickly dismisses the townspeople's rather unholy opinions of the Gudgers, the Woodses, and the Rickettses, because they fail to understand, as Agee understands, the tenant farmers' fundamental "human divinity." It also explains why Agee dismisses as a "put-up job" the tenant farmers' efforts to dress themselves and their children in their best clothes before having their pictures taken (367): as the interpreter of their "truth," he feels perfectly justified in controlling their representation.

In this concern for preserving the discrete class-based functions of cultural actors, Agee's cultural politics once again resemble Eliot's and Macdonald's, in their similar belief that cultural strata ought to remain distinct. In a controversial article, entitled "Folk Art," that appeared in the *Partisan Review* in 1944, Agee warned that the crossing of boundaries between "folk art" and highbrow art (as in, he suggested, the musical *Oklahoma*, or Paul Robeson's portrayal of the title character in *Othello*) resulted in the bastardization of both kinds of art—or, in the creation of the middlebrow:

> The non-folk crosses to the folk or the pseudo-folk . . . or . . . presumes to "dignify" the folk by "classicizing" it, the "classical" by folksifying it. Here, in the artist and in the audience, there is an essential ignorance of, contempt for, or lack of confidence in, both ends or kinds of art; and there is, on both sides, through tacit semi-conscious mutual contempt, a lowering or full dismissal of ethical and moral standards.[81]

Similarly, Agee muses in the pages of *Praise* that the traditional skills of "reading and writing" may not represent the appropriate education for "natural artists" and "natural craftsmen" such as several of the sharecroppers' children (302). To teach these children to read or to let the tenant farmers attempt to assume the trappings of middle-class respectability and be photographed in their good clothes would amount to a corruption of the tenant farmers' own unique "folk art," which would, in turn, amount to "a lowering or full dismissal of ethical and moral standards."

Yet Agee does not seem quite as interested as Macdonald in the project of policing these boundaries of cultural purity. Instead, the tenant farmers' authentic "folk" selves suggest another representational problem for Agee's project. If they are already pure, are they not also sufficient unto themselves? This problem might seem similar to the contemporary ethnographer's concerns about the politics of representing the other. But where one provisional solution to the contemporary ethnographic dilemma is offered in simply giving over representational control to one's subjects—in handing over the camera to the Gudgers—this solution was not available to Agee. For Agee, it was as if *representation itself* was already a violation of their folk authenticity. Punning interestingly on "writing," Agee at one point muses, "I have no right, here, no real right, much as I want it, and could never earn it, and should I write of it, must defend it against my kind" (410).

The tentative solution he found to the problem of not having the right to write, and of having to defend it against his "kind" (both intellectuals and the middle class) was not only to trouble the norms of representation in his revision of the documentary form, but to replace representation *with writing*, in his persistent overexplication. His repeated insistence on how we must read the book and the tenant-farmers' lives as signs of "truth" and "divinity," are, in effect, stand-ins for the very fact that Agee himself cannot say anything about them without departing from the "truth." Just as he must tell us repeatedly that the farmers are "divine" (precisely because he can't tell us why), he must also finally tell us that the book is "great," precisely because this greatness has not exactly been given content. The last pages of the book describe Agee and Evans's rapt attention at the sound of what they think must be foxes calling to one another in the dark. Agee writes,

> One time it would be sexual; another, just a casual colloquy; another, a challenge; another, a signal or warning; another, a comment on us; another, some simple and desperate effort at mutual location; another, most intense and masterful irony; another, laughter; another, triumph; another, a masterpiece of parody of any one, any combination, or all of these assigned or implicit tones: but at all times it was beyond even the illusion of full apprehension, and was noble, frightening and distinguished: a work of great, private and unambitious art which was irrelevant to audience. (466)

The sound of the foxes is clearly a kind of summary of the text of *Praise* itself, the foxes being both the tenant farmers and Agee and Evans. But it is significant that Agee must offer us this summary, only to conclude that its final effect is "a work of great, private and unambitious art . . . irrelevant to audience." After insisting that it is "beyond even the illusion of full apprehension," Agee here informs us *how* we were to read the book. With reverence sufficing in the place of understanding, we are to assume that like the tenant farmers, *Praise* is full of "divinity." In this respect, *Praise* is indeed the ultimate antidocumentary, resisting representation to the point that the meaning of the tenant-farmers' lives—and of the book—is reduced to a declarative utterance.

On the other hand, what makes this work so contradictory and frustrating is Agee's almost petulant insistence on representing in the face of its very impossibility. Indeed—and this is the part of the project that is a documentary of the tenant farmers toward a new end—in another respect, the tenant farmers become crucial to an aesthetic project of truth-telling in the book, one which ultimately concerns those very timely problems of the role of the intellectual as a preserver of "culture," and his relationship to the middle class.

Much of the text of *Praise* is given over to an extremely detailed account of exactly the kinds of things he implicitly critiqued the standard Federal Writers' Project documentaries for providing: laborious descriptions of the conditions and material surroundings of the tenant farmers. Even when Agee prowls through their houses, peering into the family Bible and revealing the contents of closets and drawers, his description of what he finds there is often the driest and minutest of reportage ("The bed, between the hall door and the front wall, in the angle of the two walls, the head toward the wall, about six inches out from each wall, the foot at the window"; 158). Once again, this is likely a parody of the mentality of bureaucratic cataloguing present in the government-sponsored documentary projects. But the actual things he uncovers ("The two parts of a broken button. / A small black hook, lying on its eye. / Another small black hook"; 169) are as meaningless as the found poems he makes out of the scraps of newspaper he also finds in their houses ("NEW STRIKE MOVE /

EARED AS PEACE / NFAB SPLITS UP"; 167). This insistence on the significance of the minutiae of the tenant farmers' lives again conforms perfectly to Greenberg's aesthetic theories: having ripped these scraps out of their context (including, of course, their political context) they are now "safe" for the production of a purely formalist art. On the other hand, there is also an incredible tedium to Agee's reportage, that not only suggests Agee's patent boredom with his enterprise, but also undercuts whatever artistic pretensions this gesture might have.

This banality of his descriptions is all the more remarkable in comparison with Agee's fascinating, and utterly passionate, explication of the similarly slim material of Louise Gudger's elementary-school textbooks, which were found by Agee to be as "rich as a poem; twisted full of contents, symptoms, and betrayals" (299). Significantly, the textbooks' "contents, symptoms, and betrayals" are not related to the lives of the tenant farmers, but are, rather, the products of the misfired good intentions of educators talking down to their charges. We return, in other words, to another version of the far more interesting problem of intellectuals' troubled relationship to the tenant farmers.

As Agee's comments on education make clear, the reader of *Praise* is explicitly implicated in this problem. Expressing his real horror at the "crime" of human beings "cheated and choked" of their potential through the failures of the educational system (one of which is, not surprisingly, to insist on uplift, when some sharecroppers' children are "naturally" where they ought to be), he confesses, "my self-disgust is less in my ignorance, and far less in my 'failure' to 'defend' or 'support' the statement, than in my inability to state it even so far as I see it, and in my inability to blow out the brains with it of you who take what it is talking of lightly, or not seriously enough" (307). In a manner typical of Agee, self-disgust thus becomes an externally projected fury. The violence of this passage is in part in the patent fact that "we" cannot possibly take the problem he locates seriously enough.

In this sense, Agee's anger, and his moral view in general, are in direct conformity with that classic ethical position of the Cold War intellectual: liberal guilt. Lionel Trilling was quick to recognize this, in his generally positive review of *Praise*, when he suggested that the book as a whole insisted on reflection on one crucial question: "How may we—'we' being the relatively fortunate middle class that reads books and experiences emotions—how may we feel about the—and the word itself proclaims the difficulty—underprivileged?"[82] Here, Trilling exactly identifies the site of Agee's central critique of the documentary form, which is to shift the work of explication from the traditional focus of the documentary, the lives of the tenant farmers, to another site altogether, the views and "feelings" of that class of people represented by the "we" of Trilling's question: the "relatively fortunate middle class," represented both by the author and his presumed readers. Moreover, the word "underprivileged" seems so apt to Trilling precisely because it situates the sharecroppers in relation to their other, the "privileged." Thus, as Trilling so astutely recognized, the work of representing the sharecroppers is turned into a project of getting at the condition of the self—specifically, one's sense of one's own sinfulness. (As Agee confessed in a letter to Father Flye, "I have a fuzzy, very middle-class, and in a bad sense of the word, very Christian mind, and a very clouded sensibility."[83])

This helps account for the fact that our real sense of the tenant farmers is structured most clearly through Agee and Evans's encounter with them. It also explains why this encounter with them often takes on the features of a fraught and embarrassed sexual seduction. In a central passage of the book describing Agee and Evans's first encounter with Mrs. Ricketts, he imagines her fear and self-consciousness at being looked at by "alien, town-dressed eyes":

> To you it was as if you and your children and your husband and these others were stood there naked in front of the cold absorption of the camera in all your shame and pitiableness to be pried into and laughed at; and your eyes were wild with fury and shame and fear, and the tendons of your little neck were tight, the whole time, and one hand continually twitched and tore in the rotted folds of your skirt like the hand of a little girl who must recite before adults, and there was not a thing you could do, nothing, not a word of remonstrance you could make, my dear, my love, my little crazy, terrified child. (363–64)

Though describing another person's acute embarrassment at being exposed to the view of strangers (resulting partially from being caught by the visitors while still wearing her tattered work clothes), Agee translates this moment of distance and antipathy—to him as much as to Evans, holding the camera—into one of intimacy and understanding. Or rather, Agee's sympathy allows an intimate understanding of Mrs. Ricketts's "pain," while she must be seduced into "trust":

> yet, at the very last, just as we left, the unforgiving face, the eyes, of Mrs. Ricketts at her door: which has since stayed as a torn wound and sickness at the center of my chest, and perhaps more than any other thing has insured what I do not yet know: that we shall have to return, even in the face of causing further pain, until that mutual wounding shall have been won and healed, until she shall fear us no further, yet not in forgetfulness but through ultimate trust, through love. (370)

The final goal of this seduction is access to the farmers' secrets: a chance for Agee (who occasionally identifies himself in the text as a "spy") to prowl alone through their houses, to open drawers and closets, and to peer into the family Bible.[84] The experience of snooping through their belongings reminds Agee of adolescent masturbations in his grandfather's house, and he writes, "It is not entirely otherwise now, in this inhuman solitude, the nakedness of this body which sleeps here before me, this tabernacle upon whose desecration I so reverentially proceed" (137). Just as he imagined Mrs. Ricketts's exposure before the "cold absorption" of Evans's camera, Agee now imagines the body of the tenant farmers' house open before him.

In this seduction, leading up to the opening of the Gudgers' house for his inspection, the seduced tenant farmers are coded as feminine: the passive, pliant, and the objects of his, and our, gaze. This role is literalized as Agee reveals his self-flattering sexual fantasies about Emma Woods and his erotic meditations about the ten-year-old Louise Gudger (62, 400–401). Agee is aware enough of this dynamic to speak of the "obscenity" of "pry[ing] intimately into the lives of an undefended and appallingly damaged group of human beings" (7), but he also justifies his actions, simply, as being in the service of the "truth:" "I would do just as badly to simplify or eliminate myself from this picture as to simplify or invent character, places, or atmospheres. A chain of truths did actually weave itself and run through: it is their texture that I want to represent, not betray, nor pretty up into art" (240). Thus, while self-flattering, the eroticism of his interaction with the tenant farmers is also metaphorical for Agee's creative process.

Much of this subject is addressed in the tripartite section of *Praise* entitled "On the Porch." This title refers specifically to the porch of the Gudgers' house, where Agee and Evans were allowed to sleep.[85] In the second part of "On the Porch," Agee details his opinions on realism, naturalism, description, art, truth, and much more. Indeed, this section may be the core of the book, for, as Agee explains in a footnote, "On the Porch" was "intended still in part as a preface or opening, but also as a frame and as an undertone and as the set stage and center of action, in relation to which all other parts of this volume are intended as flashbacks, foretastes, illuminations and contradictions" (245). The centrality of the porch, the entryway to the house, connects the accessibility of the tenant farmers' physical house, and hence their lives, with Agee's creative process. There, on the Gudgers' porch, Agee experiences a transcendence, a perception of what he calls the "totally *actual*" that is both the creation of a genuine art ("truth") and something like a spritualized description of orgasm:

> There was, by our minds, our memories, our thoughts and feelings, some combination, some generalizing, some art, and science; but none of the close-kneed priggishness of science, and none of the formalism and straining and lily-gilding of art. All the length of the body and all its parts and functions were participating, and were being realized and rewarded, inseparable from the mind, identical with it: and all, everything, that the mind touched, was actuality, and all, everything, that the mind touched . . . revealed, of its self, truth, which in its very nature was joy, which must be the end of art, of investigation, and of all anyhow human existence. (225)

Here, Agee's "truth" is opposed to both the ("close-kneed" and priggish) "science" of the dry New Deal documentary book and the ("straining" and "lily-gilding") of more middlebrow and populist representations of sharecroppers.

It involves what is in effect a coital encounter between the artist, using "the length of the body and all its parts and functions" and the material of the sharecroppers' lives, whether this be their actual bodies or their otherwise meaningless possessions. In this case, it is the porch, the same site from which he rapturously listens to the foxes' "colloquies," that seems to serve this purpose of making "art."

It is also the site and source of a transcendence of a more concrete kind—of Agee's own "middle-class" origins. This becomes clear when his raptures on the Gudgers' porch are compared to the porches of other, less penetrable, dwellings. Driving past the houses in the middle-class neighborhoods of a nearby town, Agee connects *their* porches with further masturbatory memories of his grandfather's house:

> On the cool, gray-painted, shaded boards of one of these middleclass porches my body stretched its length and became the loose and milky flesh of its childhood who listened, hours long in the terrible space and enlargement of silence, while the air lay in the metal magnolia leaves asleep, once in a while moving its dreaming mouth on the shapeless word of a dream or lifting and twisting one heavy thigh and creating in the leaves a chaffering and dry chime, and I, this eleven-year-old, male, half-shaped child, pressing between the sharp hip bone and the floor my erection, and, thinking and imagining what I was able of the world and its people and my grief and hunger and boredom, lay shaded from the bird-stifling brilliance of the afternoon and was sullen and sick, nearly crying, striking over and over again the heel of my bruised hand against the sooty floor and sweating and shaking my head in a sexual and murderous anger and despair. (379–80)

Awakened from this recollection, Agee realizes, "I was again in Centerboro driving on the slow flotation of silence, door by door and yard by yard in all its detail home by home in a town I hated that was drained, drenched, drowned in the desperateness of sunday," (380). These middle-class houses connote stillness and vapidity and piety, the antithesis of artistic transcendence, and the quintessence of middlebrow sentiment. Nevertheless, they manage to awaken in Agee whole drifts of childhood memory, including thoughts of all those he has "harmed," and they send him into a tailspin of self-doubt that encompasses his artistic ambitions, his romantic life, and even lead him to briefly consider suicide. In other words, as sites closely connected with his own history and memory, these middle-class porches are gateways to depths of despair, self-loathing, and self-recognition well beyond the interior possibilities of the houses of the Gudgers and the Rickettses. And yet, like Chester Boles's expression, they are also fundamentally, and literally, impenetrable: they are inappropriable for the purposes of art, precisely because they are connected to the middlebrow, its taboo now figured in the sexual terms of onanism or even incest. Put another way, there is a kind of sexual normativeness to Agee's preference in porches. Since the middle-class porches (associated with his grandfather and his own childhood) are too close to him, he turns instead to penetrating the houses of the (feminized) tenant farmers. In this way, he is no longer one of the things he fears he is when he flees in disgust from the houses of Centerboro, "Just an individualizing intellectual. Bad case of infantilism. And——you, too." (385).

Agee's text thus works in two ways. On the one hand, it thoroughly dismantles the project of documenting the lives of the tenant farmers as being morally bankrupt, cruel, the stuff of kitsch, and, in some sense, formally and conceptually *impossible*. On the other hand, *Praise* also develops a new project in which the tenant farmers' representation is crucial: the exploration of the interior spaces of the liberal intellectual himself. Anxious about his own southern, middle-class, and probably also middlebrow, origins, the intellectual finds in the poor tenant farmers, their lives, their struggles, their houses and porches, the objects through which he can think about and locate himself without risking contamination from the corruptive features of his own class background. And yet, he has already shown the impossibility and immorality of representing these others. His new project of self-representation is thus rendered similarly fraught with immorality and impossibility. So Agee is caught, in the impossibility and necessity of his task, which is ultimately one of self-examination.

This, I think, is the work that would find favor with Cold War literary intellectuals, many of whom were increasingly drawn to psychoanalysis, and many of whom saw in Agee's anger and hand-wringing a model for their own— infinitely complex, fascinatingly ambiguous—position of self-imposed marginality in relation to the political and ethical questions of their day. Part of this marginalization is reflected in a retreat from cultural representation of an older form, associated with the gesture of intercultural comparison, so typical of the thirties, and now discredited during the years surrounding World War II. In Agee's revision of the documentary form, the point is not to show how "they" get along (or do things differently), but to reveal *oneself*, through one's (thoroughly dissected) relation to them. The self is recentered as the object of interest, the reason for writing.

Agee's reworking of this most anthropological of literary forms may thus be a sign of the way the interests of the producers and critics of "highbrow" literature seemed in the post–World War II decades to part company with those of anthropology, whose practitioners were, of course, still in the business of describing other cultures. And yet, there is a basic way in which Agee's project also conformed to these post-Boasian "cultural" projects of the Cold War academy. In the Area Studies model, the study of other countries served as a kind of weak comparativism, in which the Soviet Union, for example, served (like Agee's tenant farmers) as a player in a larger narrative that ultimately was about the United States, its peculiarly moral democratic structure, its special role in world politics and history. In American Studies, too, there was a new emphasis on cultural self-examination, but without even this reference to the cultural other. There, the focus was on the uniqueness of the American character, and on the complexities and ambiguities of a national subject now fully seeming to be at the center of the universe.

7

On Getting Rid of Culture: An Inconclusive Conclusion

And an idea, such as that of Culture, is apt to lead
to consequences which its author cannot foresee and
probably will not like.
  (T. S. Eliot)

IN THIS FINAL CHAPTER, I will jump ahead to the present, to briefly interrogate the postmodern context of "culture," and the legacy of its modernist antecedents sketched out in the previous chapters. Obviously, "culture" is very much with us, and very much a central term of our debates, many of which have their origins in the earlier parts of this century. Culture is, moreover, still a term related to the articulation of social space—indeed, so much so, that it is not surprising that it has come under new scrutiny in the light of postmodern critiques of "totalization" and totalizing theory: frequently invoked to describe bounded space and finite identities, "culture" seems in the context of postmodernism to have its definite conceptual shortcomings.[1]

In this conclusion, I will explore both "culture's" limits and the limits of its critique by examining arguments that have been made recently by both anthropologists and literary scholars for the complete *abandonment* of "culture" as a critical term.[2] I will not suggest here that such radical arguments against "culture" comprise a dominant, or even an emergent, view among people invested in one way or another in things widely thought of as "cultural." Nor, as will become clear, am I convinced that proposals to simply abolish a critical term will do what their advocates believe it will do. But I do find the drama of this proposal fascinating. The rhetorical gesture of clearing the "cultural" decks indicates at least a severe state of terminological uncertainty. More radically, it suggests a repudiation of the historical and philosophical contexts in which "culture" is thought to be a key term. It is thus an excellent site for examining the current status of the modernist culture concept, in light of new theoretical pressures. First, however, it is important to establish some sense of the deep continuities between our "culture" and its earlier counterpart.

Culture and Totality

It is not hard to see a continuity between contemporary debates on "culture" and those constructions of culture from the recent past. Indeed, I would suggest that the lineaments of many of the most visible contemporary debates about "culture" are residua of the early Cold War era addressed in the last chapter. Most obviously, the cultural-Right's obsession with the present moment's supposed loss of standards and the falling away from the great normative truths of "Western civilization" are strongly nostalgic for this moment of nationalist triumphalism—despite their occasional references back to Matthew Arnold. Similarly, much of the hand-wringing about the political inefficacy of both literary criticism and academic professional life has its roots in the New York intellectuals' peculiar *Schadenfreude* over their own political irrelevance.

What is interesting, however, is that both of these positions have reemerged with such force in the very moment of the post–Cold War breakdown of the conditions of intellectual labor established in that period. It is as if, as the institutional structure of government-supported academia is increasingly eroded, intellectuals incline—again, nostalgically—back to the debates of the days in which this partnership was first established. In the face of cutbacks in public funding for higher education and the arts, would it be so surprising that literary intellectuals *longed* for the days when culture was what one privately worried about, in full awareness of its political insignificance? Meanwhile, it is not too hard to see attacks from the Right about such topics as relativism, isolationism, and the apparent un-Americanism of multiculturalism and "Victim Studies" as attempts to recuperate some of the nationalist cohesion—and imperialist agenda—of the United States during its last "good war."

Yet, as far as the institutions of "culture" go, there may be other, less obvious legacies worth pursuing. Immanuel Wallerstein has recently pointed out that the institutional structures of Cold War Area Studies (and, I would add, American Studies) set up the structures of the very institutional sites often attacked by the nostalgic Right: Women's, African-American, and Ethnic Studies programs. Created in response to student-, as opposed to government-generated political pressure—and operating, it might be added, with very different funding structures than their government-funded predecessors—these new emergences from the Area Studies model would not only complicate the "us" and "them" binaries of Cold War thinking, but also revive certain features of a less normative, more critically comparative "culture." As Wallerstein points out, the creation of institutional structures can have all kinds "unintended consequences"—just as (T. S. Eliot pointed out long ago) can deployments of fluid concepts like "culture."[3]

While we have thus seen the reemergence of some of the particularistic energies of earlier moments, now articulated less on regional, than on racial, ethnic, and gender lines, we have also seen new universalizations emerge around the concept of culture. New "cultural" modes of investigation, including the new historicism and cultural studies, are strongly indebted to a textual model of culture, perhaps most famously elaborated by Clifford Geertz, with his concept of "thick description."[4] While these approaches have thus to some extent revived the close allegiance between literary scholars and anthropologists, they also imply the existence of a rather fluid—indeed, a potentially illimitable—object, readable via the operations of literary criticism: the *cultural* text.

This relatively recent vision of culture as suggesting a strangely unbounded field of intellectual inquiry may have its origins, again, in the 1950s and 1960s, or rather, in an attempt to combat the reductivisms and universalizations of the kinds of theoretical work being done in the social sciences of that period. As evidence of this point, I will refer to a book review written in 1978 by anthropologist Marshall Sahlins, which makes a devastating case not only against Marvin Harris's popularizing *Cannibals and Kings*, but against Harris's version of cultural ecology: cultural materialism.[5] In his refutation of what he saw as Harris's highly reductive thesis that the Aztecs practiced ritual cannibalism for the purposes of supplementing their protein-deficient diet, Sahlins offers another account of the complexities of Aztec ritual:

> In connection with various sacrifices, different categories of people would ritually fast, bleed themselves, paint themselves, climb mountains, go into and come out of seclusion, stage farces, drink pulque, eat earth, offer valuable gifts to the gods, take ceremonial baths, parade in the streets, play games, hold sham fights, practice chastity, hunt deer, sing and dance for days on end, beg alms, erect and adorn idols, prepare and eat special delicacies, and much else.[6]

Much else, indeed. Sahlins goes on to argue that in order to really get at the meaning of the complex act of ritual cannibalism, we also needed to consider the costumes the participants wore; the range of animals and plant products that were also sacrificed; the genders, local origins, and social statuses of the various human victims; the social statuses of the people by whom the sacrifices were sponsored; the different ritual significances and roles the victims were understood to take on (45, 46). The explanation of the event—and of the "culture" of which it was a part—is in its complexity of specifics.

In the context of Sahlins's quarrel with Harris, the overall effect of this dazzling list of contextual specifics is to provide a sense of the ineffable complexity of a feature of Aztec culture. As such, the description not only offers a formidable argumentative weapon against attempts to subsume the "cultural" to the residual, ephemeral, or superstructural, but it also joins a venerable tradition of describing the cultural by resorting to the rhetorical device of enumeration. Sahlins's description thus harkens back not only to Raymond Williams's cultural bus trip through Wales, discussed in Chapter 1, not to mention the jumble of detritus in the Hollywood studio lot of Nathanael West's imagination, from Chapter 5, but recalls T. S. Eliot's famous definition of "culture" as "all the characteristic activities and interests of a people: Derby Day, Henley Regatta, Cowes, the twelfth of August, a cup final, the dog races, the pin table, the dart board, Wensleydale cheese, boiled cabbage cut into sections, beetroot in vinegar, nineteenth-century Gothic churches and the music of Elgar."[7] Culture, in this construction, winds up being both minute and tangible—indeed, as homely as beetroot in vinegar—while also amply demonstrating what Daniel Cottom has described as the relationship between "culture" and the "metaphor of totality."[8] Such cultural descriptions are, of course, endlessly inclusive; as Eliot reminds us, "The reader can make his own list."[9]

Even aside from such strategies of enumeration, however, there is much evidence to support Cottom's point about the relationship between conceptions of "culture" and various constructions of totality. From Arnold's "total perfection" and E. B. Tylor's "complex whole" to Brooks's complex dichotomies and Ruth Benedict's God-given cups of clay, cultural discourse is wrapped up in the problem of defining the whole.[10] But we should be clear that "culture's" relationship to the "metaphor of totality" extends beyond the spatial metaphorics of bounded groupings, such as in tribes or nations. As the Sahlins example shows us, this infinitely complex "culture" can also imply a mode of analysis.[11]

In Sahlins's account, Aztec ritual cannibalism is only understandable once we grasp the totality of its features; in turn, these features (from alms begging to obsidian knives) are keys to the comprehension of the whole. Of course, they do not stand alone either and require their own elucidation, doubtless replete with their own particularities. Sahlins explains in fascinating detail, for instance, how the sacrificial victim is transformed from being a prisoner of war, to being his captor's "son" (entailing various complex obligations and expectations of kinship), to being invested with a supernatural power so significant that his sacrifice and consumption have divine effects on the ritual's beneficiaries. Then Sahlins extends his analysis outward: the sacrifice thus elucidated in terms of its participants' real and symbolic social positions, Sahlins goes on to account for the ritual's function in terms of Aztec cosmology—the larger symbolic system—and explains that the symbolic relations of the ritual act are reproduced in other aspects of Aztec society, so that a woman giving birth and a merchant who acquires certain kinds of goods are both likened ritually to the warrior who takes prisoners (46–47). Though my account is of course a simplification of a simplification, the end result of such an analysis is the comprehension of a "dynamic" evolving "system" that is somehow both Aztec ritual sacrifice and "Aztec culture" itself. As Sahlins puts it, "[R]eproductive sacrifice, transforming death into life through the offering, was so implicated in social relations, politics, and economics that it ended by becoming true: Aztec culture *was* reproduced by human sacrifice" (47; italics his).

This comment should allow us to establish several important points about how Sahlins's cultural analysis operates. First, though Sahlins addresses Aztec culture in terms of such extrinsic categories as economics and politics, this analysis finally conforms very neatly to what we would assume to be the intrinsic, *Aztec* account of cannibalism: that it is part of a rite necessary to the maintenance of balance and harmony. Thus, Sahlins offers us another example of the way "culture" seems to theoretically resolve certain key oppositions: the scientific analysis and the lived experience, the view from afar and the insider's perspective. Put another way, "culture" appears here to mediate between ideology—whose simplest definition is the tales "we" (insiders) tell ourselves about the way our society works—and critique, which must presume a vantage point at least theoretically "outside." But as we shall see in attending to arguments for abandoning "culture," the possibility of the term's somehow mediating or incorporating both extrinsic and intrinsic perspectives is far from untroubled.

Another point to be learned about the logic of "culture" from Sahlins is that the complexity of culture resists simplistic models of causality. In Sahlins's account, ritual cannibalism is so multiply "implicated" in Aztec life that it does not make sense to ask whether the economic structure *caused* the "cultural" phenomenon of ritual cannibalism (or vice versa). Rather, the two are shown to be complexly inter-implicated. Indeed, one gathers from Sahlins's account that, whether one began with ritual sacrifice, the complex symbolism of the hummingbird, an analysis of the political structure, or the war cries of midwives, the "system" could be similarly interpreted. Thus, the logic that defines the "totality" that is "Aztec culture" is not one of lesser parts combining to produce the whole, but of stringed connections, where the singular "cultural" phenomenon, from the smallest hummingbird to the largest pyramid (and the concretest obsidian knife to the most abstract kinship system) is significant on the level of the more abstract conceptual "cultural" whole. "Culture" is created, in other words, not through the logic of synecdoche, but by metonymy.

It would be a significant unfairness to reduce Sahlins's long and complex quarrel with functionalism and instrumentalism—including what he sees as the Marxian instrumentalism of "base-superstructure" models—to this brief characterization.[12] Besides, my point is not to critique Sahlins's work from the slim example of a book review, but to show how compelling this construction of "culture" can be. I would argue that it has become fairly common in work dealing generally with things "cultural" to replicate such metonymic chains of association, without offering any theorization about how the features of the analysis, the links in the chain, actually connect.[13] It is hardly surprising when these relationships go untheorized that "culture" too begins to look a bit amorphous. At which point there appears something like the flip side of the old base-superstructure question: if we don't imagine "culture" as a *part* of a larger system, then what is it? The temptation, I think, is to conceive of "culture" *itself* as total, and then perhaps to worry—if one bothers to worry—that one's invocation of "culture" is either a reification, or a banality ("everything is cultural").[14]

In other words, it is difficult to generalize about the conceptual relationship between "culture" and totality. Sometimes what is at stake is the easily recognizable totality of a bounded population or grouping; sometimes it is as amorphous as the entirety of that which can be thought and said. Frequently, these different problems of totality are confused in one description or invocation of "culture." Nevertheless, we will see the persistence with which the problem of totality vexes conceptions of "culture," leading ultimately to some serious arguments for the rejection of "culture" as a critical term. Addressing the very real problems of exclusion, marginalization, and hierarchy, the theorists I shall discuss all show how various conceptions of totality, represented rhetorically by "culture," are necessarily incomplete, and are mystifications as well. These theorists also engage with questions about the limits of knowledge itself, another conceptual totality, once again described in terms of "culture." In their suspicion of these "cultural" wholes, they join theorists from diverse postmodern perspectives, who have likewise interrogated diverse modernist constructions of totality, on the grounds that these are descriptively insufficient, or else obscure relations of power and dominance.

The specific complaints against "culture" are, however, much more focused. I will concentrate first on arguments made from within the field of anthropology. Though these are in some respects predicated on assumptions about the special relationship of "culture" to that discipline, they also address the possibility that "culture" may not be an adequate framework for confronting differences among people of perspective and position. The section following will concentrate on the equally provocative argument that "culture" is a poor substitute for another disfavored description of groups of humans, namely "race." Throughout, however, we will see a strong continuity in the deployment of many of the common tropes of "culture," even as these writers argue for the term's obsolescence.

Of Eurocentrism and Cultural Relativism

Virginia R. Dominguez's "Invoking Culture: The Messy Side of 'Cultural Politics' " provides excellent evidence of the kind of terminological uneasiness over "culture" that I have described. In this essay, Dominguez, an anthropologist, complains that at a conference of social scientists she attended, their supposedly common subject matter—"cultural policies and national identities"—covered a dizzying array of national sites, methodologies, and practices, and was, indeed, united only by a largely unquestioned invocation of "culture" to address widely disparate contexts and agendas. She observes that, "For some of these scholars, culture is an object of discourse, for others an analytic concept, and for still others the empirical attributes and properties of bounded populations." Given such confusions, Dominguez sensibly concludes, "for a much-used word, culture has little communicative efficiency."[15] We shall see, however, that Dominguez is for her part clear about what "culture" means; she sees, and is disturbed by, the high-cultural, elitist, connotations of the term.

This is in some respects an interesting view for an anthropologist to hold, since it reverses the common trajectory of the modernist origin story of anthropology, in which anthropological "culture" is often said to have triumphed over an elitist "Culture." Dominguez herself relies on this narrative, and gives it a political spin, writing, " 'Culture' was strategically invoked to wrest it from the elite and make it the property of the masses" (20). For her, it is thus understandable that American-trained anthropologists have strong affective—indeed, filial—ties to the "anthropological" culture concept; as Dominguez puts it, "I have never met an anthropologist not firmly committed to a populist (rather than elitist) sense of culture" (20).

But despite what she describes as anthropologists' general commitment to "culture," Dominguez nevertheless argues that, among anthropologists today, "culture" is looking a little shabby. Clearly, the Boasians' view of "culture" as a set of easily identified properties of a bounded group of people is no longer theoretically adequate, and tends to encourage the reification of a given "culture" to a set of historically specific, and spuriously "authentic" traits. Thus, despite filial attachments, the modernist triumph of "culture" has come under review. But Dominguez does not connect this critique of an older "culture" to some postmodern renovation of the concept.[16] Rather, she emphasizes "culture's" pre-Boasian roots, as "a historically situated discursive object with a particular European origin and Eurocentric history" (22). While she is of course right to characterize "culture" in this way, she ignores other features of "culture's" complex history, in which the term was deployed, despite (or, perhaps because of) its origins, in various challenges to Eurocentrism. She argues:

> From an anthropological perspective, the commitment to employ culture [by, among others, proponents of cultural studies] at a time when anthropologists are suspicious of its referentiality or validity seems . . . curious—making us wonder why. Why, when the concept of culture has such an elitist history, would sympathetic anti-elitists contribute to its discursive objectification by trying to argue *in terms of it*? (20; italics hers)

The history of the Boasian challenge to an "elitist" deployment of "culture" has thus become strangely irrelevant, and the elitist "culture" it supposedly challenged appears to have won out.

It is tempting to speculate on the disciplinary malaise that would cause a practitioner to so thoroughly write off (or write out) the—albeit somewhat overstated—discursive influence of her discipline. But in fairness, Dominguez's emphasis on the "elitism" of "culture" may be a result of her own research (culminating in her book *People as Subjects, People as Objects*) on the cultural politics of Israel.[17] In Israel, the official national culture as promoted by state institutions is defined by a European-identified Ashkenazi elite, who promote their cherished objects and practices and diminish the value and significance of the comparable objects and practices of non-elite groups. According to Dominguez, the customs, folkways, and art forms of non-European Jews in Israel is called "heritage," not "culture" (35). Dominguez maintains (and here her point is irrefutable to the extent that it is nearly a tautology) that this official "culture" is in the service of maintaining Ashkenazi hegemony.

But in Dominguez's argument, this specific usage—as in, "Ministry of Culture"—becomes something of a horizon for the term's general connotations, to the extent that *any* usage of "culture" is for Dominguez both politically and intellectually suspect. Thus, she warns that in their invocations of "culture," "intellectuals, community activists, and politicians are, even in acts of resistance against European hegemony, perpetuating the very terms—of hierarchies of differential value—that constitute that hegemony" (38). The very word "culture," in other words, carries with it a taint of its own history—here described narrowly as Eurocentric—which cannot be expunged, even in such deployments as "multiculturalism," where the term is often used to specifically challenge traditional elites and hierarchies of value. Clearly, then, it would be inappropriate in Dominguez's view for anthropologists to keep "invoking culture."

In this contention, Dominguez is not alone. Indeed, we might say this rejection of "culture" is part of a larger internal critique of anthropology. Thus Johannes Fabian writes:

> Culture, inasmuch as it has served as anthropology's guiding concept, has always been an idea *post factum*, a notion oriented toward the past (to "custom" and "tradition"), descriptive of a state of affairs (and often of a status quo), a nostalgic idea at best (when it mixed the study of exotic societies with regret) and a reactionary ideologeme at worst (when it was used optimistically to explain away as "variation" what in many cases was the result of discrimination and violence).[18]

The problem with "culture," in other words, lies in its very connection to a discipline that historically has theorized its relationship to its object of study in a certain way. Fabian's central complaint is to be found in the status of "culture" as "a theory of knowledge": "Culture," he argues, "enshrines order as the negation of chaos. . . . It does this on the basis of an unfounded claim to occupy a position above and outside" (192–93). According to Fabian, "culture" presents itself as "occup[ying] a position above and outside" because of its relationship to "representationism." The anthropological practice that "represents" the cultural other also tends to replicate the "cultural" reifications of the other as part of some eternal ethnographic present. However, Fabian argues that through a writing practice that rejects representationism by portraying in writing the multiple perspectives and voices present in the ethnographic encounter—the sort of writing practices advocated by the proponents of "postmodern" or "reflexive" ethnography—we can get beyond "representationism," and thus, beyond "culture" (200–206).[19]

Because Fabian analyzes disciplinary rather than ideological usages of "culture," his vision of the problem with the term is different from Dominguez's in one respect. Where we might infer from her comments that it is the absence (or obsolescence) of a more "populist" (anthropological) understanding of the term that makes for its unwanted implications, Fabian laments its *centrality* to the discipline of anthropology. Nevertheless, in that it suggests a uniquely Western rendering of "order out of chaos," a will to knowledge that places the observer "above and outside," the "culture" about which he complains could also be described as hierarchical and Eurocentric. And of course, both writers advocate deleting "culture" from their discourses, a reasonable suggestion only given their view of "culture" as a kind of virus, infecting speech and thought with unfortunate premises and presuppositions—those of elitism (Dominguez) and exteriority (Fabian).

But unless we are to assume that "culture" is somehow unique among words, Fabian and Dominguez are also offering a theory of language, one in which terms somehow inherently contain, or import, specific ideas, largely irrespective of context and usage. Perhaps needless to say, this theory has some peculiar implications, one of which being that those interested in resisting European hegemony ought to avoid the importation of "Eurocentric presuppositions" by refusing to use any European or European-derived word, and thus to refrain from speaking European (and Creole) languages altogether. Though complete separatisms of this kind have been proposed, and are interesting thought experiments, it is hard to imagine their political efficacy. The unlikelihood of this project, moreover, suggests the similar difficulty of simply refusing, for political or philosophical reasons, to engage with the word "culture". Even the possible objection that I misrepresent their position by extending it to a logical absurdity—even the objection that they merely suggest that we take special care in our deployments of this word (a proposal with which I would entirely agree)—could not rescue their final point, for terminological scrupulousness would entail an intensification of our "cultural" discourse, not its banishment.

Given these accounts of the Eurocentrism of the culture concept, it is interesting to see another anthropologist, Joel S. Kahn, argue for the "demise of culture" from the opposite perspective. Diverging markedly from Dominguez or Fabian, Kahn argues that it is not a Eurocentric, but an epistemologically *relativist*, version of "culture," that has in fact "achieved a position of hegemony" in the discipline of anthropology, beginning in the 1970s under the influence of figures including Geertz, Sahlins, and Victor Turner. According to Kahn, this version of "culture" achieved its authority in the discipline through an aura of embattlement: "[T]hose who employ the concept are apparently committed to a view that their project is a direct challenge to the hege-monic discourses of 'western' thought."[20] It is the "demise" of this relativist "culture" that Kahn's essay seeks to further.

Kahn objects to this relativist version of "culture" because he sees it as leading to something he calls "the reflexive dilemma," a phenomenon clearly connected to the experiments and arguments of reflexive anthropology. Simply put, the dilemma arises from considering whether or not it is possible to repre-sent the culture of the other without importing some of one's own context into the representation. Is there, in other words, a way of representing the world of the other *in the other's own terms*? Since the only honest (to say nothing of anti-Eurocentric) answer to this question would have to be "no," Kahn suggests that this quest has led anthropologists into a dead end: They go in search of indigenous representations of indigenous practices, but in the haunting aware-ness that whatever explanations they find may turn out to be ones of their own devising.

Here again, "culture" can only be seen as the term that motivates or implies the necessity of this project if we concede what Kahn takes to be the "hege-mony" of the relativist usage of the term. Nevertheless, Kahn's account offers an interesting way to understand Dominguez and Fabian's complaints against "culture" as another manifestation of the "reflexive dilemma." Thanks to Kahn, we might summarize their predicament as follows: working under the false perception of embattlement, but in fact under the regime of a "hegemonic" anti-Eurocentric conception of "culture," Fabian and Dominguez find them-selves logically in the position of purging themselves of the very term "cul-ture," because it is of their—and not their informants'—cultural context. Kahn also helps us to understand their position by suggesting that this dilemma leads Fabian and the reflexive anthropologists to advocate "dialogue" and "nonrepre-sentationism" as a way of approximating the elusive object of interpretation (formerly known as "culture"), now relocated to the intermediary space of the ethnographic text itself. "But," complains Kahn, "the view that what we as anthropologists call culture is something that we produce, in definitive social and historical contexts, seems to me to take us so far away from the classical concept of culture, that it would be far better for the latter to be laid to rest" (16–17). Thus, it is on these grounds of its apparent self-negation that he winds up agreeing with Dominguez and Fabian on the point of the proper fate for the term: if "culture" means nothing more than some texts anthropologists pro-duce, then why bother with it?

Along the way, however, Kahn offers a practical solution for ridding his colleagues of the "reflexive dilemma," and hence, perhaps, of some of the problems he sees as associated with "culture." He notes, "[P]erhaps it is time to recognize that escaping our own concepts and categories into a world of the other is neither possible nor even necessarily desirable."[21] Significantly, there is nothing incompatible between an epistemologically relativist conception of "culture" and this generally compelling suggestion. For example, Richard Rorty, one of the more visible exponents of a pragmatist relativism, calls his position "ethnocentrism," and argues forcefully that we are constrained by the terms of our own context, or "community."[22] Though open to critique on a number of grounds, this view does not necessarily negate the project of ethnography, unless the "community" is viewed as so static an entity that it is impossible to imagine its ever responding to the pressures and influences of contact, or to believe that a new idea could ever be assimilated into the local vision.

But this is just a long way of saying that we may be able to clear up what seems like a difficulty with "culture" by thinking a little more clearly about how we imagine intercultural contact. The problem seems to relate to some conception of the relative porosity of contact *across* cultures—a theory of the other, or perhaps of communication, that assumes that interpretive schema are insufficiently commensurate across cultures for one to provide the terms for interpreting the other, but sufficiently commensurate to allow for the location and explanation of the other's terms. Since this view implies the relative powerfulness of the anthropologist's interpretive position compared to that of the cultural other, this may be the site not only of logical uncertainty, but also of anthropology's moral ambivalence about its historical mission and its relationship to its traditional "object" of study. In either case, however, purging anthropology of "culture" will rid it of neither the queasiness engendered by the discipline's historical will to knowledge of the cultural other nor the "reflexive dilemma."

But Kahn seems to realize this—or, at least, he concedes that there may be something perverse in arguing that we acknowledge the difficulty of getting outside of our own worldview, only to suggest purging that part of our worldview called "culture." So he shifts the grounds of his complaint slightly, arguing that the problem with "culture" is rather like that of "race," a term that is certainly still in use in all sorts of discourses, but that is often qualified by a series of caveats about the ugly history of its usage and its questionable scientific validity. Of course, in drawing this particular analogy between "race" and "culture," Kahn is also advancing an entirely new definition of "culture"— a definition that suggests a similarity in the two concepts that extends beyond the simple fact of their both being ambiguous, misused, and scientistic:

> I would argue that the notion of *a* culture is formally identical [to that of *a* race]; that those markers used to assign people to one or another of the world's cultures are equally ambiguous, and are far from allowing us to demarcate discrete, to say nothing of unchanging, cultural units except by reference to some boundary which is purely spatial and, hence, largely arbitrary, especially in the contemporary world. (18–19; his italics)

Kahn argues that, just as anthropology addressed and helped to debunk the quasi-scientific "folk usages" of race, so might it now find a new object in addressing similar flaws in contemporary usages—"folk" *and* anthropological—of "culture."

This proposal to examine actual usages of "culture" is entirely in keeping both with what I have tried to do in the preceding pages and, despite the conclusions they reach, with the arguments of all the writers I discuss here. As with Dominguez, however, one wonders about Kahn's readiness to make so quick a separation between "folk" (or, in Dominguez's case, official) usages and anthropological definitions of the term. Specifically, one suspects that this separation, indeed this interest in excising "culture" from the technical discourse of anthropology, is related to some desire—or better, a nostalgia—for disciplinary purity or authority. However, as my study has already shown, anthropologists are influenced in their work by political and intellectual concerns similar to those that have motivated various "folk" invocations of culture, and, despite whatever disciplinary confusions these forays into public debate have caused, they were—and will likely continue to be—a good thing both for anthropologists and for the quality of public debate. In other words, the point of the kind of rhetorical analysis of "culture" that Kahn advocates should be to *focus on* the intersection between his so-called folk and anthropological definitions of the term, for it is in this intersection of usages that we will actually understand the wider social motivations and interests of the various discourses in question.

Race and Culture

However, we must not pass so quickly over Kahn's comparison between usages of "culture" and "race." He argues not only that "culture" has become the functional equivalent of "race," but that it is not glossed with the same qualifications that at least rhetorically separate invocations of "race" from *racism* outright. Nor is this point unique to Kahn. "Culturalism," a term originally referring to a specific critical tradition (usually the Marxist or "Left culturalism" of E. P. Thompson and Raymond Williams), has increasingly come into use as a term of disparagement, largely I think because of its neat parallel construction with "racism"—as in the title of a panel Dominguez chaired in 1991 at the meetings of the American Ethnological Society, "Is Culturalism an Improvement on Racism?" The implicit argument in the comparison, one assumes, is that while invocations of "race" are central to any elaboration of racism (a big assumption), invocations of "culture" are at least similarly unreflective in their conception of difference.[23]

The basis of the comparison between these terms brings us back to another origin story of "culture"—what I'm now tempted, thanks to Kahn, to call a "folk" history of "culture"—that emphasizes "culture's" historical role as a powerful analytical alternative to racial thinking. I quote Carl N. Degler once again, with his dramatic claims about Boas's invention of "the concept of culture, which, like a powerful solvent, would in time expunge race from the literature of social science."[24] As we have seen, this dramatic narrative can be tempered by reference to certain historical considerations (see Chapter 2). While Boas was a tireless critic of scientific racism, it could be more convincingly argued that it was the rediscovery of Gregor Mendel and the development of genetic theory that ultimately delegitimated the scientific idea of distinct "racial" populations of humans, by showing the extent to which genetic material was shared across these populations. Instead of "expunging" all of the uses and connotations of "race" (a term that is still is use in both racist and antiracist discourses), I think we may more properly see the Boasian invocation of "culture" as having done some of the explanatory work of "race," offering a nonbiological and nonevolutionist way to think about collective features of human populations.

Given the complexity of this history, it should not be too surprising that some would be tempted to contend that the shift from "race" to "culture" was really no change at all (just as others were tempted to wonder about the efficacy of "culture's" putative assault on Eurocentrism). This is the case with Walter Benn Michaels, who argues that, all along, "culture" has been a Trojan Horse of racial and racist thinking.[25] While explaining this connection is Michaels's explicit agenda, I will suggest that he does a little smuggling of his own: in his argument, he offers an implicit description of "culture" that, though unnamed (he wants to get rid of "culture," after all), would doubtless make the anthropologists whose work I have been discussing shudder. I offer my description of Michaels's work as a cautionary tale for those anthropologists (and others) who would seriously propose abandoning the term.

Corresponding to my account of the intensity of the "cultural" debate of the pre–World War II decades, Michaels's essay "Race into Culture: a Critical Genealogy of Cultural Identity," and subsequent book, *Our America*, focuses on the literature of the United States in the 1920s. However, likening that period's literary interests in the cultural alienation of immigrants and Native Americans to explicitly racist literature from the 1890s, Michaels's narrative of this moment hinges on what he sees as the (non-) transition from "racial" to "cultural" forms of identity. He writes: "In Progressive racism, Confederate comrades in arms offer the image of a racial entity that breaks the organic bonds of the (multiracial) family and substitutes for them the superorganic bonds of the white 'State'; in the 1920s, the Indian embodies a racial entity that finds through the family a 'heritage' or 'culture' that transcends the (multiracial) state" (669). While the first of these historical moments creates racial difference in the service of a transfamilial nationalism, the second resists nationalism in favor of an assertion of familial bonds. Though these latter bonds are called "cultural," they are racial insofar as they imply an organic, hereditary connection between a group of people. Moreover, "cultural pluralism," rather than being a new way to conceive of the nation, is in Michaels's view a "racial pluralism [where] one prefers one's own race not because it is superior but because it is one's own" (669).[26]

Through his use of "race" to connote both moments, Michaels elides "progressive racism" with what he identifies as the 1920s fascination with "culture." From there it is a very short logical step—if a rather bigger historical one—to his main point, that "[t]he modern concept of culture is not . . . a critique of racism; it is a form of racism" (683). This argument is similar in its form and psychological appeal to what Barbara Herrnstein Smith identified as a traditional philosophical response to epistemological relativism.[27] Just as the relativist is accused of "self-refutation" (that is, of holding a position that undercuts her own grounds for asserting anything, including relativism, as in the statement "relativism is true"), Michaels makes a similar charge of self-refutation to those who would invoke the language of "cultural" difference. In his view, apparently antiracist invokers of "culture" are really appealing to "race" and are therefore themselves racists. Smith shows that the self-refutation argument against relativism is based on a prior commitment to antirelativism (e.g., the "dubious inference and dubious paraphrase" by which "relativism is true" is taken to mean "relativism is absolutely, objectively true"). Michaels's argument about "culture's" racism is based on some similarly questionable prior assumptions: on a rhetorical and conceptual collapsing of "race" and "culture," and on the inference that invocations of "race" are per se racist. Smith's observations about the psychological satisfactions of the self-refutation charge also have some relevance to Michaels's argument: "There is in self-refutation the satisfaction . . . of cognitive and pragmatic economy: the exposure and defeat of an adversary accomplished neatly, at his own cost" (89). Clearly, the payoff for Michaels's leveling of such a charge is multiple, showing that the "pathos" of racial-cultural complaint is both illogical *and* racist.

The argument with Michaels would now be over if his point rested on no more than a rhetorical elision. But in fact, he does give content to the conceptual similarity that he asserts exists between "race" and "culture." Specifically, Michaels rejects as racist any claim to a common culture based on appeals to a shared history; for example, a shared history of enslavement or colonization. His compellingly simple argument is that in order for the idea of an identity in shared history to make sense, one must infer a common genealogical, hence racial, relationship to those who actually experienced that event. To call this shared history a common "culture" is covertly to employ racial thinking, and thus "culture" becomes for him the de facto equal of "race." It bears noting that Michaels would probably understand the idea of the "nation" to be racial as well, since the invocation of a shared historical past is a typical feature of national ideologies, in support of which such histories are constantly invented and mythologized.[28]

Indeed, if we accept Michaels's basic argument about the "racial" nature of appeals to shared history, then it may be interesting to ask what is *not* a racial way of accounting for group identity (By appealing to Boas as a "father" of their discipline, are anthropologists engaging in racial thinking?). Michaels provides the answer to this question in *Our America*, through his argument that the racialized "culture" of the twenties offers a "nativist" strategy for constructing American identity that gets around the openness of "citizenship" as a category of national belonging: through citizenship, any immigrant could choose to be "American." But interestingly, Michaels rejects the possibility that belonging to a culture could be similarly voluntary, that one might see culture as something that could be similarly chosen, as the immigrant chooses to become a citizen. Instead, he specifies that (pluralist) "culture" must have a "racial" component, otherwise "our culture" does no "cultural work." "For insofar as our culture remains nothing more than what we do and believe, it is impotently descriptive" (682).

Readers familiar with Steven Knapp and Michaels's polemic, "Against Theory," may find in this otherwise astonishing statement an echo of the earlier essays, which argued for an end to theory in terms similar to this essay's support of "abandoning our idea of culture".[29] In the 1980s, Stanley Fish's assertion that theory has no practical consequences (being a kind of discursive game played by the interpretive community of the theory cognoscenti) led Knapp and Michaels to wonder, "But once theory has given up all claims to affect practice, what is there left for theory to do?"[30] In the 1990s, Michaels contends that the only "culture" that is not "impotently descriptive" is one that is somehow connected with implicitly racial justifications for behavior or belief.

This, then, is the crux of Michaels's argument for abandoning the culture concept: if "culture" is secretly racial, then it should go, because "race" should go (because invocations of "race" are racist); if it is not racial, then why should we bother with it? But is "what we do and believe" really so useless, so "impotent," and therefore so harmless a definition of "culture" as Michaels suggests? This definition is not really so different from Edward Sapir's conception of "culture" as "what a society does and thinks," and only slightly more extensive than Ruth Benedict's conjunction of "culture" with "custom" in *Patterns of Culture*. Giving descriptive content to "what we do and believe" could hardly be seen as a neutral act. Rather, such a description would do the significant, and likely very controversial work of (among other things) defining the contours of a bounded population, of marking the difference between "we" and "they." This kind of differentiation could, as Kahn suggested, have all the faults of a racial distinction between peoples, or have other descriptive flaws in not allowing for contingencies of history, contact, and migration. But these are not issues of significant consequence to Michaels. Indeed, I would suggest that, in ignoring that the "we" only exists in relation to the "they," he takes for granted how cultural description delimits belonging. Though this oversight seems peculiar in the light of his earlier account of how racial and cultural thinking helped form national identities, it does help to explain not only his rejection of simply descriptive invocations of "culture" as uninteresting, but also his repetitive and unqualified use of the phrase "our culture," as though its referent were self-evident.

This oversight would also help explain Michaels's interesting conception of why it is that someone might question another's assumptions about the boundaries of a "culture." Referring to Arthur M. Schlesinger Jr.'s controversial *The Disuniting of America*, Michaels argues, "When . . . people dispute Schlesinger-style claims about the values we ought to hold by asking who 'we' are, they assume that the answer to the question of which values are appropriate for us depends on identifying which culture we belong to."[31] I would put the case slightly differently: that the force of the gesture of questioning the content of the "we" can also be a project of negative critique rather than an expression of allegiance to another value-defining culture. Its force is to insist that claims to a unified identity are ideological—specifically, that those who are socially marked as different ("racially," "culturally," linguistically, etc.) are only imperfectly interpellated into the "we," and therefore that arguments about how "we" ought to behave should be similarly limited in terms of whom they hail. It is, in other words, a query directed at the ideological suasion of a unified social totality.

It is important to point out that Michaels's "culture" leads to a conception of identity formation that is, if not exactly voluntarist (because one cannot quite *choose* to belong to a culture), then at least unaffected by these considerations of interpellation. (This too might have a parallel in "Against Theory," which argues that the job of criticism is the recovery of authorial intent.) Tellingly, in the last footnote of his article "Race into Culture," Michaels, who seems to dislike "the melodrama of assimilation" more than anything else, concedes that "compulsory assimilation" might present a legitimate occasion for some "pathos"—as though even the happiest of instances of assimilation did not present an element of compulsion (685). The idea that individuals might be imperfectly hailed by the identities "we" choose, or indeed that identities are not only chosen but imposed upon us, is strikingly absent from Michaels's conception of identity. For indeed, if "race" were *only* a matter of claiming an identity based on a common history, then it seems that the charge of racism would lose its sting—unless, of course, the idea of people claiming certain kinds of identities is itself felt to be repugnant.[32]

This is, of course, the case with Schlesinger, for whom the claiming of distinct "cultural" or racial identities is inimical to the cohesion of the nation. But Michaels is no Schlesinger, longing for the good old days of nationalist fellow feeling and *e pluribus unum*. Rather, the issue of the nation drops out of his account somewhere in the 1920s, and thereafter he effectively forestalls questioning or even naming the existence of the larger social totality by defining "culture" as what we do and believe. The question of who "we" are is already answered in the definition: "we" are who we believe we are. In other words, the purely descriptive definition of "culture" Michaels offers is far less "impotent" than he maintains, precisely because it is there that he gets around the vexing problem of how, in the face of various challenges to identity formation, including disintegrating ideologies of nationalism, we define ourselves—for we have already decided that.

Indeed, it turns out that culture-as-belief covers an enormous amount of conceptual ground. The only thing this apparently limited "culture" doesn't do, according to Michaels, is predict who we *ought* to be and what we *ought* to do:

> The fact, in other words, that something belongs to our culture cannot count as a motive for our doing it since, if it *does* belong to our culture, we *already* do it and if we don't do it (if we've stopped, or haven't yet started doing it) it doesn't belong to our culture. . . . . It is only if we think that our culture is not whatever beliefs and practices we actually happen to have but is instead the beliefs and practices that should properly go with the sort of people we happen to be that the fact of something belonging to our culture can count as a reason for doing it. But to think this is to appeal to something that must be beyond culture and that cannot be derived from culture precisely because our sense of which culture is properly ours must be derived from it. This has been the function of race. (Michaels, 682–83)

I quote here at length not only to give some sense of the rhetorical complexities of Michaels's prose, but to show, once again, how Michaels's argument is related, in fascinatingly compressed form, to some of the major points of his and Knapp's "Against Theory" articles. A major polemic of the earlier essays held that literary theory presumed the existence of a position of critique extraneous to our belief systems. Here, Michaels emphasizes that we cannot get outside of our culture any more than we can our beliefs, because like our beliefs, our culture constrains what can be thought—including what can be thought about "culture." The only way, then, to make connections with the historical past, to understand what constitutes "our culture," is to invoke "something that must be beyond culture," in this case, race. This is, in other words, another articulation of Kahn's "reflexive dilemma," expressed not in terms of intercultural contact, but in terms of contact with our historical past and present. "Culture" is nothing less than our entire way of thinking and being, but, strangely, nothing more than an inconvenient set of blinders that prevents us from imagining our relationship to either the past or the future; the former being "racial" in that it requires an appeal to family, the latter in that it requires us to imagine something ("racial") outside our beliefs.

Imagined Totalities

We might think of Michaels's culture-as-belief as a kind of Arnoldian culture for the postnational, postpolitical (postutopian) moment. Having once done the work of "race" to shore up ideologies of the nation, "culture's" work is done—now that political and especially economic forces seem (at least in North America) to have diminished "the nation's" ideological force.[33] And yet, in its easy assumption of the self-evident quality of "our culture," Michaels's conception of "culture" also seems the perfect vehicle for perpetuating the chauvinisms that nationalism enabled. Further, though Michaels claimed to want to give up "culture" because of its excessively "racial" connotations, his implicit equation of "culture" with belief offers us the possibility that there is nothing—barring the more or less unfathomable past and future—that isn't "cultural" (since we can't get outside of our beliefs). Thus we can see that in Michaels's conception, "culture" is very large—is indeed total.

In this roundabout way, Michaels may have given us one of the most persuasive arguments I can imagine for getting rid of "culture" (though not for his reasons), and correspondingly, for resuscitating "race" as a valuable critical tool (not a project Michaels would at all endorse). For if "culture" is understood to be the totality of what we are able to conceive, then it is also impervious to interrogation—or rather, it already *contains* its interrogation, since that too is part of our beliefs. "Race," on the other hand, seems to occupy a position of critical exteriority. This is in part perhaps because Michaels seems to take for granted its inadmissibility in critical discourse (it is, in his view, *racist*), but, more specifically, because "race" speaks to the question of the constitution of the "we," and thus offers us the (only?) ideological leverage in his otherwise completely closed "cultural" milieu.

In short, barring the potentially critical possibilities of "race" in his work, Michaels's vision may be taken to be a manifestation of a frequent complaint about "culture": that it is simply ideological, offering a static conception of social life, validating the status quo, and serving to obscure the significance of other factors in the construction of human life, like social structure, economics, or the natural environment.[34] Surely, none of the anthropologists I have discussed above would find much appealing in Michaels's conception of "culture," but getting rid of the word "culture"—thus leaving unnamed and untheorized the totality that Michaels smuggles in—would give us no place from which to critique his view. Arif Dirlik's point is thus particularly salient in light of work such as Michaels's: "To avoid the question of 'culture' is to avoid questions concerning the ways in which we see the world."[35] Put another way, our options may well be to address a (problematic, ideological) totality that has a name like "culture," or a totality that doesn't—that simply exists, the way Michaels's belief simply *is*.

And thus we return to the problem of "culture's" vexatious relationship to the "metaphor of totality" in general. In a moment when most theoretical totalities have come under critical scrutiny, the apparent conceptual relationship between "culture" and totality might seem damning. Indeed, the very idea of any innocently proposed bounded site seems, at this critical moment, to cry out for interrogation and destabilization, inducing one to think not only about the instability of such constructs as the nation, but about how animal behaviorists, virologists, and science-fiction writers alike force us to question—yet again—our understanding of such basic categories as humanity, and life itself. We are, these days, justifiably, and productively, suspicious of holisms and of systems of knowledge that make claims to representing the whole. This, as I have said, is the very real force behind arguments made by Dominguez and Fabian against "culture."

However, there is a tendency in this postmodern moment of destabilized totalities, not to rigorously interrogate the reifications of totalizing knowledge, but to slip around the question of totality altogether. As in the example of Michaels, constructs such as "culture" or the "nation" disappear and reappear chimerically, and questions about perspective and the nature of the collectivity are simply dismissed—like "culture" itself—as irrelevancies. At least Michaels is consistent, and has methodically theorized his position "against theory." But there are certainly others who work from the unarticulated premise that "culture" is coextensive with what one is writing about, and then proceed, via some version of the logic of metonymy, to assume that everything somehow connects to everything else. In these conditions, "culture" does become a meaningless abstraction, among other abstractions. And, in such circumstances of critical unselfconsciousness, the possibility is left open for some undesirable version of totality to be snuck in the back door.

In other words, I do not think we are entirely "beyond" thinking in terms of totality. Nor, indeed, do I consider totalizing knowledges or constructs illegitimate as ways of thinking.[36] Postmodern "antitotalizing" critical positions usefully teach us not that we are confined in our knowledges to the local and the personal, but rather that the totalities we propose are *provisional*—that total knowledge only exists in the moment before we shift our perspective, or take into account the next bit of evidence, the next voice. And as far as spatial totalities are concerned, there is some odd truth to the saying that beneath the turtle who carries the world on its shell there are turtles all the way down: our borders are only as small, as large, as permeable, as stable as the systems of exclusion and inclusion that produce them. This point should encourage us to regard as a reification any easy equation of "culture" with a self-evident or stable totality. But it should also remind us that totalizing knowledge can be thought of as an instance in a dialectical process which is challenged and changed by the pressures of the local, the contingent, and the specific.

Given the term's much commented-upon descriptive affinity for the local instance *and* the conceptual whole, the ethnographic concrete *and* the Arnoldian ideal, technical *and* "folk" discourses, "culture" is ideally situated, discursively, to think through this dialectic. It is in deployments of metaphors of spatial and conceptual wholes where "culture" may find its current utility and its charge. I would suggest that the debates about the meaning and deployment of "culture"—even ones that gesture toward rejecting the term altogether—represent exactly this kind of work, indicating the conceptual sites in which the tension between the local and the global, between the specific instance and the grand theory, are being rethought and redeployed. This is not to say, of course, that the "cultural" is the only register in which we can imagine conceptual wholes. But this is an understandable assumption to make, since, as we have seen, some views equate "culture" with the mode and extent of thought itself. The mistake goes something like this: if our thoughts are somehow defined by cultural context, then aren't the very limits and extent of what we can think somehow "cultural"? This is only true if we banally assume (with Michaels) that "culture" is coextensive with what we think, rather than a register, a category, among others for thinking about what we think. Obviously, we need to renovate models in which "culture" is once again described as part of other (yes, probably totalizing) conceptions of, among other things, society, human life, biological life, and so on. Only in this way will "culture" regain some of the critical force it has had in various historical deployments: in Matthew Arnold's writing (where, for all its conservatism and logical shortcomings, "culture" nevertheless connoted a utopian horizon of "perfection"); in Franz Boas's antiracist polemics; in Randolph Bourne's conception of a nation built upon the premise of internationalism; in Edward Sapir, Van Wyck Brooks, and Ruth Benedict's attempts to imagine the integration of the individual with the social.

Meanwhile, it might be good to make some changes in our "cultural" rhetoric, especially in our reliance on modernist constructions of "culture's" history as a concept. Rather than invoking the language of radical breaks, revolutions, and epistemic shifts to describe conceptual usages, we could try grappling with the cacophony of ideas "culture" evokes, and the accretion of histories that have contributed to its rhetorical formation. This change in how we describe "culture" would more logically reveal the necessity of coming to terms (as it were) with the tensions of the local and the global, the concrete and the ideal. Moreover (as some have noted with despair), "culture" allows us to tack back and forth interestingly between the minutiae of academic border skirmishes and the messy sweeps of public discourse. What would happen if we opened up our disciplinary understandings of the term to considerations of such interesting usages as "corporate culture" (to describe, I guess, the esprit imposed by a company on its employees), or a recent papal encyclical's use of the phrase "the culture of death"? I am, in other words, suggesting that, rather than dispense with the concept in light of its imprecision, or, following Kahn, address it by way of a long list of caveats—interrogating "culture" as (we congratulate ourselves in believing) we have interrogated "race"—we should consider its limits in some complex relation to what it promises to describe, through its deployment in many different sites. Let us, moreover, consider the intensity of the debates surrounding the term as above all the measure of its continued rhetorical utility.

Notes

Introduction
The Domestication of Culture

1. A. L. Kroeber and Clyde Kluckhohn, *Culture: A Critical Review of Concepts and Definitions* (New York: Vintage, 1952), 3.

2. See Raymond Williams, *Keywords: A Vocabulary of Culture and Society* (London: Croom Helm, 1973).

3. The most influential treatment of this earlier history of "culture" in the British context is Williams, *Culture and Society: 1780–1950* (1958; reprint, New York: Columbia University Press, 1983); see also Kroeber and Kluckhohn, *Culture*.

4. Christopher Herbert's important work on the Victorian context of the culture concept supports my point about the significance of this period for the development of the discourse of "culture." Though Herbert's study focuses on authors and issues of this other, earlier, context, he nevertheless views figures central to my study—especially Ruth Benedict, whom he describes as "possibly the most influential of all writers in crystallizing the discourse of culture"—as expressing the concept of culture in its most complete form. In other words, his study to some degree locates traces of their "culture" in its Victorian antecedents. Christopher Herbert, *Culture and Anomie: Ethnographic Imagination in the Nineteenth Century* (Chicago: University of Chicago Press, 1991), 7, 23–24.

5. Warren I. Susman, "The Culture of the Thirties," in *Culture as History: The Transformation of American Society in the Twentieth Century* (New York: Pantheon, 1984), 154.

6. Ralph Waldo Emerson, "The Progress of Culture," in *The Complete Works of Ralph Waldo Emerson* (New York: Houghton Mifflin, 1917), 8:205–34.

7. Lewis Mumford, *The Golden Day: A Study in American Experience and Culture* (New York: Boni and Liveright, 1926), 3. Historians Charles and Mary Beard showed that "civilization" also comprised an important keyword of this same moment, particularly in the early years of the twentieth century, and in those surrounding World War II. The Beards's usage of "civilization" both overlaps and differs from typical conceptions of "culture" in the period, at times suggesting something more technological or more teleological than "culture," at times meaning something only perhaps a little grander than "culture." Some of this complexity is reflected in their statement in the preface of *The American Spirit*: "Out of our studies extending over many years we have reached the conviction that no idea, such as democracy, liberty, or the American way of life, expresses the American spirit so coherently, comprehensively, and systematically as does the idea of civilization." Charles A. Beard and Mary R. Beard, *The American Spirit* (1942; reprint, New York: Collier, 1971), 7, 19–93. See also their popularly influential history, *The Rise of American Civilization* (New York: Macmillan, 1930).

8. Randolph Bourne, "A Mirror of the Middle West," in *The Radical Will: Selected Writings 1911–1918*, ed. Olaf Hansen (New York: Urizen, 1977), 265.

9. Kroeber and Kluckhohn, *Culture*, 19–30.

10. Edward Sapir, "Culture, Genuine and Spurious," in *Selected Writings of Edward Sapir in Language, Culture, and Personality,* ed. David G. Mandelbaum (Berkeley: University of California Press, 1949), 311.

11. The complexity of the relationship between "culture" and "civilization" is, however, also revealed in Morgan's work, where he also specifies that each of his "ethnical periods" "has a distinct culture and exhibits a mode of life more or less special and peculiar to itself." In other words, the road to civilization accommodates myriad cultures. This relationship between the two concepts would be reversed in Oswald Spengler's extremely influential *The Decline of the West* (translated into English in 1926), where "civilization" represented the final, decadent stage of the development of "culture." Lewis Henry Morgan, *Ancient Society,* ed. Leslie A. White (1877; reprint, Cambridge: Harvard University Press, 1964), 18; Kroeber and Kluckhohn, *Culture,* 28, 48–49.

12. Raymond Williams's widely influential work on the idea of "culture" challenged the rhetorical separability of these two strains of the definition of the word (see, for example, Williams, *Culture and Society;* and "Culture," in *Keywords.* Nevertheless, the assumption of two discrete traditions of "cultural" thought continues. For recent examples of this view of the history of culture, see Russell Jacoby, "The Myth of Multiculturalism," *New Left Review,* no. 208 (November–December 1994): 121–26; and Virginia Dominguez, "The Messy Side of 'Cultural Politics,' " *South Atlantic Quarterly* 91, no. 1 (Winter 1992): 19–42. Dominguez's article is discussed at length in Chapter 7.

13. Franz Boas's work is a good example of this: not only was Boas committed to the empirical project of science, and to an understanding of a universal humanity, but he had little trouble making distinctions between the "primitive" and the "civilized" in matters of, for example, technological superiority. What he adamantly refused to consider was the possibility that "primitives" were in any broader, human sense "inferior." See Boas, "Modern Life and Primitive Culture," in *Anthropology and Modern Life* (1928; reprint, New York: Norton, 1962), 202–46. See also Melford E. Spiro, who offers a useful taxonomy of cultural relativisms in anthropology and usefully points out that *epistemological* relativism—the kind we may attribute to B. L. Whorf, Clifford Geertz, and the symbolic anthropologists generally—was a comparatively recent theoretical development in the field. Spiro, "Cultural Relativism and the Future of Anthropology," in *Rereading Cultural Anthropology,* ed. George E. Marcus (Durham, N.C.: Duke University Press, 1992), 124–51; and, for an extended philosophical critique of moral relativism, see Michele M. Moody-Adams, *Fieldwork in Familiar Places: Morality, Culture, and Philosophy* (Cambridge: Harvard University Press, 1997).

14. For a brief overview of the very different British context of disciplinary understandings of "culture," see Elman R. Service, "Cultural Anthropology Versus Social Anthropology," in *A Century of Controversy: Ethnological Issues from 1860 to 1960* (Orlando, Fla.: Academic Press, 1985), 251–57.

15. Margaret Mead would be the exception who proves the rule here: though her primary source of institutional support was as a curator at the American Museum of Natural History, she did nevertheless obtain the academic credentials of a PhD, and maintained strong ties to Columbia's anthropology department throughout her career. See Jane Howard, *Margaret Mead: A Life* (New York: Simon and Schuster, 1984).

16. This "professional-managerial" designation is, I am aware, historically vexed. In 1977 Barbara Ehrenreich and John Ehrenreich proposed the existence of the "professional-managerial class" (PMC), to designate the doctors, lawyers, teachers, social workers, and professional managers who emerged as a coherent social group at the turn of the century in the United States. The designation has drawn debate in Marxist circles largely over the question of where this group's class allegiances lie, and thus whether or not it is properly a class separate from that of the capitalists, the workers, or the traditional petite bourgeoisie. Though I defer to these criticisms, and with Stanley Aronowitz describe the PMC as a "strata" of the middle class, I think it is worth noting that at the turn of the century this group does seem to have acted very like a class, in its promotion and protection of interests related to the central issue of professionalization—notably, the production and protection of monopolies of information and expertise. Barbara Ehrenreich and John Ehrenreich, "The Professional-Managerial Class," in *Between Labor and Capital*, ed. Pat Walker (Montreal: Black Rose, 1978), 5–48; and Stanley Aronowitz, "The Professional-Managerial Class or Middle Strata," in *Between Labor and Capital*, 213–42; see also Robert H. Wiebe, *The Search for Order 1877–1920*, The Making of America Series, ed. David Donald (New York: Hill and Wang, 1967), 111–32.

17. Though important work was done on African-American culture by Boasian anthropologists (notably Melville Herskovits), it would not be fair to say that anthropology as a field offered exceptional opportunities for blacks. Zora Neale Hurston's widely discussed relationship with the Columbia anthropology department is a case in point. Not only was Hurston's academic career so plagued by financial troubles that she left Columbia without ever taking an advanced degree, but she occupied a strange status in anthropology (similar to that of the several Native American anthropologists of this period, including the Boas-trained Ella Cara Deloria), as both anthropologist and a species of native informant. Vernon J. Williams Jr., *Rethinking Race: Franz Boas and His Contemporaries* (Lexington: University Press of Kentucky, 1996), 48–51; Ruth Behar, "Introduction: Out of Exile," Janet L. Finn, "Ella Cara Deloria and Mourning Dove: Writing for Cultures, Writing Against the Grain," and Graciela Hernández, "Multiple Subjectivities and Strategic Positionality: Zora Neale Hurston's Experimental Ethnographies," in *Women Writing Culture*, ed. Ruth Behar and Deborah A. Gordon (Berkeley: University of California Press, 1995), 18, 131–47, 148–65.

18. Such financial arrangements were not unusual in the early years of anthropology. Both Boas and Benedict also supported students and paid for departmental expenses out of their own pockets. Judith Modell, "Ruth Benedict, Anthropologist: The Reconciliation of Science and Humanism," in *Toward a Science of Man: Essays in the History of Anthropology*, ed. Timothy H. H. Thoresen (Paris: Mouton, 1975), 195; Louise Lamphere, "Feminist Anthropology: The Legacy of Elsie Clews Parsons," in *Women Writing Culture*, 85–103; Esther S. Goldfrank, *Notes on an Undirected Life: As One Anthropologist Tells It* (Flushing, N.Y.: Queens College Press, 1978), 4, 21–35; Margaret M. Caffrey, *Ruth Benedict: Stranger in this Land* (Austin: University of Texas Press, 1989), 272.

19. See Robert F. Murphy, "Anthropology at Columbia: A Reminiscence," *Dialectical Anthropology* 16 (1991): 65–81.

20. Marshall Sahlins, *Culture and Practical Reason* (Chicago: University of Chicago Press, 1976); and see Murphy, "Anthropology at Columbia." Another strain of the

Boasian tradition, invested primarily in analyzing social behavior (Sahlins's "practical reason"), would include the work of Robert Lowie, Paul Radin, and Julian Steward.

21. Waldo Frank, "Note on American Cultural Criticism Since 1909," in *The Re-Discovery of America* (New York: Scribners, 1929), 313–26.

22. Russell Jacoby, *The Last Intellectuals: American Culture in the Age of Academe* (New York: Noonday, 1987), 17. For an extended discussion of the connections between Mumford and Brooks, Frank, and Bourne, see Casey Nelson Blake, *Beloved Community: The Cultural Criticism of Randolph Bourne, Van Wyck Brooks, Waldo Frank, and Lewis Mumford* (Chapel Hill: University of North Carolina Press, 1990); the relationship between Burke and these men was more fraught, but nevertheless filial. Shortly after the twenty-five-year-old Burke published an extremely negative review of Brooks's *The Ordeal of Mark Twain* which also savaged the work of Waldo Frank, Burke wrote to Malcolm Cowley to express his delight at meeting Brooks and Frank, who were not only friendly but supportive of his career: "I have felt the solidest elation of my life when I think that I could go at the very basis of these men's work, could muster every argument against it that I could invent, could convince them that my objections were of validity, and could retain their respect. . . . I have gotten closer to two people who share my new religion, the desire to be decent." Kenneth Burke, "Art and the Hope Chest," *Vanity Fair*, December 1922, 59, 102; Paul Jay, ed. *The Selected Correspondence of Kenneth Burke and Malcolm Cowley* (New York: Viking, 1988), 133–34.

23. Robert H. Lowie, "Comments on Edward Sapir, His Personality and Scholarship," in *Edward Sapir: Appraisals of His Life and Work*, ed. Konrad Koerner, Amsterdam Studies in the Theory and History of Linguistic Science, vol. 36 (Philadelphia: John Benjamins, 1984), 122.

24. See George E. Marcus and Michael M. J. Fischer, *Anthropology as Cultural Critique: An Experimental Moment in the Human Sciences* (Chicago: University of Chicago Press, 1986), 125–31.

Chapter 1
Modernism, Anthropology, Culture

1. Raymond Williams, "Culture," in *Keywords: A Vocabulary of Culture and Society* (London: Croom Helm, 1973), 87; Eric R. Wolf, "Perilous Ideas: Race, Culture, People," *Current Anthropology* 35, no. 1 (February 1994): 1–7; and Stephen Greenblatt, "Culture," in *Critical Terms for Literary Study*, ed. Frank Lentricchia and Thomas McLaughlin (Chicago: University of Chicago Press, 1990), 225.

2. Clifford Geertz, "The Impact of the Concept of Culture on the Concept of Man," in *The Interpretation of Cultures* (New York: Basic, 1973), 35.

3. Indeed, one might say that there is a rather *modernist* desire on the part of anthropology's historians to find vanguards and dramatic breaks with the past in its disciplinary founders. Edwin Ardener goes so far as to describe Boas's British counterpart, Malinowski, as an anthropological Breton or Marinetti, whose avant-garde movement was British Functionalism and whose manifesto was *Argonauts of the Western Pacific*. Against this heroic account, Marilyn Strathern rightly points out that Malinowski's technical innovations of functionalist theory and participant observation were not really so much "masterminded" as heavily promulgated by him. Ardener, "Social Anthropol-

ogy and the Decline of Modernism," in *Reason and Morality*, ed. Joanna Overing (London: Tavistock Publications, 1985), 47–70; Strathern, "Out of Context: The Persuasive Fictions of Anthropology," in *Modernist Anthropology: From Fieldwork to Text*, ed. Marc Manganaro (Princeton, N.J.: Princeton University Press, 1990), 96.

4. Carl N. Degler, *In Search of Human Nature: The Decline and Revival of Darwinism in American Social Thought* (New York: Oxford University Press, 1991), 71.

5. See Christopher Herbert, *Culture and Anomie: Ethnographic Imagination in the Nineteenth Century* (Chicago: University of Chicago Press, 1991), and George W. Stocking Jr., *Race, Culture, and Evolution: Essays in the History of Anthropology* (New York: Free Press, 1968).

6. Marc Manganaro, *Myth, Rhetoric, and the Voice of Authority: A Critique of Frazer, Eliot, Frye, and Campbell* (New Haven, Conn.: Yale University Press, 1992).

7. T. S. Eliot, "Tradition and the Individual Talent," in *Critical Theory Since Plato*, ed. Hazard Adams (New York: Harcourt Brace Jovanovich, 1971), 785.

8. Lawrence W. Levine, *Highbrow/Lowbrow: The Emergence of Cultural Hierarchy in America* (Cambridge: Harvard University Press, 1988), 235.

9. Andreas Huyssen, *After the Great Divide: Modernism, Mass Culture, Postmodernism* (Bloomington: Indiana University Press, 1986); see also Fredric Jameson, "Reification and Utopia in Mass Culture," in *Signatures of the Visible* (New York: Routledge, 1990), 9–34.

10. Paul DiMaggio, "Cultural Entrepreneurship in Nineteenth-Century Boston: The Creation of an Organizational Base for High Culture in America," *Media, Culture, and Society* 4 (1982): 33–50; DiMaggio, "Cultural Entrepreneurship in Nineteenth-Century Boston, Part II: The Classification and Framing of American Art," *Media, Culture, and Society* 4 (1982): 303–22; Lary May, *Screening Out the Past: The Birth of Mass Culture and the Motion Picture Industry* (Chicago: University of Chicago Press, 1983); David Nasaw, *Going Out: The Rise and Fall of Public Amusements* (New York: Harper Collins, 1993); and Levine, *Highbrow/Lowbrow*.

11. The use of the "low" in the creation of "high" modernist art has been widely discussed. See, for example, the catalogue of a recent exhibit at New York's Museum of Modern Art, and its accompanying book of essays: Kirk Varnedoe and Adam Gopnik, *High and Low: Modern Art and Popular Culture* (New York: Museum of Modern Art, 1990); and Varnedoe and Gopnik, eds., *Modern Art and Popular Culture: Readings in High and Low* (New York: Harry N. Abrams in association with the Museum of Modern Art, 1990).

12. Alice G. Marquis, *Hopes and Ashes: The Birth of Modern Times 1929–1939* (New York: Free Press, 1986), 37–39.

13. Ann Douglas, *Terrible Honesty: Mongrel Manhattan in the 1920s* (New York: Farrar, Straus and Giroux, 1995), 70; Waldo Frank, *Memoirs*, ed. Alan Trachtenberg (Amherst: University of Massachusetts Press, 1973), 120; Charles J. Maland, *Chaplin and American Culture: The Evolution of a Star Image* (Princeton, N.J.: Princeton University Press, 1989), 84–93; and Susan Buck-Morss, *The Dialectics of Seeing: Walter Benjamin and the Arcades Project* (Cambridge: MIT Press, 1989), 269–70.

14. A. L. Kroeber and Clyde Kluckhohn, *Culture: A Critical Review of Concepts and Definitions*, (New York: Vintage, 1952), 68.

15. For example, Arnold's characterization of social classes in *Culture and Anarchy* as "Barbarians," "Philistines," and "Populace" is an interestingly deracinated version

of his ethnological racial typology of the "Celtic," "Norman," and "Teuton" "bloods" that he had earlier described as commingling to produce an ideal "English" character type. Matthew Arnold, *On the Study of Celtic Literature*, vol. 5 of *The Works of Matthew Arnold* (New York: Macmillan, 1903); Arnold, *Culture and Anarchy*, ed. J. Dover Wilson (New York: Cambridge University Press, 1990), 98–128; and see Frederic E. Faverty, *Matthew Arnold the Ethnologist* (Evanston, Ill.: Northwestern University Press, 1951). For a discussion of how the "culture" in *Culture and Anarchy* is similar to the concept as articulated by twentieth-century American anthropologists, see Herbert, *Culture and Anomie*, 55–57; and Stocking, *Race, Culture, and Evolution*, 72–90.

16. Williams, "Culture is Ordinary," in *Convictions* (London: Macgibbon and Kee, 1958), 74.

17. In this respect, I follow Perry Anderson, who addressed a set of historically specific "coordinates" in the "sociopolitical conjuncture" of modernism. Anderson, "Modernity and Revolution," in *Marxism and the Interpretation of Culture*, ed. Cary Nelson and Lawrence Grossberg (Chicago: University of Illinois Press, 1988), 317–33.

18. Anderson, "Modernity and Revolution," 324–25; see also Stephen Kern, *The Culture of Time and Space, 1880–1918* (Cambridge: Harvard University Press, 1983).

19. On this point, see Williams, *The Politics of Modernism*, ed. and introduced by Tony Pinkney (New York: Verso, 1989), 35; and see Pinkney's introduction, 2.

20. For an example (belying its title) of this bias in more traditional scholarship on modernism, see Hugh Kenner, *A Homemade World: The American Modernist Writers* (Baltimore: Johns Hopkins University Press, 1975).

21. See Ann Douglas, *Terrible Honesty: Mongrel Manhattan in the 1920s* (New York: Farrar, Straus and Giroux, 1995); Houston A. Baker Jr., *Modernism and the Harlem Renaissance* (Chicago: University of Chicago Press, 1987); Cary Nelson, *Repression and Recovery: Modern American Poetry and the Politics of Cultural Memory, 1910–1945* (Madison: University of Wisconsin Press, 1989); Walter Kalaidjian, *American Culture Between the Wars: Revisionary Modernism and Postmodern Critique* (New York: Columbia University Press, 1993).

22. Steven Watson provides an interesting collective biography of the "American avant-garde" and its various locales, even offering evidence of the importance, as "cradles of modernism," of such provincial locations as Davenport, Iowa, once the home of Floyd Dell, George Cram Cook, Susan Glaspell, and Margery Currey. Watson, *Strange Bedfellows: The First American Avant-Garde* (New York: Abbeville, 1991), 15–20.

23. Peter Wollen, "Modern Times: Cinema / Americanism / The Robot," in *Raiding the Icebox: Reflections on Twentieth-Century Culture* (Bloomington: Indiana University Press, 1993), 35–71; H. D. Harootunian, "America's Japan / Japan's Japan," in *Japan in the World*, ed. Masao Miyoshi and Harootunian (Durham, N.C.: Duke University Press, 1993), 198; Antonio Gramsci, "Americanism and Fordism," *Selections from the Prison Notebooks*, ed. and trans. Quintin Hoare and Geoffrey Nowell Smith (New York: International, 1971); Max Horkheimer and Theodor W. Adorno, *Dialectic of Enlightenment*, trans. John Cumming (1944; reprint, New York: Continuum, 1995); Le Corbusier, *Towards a New Architecture*, trans. Frederick Etchells (New York: Dover, 1986); first printed in 1923 as *Vers une architecture*.

24. This is not, of course, to say that American artists were unaffected by the technological sublime; for an account of this feature of the American context, see Cecilia

Tichi, *Shifting Gears: Technology, Literature, Culture in Modernist America* (Chapel Hill: University of North Carolina Press, 1987).

25. The central discussion of modernity in this context is Marshall Berman, *All That is Solid Melts into Air: The Experience of Modernity* (New York: Penguin, 1982); see also Anderson, "Modernity and Revolution."

26. Fredric Jameson, *Postmodernism; or, the Cultural Logic of Late Capitalism* (Durham, N.C.: Duke University Press, 1991), 307. This point is central not only to Jameson's characterization of modernism, but to his differentiation between modernism and postmodernism, which he sees as expressing a much more completely realized modernity.

27. Marquis, *Hopes and Ashes*, 27.

28. For a fascinating comparison between Gramsci's southern Italy and the southern United States as portrayed in W. J. Cash's classic, *The Mind of the South*, see Anne Goodwyn Jones, "The Cash Nexus," in *The Mind of the South: Fifty Years Later*, ed. Charles W. Eagles (Jackson: University Press of Mississippi, 1992), 23–51.

29. Unlike western Europe, New Zealand, and even Canada, where rural electrification was a matter of government policy, the United States left it to the initiative of the corporate sector until the institution of the New Deal. Even after the significant impact of the Tennessee Valley Authority and the Rural Electrification Administration, by 1946 only half of the farms in the United States were electrified—compared to France and Germany, which had both achieved rates of 90 percent rural electrification a decade earlier. David E. Nye, *Electrifying America: Social Meanings of a New Technology, 1880–1940* (Cambridge: MIT Press, 1990), 287, 299, 320.

30. Of course, the development of infrastructure was just one part of the rural modernization process. Crucially, farmers also had to be taught that electricity, electrical appliances, and indoor plumbing were worth the significant expense. For a fascinating account of the pedagogy of rural modernization, and the particular role of women as recipients of this training, see Marilyn Irvin Holt, *Linoleum, Better Babies, and the Modern Farm Woman, 1890–1930* (Albuquerque: University of New Mexico Press, 1995).

31. Marquis, *Hopes and Ashes*, 27.

32. Twelve Southerners, *I'll Take My Stand: The South and the Agrarian Tradition* (New York: Harper, 1930).

33. See Wendy Kaplan, *"The Art that is Life": The Arts & Crafts Movement in America, 1875–1920* (Boston: Little, Brown, 1987).

34. The most influential book on American antimodernism to date has been Jackson Lears, *No Place of Grace: Antimodernism and the Transformation of American Culture* (New York: Pantheon, 1981); on nostalgic appropriations of Appalachia, see David E. Whisnant, *All That is Native and Fine: The Politics of Culture in an American Region* (Chapel Hill: University of North Carolina Press, 1983); and for a discussion of similar tendencies in the American Southwest, see Molly H. Mullin, *Consuming The American Southwest: Culture, Art, and Difference* (Durham, N.C.: Duke University Press, forthcoming).

35. See James Clifford, *The Predicament of Culture: Twentieth-Century Ethnography, Literature, and Art* (Cambridge: Harvard University Press, 1988), 117–214; Marianna Torgovnick, *Gone Primitive: Savage Intellects, Modern Lives* (Chicago: Univer-

sity of Chicago Press, 1990); and Wollen, "Out of the Past: Fashion / Orientalism / The Body," in *Raiding the Icebox*, 1–34.

36. Fredric Jameson, "Modernism and Imperialism," in *Nationalism, Colonialism, and Literature*, Field Day Pamphlet 14 (Lawrence Hill, Derry, N. Ireland: Field Day Theatre Company, 1988), 9; reprinted in *Nationalism, Colonialism, and Literature*, ed. Terry Eagleton, Jameson, and Edward W. Said (Minneapolis: University of Minnesota Press, 1990). See also Edward W. Said, "Representing the Colonized: Anthropology's Interlocutors," *Critical Inquiry*, 15 (Winter 1989): 222–23.

37. Said, *Culture and Imperialism* (New York: Knopf, 1993), 189.

38. The exceptionalist claim that the United States was fundamentally different from the European powers because of its rather late engagement in imperialist adventures has recently been subjected to important scrutiny; see Amy Kaplan and Donald E. Pease, eds., *Cultures of United States Imperialism* (Durham, N.C.: Duke University Press, 1993).

39. F. Scott Fitzgerald, *The Great Gatsby* (New York: Scribner's, 1953), 12; and see Baker, *Modernism and the Harlem Renaissance*, 4–5.

40. Mabel Dodge Luhan, *Movers and Shakers* (New York: Harcourt, Brace, 1936), 534.

41. See Mullin, "The Patronage of Difference: Making Indian Art 'Art, Not Ethnography,' " in *The Traffic in Culture: Refiguring Art and Anthropology*, ed. George E. Marcus and Fred R. Myers (Berkeley: University of California Press, 1995), 166–98.

42. Manganaro, *Myth, Rhetoric, and the Voice of Authority*.

43. The work of Janice Radway remains exemplary in its use of ethnographic techniques to address both questions of readers' practices and the construction of taste. See Janice A. Radway, *A Feeling for Books: The Book-of-the Month Club, Literary Taste, and Middle Class Desire* (Chapel Hill: University of North Carolina Press, 1997); and Radway, *Reading the Romance* (Chapel Hill: University of North Carolina Press, 1984).

44. See especially the essays by Marcus, Tyler, Fischer, and Rabinow in *Writing Culture: The Poetics and Politics of Ethnography*, ed. James Clifford and George E. Marcus (Berkeley: University of California Press, 1986); and Marcus and Michael M. J. Fischer, *Anthropology as Cultural Critique: An Experimental Moment in the Human Sciences* (Chicago: University of Chicago Press, 1986), 67–73; and for an overview of the demarcations of "modernist anthropology" (and other peculiarities of this juxtaposition of terms), see Manganaro's introduction to *Modernist Anthropology*.

45. See Ardener, "Social Anthropology and the Decline of Modernism."

46. On anthropology's "classical phase," see Stocking, "The Ethnographic Sensibility of the 1920s and the Dualism of the Anthropological Tradition," in *Romantic Motives*, 208–76.

47. Tzvetan Todorov, *The Conquest of America*, trans. Richard Howard (New York: Harper Perennial, 1984), 250.

48. William H. Goetzmann, *New Lands, New Men: America and the Second Great Age of Discovery* (New York: Viking, 1986), 406–9.

49. Julia E. Liss, "Patterns of Strangeness: Franz Boas, Modernism, and the Origins of Anthropology," in *Prehistories of the Future: The Primitivist Project and the Culture of Modernism*, ed. Elazar Barkan and Ronald Bush (Stanford, Calif.: Stanford University Press, 1995), 114–30.

50. "Cultural lag," a fairly common term of the social sciences in the earlier decades of this century, refers to manifestations of the experience of uneven development. It was first offered as a concept in William Fielding Ogburn, *Social Change with Respect to Culture and Original Nature* (New York: Huebsch, 1922).

Chapter 2
Dry Salvages

1. Frank Lentricchia, *Modernist Quartet* (New York: Cambridge University Press, 1994), 249.

2. On the "Americanness" of "The Dry Salvages," see John Xiros Cooper, *T. S. Eliot and the Ideology of Four Quartets* (Cambridge: Cambridge University Press, 1995); and Lyndall Gordon, "The American Eliot and 'The Dry Salvages,' " in *Words in Time: New Essays on Eliot's Four Quartets.* ed. Edward Lobb (Ann Arbor: University of Michigan Press, 1993), 38–51.

3. Curtis M. Hinsley Jr., "Zunis and Brahmins: Cultural Ambivalence in the Gilded Age," in *Romantic Motives: Essays on Anthropological Sensibility*, vol. 6 of *History of Anthropology*, ed. George W. Stacking Jr. (Madison: University of Wisconsin Press, 1989), 169–70.

4. Hinsley, *Savages and Scientists: The Smithsonian Institution and the Development of American Anthropology 1846–1910* (Washington, D.C.: Smithsonian Institution Press, 1981), 89.

5. Stocking, "The Ethnographic Sensibility of the 1920s and the Dualism of the Anthropological Tradition," in *Romantic Motives*, 210.

6. James Clifford, "On Ethnographic Allegory," in *Writing Culture: The Poetics and Politics of Ethnography*, ed. Clifford and George E. Marcus (Berkeley: University of California Press, 1986), 112–13.

7. Marc Manganaro, *Myth, Rhetoric, and the Voice of Authority: A Critique of Frazer, Eliot, Frye, and Campbell* (New Haven, Conn.: Yale University Press, 1992), 78–79.

8. Eliot's scorn for the embrace of evolutionary theory in "the popular mind" is even clearer in various drafts of the poem, in which he rendered "development" with scare-quotes, "evolution" with a capital *E*, and "a partial fallacy" as "a cheerful fallacy." Helen Gardner, *The Composition of the Four Quartets* (New York: Oxford University Press, 1978), 132–33.

9. Wyndham Lewis, *Time and Western Man* (Boston: Beacon, 1957).

10. Perry Anderson's account of characteristic features of modernism has influenced my description here. Anderson, "Modernity and Revolution," in *Marxism and the Interpretation of Culture*, ed. Cary Nelson and Lawrence Grossberg (Chicago: University of Illinois Press, 1988), 317–33.

11. For a classic example of the elaboration of this point, see Edward Sapir, *Language* (New York: Harcourt, Brace, 1921).

12. My story is derived from Hinsley, *Savages and Scientists*, 98–100, 250–52, 267–70; and Ira Jacknis, "Franz Boas and Exhibits: On the Limitations of the Museum Method of Anthropology," in *Objects and Others: Essays on Museums and Material Culture*, vol. 3 of *History of Anthropology*, 75–111.

13. Franz Boas, "The Principles of Ethnological Classification," in *The Shaping of American Anthropology 1883–1911: A Franz Boas Reader*, ed. Stocking (New York: Basic, 1974), 61.

14. Stocking, "Franz Boas and the Culture Concept in Historical Perspective," in *Race, Culture, and Evolution: Essays in the History of Anthropology* (New York: Free Press, 1968), 205; Boas, "Principles," 61.

15. The connection I am making here between spatiality and modernism should be distinguished from an earlier argument made by Joseph Frank. For Frank, the spatiality of modernism was rather more a formal, and negative, concept, related to what he described as the modernists' attempt to deny the temporality of language. See Frank, "Spatial Form in Modern Literature," in *The Widening Gyre: Crisis and Mastery in Modern Literature* (New Brunswick, N.J.: Rutgers University Press, 1963), 3–62.

16. Alexander Lesser aptly qualifies Boas's reputation as an "antievolutionary" thinker by explaining that what he really objected to was the element of teleology in most social appropriations of Darwinian theory. Lesser, "Franz Boas," in *Totems and Teachers: Perspectives on the History of Anthropology*, ed. Sydel Silverman (New York: Columbia University Press, 1981), 22–24. For a discussion of Eliot's relationship to evolutionary theory, see Manganaro, *Myth*, 68–110; on the distinction between evolution and teleology, see also John Dewey, "The Influence of Darwin on Philosophy," in *The Influence of Darwin on Philosophy and Other Essays on Contemporary Thought* (New York: Henry Holt, 1910), 1–19; and, on the complex relationship between historical thinking and this spatial turn in Boas's early work, see Boas, "The Study of Geography," in *Volksgeist as Method and Ethic: Essays on Boasian Ethnography and the German Anthropological Tradition*, vol. 8 of *History of Anthropology*, 16. First printed in *Science*, 11 February 1887, 137–41.

17. Jacknis, "The Ethnographic Object and the Object of Ethnology in the Early Career of Franz Boas," in *Volksgeist as Method and Ethic*, 185–214.

18. Hinsley, *Savages and Scientists*, 267–8; Paul Radin, *The Method and Theory of Ethnology* (1933; reprint, South Hadley, Mass.: Bergin and Garvey Publishers, 1987), 24–60; Robert H. Lowie, *The History of Ethnological Theory* (New York: Farrar and Rinehart, 1937), 128–55; Marvin Harris, *The Rise of Anthropological Theory* (New York: Thomas Y. Crowell, 1968), 250–463.

19. Marshall Hyatt, *Franz Boas Social Activist: The Dynamics of Ethnicity,* vol. 6 of *Contributions to the Study of Anthropology* (New York: Greenwood, 1990); see also George Hutchinson, *The Harlem Renaissance in Black and White* (Cambridge: Harvard University Press, 1995), 62–77.

20. Benedict apparently saw Boas's endorsement to be especially important since (as she wrote her publisher), "most anthropologists will be amazed at his approval of my theme." Quoted in Margaret M. Caffrey, *Ruth Benedict: Stranger in this Land* (Austin: University of Texas Press, 1989), 207; Boas, foreword to *Coming of Age in Samoa*, by Margaret Mead (New York: Morrow Quill Paperbacks, 1961); Boas, introduction to *Patterns of Culture*, by Ruth Benedict, with a preface by Margaret Mead and a new foreword by Mary Catherine Bateson (Boston: Houghton Mifflin, 1989), xix–xxi.

21. Edward Sapir, "Franz Boas," review of *Anthropology and Modern Life*, by Franz Boas, *New Republic*, 23 January 1929, 278–79; and see Harris, *The Rise of Anthropological Theory*, 250–463. Though Stocking cites Leslie White as making a point very similar to Sapir's about Boas's theoretical conservatism, he nevertheless emphasizes

the theoretical coherence of Boas's legacy, and indeed argues for Boas's early centrality to the development of the culture concept despite Boas's reticence on the topic. Stocking, "Franz Boas and the Culture Concept," 212.

22. See A. L. Kroeber and Clyde Kluckhohn, *Culture: A Critical Review of Concepts and Definitions* (New York: Vintage, 1952), 82.

23. Lesser, "Franz Boas," 22–24.

24. Boas, "Principles," 61.

25. Ibid., 65.

26. Stocking, "Franz Boas and the Culture Concept," 205; Boas, "Principles," 61. It should also be noted that Boas later warned that diffusion was not necessarily the most economical explanation for cultural phenomena, and could thus be dangerously overused. Harris, *The Rise of Anthropological Theory*, 260.

27. Boas, "Principles," 61.

28. Ibid., 62.

29. Ibid., 65–66.

30. Boas, "Museums of Ethnology and their Classification," *Science*, 17 June 1887, 687–89.

31. Hinsley, *Savages and Scientists*, 98–100.

32. Jacknis, "Franz Boas and Exhibits," 86. Jacknis suggests (107) that the museum leadership may also have been interested in displays that illustrated social evolutionary principles—something Boas may have refused to support on intellectual grounds; see also Hyatt, *Franz Boas Social Activist*, 67–72.

33. David Jenkins, "Object Lessons and Ethnographic Displays: Museum Exhibitions and the Making of American Anthropology," *Comparative Studies in Society and History* 36, no. 2 (April 1994): 242–70; Simon J. Bronner, "Object Lessons: The Work of Ethnological Museums and Collections," in *Consuming Visions: Accumulation and Display of Goods in America 1880–1920*, ed. Bronner (New York: Norton, 1989), 217–54.

34. Paul DiMaggio, "Cultural Entrepreneurship in Nineteenth-Century Boston, Part II: The Classification and Framing of American Art," *Media, Culture and Society* 4 (1982): 304.

35. On the topic of the era's obsessions with hierarchies of taste, see DiMaggio, "Cultural Entrepreneurship in Nineteenth-Century Boston, Part I: The Creation of an Organizational Base for High Culture in America," *Media, Culture and Society* 4 (1982): 33–50; DiMaggio, "Cultural Entrepreneurship, Part II"; and Lawrence W. Levine, *Highbrow/Lowbrow: The Emergence of Cultural Hierarchy in America* (Cambridge: Harvard University Press, 1988).

36. Jacknis, "Ethnographic Object."

37. Jacknis, "Ethnographic Object," 203.

38. Burton J. Bledstein, *The Culture of Professionalism: The Middle Class and the Development of Higher Education in America* (New York: Norton, 1976).

39. Hinsley, *Savages and Scientists*, 85–86.

40. Raymond Williams, *The Politics of Modernism*, ed. Tony Pinkney (New York: Verso, 1989), 56–57.

41. Besides the separation from the museum, another exemplary site for this kind of struggle in Boasian anthropology took place within the area of folklore studies. As Rosemary Lévy Zumwalt has shown, Boas took a leading role both in defining profes-

sional practices within the study of folklore and in wresting control of its major organs, including the *Journal of American Folklore*, from scholars with a more "literary" approach to the field. According to Zumwalt, Boas's control over this journal was also related to his disassociation from the Washington establishment; he saw it as a publishing venue that would make him and his students that much less dependent on the publications of the Bureau of American Ethnology. Boas was editor of the journal for sixteen years. Rosemary Lévy Zumwalt, *American Folklore Scholarship: A Dialogue in Dissent* (Bloomington: Indiana University Press, 1988), 30–31, 68–69.

42. Bruce Robbins, *Secular Vocations: Intellectuals, Professionalism, Culture* (New York: Verso, 1993), 13–20, 57–83; see also Robert H. Wiebe, *The Search for Order 1877–1920*, The Making of America Series, ed. David Donald (New York: Hill and Wang, 1967), 111–32; and Peter Dobkin Hall, *The Organization of American Culture, 1700–1900: Private Institutions, Elites, and the Origins of American Nationality* (New York: New York University Press, 1984), 240–70. For a discussion of these issues in the British context, see Harold Perkin, *The Rise of Professional Society: England Since 1880* (New York: Routledge, 1989).

43. See Virginia Dominguez, "The Messy Side of 'Cultural Politics,' " *South Atlantic Quarterly* 91, no. 1 (Winter 1992): 19–42; and Chapter 7 of the present book.

44. Mead, *Coming of Age in Samoa*; Ruth Benedict, *Patterns of Culture* (Boston: Houghton Mifflin, 1989); Boas, *The Mind of Primitive Man* (New York: Macmillan, 1911); Boas, *Anthropology and Modern Life* (New York: Norton, 1928).

45. Leonard B. Glick, "Types Distinct From our Own: Franz Boas on Jewish Identity and Assimilation," *American Anthropologist* 84, no. 3 (1982): 557.

46. John S. Allen, "Franz Boas's Physical Anthropology: The Critique of Racial Formalism Revisited," *Current Anthropology* 30, no. 1 (1989): 79–84.

47. On Boas's propensity for argument by the negative instance, see Lesser, "Franz Boas," 4; and see Marvin Harris, *The Rise of Anthropological Theory*, 258–60.

48. Glick, "Types Distinct From our Own."

49. Ibid., 554, 556; Hyatt, *Franz Boas Social Activist*, 72; see also Ellen Messer, "Franz Boas and Kaufmann Kohler: Anthropology and Reform Judaism," *Jewish Social Studies* 48, no. 2 (1986): 127–40.

50. As I suggested in the Introduction, "cultural relativism" can be as slippery a concept as "culture" itself. Here, Glick's understanding of the term might be considered an example of what Melford E. Spiro taxonomized as "moral cultural relativism," which serves to refute the validity of intercultural judgments of worth, value, taste, and so on. As Richard Rorty has shown from the perspective of a more strictly *epistemological* relativism, it is hard to imagine how one might actually enact this kind of moral cultural relativism. In short, what if *my* cultural context precludes considering yours as worthy of respect? See Spiro, "Cultural Relativism and the Future of Anthropology," in *Rereading Cultural Anthropology*, ed. George E. Marcus (Durham, N.C.: Duke University Press, 1992), 124–51; and Rorty, "On Ethnocentrism: A Reply to Clifford Geertz," *Michigan Quarterly Review* 25, no. 3 (1986): 525–35.

51. Glick points out, from his careful observation of the pronouns Boas used in a talk he gave, entitled, "Race Problems in America," that Boas considered himself part of the "physical type of northwestern Europe," while the new immigrants from southern and eastern Europe were "types distinct from our own." Glick, "Types Distinct From our Own," 545.

52. Boas, "The Outlook for the American Negro," in *The Shaping of American Anthropology*, 314.

53. Ibid., 311.

54. Ibid., 313.

55. W. E. B. Du Bois, "Is Race Separation Practicable?" in *W. E. B. Du Bois Speaks: Speeches and Addresses 1890–1919*, ed. Philip S. Foner (New York: Pathfinder, 1970), 179–86.

56. Arnold Rampersad, *The Art and Imagination of W. E. B. Du Bois* (New York: Schocken, 1990), 228–33; and see Thomas C. Holt, "The Political Uses of Alienation: W. E. B. Du Bois on Politics, Race, and Culture, 1903–1940," *American Quarterly* 42, no. 2 (June 1990): 301–23.

57. Hutchinson, *The Harlem Renaissance in Black and White*, 62–77.

58. Richard Hofstadter, *Social Darwinism in American Thought* (Boston: Beacon, 1966), 105–42. From abroad, Henri Bergson, who also critiqued Darwinian theory from an essentially Lamarckian perspective, was enjoying a remarkable popularity in the United States; his first American lecture at Boas's Columbia in 1913 caused traffic jams on Broadway. Henry F. May, *The End of American Innocence* (1959; reprint, Chicago: Quadrangle, 1969), 228–29.

59. May, *The End of American Innocence*, 372; Lesser, "Franz Boas," 14; see also "The German-American Problem," *New Republic*, 30 March 1918, 252–53.

60. The German word *Kultur* has its own complex history, one strongly tied to debates about the place of the German nation in relation to the rest of Europe. For a brief overview of this history, see Alfred G. Meyer, "Historical Notes on Ideological Aspects of the Concept of Culture in Germany and Russia," in Kroeber and Kluckhohn, *Culture*, 403–13.

61. See May, *The End of American Innocence*, 364.

62. Christian Gauss, *Why We Went To War* (New York: Scribner's, 1918), 20. Gauss went to great pains in this book to suggest that the war was the fault of a malignant "Prussian" character type, distinct from his own "southern German" heritage.

63. See Hyatt, *Franz Boas Social Activist*, 123–38.

64. Boas, letter to the editor, *New York Times*, 8 January 1916; reprinted in *The Shaping of American Anthropology*, 333.

65. Ibid., 335.

66. May, *The End of American Innocence*, 388.

67. "Lynching: An American Kultur?," *New Republic*, 13 April 1918, 311–12.

68. Stocking, *The Shaping of American Anthropology*, 335.

69. Hyatt, *Franz Boas Social Activist*, 127, 129; Thomas Bender, *New York Intellect* (New York: Knopf, 1987), 295–300. It has been speculated that this conflict with the Columbia administration and his other publicly antiwar statements prevented the otherwise enormously powerful Boas from designating his successor as department chair at the time of his retirement in 1936. This fact, in turn, produced a lasting enmity between Boas's chosen successor, Ruth Benedict, and the administration's choice, Ralph Linton. Murphy, "Anthropology at Columbia," 72.

70. Boas, "Scientists as Spies," *Nation*, 16 October 1919, 797; Esther S. Goldfrank, *Notes on an Undirected Life: As One Anthropologist Tells It* (Flushing, N.Y.: Queens College Press, 1978), 10–15; Virginia Yans-McLaughlin, "Science, Democracy, and Ethics: Mobilizing Culture and Personality for World War II," in *Malinowski, Rivers,*

Benedict, and Others: Essays on Culture and Personality, vol. 4 of *History of Anthro-pology* (Madison: University of Wisconsin Press, 1986), 185–86. George Stocking con-textualizes this professional condemnation of Boas as the product of jealousies and animosities provoked during the years of Boas's consolidation of position in the profes-sion. Stocking, "The Scientific Reaction Against Cultural Anthropology, 1917–1920," in *Race, Culture, and Evolution*, 270–307.

71. Romain Rolland, *Above the Battle*, trans. C. K. Ogden (Chicago: Open Court, 1916); Julien Benda, *Treason of the Intellectuals*, trans. Richard Aldington (New York: Morrow, 1928); see also Martha Hanna, *The Mobilization of Intellect: French Scholars and Writers During the Great War* (Cambridge: Harvard University Press, 1996).

72. Boas, "Nationalism," *Dial* 66 (8 March 1919): 232–7; Boas, "The Mental Atti-tude of the Educated Classes," *Dial* 65 (5 September 1918): 145–48.

73. Harris, *The Rise of Anthropological Theory*, 280–81.

74. Gauss was willing to concede that it is none of Americans' business if the Ger-mans "worship Thor under a new name, or even the Grand Llama, or their Emperor's great toe. . . . But when their masters tell us that God has changed his mind and has decided that henceforth the Prussians and not the peacemakers shall inherit the earth, . . . it has become our most serious business." Gauss, *Why We Went To War*, 29.

75. See Werner Sollors, *Beyond Ethnicity* (New York: Oxford University Press, 1986), 66–101.

76. Horace Kallen, "Democracy Versus the Melting-Pot," *Nation*, 18 February 1915 and 25 February 1915, 190–94, 217–20; hereafter, page numbers cited in text.

77. Bourne, "Trans-National America," in *The Radical Will: Selected Writings 1911–1918*, ed. Olaf Hansen (New York: Urizen, 1977), 248–64; first published in the *Atlantic Monthly*, July 1916, 86–97. Hereafter, page numbers cited in text.

78. Bourne, "The War and The Intellectuals," in *The Radical Will*, 317; first pub-lished in the *Seven Arts* (June 1917): 133–46.

79. Romain Rolland, the 1915 Nobel Laureate in Literature, was an important figure to Bourne, and it is likely that he read Rolland's controversial statement "Au-dessus de la mêlée," either in the original (first published in the *Journal de Genève*, 15 September 1914), or in translation, "Above the Battle," in *Above the Battle*, trans. C. K. Ogden (Chicago: Open Court, 1916), 37–55.

80. Eric J. Sandeen, "Bourne Again: The Correspondence Between Randolph Bourne and Elsie Clews Parsons," *American Literary History* 1, no. 3 (Fall 1989): 497. For a discussion of Bourne's frequent disappointment with his friends, see Christopher Lasch, *The New Radicalism in America, 1889–1963: The Intellectual as Social Type* (New York: Norton, 1965), 69–103.

81. Bourne, "Continental Cultures," *New Republic*, 16 January 1915, 14–16.

82. Benedict Anderson has argued that while citizens of the United States were rela-tively quick to create for themselves a national identity, the United States has also experienced significant moments of "failure" in its cohesion as a cultural, linguistic, and bureaucratic unit—including its failure to absorb English-speaking Canada, the short-lived Texan independence, and, of course, the Civil War. Following Anderson's argument that bureaucratic centralization is a vital component in the creation of nation-alist identity, it might be noted further that the United States has never—by design—had one political, economic, military, and cultural center comparable to France's Paris or England's London. Its nationalism has thus, arguably, always been complicated by

various versions of regionalism, including the recurrent struggles related to "states' rights." Anderson, *Imagined Communities: Reflections on the Origin and Spread of Nationalism* (New York: Verso, 1983), 50–65.

83. Bourne, "American Use For German Ideals," *New Republic*, 4 September 1915, 117–19.

84. See Bourne, "The Puritan's Will to Power," in *The Radical Will*, 301–6; and see Van Wyck Brooks, "The Wine of the Puritans," "America's Coming-of-Age," "Toward a National Culture," in *Van Wyck Brooks: The Early Years*, ed. Claire Sprague (New York: Harper and Row, 1968), 1–60, 79–158, 180–91.

85. Bourne, "Education in Taste," *New Republic*, 4 March 1916, 122–24; Bourne, "Our Cultural Humility," in *The History of a Literary Radical*, ed. Van Wyck Brooks (New York: Huebsch, 1920), 31–44; see also Bourne, "Continental Cultures."

86. For examples of contemporary usages of *transnationalism*, see Inderpal Grewal and Caren Kaplan, eds., *Scattered Hegemonies: Postmodernity and Transnational Feminist Practices* (Minneapolis: University of Minnesota Press, 1994); and Paul Gilroy, *The Black Atlantic: Modernity and Double Consciousness* (Cambridge: Harvard University Press, 1993), 15.

87. If there is any irony at all in Macdonald's quotation of Bourne, it is that in tracing "masscult's" origin to those "bottom-dogs of Europe," Macdonald recuperates the category of the "Puritan," to locate the immigrants' social flaw (besides their penchant for assimilation) in the fact that they weren't *sufficiently* Puritan. Dwight Macdonald, "Masscult and Midcult," in *Against the American Grain: Essays on the Effects of Mass Culture* (New York: Da Capo, 1962), 35–36.

88. See Casey Nelson Blake, *Beloved Community: the Cultural Criticism of Randolph Bourne, Van Wyck Brooks, Waldo Frank, and Lewis Mumford* (Chapel Hill: University of North Carolina Press, 1990).

89. T. S. Eliot, "Tradition and the Individual Talent," in *The Sacred Wood* (1928; reprint, London: Methuen, 1964), 47–59; Eliot, *After Strange Gods: A Primer on Modern Heresy* (New York: Harcourt, Brace, 1933), 18; see also Eliot, *Christianity and Culture* (New York: Harcourt Brace Jovanovich, 1988).

Chapter 3
The National Genius

1. Regna Darnell, *Edward Sapir: Linguist, Anthropologist, Humanist* (Berkeley: University of California Press, 1990), 10–11, 133–36, 198–200, 379–80. Both Zora Neale Hurston and Esther Goldfrank take credit for first calling Boas "Papa Franz" to his face; see Ann Douglas, *Terrible Honesty: Mongrel Manhattan in the 1920s* (New York: Farrar, Straus, and Giroux, 1995), 283–84; and Goldfrank, *Notes on an Undirected Life: As One Anthropologist Tells It* (Flushing, N.Y.: Queens College Press, 1978), 19–20, 39–40.

2. Edward Sapir, "Randolph Bourne," *Dial*, 11 January 1919, 45; Darnell, *Edward Sapir: Linguist, Anthropologist, Humanist*, 176–77. For a discussion of the theoretical connections between Bourne's and Sapir's thought, see Richard Handler, "Anti-Romantic Romanticism: Edward Sapir and the Critique of American Individualism," *Anthropological Quarterly* 61, no. 1 (1989): 1–13.

3. In his account of the folding of the *Seven Arts*, Waldo Frank insists that circulation actually improved when it made its most vehement antiwar statements. Instead, he points to a less heroic story, in which the war caused the magazine's decline by precipitating fighting among the staff members and the publication of political pieces that compromised their literary standards. No doubt aiding in its demise was the suicide of its primary financial supporter, Mrs. A. K. Rankine, prompted, Frank hints, by her inability to cope with the social ostracism resulting from the magazine's antiwar position. Frank, *Memoirs*, ed. Alan Trachtenberg (Amherst: University of Massachusetts Press, 1973), 92–95.

4. Frank, introduction to *The Bridge*, by Hart Crane (1933, New York: Liveright, 1970), xxi; Frank, *Memoirs*, 242.

5. Lewis Mumford, "Lyric Wisdom," in *Paul Rosenfeld: Voyager in the Arts*, ed. Jerome Mellquist and Lucie Wiese (New York: Creative Age, 1948), 43.

6. Frank, *Our America* (New York: Boni and Liveright, 1919), xi. Nor, of course, would I categorize these writers as "nativists," as I suspect Walter Benn Michaels would; see his *Our America: Nativism, Modernism, and Pluralism* (Durham, N.C.: Duke University Press, 1995). For a fuller discussion and bibliography of the historical debate over the *Seven Arts* group and their status as "cultural nationalists," see Casey Nelson Blake, *Beloved Community: The Cultural Criticism of Randolph Bourne, Van Wyck Brooks, Waldo Frank, and Lewis Mumford* (Chapel Hill: University of North Carolina Press, 1990), 123, 318–19, note 3.

7. Van Wyck Brooks, "Young America," *Seven Arts* (December 1916): 144–51; Seichi Neruse, "Young Japan," *Seven Arts* (April 1917): 616–26; John Dos Passos, "Young Spain," *Seven Arts* (August 1917): 473–88; and Padraic Colum, "Youngest Ireland," *Seven Arts* (September 1917): 608–23. In his memoirs, Waldo Frank refers to these articles as an important "inner grouping of the magazine." Frank, *Memoirs*, 88.

8. Brooks, "The Wine of the Puritans," in *Van Wyck Brooks: The Early Years*, 50–52; hereafter, cited in text as "Wine."

9. Brooks, "America's Coming-of-Age," in *Van Wyck Brooks: The Early Years*, 95; hereafter, cited in text as "America's."

10. Brooks, "Toward a National Culture," and "The Culture of Industrialism," *Van Wyck Brooks: The Early Years*, 190–202; first printed in the *Seven Arts* (March 1917): 535–47, and (April 1917): 655–66.

11. See Warren I. Susman, "Uses of the Puritan Past," in *Culture as History: The Transformation of American Society in the Twentieth Century* (New York: Pantheon, 1984), 39–49. Though Susman's history of the uses of the Puritan past is invaluable, I disagree with his assertion, "During the nineteenth-century, the Puritan generally enjoyed a good press." To argue this, he had to ignore the fact that American Calvinism (and Puritans as its representatives) had come under siege by what was arguably one of the most important cultural events of the century, the rise of evangelical religion. See James Turner, *Without God, Without Creed: The Origins of Unbelief in America* (Baltimore: Johns Hopkins Press, 1985).

12. For example, Ann Douglas identifies a subgenre of the nineteenth-century historical novel, set in Puritan New England, in which an innocent young girl comes into conflict with a strict Puritan father or doctrinaire minister. The girl suffers severe punishments for disobeying some point of Calvinist dogma, to follow her heart's guidance instead. Douglas, *The Feminization of American Culture* (New York: Knopf, 1979),

107; see also Jane Tompkins, *Sensational Designs* (New York: Oxford University Press, 1985).

13. The phrase "Protestant ethic" as a referent for the American Puritans was apparently not indebted to Max Weber. Though Weber's classic essay appeared in German in 1905, it was not widely read in the United States until it was translated into English in 1930. Susman, "Uses," 46; Talcott Parsons, preface of *The Protestant Ethic and the Spirit of Capitalism*, by Max Weber, trans. Talcott Parsons (New York: Scribner's, 1958), xiii.

14. For another discussion of Brooks as an "Arnoldian" thinker, see John Henry Raleigh, *Matthew Arnold and American Culture* (Berkeley: University of California Press, 1961), 151–53.

15. Matthew Arnold, *Culture and Anarchy*, ed. J. Dover Wilson (New York: Cambridge University Press, 1990), 54.

16. See Williams, *Culture and Society: 1780–1950* (New York: Columbia University Press, 1983), 110–29; and Lionel Trilling, *Matthew Arnold* (New York: Norton, 1965).

17. Brooks, "Toward a National Culture," 191; "America's," 149.

18. See Frederick J. Hoffman, *The Twenties: American Writing in the Postwar Decade* (New York: Viking, 1955), 314–27.

19. Richard Chase, *The American Novel and Its Tradition* (Garden City, N.Y.: Doubleday, 1957), 9–10. Leslie Fiedler may have had some similar notion of the "middlebrow" as a resolution to the positions of high and low when he described as "cheery, middlebrow" Hawthorne's *The House of the Seven Gables*—a tale full of doleful, historically cursed Puritans and irresolute technical Pioneers, joined together by the sunny ministrations of Phoebe, the social housekeeper. Fiedler, *Love and Death in the American Novel* (New York: Meridian, 1964), 229.

20. See Janice Radway, "The Scandal of the Middlebrow: The Book-of-the-Month Club, Class Fracture, and Cultural Authority," *South Atlantic Quarterly* 89, no. 4 (Fall 1990): 703–36; Joan Shelley Rubin, *The Making of Middlebrow Culture* (Chapel Hill: University of North Carolina Press, 1992); Russell Lynes, *The Tastemakers: The Shaping of American Popular Taste* (New York: Dover, 1949).

21. Vernon Louis Parrington, *Main Currents in American Thought* (New York: Harcourt, Brace, 1930), 3–88.

22. This difference in social and economic background between the writers of the *Seven Arts* did produce its conflicts. According to Bourne, Brooks occasionally felt alienated by his fellow *Seven Arts* editors, explaining that the magazine was somewhat too "Jewish" and "Freudian" in character (this last description being especially ironic, since he was himself later castigated for being a vulgar Freudian critic). Blake, *Beloved Community*, 14, 318–19.

23. Randolph Bourne, "Old Tyrannies," in *The Radical Will: Selected Writings of Randolph Bourne, 1911–1918*, ed. Olaf Hansen (New York: Urizen, 1977), 169.

24. See Robert Fishman, *Bourgeois Utopias: The Rise and Fall of Suburbia* (New York: Basic, 1987), 134–54.

25. See Jackson Lears, *No Place of Grace: Antimodernism and the Transformation of American Culture* (New York: Pantheon, 1981).

26. Theodore Roosevelt, "The Strenuous Life," in *The Call of the Wild*, ed. Roderick Nash (New York: George Braziller, 1970), 79–84.

27. Brooks, "Wine," 34–40. Brooks rightly connected naturalism with the imperialism of the period, but he also suggested that its popularity was the result of Americans' poor literary education, which, because of its emphasis on models related to the Puritan past, made readers inadequate judges of the literature of their moment.

28. Blake, "The Young Intellectuals and the Culture of Personality," *American Literary History* 1, no. 3 (Fall 1989): 510–34.

29. George Santayana, "The Genteel Tradition in American Philosophy," *The Genteel Tradition: Nine Essays*, ed. Douglas L. Wilson (Cambridge, Harvard University Press, 1967), 36–56; Blake, *Beloved Community*, 116. See also John Dos Passos's early article "Against American Literature," which is also indebted to Brooks's writing, and which criticizes contemporary American letters as hopelessly feminized. J. R. Dos Passos Jr., "Against American Literature," *New Republic*, 14 October 1916, 269–71.

30. Paul DiMaggio, "Cultural Entrepreneurship in Nineteenth-Century Boston: The Creation of an Organizational Base for High Culture in America," *Media, Culture, and Society* 4 (1982): 33–50; and DiMaggio, "Cultural Entrepreneurship in Nineteenth-Century Boston, Part II: The Classification and Framing of American Art," *Media, Culture, and Society* 4 (1982): 303–22.

31. Brooks, *The Ordeal of Mark Twain* (New York: Dutton, 1920), and *The Pilgrimage of Henry James* (New York: Dutton, 1925).

32. See Brooks, *An Autobiography* (New York: Dutton, 1965), 435–50; Robert E. Spiller, ed., *The Van Wyck Brooks Lewis Mumford Letters* (New York: Dutton, 1970), 219; and Raymond Nelson, *Van Wyck Brooks: A Writer's Life* (New York: Dutton, 1981), 182–95.

33. Brooks, *The Life of Emerson* (New York: Dutton, 1932); *The Flowering of New England* (New York: Dutton, 1936); Lewis Mumford, *The Golden Day* (New York: Boni and Liveright, 1926).

34. Brooks, *Opinions of Oliver Allston* (New York: Dutton, 1941), 190–246. Several of the most infamous chapters of *Oliver Allston* were first delivered as speeches at the First and Second Annual Conferences on Science, Philosophy, and Religion in New York City. These were, respectively, "On Literature Today" (10 October 1940), and "Primary Literature and Coterie Literature" (10 September 1941).

35. Dwight Macdonald, "Kulturbolschewismus is Here," *Partisan Review* 8, no. 6 (November–December 1941): 442–51; Allen Tate and others, "On the 'Brooks-MacLeish Thesis,' " *Partisan Review* 9, no. 1 (January–February 1942): 38–47; T. S. Eliot, "A Letter to the Editors," *Partisan Review* 9, no. 2 (March–April 1942): 115–16; and see Chapter 6.

36. See Stanley Edgar Hyman, *The Armed Vision: A Study in the Methods of Modern Literary Criticism* (1947; reprint, New York: Vintage, 1955), 92–113. For another, less dismissive, view of Brooks in roughly the same years, see Edmund Wilson, "A Picture to Hang in the Library: Brooks's *Age of Irving*," in *Classics and Commercials* (New York: Vintage, 1964), 224–30. For an overview of his critical reputation, see William Wasserstrom, ed., *Van Wyck Brooks: the Critic and his Critics* (Port Washington, N.Y.: Kennikat, 1979).

37. Brooks, *The Confident Years: 1885–1915* (New York: Dutton, 1952), 581–611.

38. While Sapir was, by all accounts, one of the most gifted anthropological linguists of the early years of the professional discipline, Kroeber's initiation to anthropology was also via linguistics and his lifetime contributions in that area were prodigious; for

an overview of Sapir's work in linguistics, see *Selected Writings of Edward Sapir in Language, Culture, and Personality*, ed. David G. Mandelbaum (Berkeley: University of California Press, 1949). On Kroeber's contributions to linguistics, see Dell Hymes, "Alfred Louis Kroeber," in *Language in Culture and Society*, ed. Hymes (New York: Harper and Row, 1964), 689–710.

39. A. L. Kroeber, "The Superorganic," in *The Nature of Culture* (Chicago: University of Chicago Press, 1952), 23; first printed in *American Anthropologist* 19, no. 2 (April–June 1917): 163–213.

40. A. L. Kroeber and Clyde Kluckhohn, *Culture: A Critical Review of Concepts and Definitions* (New York: Vintage, 1952), 53.

41. Kroeber, "Superorganic," 22.

42. Ibid., 40.

43. Ibid., 40, 43–45.

44. Ibid., 22.

45. Alexander Goldenweiser, for example, saw Kroeber as offering a theory of "cultural determinism," in which "events occur when they must occur" according to a kind of cultural necessity. Similarly, Edward Sapir noted both a "social determinism" in Kroeber's theory and a certain conceptual vagueness to his understanding of how the superorganic "force" related to the organic sphere: it was autonomous of the organic, and yet it still seemed to mysteriously act upon organic human entities. A. A. Goldenweiser, "The Autonomy of the Social," *American Anthropologist* 19, no. 3 (July–September 1917): 448; Sapir, "Do We Need a 'Superorganic'?" *American Anthropologist* 19, no. 3 (July–September 1917): 442–43.

46. Sapir, "Do We Need a 'Superorganic'?," 441.

47. Ibid., 443.

48. Ibid., 45.

49. Darnell, *Edward Sapir: Linguist, Anthropologist, Humanist*, 143–47; Theodora Kroeber, *Alfred Kroeber: A Personal Configuration* (Berkeley: University of California Press, 1970), 101–2.

50. A. L. Kroeber, "Totem and Taboo: An Ethnologic Psychoanalysis," *American Anthropologist* 22, no. 1 (January–March 1920): 48–55.

51. See Weston A. La Barre, "The Influence of Freud on Anthropology," *American Imago* 46, nos. 2–3 (1989): 203–45.

52. Clark Wissler, "Opportunities for Coördination in Anthropological and Psychological Research," *American Anthropologist* 22, no. 1 (January–March 1920): 4.

53. Darnell, *Edward Sapir: Linguist, Anthropologist, Humanist*, 289–94.

54. Sapir, "From a Review of Oskar Pfister, 'The Psychoanalytic Method,' " in *Selected Writings of Edward Sapir in Language, Culture, and Personality*, ed. David G. Mandelbaum (Berkeley: University of California Press, 1949), 522.

55. Sapir, "A Freudian Half-Holiday," review of *Delusion and Dream*, by Sigmund Freud, in the *Dial* 63 (20 December 1917): 636.

56. Sapir, "From a Review of Oskar Pfister," 523; Sapir, "From a Review of C. G. Jung, 'Psychological Types,' " in *Selected Writings*, 532.

57. Robert Lowie, for example, expressed to Ruth Benedict his irritation at being labeled an "extrovert." See Darnell, *Edward Sapir: Linguist, Anthropologist, Humanist*, 139–43; and see Mead, *An Anthropologist at Work*, 72–73.

58. See Mead, *Blackberry Winter: My Earlier Years* (New York: Pocket Books, 1975), 135. Alfred Kroeber also may have recognized this fact when, in a discussion of Benedict's theories of culture, he referred to her interest in locating cultural "patterns or configurations or Gestalts"; Kroeber, *Nature of Culture*, 5.

59. Sapir, *Language* (New York: Harcourt, Brace, 1921), 233–34. Sapir's argument against the connection between language, race, and culture may have been directed against Clark Wissler's recently published landmark work, *The American Indian*, which made tentative claims for such connections; see Sapir, "The American Indian," review of *The American Indian*, by Clark Wissler, *New Republic,* 7 June 1919, 189–91; and Clark Wissler, *The American Indian, an Introduction to the Anthropology of the New World* (New York: McMurrie, 1919).

60. Sapir, *Language*, 232, 233.

61. Whorf's hypothesis of "linguistic relativism," which held that speakers of different languages *thought* in fundamentally distinct ways, was widely influential in the 1950s, when compilations of his essays were first published in book form. In 1953, his work was the subject of a conference whose participants included Claude Lévi-Strauss, Roman Jakobson, Thomas Sebeok, and C. F. Voegelin. In 1956, art historian E. H. Gombrich cited Whorf's theories approvingly in his classic *Art and Illusion.* Though subsequently marginalized in contemporary linguistic theory, Whorf's theories continue to be of some interest for, among others, philosophers of language. See Benjamin Lee Whorf, *Language, Thought, and Reality: Selected Writings*, ed. John B. Carroll (Cambridge: Technology Press of the Massachusetts Institute of Technology, 1956); E. H. Gombrich, *Art and Illusion: A Study in the Psychology of Pictorial Representation* (1956, Princeton, N.J.: Princeton University Press, 1969); Emily A. Schultz, *Dialogue at the Margins : Whorf, Bakhtin, and Linguistic Relativity* (Madison: University of Wisconsin Press, 1990); and Donald Davidson, "On the Very Idea of a Conceptual Scheme," in *Inquiries into Truth and Interpretation* (New York: Oxford University Press, 1990), 183–98.

62. Kroeber, "Reflections on Edward Sapir, Scholar and Man," in *Edward Sapir: Appraisals of His Life and Work*, 136; see also Darnell, *Edward Sapir: Linguist, Anthropologist, Humanist*, 381–82.

63. Handler, "The Dainty and the Hungry Man: Literature and Anthropology in the Work of Edward Sapir," in *Observers Observed: Essays on Ethnographic Fieldwork*, vol. 1 of *History of Anthropology*, ed. George W. Stocking Jr. (Madison: University of Wisconsin Press, 1983), 208–31.

64. See especially "The King of Thule" and "This Age," quoted in Toni Flores, "The Poetry of Edward Sapir," *Dialectical Anthropology* 11 (1986): 152, 161.

65. Judith Modell, *Ruth Benedict: Patterns of a Life* (Philadelphia: University of Pennsylvania Press, 1983), 155; Margaret Mead, *An Anthropologist at Work: Writings of Ruth Benedict* (Boston: Houghton Mifflin, 1959), 93.

66. Emanuel Carnevali, "A Few First Books," *Poetry* 15, no. 3 (December 1919): 170; Sapir, *Dreams and Gibes* (Boston: Poet Lore, 1917).

67. For a comprehensive account of the free-verse controversy in this period, see Eddie G. Cone, "The Free-Verse Controversy in American Magazines: 1912–1922" (PhD diss., Duke University, 1970).

68. Sapir, "The Twilight of Rhyme," *Dial* 63 (16 August 1917): 100.

69. Ibid., 99.

70. Ibid., 98.

71. Ibid., 100.

72. Ibid., 99.

73. Handler, "Dainty Man," 219–21.

74. Sapir, "Culture, Genuine and Spurious," in *Selected Writings*, 311; first printed in *American Journal of Sociology*, 29 (1924): 401–29; portions were also printed as "Civilization and Culture," *Dial* 67 (September 1919): 233–36; and as "Culture in New Countries," *Dalhousie Review* 2 (1922): 358–68. Hereafter, cited in the text.

75. Ibid., 316; Sapir, "The Stenographer," quoted in Flores, "The Poetry of Edward Sapir," 154.

76. Sapir to Benedict, 29 April 1929, quoted in Darnell, *Edward Sapir: Linguist, Anthropologist, Humanist*, 180.

Chapter 4
Terrains of Culture

1. See Waldo Frank, *Our America* (New York: Boni and Liveright, 1919), 222–32. The "pessimism" model of the twenties is propagated by the influence of such important works as Henry F. May, *The End of American Innocence* (New York: Knopf, 1969); and Alfred Kazin, *On Native Grounds* (1942; reprint, New York: Harcourt Brace Jovanovich, 1982). For recent corrections of this view, see Charles C. Alexander, *Here The Country Lies: Nationalism and the Arts in Twentieth Century America* (Bloomington: Indiana University Press, 1980), 85–86; and George Hutchinson, *The Harlem Renaissance in Black and White* (Cambridge: Harvard University Press, 1995), 105–9.

2. Edward Sapir, "The Woman's Man," *New Republic*, 16 September 1916, 167.

3. See Ellen Kay Trimberger, "Feminism, Men, and Modern Love: Greenwich Village 1900–1925," in *Powers of Desire: The Politics of Sexuality*, ed. Ann Snitow, Christine Stansell, and Sharon Thompson (New York: Monthly Review Press, 1983), 131–52.

4. Margaret Mead, *Blackberry Winter: My Earlier Years* (New York: Pocket Books, 1975), 313–14.

5. The Lyricists—described by Amy Lowell as the heirs to the American poetic vanguard after her own Imagists—were particularly well represented in the 1920s in the pages of *Poetry*. Though their work has to a large extent been removed from the modernist canon (one suspects because many of its best practitioners were widely popular, and were women), the Lyricists possessed a typically modernist interest in expanding the possibilities of lyric form. Louis Untermeyer's *American Poetry Since 1900* devotes two—gender-segregated—chapters to the Lyricists, among whom he lists (for the women) Harriet Monroe, Edna St. Vincent Millay, Sara Teasdale, Elinor Wylie, Louise Bogan, Léonie Adams, and Genevieve Taggard, and (for the less impressive group of men) William Rose Benét, Stephen Vincent Benét, Witter Bynner, and John Hall Wheelock. In his 1930 anthology, *Modern American Poetry*, Untermeyer included in this company the poetry of "Anne Singleton—the pseudonym under which a well-known anthropologist writes her poems." Untermeyer, ed., *American Poetry Since 1900* (New York: Henry Holt, 1923), 205–61; Untermeyer, ed., *Modern American Poetry* (New York: Harcourt, Brace, 1930), 518–19; Mead, *An Anthropologist at Work: Writ-*

ings of Ruth Benedict (Boston: Houghton Mifflin, 1959), 92; Margaret M. Caffrey, *Ruth Benedict: Stranger in this Land* (Austin: University of Texas Press, 1989), 172–77.

6. Caffrey, *Ruth Benedict*, 188. Clifford Geertz has recently argued that Mead's proprietary relationship to Benedict's work has contributed to Benedict's subsequent devaluation as an important theorist of her period. Whether or not this is true, it is clear that interpretations of Benedict's work have tended to be filtered through Mead's interpretations of them, and through analyses of Mead's place in anthropological history. Geertz, *Works and Lives: The Anthropologist as Author* (Stanford, Calif.: Stanford University Press, 1988), 105–6; Mead, *Blackberry Winter*, 122–25; Jane Howard, *Margaret Mead: A Life* (New York: Simon and Schuster, 1984), 57; see also Gail Dimitroff, "Guiding Spirits: An Inquiry into the Nature of the Bond Between Ruth Benedict and Margaret Mead" (PhD diss., United States International University, 1983).

7. Regna Darnell, *Edward Sapir: Linguist, Anthropologist, Humanist* (Berkeley: University of California Press, 1990), 183–88; Mead, *Anthropologist at Work*, 288.

8. I think it is indicative of Mead's lingering anger at Sapir that in *Blackberry Winter* she *twice* mentions—in similar language—that Sapir told her she "would do better to stay home and have children than to go off to the South Seas to study adolescent girls." Mead, *Blackberry Winter*, 9, 266.

9. Sapir, "Observations on the Sex Problem in America," *American Journal of Psychiatry* 8 (November 1928): 519–34. Helen Swick Perry, biographer of the psychiatrist Harry Stack Sullivan, considers Sapir's "Observations" a direct reflection of Sullivan's opinions on sexuality in America, and indeed suggests that it was written at Sullivan's urging—though Sapir "somewhat resented the assignment." This suggestion, if it is true, may have a tragic element, considering the article's disparagement of homosexuality, and the widespread assumption that Sullivan was himself involved in a long-term homosexual relationship during the time of his acquaintance with Sapir. Perry is agonizingly discrete on the point of her subject's sexual orientation, an issue not irrelevant in light of Sullivan's professional statements concerning homosexuality. Helen Swick Perry, *Psychiatrist of America: The Life of Harry Stack Sullivan* (Cambridge, Mass.: Belknap, 1982), 209–11, 339–40; Darnell, *Edward Sapir*, 291–92.

10. Darnell, *Edward Sapir*, 180. Sapir's poor opinion of Mead's work was a matter of public record. In 1929 he described *Coming of Age in Samoa* as "cheap and dull"; Sapir, "Franz Boas," review of *Anthropology and Modern Life*, by Franz Boas, *New Republic*, 23 January 1929, 279.

11. As Richard Handler wittily puts it, "Pound is to Eliot as Sapir is to Benedict." Handler, "Ruth Benedict and the Modernist Sensibility," in *Modernist Anthropology: From Fieldwork to Text*, ed. Marc Manganaro (Princeton, N.J.: Princeton University Press, 1990), 163.

12. Ruth Benedict, "Anthropology and the Abnormal," *Journal of General Psychology* 10, no. 1 (1934): 76.

13. Geertz, *Works and Lives*, 106.

14. Benedict, *Patterns of Culture* (Boston: Houghton Mifflin, 1989), 278; hereafter, cited in text.

15. For a reading that suggests that Benedict's work "was less reificationist and psychologistic than she was later reputed to be," see James A. Boon, *Other Tribes, Other Scribes* (New York: Cambridge University Press, 1982), 105–8. For a thoroughgoing contemporary critique of the "culture and personality" approach, see Alfred R.

Lindesmith and Anselm L. Strauss, "A Critique of Culture-Personality Writings," *American Sociological Review* 15, no. 5 (October 1950): 587–600.

16. Victor Barnouw, "Ruth Benedict," *American Scholar* 49, no. 4 (Autumn 1980): 506.

17. A. L. Kroeber, review of *Patterns of Culture*, by Ruth Benedict, *American Anthropologist* 37 (1935): 690.

18. Geertz, *Works and Lives*, 102–28.

19. Boon, *Other Tribes, Other Scribes*, 107.

20. Benedict, "Configurations of Culture in North America," *American Anthropologist* 34 (1932): 1–27.

21. See, for example, Li An-che, "Zuñi: Some Observations and Queries," *American Anthropologist*, 39 (1937); and Esther S. Goldfrank, "Socialization, Personality, and the Structure of Pueblo Society," *American Anthropologist*, 47 (1945): 513–37.

22. Caffrey, *Ruth Benedict*, 223.

23. Boon, *Other Tribes, Other Scribes*, 107.

24. Caffrey, *Ruth Benedict*, 214; Goldfrank, *Notes on an Undirected Life: As One Anthropologist Tells It* (Flushing, N.Y.: Queens College Press, 1978), 39.

25. Kroeber, review of *Patterns of Culture*, 689; see also Carl N. Degler, *In Search of Human Nature: The Decline and Revival of Darwinism in American Social Thought* (New York: Oxford University Press, 1991), 206.

26. D. H. Lawrence, *Studies in Classic American Literature* (1923; reprint, New York: Viking, 1968).

27. Edward Sapir, review of *The Re-Discovery of America: An Introduction to a Philosophy of American Life*, by Waldo Frank, *American Journal of Sociology* 35 (1929): 336.

28. Frank, *Memoirs*, ed. Alan Trachtenberg (Amherst: University of Massachusetts Press, 1973). On Frank's influence in Latin America, see Michael A. Ogorzaly, *Waldo Frank: Prophet of Hispanic Regeneration* (Lewisburg, Pa.: Bucknell University Press, 1994).

29. Frank, *Our America*, ix–xi; hereafter, cited in the text. Given Frank's ties to Latin America, it would be tempting to assume a connection between his long essay and the Cuban poet José Martí,'s earlier "Nuestra America" (1891), an important plea for pan-American identity and autonomy from Europe, but Frank stated that he was not yet aware of Martí,'s work when he wrote *Our America*. Frank, *Memoirs*, 114.

30. For another discussion of the significance of the figures of the Indian and the Jew, see Walter Benn Michaels, *Our America: Nativism, Modernism, and Pluralism* (Durham, N.C.: Duke University Press, 1995).

31. Frank, *Memoirs*, 99; italics his.

32. Mabel Dodge Luhan, *Movers and Shakers* (New York: Harcourt, Brace, 1936), 534.

33. For an important discussion of the art colony's fascination with Indian and Hispanic culture, and its effective "mystification" of the social conditions of the region, see Sylvia Rodriguez, "Art, Tourism, and Race Relations in Taos: Toward a Sociology of the Art Colony," *Journal of Anthropological Research* 45, no. 1 (Spring 1989): 77–97.

34. Sheldon Reich, *Andrew Dasburg: His Life and Art* (Cranbury, N.J.: Associated University Presses, 1989), 52.

35. See Reich, 54; and *Picturesque Images From Taos and Santa Fe* (exhibition catalogue, the Denver Art Museum, 12 January–17 March 1974), 57–66, 93–97, 145–50.

36. Lewis Mumford, *Herman Melville* (New York: Harcourt, Brace, 1929), 361.

37. D. H. Lawrence, "America, Listen to Your Own," *New Republic*, 15 December 1920, 70. See also Walter Lippmann, "Apropos of Mr. Lawrence: The Crude Barbarian and the Noble Savage," *New Republic*, 15 December 1920, 70–71. In his reply to Lawrence, Lippmann argued that the Aztec empire was more culturally remote to Americans than the antique traditions of Europe, and somewhat tartly suggested that a country such as the United States, where Lawrence's own novels could not be carried through the mails in their unexpurgated form, was hardly in danger of becoming overwhelmed by an excessive reverence for European culture.

38. Besides Frank and Lawrence, residents of Mexico City in these decades included Langston Hughes, John Dos Passos, Katherine Ann Porter, Marsden Hartley, Henri Cartier-Bresson, Sergei Eisenstein, Graham Greene, Aldous Huxley, Archibald Mac-Leish, and Frank's protégé, Hart Crane, who died while returning to the United States from Mexico. These artists were attracted not only to the work of the important Mexican artists of the period—notably, Diego Rivera, Frida Kahlo, David Alfaro Siquieros, and José Clemente Orozco—but also, as with the New Mexico colonists, to the ancient and contemporary Indian presence in Mexico. Daniel Cooper Alarcón, *The Aztec Palimpsest: Mexico in the Modern Imagination* (Tucson: University of Arizona Press, 1997), 60–68; Drewey Wayne Gunn, *American and British Writers in Mexico, 1556–1973* (Austin: University of Texas Press, 1974), 76–163; Frank, *America Hispana: A Portrait and a Prospect* (New York: Scribner's, 1931).

39. Frank seems to have regretted his secular upbringing. In the decades following the publication of *Our America*, Frank would explore his connection to a specifically Jewish religiosity, becoming passionately interested in Spinoza, and visiting both Palestine and the shtetls of eastern Europe. Frank, *Memoirs*, 32, 37–39, 173–76.

40. Abraham Cahan, *The Rise of David Levinsky* (New York: Harper, 1917), 284.

41. Hutchins Hapgood, *The Spirit of the Ghetto: Studies of the Jewish Quarter of New York*, ed. Harry Golden (New York: Funk and Wagnalls, 1965). Hapgood's guide through the East Side was Cahan.

42. Ibid., 136–48, 201–11, 243–60.

43. Though "The Intellectuals" were a third category in Hapgood's sociology of the ghetto, he dismisses them as largely uninfluential to the young, and therefore outside of the opposition of old and new. Hapgood tended to refer to these people (who were, of course, writing the plays and painting the pictures he spent the better part of the book enthusiastically describing) as the more explicitly foreign "Russian" element of the ghetto. Though this label was accurate to the extent that many of these intellectuals strongly identified with Russian culture, it may also be reflective of Hapgood's ambivalence about some of the ("foreign"?) political views held by this group, particularly anarchism. Ibid., 3–52.

44. Ibid., 46.

45. See Theodore Roosevelt, "Americanism," *Collected Works* (New York: Scribner's, 1926), 18:388–405. Interest in preserving folk customs was also evident in Jane Addams's settlement house movement. There, efforts at assimilating immigrants as speedily as possible went cheek by jowl with a rather melancholy effort to maintain

the folkways which she felt the immigrants would inevitably lose. Hence, her plan, for example, to set up a museum of handicraft. For a fascinating account of the (occasionally misguided) preservationist impulses of settlement workers in Appalachia, see David Whisnant, *All That is Native and Fine: The Politics of Culture in an American Region* (Chapel Hill: University of North Carolina Press, 1983).

46. Randolph Bourne, "A Mirror of the Middle West," in *The Radical Will*, 265; see also "Morals and Art From the West," *Dial* (14 December 1918): 556–57.

47. See May, *End of American Innocence*, 298.

48. Frank, "Sherwood Anderson," *In the American Jungle* (New York: Farrar and Rinehart, 1937), 93.

49. See Kazin, *On Native Grounds*, 213–15; and Hugh Kenner, *A Homemade World: The American Modernist Writers* (Baltimore: Johns Hopkins University Press, 1975), 149.

50. Frank, "Sherwood Anderson," 93.

51. Brooks, "America's Coming-of-Age," in *Van Wyck Brooks: The Early Years*, ed. Claire Sprague (New York: Harper and Row, 1968), 135.

52. Just one example of this still current use of Whitman should suffice: in "A Nation of Nations," a semipermanent exhibit installed at the Smithsonian Museum for the U.S. Bicentennial, the phrase "I contain multitudes" is used as a caption for a series of portraits of (mostly famous) Americans of a conspicuous variety of races and ethnicities. The effect of this display, which juxtaposes portraits of Billie Holliday, Grace Kelly, Anthony Quinn, and Benny Goodman, is, like the ideology of multiculturalism in general, to simultaneously celebrate difference, and to imply a basic, transhistorical similarity between the social conditions and privileges of people regardless of ethnicity, race, gender, or social class. See Susan Hegeman, "Shopping for Identities: 'A Nation of Nations' and the Weak Ethnicity of Objects," *Public Culture* 3, no. 2 (Spring 1991): 71–92.

53. John Dos Passos, *The Big Money* (1933, reprint, New York: Harcourt, Brace, 1936), 561.

54. Frank, *Memoirs*, 99.

55. Nellie Y. McKay, *Jean Toomer, Artist: A Study of His Literary Life and Work, 1894–1936* (Chapel Hill: University of North Carolina Press, 1984), 50.

56. Though Toomer's work was undeniably influential to this movement, it is one of the central ironies of his career that at the height of his prestige and influence after the publication of *Cane*, Toomer had already distanced himself from Harlem intellectual circles, turning instead to the teachings of the mystical healer, Georgi Ivanovitch Gurdjieff. David Levering Lewis, *When Harlem Was in Vogue* (New York: Oxford University Press, 1981), 70–71.

57. Jean Toomer, *Cane* (1923; reprint, New York: Liveright, 1975), 83; hereafter, cited in text. For a discussion of the influence of Frank and other advocates of "vernacular" tradition on the development of the Harlem Renaissance, see Hutchinson, *Harlem Renaissance*, 106–24.

58. Robert B. Jones, introduction, to *The Collected Poems of Jean Toomer*, ed. Robert B. Jones and Margery Toomer Latimer (Chapel Hill: University of North Carolina Press, 1988), xiv.

59. Toomer, "Blue Meridian," *The Collected Poems of Jean Toomer*, 72.

60. Toomer and Frank's relationship was disrupted shortly after the publication of *Cane*, when Toomer had a marriage-ending affair with Frank's wife, the radical educator Margaret Naumberg. See McKay, *Jean Toomer, Artist*; Lewis, *When Harlem Was in Vogue*, 71–72; and Charles R. Larson, *Invisible Darkness: Jean Toomer and Nella Larsen* (Iowa City: University of Iowa Press, 1993).

61. For an extended discussion of the shared usage of curve imagery in Toomer, Crane, and Frank, see Robert L. Perry, *The Shared Vision of Waldo Frank and Hart Crane*, vol. 33 of *University of Nebraska Studies* (Lincoln: University of Nebraska Press, May 1966), 43–67.

62. Hart Crane, *The Bridge* (1933; reprint, New York: Liveright, 1970), 55; hereafter, cited in text.

63. Brom Weber, ed., *The Letters of Hart Crane, 1916–1932* (Berkeley: University of California Press, 1965), 27.

64. Margaret Dickie, *On the Modernist Long Poem* (Iowa C›ity: University of Iowa Press, 1986), 47–76; and see Weber, *The Letters of Hart Crane*, 305.

65. On Crane's knowledge of the theory of relativity, see Paul Giles, *Hart Crane: The Contexts of* The Bridge (New York: Cambridge University Press, 1986), 19–28.

66. It has been suggested by several critics that this reference to blackmail is an autobiographical allusion to Crane's experience of being blackmailed over his homosexuality. This reading is not out of keeping with mine, in that Crane is suggesting that "a new destiny" must come from sources that are viewed in the present as impure, taboo, or debased. See Giles, 164; and see Thomas E. Yingling, *Hart Crane and the Homosexual Text* (Chicago: University of Chicago Press, 1990).

67. Sherwood Anderson, *Poor White* (New York: Huebsch, 1920); hereafter, cited in text; Cecilia Tichi, *Shifting Gears: Technology, Literature, Culture in Modernist America* (Chapel Hill: University of North Carolina Press, 1987), 183–94.

68. Anderson, *Home Town*, The Face of America Series, ed. Edwin Rosskam (New York: Alliance, 1940), 4.

Chapter 5
The Culture of the Middle

1. Stuart Chase, quoted in "From the Bill of Fare," *Nation*, 18 May 1940, 624.

2. Chase, *Mexico: A Study of Two Americas* (New York: Macmillan, 1931), 216. Chase's comparisons of Tepoztlan and Middletown were based upon the findings of two classic community studies of the period, Robert Redfield, *Tepoztlan, A Mexican Village; A Study of Folk Life* (Chicago: University of Chicago Press, 1930); and Robert S. Lynd and Helen Merrell Lynd, *Middletown* (New York: Harcourt, Brace, 1957).

3. See Mabel S. Ulrich, "Salvaging Culture for the WPA," *Harper's*, May 1939, 653–64; and Jerre Mangione, *The Dream and the Deal: The Federal Writers' Project, 1935–1943* (Boston: Little, Brown, 1972), 265–75, 375–96.

4. Warren I. Susman, "The Culture of the Thirties," *Culture as History: The Transformation of American Society in the Twentieth Century* (New York: Pantheon, 1984), 154.

5. See Constance Rourke, *The Roots of American Culture and Other Essays*, ed., with a preface by Van Wyck Brooks (Port Washington, N.Y.: Kennikat, 1965).

6. George E. Marcus and Michael M. J. Fischer, *Anthropology as Cultural Critique: An Experimental Moment in the Human Sciences* (Chicago: University of Chicago Press, 1986), 125; see also William Stott, *Documentary Expression and Thirties America* (New York: Oxford University Press, 1973).

7. On this point, Stott goes so far as to turn "the primacy of feeling" into a feature of the thirties documentary as a genre. *Documentary Expression,* 8–17.

8. Joan Shelley Rubin, *Constance Rourke and American Culture* (Chapel Hill: University of North Carolina Press, 1980), 57.

9. Twelve Southerners, *I'll Take My Stand: The South and the Agrarian Tradition* (New York: Harper, 1930).

10. Howard W. Odum and Harry Estill Moore, *American Regionalism: A Cultural-Historical Approach to National Integration* (New York: Henry Holt, 1938), 1–2.

11. James Agee, "Period Pieces from the Mid-Thirties," in *The Collected Poems of James Agee,* ed. Robert Fitzgerald (New York: Ballantine, 1970), 184.

12. James Burkhart Gilbert, *Writers and Partisans: A History of Literary Radicalism in the United States* (New York: John Wiley, 1968), 93–94.

13. See Marcus Klein, *Foreigners: The Making of American Literature 1900–1940* (Chicago: University of Chicago Press, 1981).

14. Mangione, *The Dream and the Deal,* 49. Frank was clearly the most vanguardist and the most politically leftist of the older group, although his politics (like his vanguardism) tended to run toward the romantic and religious.

15. For a discussion of radicals' fascination with popular culture, see Paul Buhle, *Marxism in the United States* (New York: Verso, 1991), 177–83. I take my history of the emergence of these terms from Janice Radway, who places the emergence of the term "middlebrow" in the late 1920s. Radway, "The Scandal of the Middlebrow: The Book-of-the-Month Club, Class Fracture, and Cultural Authority," *South Atlantic Quarterly* 89, no. 4 (Fall 1990): 707.

16. For a crucial discussion of the debates on "standardization," its antithetical relationship to "democracy," and its association with the middlebrow, see Radway, *A Feeling for Books: The Book-of-the-Month Club, Literary Taste, and Middle-Class Desire* (Chapel Hill: University of North Carolina Press, 1997), 205–20.

17. Constance Rourke, "The Significance of Sections," *New Republic,* September 1933, 148–49.

18. Henry Hart, ed., *American Writers' Congress* (New York: International, 1935), 188–89. Among the other members of the Executive Committee and the National Council were Kenneth Burke, Malcolm Cowley, Matthew Josephson, Nelson Algren, Edward Dahlberg, James T. Farrell, Kenneth Fearing, Robert Herrick, Lewis Mumford, Clifford Odets, Agnes Smedley, Lincoln Steffens, and Richard Wright. For a discussion of the impact of the League on American culture, see Michael Denning, *The Cultural Front* (New York: Verso, 1996), 223–26.

19. Hart, *American Writers' Congress,* 87–94. For other discussions of "Revolutionary Symbolism in America," see Frank Lentricchia, *Criticism and Social Change* (Chicago: University of Chicago Press, 1985), 21–38; and Denning, *Cultural Front,* 102–3 and 440–44.

20. Hart, *American Writers' Congress,* 165–71.

21. Malcolm Cowley, "The Writers' International," *The Social Record*, ed. Henry Dan Piper (Carbondale: Southern Illinois University Press, 1967), 99; first published in the *New Republic*, 31 July 1935, 339.

22. André Breton, "Du Temps que les Surréalistes avaient raison," in *Position politique du Surréalisme* (Paris: Editions du Sagittaire, 1935), 99–119; Maurice Nadeau, *The History of Surrealism*, trans. Richard Howard (Harmondsworth, England: Penguin, 1973), 191–98, 208–15. See also Serge Guilbaut, *How New York Stole the Idea of Modern Art: Abstract Expressionism, Freedom, and the Cold War* (Chicago: University of Chicago Press, 1983), 22.

23. Pierre Bourdieu, *Distinction: A Social Critique of the Judgment of Taste* (Cambridge: Harvard University Press, 1984), 319–28.

24. Radway, *A Feeling for Books*; Rubin, *The Making of Middlebrow Culture* (Chapel Hill: University of North Carolina Press, 1992); and Henry F. Pringle, "Chautauqua in the Jazz Age," *American Mercury* 16, no. 61 (January 1929): 85–93.

25. Lynd and Lynd, *Middletown*, 12.

26. The Lynds provide an especially stunning account of the social changes brought about by the automobile, writing, "Into the equilibrium of habits which constitutes for each individual some integration in living has come this new habit, upsetting old adjustments, and blasting its way through such accustomed and unquestioned dicta as 'Rain or shine, I never miss a Sunday morning at church'; 'A high school boy does not need much spending money'; 'I don't need exercise, walking to the office keeps me fit'; 'I wouldn't think of moving out of town and being so far from my friends'; 'Parents ought always to know where their children are,' " Lynd, *Middletown,* 253–54; for details of Robert Lynd's education and sponsorship, see Richard Wightman Fox, "Epitaph for Middletown: Robert S. Lynd and the Analysis of Consumer Culture," in *The Culture of Consumption: Critical Essays in American History 1880–1980*, ed. Richard Wightman Fox and T. J. Jackson Lears (New York: Pantheon, 1983), 103–41.

27. Lynd and Lynd, *Middletown*, 3–9; Fox, "Epitaph." *Middletown*, and Lynd's follow-up study, *Middletown in Transition* (1937) made Muncie one of the most studied communities on earth. Middletown III, a third major research project in Muncie, was started in 1975 by Theodore Caplow, Howard M. Bahr, and Bruce A. Chadwick. Popularly perceived as the "typical" American city, Muncie has also been the site of numerous political-opinion polls, the test market for countless new products, and the subject of film and television documentaries by producers from as far away as Finland and Japan. Especially controversial among Muncie residents themselves were a 1937 *Life* magazine photo essay by Margaret Bourke-White and a 1982 PBS documentary series—one particularly disturbing episode of which, on the lives of Muncie teenagers, was never aired. For a comprehensive account of Muncie as the site of community studies, and a fascinating look at how this attention was received in the community, see David C. Tambo, Dwight W. Hoover, and John D. Hewitt, *Middletown: An Annotated Bibliography* (New York: Garland, 1988).

28. Lynd and Lynd, *Middletown,* 315–409, 415.

29. Robert S. Lynd, *Knowledge for What? The Place of Social Science in American Culture* (Princeton, N.J.: Princeton University Press, 1939).

30. H. L. Mencken, "A City in Moronia," review of *Middletown: A Study in Contemporary American Culture*, by Robert S. Lynd and Helen Merrill Lynd, *American Mercury* 16, no. 63 (March 1929): 379.

31. Whiting Williams, "Through the Looking Glass," review of *Middletown: A Study in Contemporary American Culture*, by Robert S. and Helen Merrill Lynd, *Saturday Review of Literature*, 30 March 1929, 324.

32. "U.S. Scene," *Time* 24 December 1934, 24–27. When these artists are addressed together, they are usually referred to as "American Scene Painters"; only a few of them are also regionalists.

33. For an account of a similar construction of an oppositional middlebrow aesthetic at the Book-of-the-Month Club, see Radway, *A Feeling for Books*.

34. "U.S. Scene," 24.

35. Ibid., 25; Charles Burchfield, "On the Middle Border," *Creative Art* 3 (September 1929): xxix.

36. Burchfield, "On the Middle Border," xxx.

37. Henry Adams, *Thomas Hart Benton: An American Original* (New York: Knopf, 1989), 220–21. For an extended study of Curry's reception in Kansas, see M. Sue Kendall, *Rethinking Regionalism: John Steuart Curry and the Kansas Mural Controversy* (Washington D.C.: Smithsonian Institution Press, 1986).

38. Adams, *Thomas Hart Benton,* 221. Though Benton famously boasted that he would rather have his work hang in saloons than in museums, he would eventually turn his back on New York altogether, and seek the institutional support he needed at Kansas City's Nelson-Atkins Museum of Art. After a series of squabbles with the museum administrators, Benton was finally led to bemoan the provincialism, and the (yes) middlebrow sensibilities of his new patrons; see Adams, *Thomas Hart Benton,* 236–313.

39. Alan Wallach, indicating the importance of the *Time* cover to Benton's career, suggested that a study of Benton ought to be titled, "The Work of Art in the Age of *Time* Magazine"; Wallach, "Regionalism Redux," *American Quarterly* 43, no. 2 (June 1991): 259–78. For an extended discussion of Benton's reliance on corporate sponsorship, see Erika Doss, *Benton, Pollock, and the Politics of Modernism: From Regionalism to Abstract Expressionism* (Chicago: University of Chicago Press, 1991), especially chapters 3 and 4.

40. "U.S. Scene," 24.

41. Benton, "America and/or Alfred Stieglitz," in *A Thomas Hart Benton Miscellany: Selections from His Published Opinions 1916–1960*, ed. Matthew Baigell (Lawrence: University Press of Kansas, 1971), 66; originally published in *Common Sense* 4, no. 1 (January 1935): 22–25; see also Adams, *Thomas Hart Benton*, 73–78.

42. Benton, "Interview in *Art Front*," in *A Thomas Hart Benton Miscellany,* 59; originally appeared in *Art Front* 1 (April 1935): 2.

43. Ibid., 59.

44. Benton, "Art and Social Struggle: Reply to Rivera," in *A Thomas Hart Benton Miscellany,* 39; first appeared in *The University Review* 2 (Winter 1935): 71–78.

45. Baigell, "Thomas Hart Benton and the Left," in *Thomas Hart Benton: Artist, Writer, and Intellectual*, ed. R. Douglas Hurt and Mary K. Dains (State Historical Society of Missouri, 1989), 11; Benton, "America and/or Alfred Stieglitz," 74.

46. Adams, *Thomas Hart Benton,* 214–16.

47. Thomas Craven, *Modern Art: The Men, The Movements, The Meaning* (New York: Simon and Schuster, 1940), 160–61, 181.

48. Ibid., 312.

49. Ibid., 315–16.

50. Waldo Frank and others, eds., *America and Alfred Stieglitz: A Collective Portrait* (New York: The Literary Guild, 1934). Stieglitz himself participated actively in the volume's preparation.

51. Benton, "America and/or Alfred Stieglitz," 65–73. In a somewhat confused sexual analogy, Benton also wrote of Stieglitz and his circle, "This man and his confreres are like boys addicted to bad habits whose imaginative constructions have so defined the qualities of 'life' that they are impotent before the fact" (71).

52. Adams (to my mind somewhat unconvincingly) argues that Craven's racist and anti-Semitic comments were unfairly taken to reflect Benton's views. Regarding what Benton's own sister described as his "violent hatred of homosexuals," however, there is very little dispute. Benton contributed to the publicity surrounding his departure from New York in 1937 by writing a parting ad hominem against the New York art world, which he said was dominated by "precious fairies" whose "overdelicate refinements" controlled the art market. Though he claimed that their "aberration" would never be tolerated in the Midwest to which he was fleeing, he would later comment publicly, during a dispute with the administrators of the Nelson-Atkins Museum, upon the pernicious association between "the third sex and the museums." Adams, *Thomas Hart Benton*, 243, 246–51, 302–13; see also Doss, *Benton, Pollock, and the Politics of Modernism*, 280–81.

53. Cécile Whiting, *Antifascism in American Art* (New Haven, Conn.: Yale University Press, 1989), 76; Benton, "Art and Nationalism," in *A Thomas Hart Benton Miscellany*, 53. The First American Artists' Congress Against War and Fascism, though connected with its counterpart for writers, was (as its full title suggests) somewhat more liberal, reflecting the politics of the antifascist Popular Front. For contemporary views of Craven as reflected in the congress proceedings, see Stuart Davis, "Why an American Artists' Congress?," 5, and Saul Schary, "Tendencies in American Art," 62, both in *First American Artists' Congress* (New York: n.p. 1936).

54. Whiting, *Antifascism*, 99.

55. Adams, *Thomas Hart Benton*, 221, 233.

56. See Benton, *Political Business and Intellectual Ballyhoo*, as reproduced in Adams, *Thomas Hart Benton*, 189.

57. Paul Rosenfeld, "Ex-Reading Room," *New Republic*, 12 April 1933, 246; and see Meyer Schapiro "Populist Realism," review of *An Artist in America*, by Thomas Hart Benton, *Partisan Review* 4 (January 1938): 53–57.

58. Adams, *Thomas Hart Benton*, 190.

59. Though *Time* makes much of Benton's navy career, Benton apparently enlisted in the navy to avoid being drafted into a combat unit. His mother used her political influence on his behalf because Benton did not meet the navy's height requirements. Adams, *Thomas Hart Benton*, 84–88.

60. Radway, "Scandal," 724.

61. After the bombing of Pearl Harbor, Benton devoted his talents to war propaganda in a series of paintings entitled *The Year of Peril*. His drooling, apelike caricatures of the enemy—as Christ-killers and the defilers of white femininity—bear a close resemblance to the racist comic-book art of the period. Erika Doss observes that these paintings are so bleak as to make poor propaganda, and thus reads their brutality as reflecting a shift for Benton into surrealism, precipitated by a disillusionment with his aesthetic politics and the limitations imposed on him by his corporate sponsors. However, I think Benton's gift for racist caricature must also be understood in the context of his populist

identity politics, which made him adept at locating enemies and/as outsiders. Doss, *Benton, Pollock, and the Politics of Modernism*, 279–89.

62. Clement Greenberg, "Avant-garde and Kitsch," in *Art and Culture: Critical Essays* (Boston: Beacon, 1961), 3–21.

63. See Doss, *Benton, Pollock, and the Politics of Modernism*; and Guilbaut, *How New York Stole the Idea of Modern Art*.

64. Denning's argument in *The Cultural Front* about the larger impact of left cultural politics of the thirties on post-war America is an extremely important, and refreshing, antidote both to the New York intellectuals' endless, and often deeply self-serving, lamentations about the various failures of (their various youthful experiences with) the left and the equally endless examinations of political affiliations of various figures in the Popular Front.

65. Though opinions on the history of the "consumer society" vary, I think it is clear that a fully developed consumer culture did not exist in the United States until after World War II, when the wartime factories were retooled for domestic consumer goods, and the government officially encouraged citizens to be consumers. It was not until this moment that Americans of all classes were both urged to consume *and* had the means to do it. See Michel Aglietta, *A Theory of Capitalist Regulation: The U.S. Experience* (New York: Verso, 1987). This is not to say, however, that many of the institutions and ideologies of consumerism were not in place well before the postwar period. Lynd's *Middletown* alone offers sufficient evidence that by the late twenties many middle-class Americans considered the consumption of autos and other goods both a road to personal fulfillment and a social obligation. For a persuasive argument that the thirties marked a key moment in the creation of a consumer ethos, see Rita Barnard, *The Great Depression and the Culture of Abundance: Literature and Mass Culture in the 1930s* (New York: Cambridge University Press, 1994). My reading of West's work is indebted to Barnard's, and also to Robert Seguin's discussion of *Day of the Locust* in *Around Quitting Time: Work and Middle-Class Fantasy in American Fiction* (Durham, N.C.: Duke University Press, forthcoming).

66. Jay Martin, author of the definitive West biography, suggests that West's habitual cynicism made him disdainful of the pieties of many of his contemporaries on the left. He was, nevertheless, active in the cause of labor, including his own Screen Writers' Guild. West was also one of the signers of the call to form the first American Writers' Congress, though he did not attend the congress itself. Later, however, he helped organize a Western Writers' Congress, and was active in the California chapter of the American Artists' Congress; Martin, *Nathanael West: The Art of His Life* (New York: Hayden, 1970), 244–64, 346–47; Hart, *American Writers' Congress*, 12.

67. See Martin, *Nathanael West*, 46–120.

68. Nathanael West, *A Cool Million*, in *The Complete Works of Nathanael West* (New York: Farrar, Straus, and Cudahy, 1957), 239; hereafter, *CM*.

69. West, *The Day of the Locust*, in *The Complete Works of Nathanael West*, 405; hereafter, *DOL*; "Vas you dere, Sharley?" was the signature of radio performer Jack Pearl. Stott, *Documentary Expression*, 36.

70. Karal Ann Marling, *George Washington Slept Here: Colonial Revivals and American Culture* (Cambridge: Harvard University Press, 1988), 269–70, 283–90.

71. On Williamsburg, see Richard Handler and Eric Gable, *The New History in an Old Museum: Creating the Past at Colonial Williamsburg* (Durham, N.C: Duke University Press, 1997). For a discussion of both the "craze" for early Americana, and the

general fascination with the reproduction of historical decorative styles in the twenties and thirties, see Marling, *George Washington*; and Russell Lynes, *The Tastemakers: The Shaping of American Popular Taste* (1949; reprint, New York: Dover, 1980), 238–42. The same interests in historical styles were also clearly present in the haute couture of the thirties. For example, in his memoir "New York in 1941," Claude Lévi-Strauss wrote, "In New York, as we used to say to one another, women do not 'dress': they disguise themselves. When we saw them dressed like little sailors, Egyptian dancing girls, or pioneer women of the Far West, we knew that they were 'dressed to kill.' " Lévi-Strauss, "New York in 1941," in *The View From Afar*, trans. Joachim Neugroschel and Phoebe Hoss (New York: Basic, 1985), 265.

72. As with a number of his contemporaries, Frank's populism was more an article of faith than a firmly held proposition. Indeed, as Janice Radway has noted, Frank's brief 1925 essay "Pseudo-Literature" is a classic statement of highbrow anxieties about the encroachments of both mass culture and a snobbish, middlebrow "pseudo-literature." Yet even in this excoriation of the false tastes of the many, Frank also expresses a populist optimism about the positive effects of mass literacy, which, he asserts, can only swell the ranks of "the potential public for what is good." Frank, "Pseudo-Literature," *New Republic*, 2 December 1925, 46–47; and Radway, *A Feeling for Books*, 213–17.

73. West, *Cool Million*, 232; Andrew Ross, *No Respect: Intellectuals and Popular Culture* (New York: Routledge, 1989), 45. The cultural "germophobia" that Ross describes was not exclusively a product of the Cold War. Indeed, as Stuart Chase's comments, quoted in the beginning of this chapter, reveal, the "organic" vision of "culture" may have encouraged a similar fascination with the idea of "microbial" contamination of the cultural body.

74. Dwight Macdonald, "Masscult and Midcult," in *Against the American Grain: Essays on the Effects of Mass Culture* (New York: Da Capo, 1962), 3–75.

75. Mike Davis, *City of Quartz* (New York: Verso, 1990), 21; see also Chapter 4, above.

76. Max Horkheimer and Theodor W. Adorno, *Dialectic of Enlightenment*, trans. John Cumming (1944; reprint, New York: Continuum, 1995), 120–67.

77. Davis writes further, "For more than a quarter century, an unprecedented mass migration of retired farmers, small-town dentists, wealthy spinsters, tubercular schoolteachers, petty stock speculators, Iowa lawyers, and devotees of the Chautauqua circuit transferred their savings and small fortunes into Southern California real estate. The massive flow of wealth between regions produced population, income and consumption structures seemingly out of all proportion to Los Angeles's actual production base: the paradox of the first 'postindustrial' city in its preindustrial guise." *City of Quartz*, 25.

Chapter 6
"Beyond Relativity"

1. Rushton Coulborn, Clyde Kluckhohn, and John Peale Bishop, "The American Culture: A Symposium," *Kenyon Review* 3, no. 2 (Spring 1941): 143–90.

2. Coulborn, Kluckhohn, and Bishop, "American Culture," 183–84.

3. Henry R. Luce, *The American Century* (New York: Farrar & Rinehart, 1941).

4. Peter Novick, *That Noble Dream: The "Objectivity Question" and the American Historical Profession* (New York: Cambridge University Press, 1988), 312. See Novick also for a discussion of the general attack on "relativism" in this period, 281–314.

5. Archibald MacLeish, *The Irresponsibles* (New York: Duell, Sloan and Pierce, 1940), 12; first published in the *Nation*, 18 May 1940, 618–23.

6. MacLeish clearly influenced the opinions of, among other conference participants, Van Wyck Brooks, Louis Finkelstein, and Mortimer J. Adler. However, it was not until the second Conference on Science, Philosophy, and Religion that a presentation explicitly addressed his argument. See Brooks, "Conference on Science, Philosophy, and Religion in their Relation to the Democratic Way of Life," Finkelstein, "The Aims of the Conference," and Adler, "God and the Professors," in *Science, Philosophy, and Religion: A Symposium* (New York: Conference on Science, Philosophy, and Religion in their Relation to the Democratic Way of Life, 1941), 3–4, 11, 120–38; and Douglas Bush, " 'The Irresponsibles,': A Comment," with comments by Hoxie N. Fairchild, Harry S. V. Jones, Edward K. Rand, and Warner G. Rice, in *Science, Philosophy, and Religion: Second Symposium* (New York: Conference on Science, Philosophy, and Religion in their Relation to the Democratic Way of Life, 1942), 307–335.

7. Finkelstein, "The Aims of the Conference," 15.

8. Phillip Frank, one of the participants in the first conference, wrote in a retrospective essay on the conferences' historic function, "The members were anxious to prove that the danger of 'relativism' which was, in a way, a frequent companion of liberalism and democracy, could be avoided by democratic methods without enforcing a belief in certain values by a 'leader' or dictator." Frank, "Relativity, Truth, and Values," in *Perspectives on a Troubled Decade: Science, Philosophy and Religion, 1939–1949*, ed. Lyman Bryson, Louis Finkelstein, and R. M. MacIver (New York: Conference on Science, Philosophy, and Religion in Their Relation to the Democratic Way of Life, 1950), 203; for a representative attack on relativism in the first conference proceedings, see Adler, "God and the Professors."

9. Raymond Nelson, *Van Wyck Brooks: A Writer's Life* (New York: Dutton, 1981), 220–31.

10. Brooks, "On Our Literature Today," in *Science, Philosophy, and Religion*, 307–18; on Brooks's support of MacLeish's views, see Brooks, "On 'The Irresponsibles,' " *Nation*, 8 June 1940, 718; and Nelson, *Van Wyck Brooks*, 236.

11. Brooks, "Conference on Science, Philosophy, and Religion in their Relation to the Democratic Way of Life," in *Science, Philosophy, and Religion*, 1–2.

12. Melville J. Herskovits, *Franz Boas: The Science of Man in the Making* (New York: Scribner, 1953), 117–22; Marshall Hyatt, *Franz Boas Social Activist: The Dynamics of Ethnicity*, vol. 6 of *Contributions to the Study of Anthropology* (New York: Greenwood, 1990), 145–51.

13. Margaret Mead, "The Comparative Study of Culture and the Purposive Cultivation of Democratic Values," with comments by Ruth F. Benedict, Clyde Kluckhohn, Dorothy D. Lee, Geoffrey Gorer, and Gregory Bateson, in *Science, Philosophy, and Religion: Second Symposium* (New York: Conference on Science, Philosophy, and Religion in their Relation to the Democratic Way of Life, 1942), 57–58. The remainder of the paper was dedicated to arguing a point probably indebted to the influence of Mead's husband at the time, Gregory Bateson. Mead argued, and Bateson's "comment" defended at length, the proposition that social-scientific attempts to change or control the

development of particular cultural traits were, in effect, fascistic, and that the only proper role of the social scientist was to understand, and thereby influence, the direction of the values of a whole way of life. Mead, 65–69, 81–97. For a discussion of Bateson's attitudes toward applied social science, see Virginia Yans-McLaughlin, "Science, Democracy, and Ethics: Mobilizing Culture and Personality for World War II," in *Malinowski, Rivers, Benedict, and Other: Essays on Culture and Personality*, vol. 4 of *History of Anthropology*, ed. George W. Stocking Jr. (Madison: University of Wisconsin Press, 1986), 194.

14. Boas, letter to the editor, *New York Times*, 8 January 1916, 8; reprinted in George W. Stocking Jr., ed., *The Shaping of American Anthropology 1883–1911: A Franz Boas Reader* (New York: Basic, 1974), 333.

15. Benedict, "Anthropology and the Abnormal," *Journal of General Psychology* 10, no. 1 (1934): 59–82; Benedict, *Patterns of Culture* (Boston: Houghton Mifflin, 1989); Mead, *Coming of Age in Samoa* (1928; reprint, New York: Morrow, 1961), 195–248.

16. Mead, "Comparative Study," 73; see also Gorer's comments, 78–79.

17. Ibid., 69–70.

18. Benedict, "Ideologies in the Light of Comparative Data," in Mead, *An Anthropologist at Work: The Writings of Ruth Benedict* (New York: Houghton Mifflin, 1959), 383. The same questions about the public's potential misapprehension of the political implications of cultural relativism carried over into the postwar period. In a 1947 review of the new paperback version of Benedict's *Patterns of Culture*, Elgin Williams fretted that "relativism," the book's "real message," was incompatible with the war's recent "mass education in 'cultural divergences,' " and that the book might produce a "public hue-and-cry against anthropology." Williams, "Anthropology for the Common Man," *American Anthropologist* 49, no. 1 (January–March 1947): 85.

19. Benedict, "Ideologies," 385: italics are Benedict's.

20. Mead, "Comparative Study," 65.

21. Yans-McLaughlin, "Science, Democracy, and Ethics," 194.

22. For a full discussion of the wartime efforts of the "culture and personality" anthropologists connected to Mead, see Yans-McLaughlin, "Science, Democracy, and Ethics"; Margaret M. Caffrey, *Ruth Benedict: Stranger in this Land* (Austin: University of Texas Press, 1989), 318–21; and Mead, "Anthropological Contributions to National Policies During and Immediately After World War II," in *The Uses of Anthropology*, ed. Walter Goldschmidt (Washington, D.C.: American Anthropological Association, 1979), 145–57.

23. Robert A. McCaughey, *International Studies and Academic Enterprise: A Chapter in the Enclosure of American Learning* (New York: Columbia University Press, 1984), 111, 118; Terence Ball, "The Politics of Social Science in Postwar America," in *Recasting America: Culture and Politics in the Age of the Cold War*, ed. Lary May (Chicago: University of Chicago Press, 1989), 81.

24. See Chapter 2. For details on Boas's activism on behalf of the principle of academic freedom in the pre–World War II years, see Hyatt, *Franz Boas Social Activist*, 143–51.

25. The classic text of this critique of intellectuals' participation in the Cold War is Noam Chomsky, *American Power and the New Mandarins* (New York: Random House, 1967).

26. See Glenn Alcalay, "The United States Anthropologist in Micronesia: Toward a Counter-Hegemonic Study of Sapiens," in *Confronting the Margaret Mead Legacy: Scholarship, Empire, and the South Pacific,* ed. Lenora Foerstel and Angela Gilliam (Philadelphia: Temple University Press, 1992), 173–204; and Laura Nader, "The Fantom Factor: Impact of the Cold War on Anthropology," in Chomsky and others, *The Cold War and the University: Toward an Intellectual History of the Postwar Years* (New York: New Press, 1997), 107–46.

27. Benedict, *The Chrysanthemum and the Sword: Patterns of Japanese Culture* (Boston: Houghton Mifflin, 1946), 180–81; and see Clifford Geertz, *Works and Lives: The Anthropologist as Author* (Stanford, Calif.: Stanford University Press, 1988), 116–28. Geertz's reading of *Chrysanthemum and the Sword* is extremely sympathetic, suggesting that the features of the text that conform to Benedict's war work and to the intellectual agenda of "culture-and-personality" scholarship were somehow alien to Benedict's more naturally "aesthetic" impulses. To make his case, he places severe blame on Margaret Mead for distorting Benedict's legacy to create a figure whose interests more closely conformed with Mead's own work.

28. Mead, quoted in Jane Howard, *Margaret Mead: A Life* (New York: Simon and Schuster, 1984), 270–71. For an example of the enduring impact of national character studies in intelligence circles, see Washington Platt (Brigadier General, U.S. Army, retired), *National Character in Action: Intelligence Factors in Foreign Relations* (New Brunswick, N.J.: Rutgers University, 1961).

29. Geoffrey Gorer, "Themes in Japanese Culture," *Transactions of the New York Academy of Sciences* 5, no. 1 (November, 1943): 106–24; and John W. Dower, *War Without Mercy: Race and Power in the Pacific War* (New York: Pantheon, 1986), 124–33.

30. Mead, "Anthropological Contributions," 148.

31. Ibid., 148.

32. Ibid., 149; Gorer and John Rickman, *The People of Great Russia: A Psychological Study* (London: Cresset, 1949); Mead, *Soviet Attitudes Toward Authority: An Interdisciplinary Approach to Problems of Soviet Character* (New York: McGraw-Hill, 1951).

33. See Rickman, "A Note on the Swaddling Hypothesis," in Gorer, *The People of Great Russia*, 223–26.

34. Gorer, *The People of Great Russia*, 192.

35. See Robert F. Murphy, "Anthropology at Columbia: A Reminiscence," *Dialectical Anthropology* 16 (1991): 65–81; and Sherry B. Ortner, "Theory in Anthropology since the Sixties," *Comparative Studies in Society and History* 26, no. 1 (1984): 126–66. Sapir, who died in 1939, would also turn to a psychological study of culture, though he diverged theoretically from culture and personality studies, which he regarded as reductive. Rather, Sapir's emphasis lay in addressing the individual as a cultural actor; see Regna Darnell, "Personality and Culture: The Fate of the Sapirian Alternative," in *Malinowski, Rivers, Benedict, and Others: Essays on Culture and Personality*, 156–83.

36. Julian Steward, "Evolution and Process," in *Anthropology Today: An Encyclopedic Inventory*, ed. A. L. Kroeber (Chicago: University of Chicago Press, 1953), 325.

37. Ibid., 314.

38. Mead, *An Anthropologist at Work: Writings of Ruth Benedict* (Boston: Houghton Mifflin, 1959), 432–38; Howard, *Margaret Mead*, 273–75.

39. Mead, "Anthropological Contributions," 151.

40. Carl E. Pletsch, "The Three Worlds, or the Division of Social Scientific Labor, circa 1950–1975," *Comparative Studies in Society and History* 23, no. 5 (1981): 565–90.

41. H. D. Harootunian, "America's Japan / Japan's Japan," in *Japan in the World*, ed. Masao Miyoshi and H. D. Harootunian (Durham, N.C.: Duke University Press, 1993), 196–221.

42. For an overview of the influence of culture-and-personality in American studies, see Richard E. Sykes, "American Studies and the Concept of Culture: A Theory and Method," *American Quarterly* 15, no. 2 (Summer 1963): 253–70; and the bibliographical essay, Michael McGiffert, "Selected Writings on American National Character," *American Quarterly* 15, no. 2 (Summer 1963): 271–88.

43. See David W. Noble, "The Reconstruction of Progress: Charles Beard, Richard Hofstadter, and Postwar Historical Thought," in *Recasting America: Culture and Politics in the Age of the Cold War*, ed. Lary May (Chicago: University of Chicago Press, 1989) 61–75; and Robert Berkhofer, "Clio and the Culture Concept: Some Impressions of a Changing Relationship in American Historiography," in *The Idea of Culture in the Social Sciences*, ed. Louis Schneider and Charles Bonjean (New York: Cambridge University Press, 1973), 77–100.

44. David Riesman, Nathan Glazer, and Reuel Denney, *The Lonely Crowd: A Study of the Changing American Character* (New Haven, Conn.: Yale University Press, 1950); William H. Whyte Jr., *The Organization Man* (New York: Simon and Schuster, 1956); Charles Reich, *The Greening of America: How the Youth Revolution is Trying to Make America Livable* (New York: Random House, 1970); Christopher Lasch, *The Culture of Narcissism: American Life in an Age of Diminishing Expectations* (New York: Norton, 1979); and Robert Bellah and others, *Habits of the Heart* (Berkeley: University of California Press, 1985). On national-character studies as a genre, see Rupert Wilkinson, *The Pursuit of American Character* (New York: Harper and Row, 1988).

45. Williams, "Anthropology for the Common Man," 85.

46. As Bruce Robbins has noted, Steiner made something of a career of worrying over this theme; see Steiner, *Language and Silence: Essays on Language, Literature, and the Inhuman* (New York: Atheneum, 1967), ix–x, 5.; Robbins, *Secular Vocations: Intellectuals, Professionalism, Culture* (New York: Verso, 1993), 128–31.

47. Robbins, *Secular Vocations*, 15.

48. Brooks, *Opinions of Oliver Allston* (New York: Dutton, 1941), 224; also quoted in part in Dwight Macdonald, "Kulturbolschewismus is Here," *Partisan Review* 8, no. 6 (November–December 1941): 447.

49. Brooks, *Opinions of Oliver Allston*, 146.

50. See Nelson, *Van Wyck Brooks*, 238–40.

51. Writers from whom statements were solicited also included Allen Tate, William Carlos Williams, Louise Bogan, Henry Miller, James T. Farrell, and Lionel Trilling. Tate and others, "On the 'Brooks-MacLeish Thesis,' " *Partisan Review* 9, no. 1 (January–February 1942): 38–47; T. S. Eliot, "A Letter to the Editors," *Partisan Review* 9, no. 2 (March-April 1942): 115–16. Thomas Mann, the only living writer Brooks included in his list of literary greats, wrote to the *Partisan Review* in qualified support of Brooks's views. Macdonald dismissed Mann's support of Brooks as the result of "flat-

tery," and described Mann's comments as lacking "courage." Macdonald, "Kultur-bolschewismus," 444–45.

52. Tate, "On the 'Brooks-MacLeish Thesis,' " 40.

53. Macdonald, "Kulturbolschewismus," 449.

54. Clement Greenberg, "Avant-Garde and Kitsch," in *Art and Culture: Critical Essays* (Boston: Beacon, 1961), 3–21.

55. See Serge Guilbaut, *How New York Stole the Idea of Modern Art: Abstract Expressionism, Freedom, and the Cold War*, trans. Arthur Goldhammer (Chicago: University of Chicago Press, 1983).

56. For a fuller discussion of the ideological similarities in the work of New York intellectuals such as Greenberg and Macdonald and that of the New Critics, see Thomas Hill Schaub, *American Fiction in the Cold War* (Madison: University of Wisconsin Press, 1991), 25–49.

57. See Schaub, *American Fiction in the Cold War*; and Cary Nelson, *Repression and Recovery: Modern American Poetry and the Politics of Cultural Memory, 1910–1945* (Madison: University of Wisconsin Press, 1989).

58. Tate, "On the 'Brooks-MacLeish Thesis,' " 41.

59. William Barrett, "Declining Fortunes of the Literary Review: 1945–57," *Anchor Review* 2 (1957): 154.

60. Barrett, "Declining Fortunes," 152.

61. Macdonald, *Against the American Grain: Essays on the Effects of Mass Culture* (New York: Da Capo, 1962), 50. For Macdonald and his generation of highbrow critics, the lowbrow, or "masscult," as Macdonald would have it, was the frankly commercial nonculture of the masses.

62. Eliot, *Notes towards the Definition of Culture*, in *Christianity and Culture* (New York: Harcourt Brace Jovanovich, 1988), 78–202; Macdonald, *Against the American Grain*, 55; hereafter, cited in the text.

63. For accounts of the decay of these distinctions, see Susan Sontag, "Notes on 'Camp,' " in *Against Interpretation* (New York: Delta, 1966), 275–92; and Umberto Eco, "Lowbrow Highbrow, Highbrow Lowbrow," in *Pop Art: The Critical Dialogue*, ed. Carol Anne Mahsun (Ann Arbor, Mich.: UMI Research Press, 1989), 219–32.

64. Roland Barthes, *Mythologies*, trans. Annette Lavers (1957; reprint, New York: Hill and Wang, 1985).

65. Compare, for example, the attempts at categorizing these strata of taste in Russell Lynes, *The Tastemakers: The Shaping of American Popular Taste* (New York: Dover, 1949); and Tad Friend, "In Praise of the Middlebrow: Daring to Admit a Fondness for Gershwin, Monet, and Anne Tyler," *Utne Reader*, October 1992, 77–83 (reprinted from the *New Republic*, 2 March 1992). The increasing meaninglessness of these distinctions is made most apparent in the charts accompanying both works, locating where various kinds of objects fit in the hierarchy of brows. Where Lynes signaled the highbrow connotations of Eames chairs versus the lowbrow connotations of a "mail order overstuffed chair," the chart accompanying the more recent article ranks characters from the TV show "The Simpsons" (Lisa is highbrow, Homer is lowbrow).

66. James Agee and Walker Evans, *Let Us Now Praise Famous Men*, new ed., with an introduction by John Hersey (Boston: Houghton Mifflin, 1988); hereafter, cited in the text.

67. Macdonald, *Against the American Grain*, 156; Robert Fitzgerald, "A Memoir," in *The Collected Short Prose of James Agee*, by James Agee, ed. Robert Fitzgerald (New York: Ballantine, 1970), 56–57. Macdonald's essay "James Agee," in *Against the American Grain*, was first published as "Death of a Poet," in the *New Yorker*, 16 November 1957. Fitzgerald's elegant "Memoir," first published in the *Kenyon Review* in 1968, was in some respects an answer to Macdonald's earlier assertion that Agee's life represented a case of tragically wasted genius. However, Fitzgerald also supports key aspects of the Agee mythology—notably, the claim that Agee's *Praise* was a critical failure.

68. Fitzgerald, "A Memoir," 51; Ross Spears, *Agee*, 88 min., Johnson City, TN: The James Agee Film Project, Johnson City, Tenn. 1985, videocassette; Agee, "Victory," *Time*, 20 August 1945, 19–22.

69. Macdonald, *Against the American Grain*, 150, 156; John Hersey, "Agee," Introduction to *Praise*, x, xxxvi–xxviii.

70. Warren I. Susman, "The Culture of the Thirties," chap. in *Culture as History: The Transformation of American Society in the Twentieth Century* (New York: Pantheon Books, 1984), 182; see also Chapter 5.

71. Alfred Kazin, *On Native Grounds*, fortieth anniv. ed. (New York: Harcourt Brace Jovanovich, 1982), 495.

72. Lewis Hine, "Social Photography," in *Classic Essays on Photography*, ed. Alan Trachtenberg (New Haven, Conn.: Leete's Island Books, 1980); first published as "Social Photography, How the Camera May Help in the Social Uplift," in *Proceedings, National Conference of Charities and Corrections*, June 1909.

73. William Stott, *Documentary Expression and Thirties America* (New York: Oxford University Press, 1973), 275.

74. Hersey, "Agee," xxxix. Evans's *American Photographs* collection shows another close-up of Annie Mae Gudger smiling, which presents a very different image than her famously pained expression captured in her portrait in *Praise*. Also excluded from *Praise* was a photo of a proud and self-confident-looking George Gudger standing with his family in their Sunday best, his arms around his wife and sister-in-law; Stott, *Documentary Expression*, 284–86. For a revealing look at the complex and ambivalent reaction of the families to the way they were represented by Agee and Evans, see Dale Maharidge and Michael Williamson, *And Their Children After Them*, with a foreword by Carl Mydans (New York: Pantheon, 1989), 139–44, 173–75.

75. For another reading of middle-class consciousness in *Praise*, see Paula Rabinowitz, *They Must Be Represented: The Politics of Documentary* (New York: Verso, 1994), 35–55.

76. Erskine Caldwell and Margaret Bourke-White, *You Have Seen their Faces* (New York: Modern Age, 1937); Stott, *Documentary Expression*, 216, 220.

77. Federal Writers' Project, "Instructions to Writers," in *These Are Our Lives* (1939; reprint, New York: Norton, 1975), 417–18.

78. Federal Writers' Project, *These Are Our Lives*, 420–21.

79. If Agee's use of this article is meant as a comment upon the documentary tradition as exemplified in *You Have Seen Their Faces*, it is interesting to speculate on why he directed his attack on the photographer Bourke-White, and not on Erskine Caldwell, the man who wrote the text and the sensationalistic captions for the photos. Rabinowitz argues convincingly that Agee's venom against Bourke-White was both a reaction to her condescending attitude toward her poor, rural, subjects and the product of his own

sexism and envy. Also, Bourke-White, a highly paid, highly public figure with no firm political allegiances, may simply have been an easier target than Caldwell, a working-class southerner with good leftist credentials. Rabinowitz, *They Must Be Represented*, 56–74; and see Kazin, *On Native Grounds*, 378–80.

80. Agee, *Praise*, 7–16; Agee, *Letters of James Agee to Father Flye* (New York: George Braziller, 1962), 131.

81. Agee, "Folk Art," in *Agee on Film: Reviews and Comments* (Boston: Beacon, 1958), 408.

82. Lionel Trilling, "Greatness with One Fault in It," review of *Let Us Now Praise Famous Men*, by James Agee and Walker Evans, *Kenyon Review* 4, vol. 1 (Winter 1942): 99.

83. Agee, *Letters*, 129.

84. Maharidge reveals that this snooping was not one-sided. Unbeknownst to Agee and Evans, "Emma Woods" prowled through their belongings, and even tried on a pair of Agee's pajamas. The complexity of the relationship between the tenant farmers and Agee and Evans is also revealed in the fact that Emma, finding that they had also left money lying about, suspected that Agee and Evans had done this to test the farmers' honesty. Maharidge, *And Their Children After Them*, 55–56.

85. According to the recollections of the family members, Evans was aloof and somewhat cold. Though Agee indicated otherwise in *Praise*, Evans did not in fact stay very often at the Gudgers's, preferring the hotel in town. Maharidge, *And Their Children After Them*, 39–40.

Chapter 7
On Getting Rid of Culture

1. Diverse theoretical developments of the last twenty years—including deconstruction, some critical feminisms and standpoint epistemologies, and various "post-" theoretical positions (post-Marxism, post-Freudianism, poststructuralism, postmodernism)—have been described as being united precisely in their opposition to totalizing discourses generally. Though the enumeration of these positions and their variations would be endless, it probably suffices to cite the following as elaborations of this antitotalizing polemic: Ernesto Laclau and Chantal Mouffe, *Hegemony and Socialist Strategy* (London: Verso, 1985), and Linda Hutcheon, *A Poetics of Postmodernism: History, Theory, Fiction* (New York: Routledge, 1988). For an attempt to recuperate totalizing theory for a theory of postmodernism, see Fredric Jameson, *Postmodernism; or, the Cultural Logic of Late Capitalism* (Durham, N.C.: Duke University Press, 1991).

2. Historical precedent also exists for this resistance to the use of "culture" as a critical term. See A. L. Kroeber and Clyde Kluckhohn, *Culture: A Critical Review of Concepts and Definitions*, (New York: Vintage, 1952), 7–8.

3. Immanuel Wallerstein, "The Unintended Consequences of Cold War Area Studies," in Noam Chomsky and others, *The Cold War and the University: Toward an Intellectual History of the Postwar Years* (New York: New Press, 1997), 195–231.

4. For evidence of the influence of Geertz on these movements, see, for example, the seminal text of new historicism, Stephen Greenblatt's *Renaissance Self-Fashioning: From More to Shakespeare* (Chicago: University of Chicago Press, 1980), 3–4; and see Jameson, *Postmodernism*, 190.

5. Marvin Harris, *Cannibals and Kings* (New York: Random House, 1978). For a specific discussion of the relationship between cultural ecology and cultural materialism, see Harris, *The Rise of Anthropological Theory* (New York: Thomas Y. Crowell, 1968), 634–87.

6. Marshall Sahlins, "Culture as Protein and Profit," review of Harris, *Cannibals and Kings, New York Review of Books* 25, no. 18 (21 November 1978): 45; hereafter, cited in the text. Harris's book popularizes Michael Harner's "protein capture" theory of Aztec cannibalism, which argues, in essence, that a scarcity of animal protein from livestock or game sources led to the practice of sacrificing and consuming the flesh of slaves and prisoners of war. See Harner, "The Ecological Basis for Aztec Sacrifice," *American Ethnologist* 4, no. 1 (February 1977): 117–35.

7. T. S. Eliot, *Notes towards the Definition of Culture*, in *Christianity and Culture* (New York: Harcourt Brace Jovanovich, 1988), 104.

8. Daniel Cottom, "Ethnographia Mundi," in *Text and Culture* (Minneapolis: University of Minnesota Press, 1989), 54–57.

9. Eliot, *Notes*, 104.

10. Matthew Arnold, *Culture and Anarchy*, ed. J. Dover Wilson (New York: Cambridge University Press, 1990), 6; E. B. Tylor, *Primitive Culture* (New York, 1924), 1. See also Chapters 3 and 4.

11. In the final pages of his admirable book *Culture and Anomie*, Christopher Herbert notes some of the complexities of this fact—and of the resulting quasi-paradox of thinking about "culture" (and cultures) using "the dubious theory of culture itself." *Culture and Anomie: Ethnographic Imagination in the Nineteenth Century* (Chicago: University of Chicago Press, 1991), 304.

12. See Sahlins, *Culture and Practical Reason* (Chicago: University of Chicago Press, 1976); and "Structure and History," in *Islands of History* (Chicago: University of Chicago Press, 1985).

13. I am indebted in this account to Jameson's description of the new historicism as partaking of a structuralist logic of homology, even while it "eschews homology's theory and abandons the concept of 'structure.' " Jameson, *Postmodernism*, 188.

14. An interesting example of this problem is in Catherine Gallagher's essay, "Raymond Williams and Cultural Studies," in which Gallagher worries that in contemporary discussions of "culture" there is an "almost programmatic refusal to tell us what *isn't* culture," and then goes on to critique Williams's attempt to produce just such a distinction. *Social Text* 30 (Spring 1992): 80: see also Stanley Aronowitz, "On Catherine Gallagher's Critique of Raymond Williams," Andrew Ross, "Giving Culture Hell: A Response to Catherine Gallagher," *Social Text* 30 (Spring 1992): 90–101, and Gallagher, "Response to Aronowitz and Ross," *Social Text* 31–32 (Summer–Fall 1992): 283–85. Aronowitz and Ross both wildly miss her argument (and its contradiction) largely because they too are convinced by the proposition that "everything is cultural."

15. Virginia R. Dominguez, "The Messy Side of 'Cultural Politics,' " *South Atlantic Quarterly* 91, no. 1 (Winter 1992): 28, 29; hereafter, cited in the text.

16. Such postmodern rewritings of "culture" are legion, comprising, among other things, recent attempts to conceive of transcultural and transnational identities and spaces, and critiques from a number of disciplinary perspectives of the ideologies of cultural authenticity. For examples of the first, see, Inderpal Grewal and Caren Kaplan, eds., *Scattered Hegemonies: Postmodernity and Transnational Feminist Practices*

(Minneapolis: University of Minnesota Press, 1994); Gloria Anzaldua, *Borderlands / La Frontera: The New Mestiza* (San Francisco: Aunt Lute, 1987); and James Clifford, *Routes: Travel and Translation in the Late Twentieth Century* (Cambridge: Harvard University Press, 1997). For examples of critiques of authenticity, see Clifford, *The Predicament of Culture: Twentieth Century Ethnography, Literature, and Art* (Cambridge: Harvard University Press, 1988); and Hegeman, "Native American 'Texts' and the Problem of Authenticity," *American Quarterly* 41, no. 2 (June 1989): 265–83.

17. Dominguez, *People as Subject, People as Object: Selfhood and Peoplehood in Contemporary Israel* (Madison: University of Wisconsin Press, 1989).

18. Johannes Fabian, "Culture, Time, and the Object of Anthropology," *Time and the Work of Anthropology: Critical Essays 1971–1991* (Philadelphia: Harwood Academic Publishers, 1991), 193; hereafter, cited in the text.

19. The "reflexive" or (confusingly labeled) "postmodern" critique of traditional ethnographic practice was canonically described in two volumes: James Clifford and George E. Marcus, ed., *Writing Culture: The Poetics and Politics of Ethnography* (Berkeley: University of California Press, 1986); and Marcus and Michael M. J. Fischer, *Anthropology as Cultural Critique: An Experimental Moment in the Human Sciences* (Chicago: University of Chicago Press, 1986). Fabian's *Time and the Other: How Anthropology Makes its Object* (New York: Columbia University Press, 1983) was strongly influential in this movement.

20. Joel S. Kahn, "Culture: Demise or Resurrection?" *Critique of Anthropology* 9, no. 2 (Autumn 1989): 9; hereafter cited in text. Kahn is indebted in this account to Sherry B. Ortner's useful history of "Theory in Anthropology since the Sixties," *Comparative Studies in Society and History* 26, no. 1 (1984): 126–66.

21. Kahn, "Culture: Demise or Resurrection?" 11. This argument is, in part, in service of a case Kahn makes elsewhere for reviving the "economic" as one of the valuable interpretive categories he believes was displaced as "Eurocentric." Kahn, "Towards a History of the Critique of Economism: The Nineteenth Century German Origins of the Ethnographer's Dilemma," *Man* 25, no. 2 (June 1990): 230–49.

22. Richard Rorty, "Solidarity or Objectivity?" in *Post-Analytic Philosophy*, ed. John Rajchman and Cornel West (New York: Columbia University Press, 1985), 3–19. See also a debate between Rorty and Clifford Geertz that hinges on the question of "ethnocentrism": Geertz, "The Uses of Diversity," *Michigan Quarterly Review* 25, no. 1 (1986): 105–23; and Rorty, "On Ethnocentrism: A Reply to Clifford Geertz," *Michigan Quarterly Review* 25, no. 3 (1986): 525–35. For critiques of Rorty's "ethnocentrism," see Barbara Herrnstein Smith, *Contingencies of Value: Alternative Perspectives for Critical Theory* (Cambridge: Harvard University Press, 1988), 166–73.

23. Dominguez, "The Messy Side of 'Cultural Politics,' " 39, note 2; and see Dominguez, 21. David Bromwich has recently defined "culturalism" as "the thesis that there is a universal human need to belong to a culture—to belong, that is, to a self-conscious group with a known history, a group that by preserving and transmitting its customs, memories, and common practices confers the primary *pigment* of individual identity on the persons it comprehends" (italics mine). "Culturalism, the Euthanasia of Liberalism," *Dissent* (Winter 1995): 89; see also replies to Bromwich by Charles Taylor and Michael Walzer, same issue; and on "Left culturalism," see Arif Dirlik, "Culturalism as Hegemonic Ideology and Liberating Practice," in *The Nature and Context of Minority Discourse*, ed. Abdul R. JanMohamed and David Lloyd (New York: Oxford University

Press, 1990), 394–431; and Andrew Milner, "Cultural Materialism, Culturalism and Post-Culturalism: The Legacy of Raymond Williams," *Theory, Culture, and Society* 11, no. 1 (February 1994): 43–73.

24. Carl N. Degler, *In Search of Human Nature: The Decline and Revival of Darwinism in American Social Thought* (New York: Oxford University Press, 1991), 71.

25. Walter Benn Michaels, "Race into Culture: A Critical Genealogy of Cultural Identity," *Critical Inquiry* 18 (Summer 1992); hereafter cited in the text. The material of this essay has since been republished in Michaels, *Our America: Nativism, Modernism, and Pluralism* (Durham, N.C.: Duke University Press, 1995), 16–23, 44–47, 67–72, 123–30, 139–40. Because the book does not significantly revise the essay's argument about "culture," and because my focus is on the rhetorical move of advocating an "abandoning" of "culture," which is less structurally central to the book than to the essay, I will base my argument on the 1992 essay. However, because the book in many respects expands on the essay, I have been careful to give an account of the essay which does not falsely represent the more recent and more fully elaborated argument of the book.

26. In *Our America*, Michaels significantly sharpens his criticism of "pluralism," arguing, "the commitment to difference itself represents a theoretical intensification rather than diminution of racism, an intensification that has nothing to do with feelings of tolerance or intolerance toward other races and everything to do with the conceptual apparatus of pluralist racism"; 65.

27. Barbara Hernstein Smith, "Unloading the Self-Refutation Charge," *Common Knowledge* 2, no. 2 (1993): 81–95.

28. See Dominguez, "The Messy Side of 'Cultural Politics' "; and Eric Hobsbawm and Terence Ranger, eds., *The Invention of Tradition* (New York: Cambridge University Press, 1983).

29. Michaels, "Race into Culture," 685; Steven Knapp and Michaels, "Against Theory," *Critical Inquiry* 8 (Summer 1982): 723–42; Knapp and Michaels, "Against Theory 2: Hermeneutics and Deconstruction," *Critical Inquiry* 14 (Autumn 1987): 49–68. As Jameson notes, Knapp and Michaels's definition of theory is an oddly narrow one that, in the very moment of the importation of continental philosophy to the United States, confines "theory" to the provincial questions and participants of the Anglo-American literary academy. Jameson, *Postmodernism*, 181–82.

30. Knapp and Michaels, "Against Theory," 738.

31. Michaels, "Race into Culture," 684; Arthur M. Schlesinger Jr., *The Disuniting of America: Reflections on a Multicultural Society* (New York: Norton, 1992).

32. Michaels makes it clear in *Our America* that he would just as soon dispense with "race" as a category of identity; 134–35. However, his interest in delegitimating "race" (under the guise of "abandoning" "culture"), was already apparent in the 1992 essay. In their critical response to the essay, Avery Gordon and Christopher Newfield suggested that Michaels's secret target was "race consciousness," and linked his argument to a tradition of "liberal racism" that sees racial differentiation as *itself* the source of racial ills. Gordon and Newfield, "White Philosophy," *Critical Inquiry*, 20 (Summer 1994): 737–41; see also Michaels's reply, "The No-Drop Rule," *Critical Inquiry* (Summer 1994): 758–69.

33. Though this post–Cold War NAFTA-era vision has some currency among U.S. intellectuals, it need hardly be said that the rest of the world may not take similar

comfort in postnationalism. Particularly in postcolonial contexts, nationalism has strong liberatory and antiimperialist implications, and (like cultural politics) should not be simplistically dismissed as a political evil. See Dirlik, "Culturalism," and Partha Chatterjee, *The Nation and its Fragments: Colonial and Postcolonial Histories* (Princeton, N.J.: Princeton University Press, 1993).

34. This criticism is distinct from *equating* "culture" with ideology, a position not uncommon in Marxist theory, but related to specific debates about base and superstructure, and other models of determination. See Williams, "Base and Superstructure in Marxist Cultural Theory," in *Problems in Materialism and Culture* (London: Verso, 1980), 31–49; and Ortner, "Theory in Anthropology since the Sixties," 140.

35. Dirlik, "Culturalism," 395.

36. David Simpson has recently addressed the moral tone of some critiques of totality, commenting usefully, "Totality is not by definition totalitarian." "Literary Criticism, Localism, and Local Knowledge," *Raritan* 14, no. 1 (Summer 1994): 78; reprinted in a slightly different form in Simpson, *The Academic Postmodern and the Rule of Literature* (Chicago: University of Chicago Press, 1995).

Index